This volume is sponsored by the
Center for Chinese Studies
University of California, Berkeley

Revolutionary Struggle in Manchuria

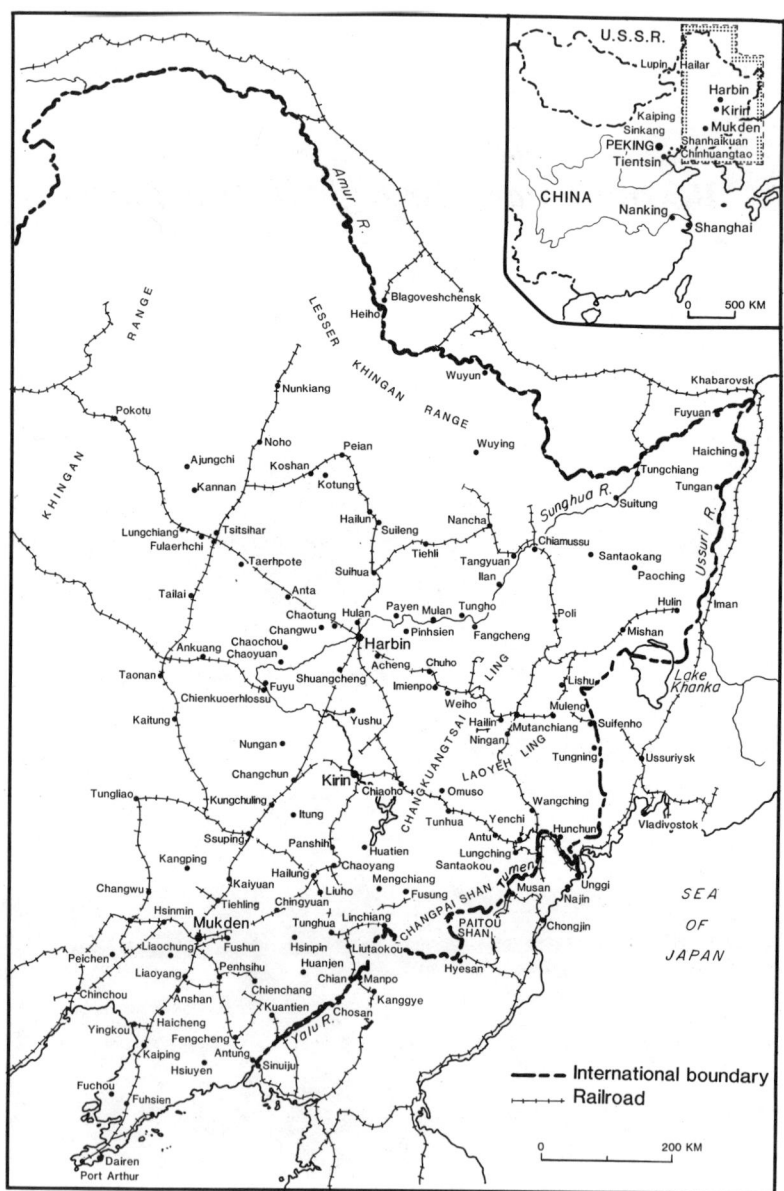

Map 1. Manchuria

Revolutionary Struggle in Manchuria

Chinese Communism and Soviet Interest, 1922–1945 **Chong-Sik Lee**

University of California Press   Berkeley · Los Angeles · London

University of California Press
Berkeley and Los Angeles, California

University of California Press, Ltd.
London, England

© 1983 by
The Regents of the University of California

Printed in the United States of America
1 2 3 4 5 6 7 8 9

Library of Congress Cataloging in Publication Data

Lee, Chong-Sik.
  Revolutionary struggle in Manchuria.

  Includes index.
    1. Communism—China—Manchuria—History—20th century.
  2. Communism—China—History—20th century. 3. China—
  History—20th century. 4. Sino-Japanese Conflict, 1937–
  1945. 5. China—Foreign relations—Japan. 6. Japan—
  Foreign relations—China. 7. China—Foreign relations—
  Soviet Union. 8. Soviet Union—Foreign relations—China.
  I. Title.
  HX420.M36L4   951'.804   82-7083
  ISBN 0-520-04375-8   AACR2

**To my old friends at
Liaoyang Ya-hua-ch'ang
(Liaoyang Cotton Gin)**

为记念
辽阳轧花厂的老朋友们
李庭植

Contents

List of Tables	viii
List of Maps	x
Preface	xi
List of Abbreviations	xv
Introduction	1
1. Manchuria in the 1920s	7
2. The Chinese Communist Party among the Urban Workers	36
3. Fetters of Soviet National Interest	62
4. Sino-Soviet Conflict of 1929 and the Li Li-san Line	95
5. Japanese Takeover of Manchuria and the Chinese Communist Party	127
6. The Comintern versus the Chinese Communist Party on United Front, 1933	158
7. Radicalism versus United Front among the Guerrillas	189
8. United Front and Guerrilla Communism	229
9. The Final Confrontation	268
10. Summary and Conclusions	307
Glossary	323
Index	345

Tables

1. Wages and Cost of Living of Manchurian Workers, 1925 — 16
2. Exchange Rate of Major Manchurian Currencies against Japanese Gold Yen, 1912–1931 — 17
3. Landholdings in Manchuria, 1934–1935 — 19
4. Land Tenure in Manchuria, 1917 and 1926 — 19
5. Wholesale Price Index of Soybeans in Manchuria, 1917–1934 — 21
6. Estimates of the Chinese Population in Manchuria, 1860–1931 — 22
7. Migration of Chinese to and from Manchuria, 1923–1934 — 23
8. Workers' Strikes in Manchuria, 1905–1925 — 29
9. Labor Strikes in Manchuria, 1916–1932 — 45
10. Appearances of Anti-Japanese Forces in Manchuria, 1932–1934 — 130
11. Losses Suffered by Anti-Japanese Forces in Manchuria, 1932–1934 — 130
12. Communist Strength in Chientao, June 1931 — 143
13. Declarations and Leaflets Issued by Communist Organizations in Manchuria after the Japanese Invasion, 1931 — 144
14. Soviets in East Manchuria, 1932–1933 — 204
15. Communist Strength in Chientao, 1933–1934 — 207
16. Communist Strength in Manchuria as of October 1934 — 227
17. Anti-Japanese Fighters in Sanchiang Province, January 1935–June 1936 — 245
18. Occupation of Chinese Communist Party Members and Party Affiliates Arrested in June 1937 — 254

19. Age of Chinese Communist Party Members and
    Party Affiliates Arrested in June 1937   255
20. Numbers of Anti-Japanese Fighters in Manchuria
    by Province, June–October 1937   263
21. The Anti-Japanese Struggle in Manchuria and
    Losses Suffered by the Anti-Japanese Forces,
    1932–1940   264

Maps

1. Manchuria   frontispiece
2. Provinces of Manchukuo, 1932–1945   167
3. Mountain and Forest Terrain in Manchuria   170

Preface

I CONCEIVED THE IDEA OF WRITING A BOOK OF THIS kind in the early 1960s, when I had accumulated a fairly substantial amount of source material on the resistance movement in Manchuria and the Communist movement in particular. I had been working on the Korean nationalist and Communist movements since 1957, and since many of the Koreans operated in Manchuria, it was natural for me to come into contact with materials concerning their Chinese counterparts operating in the same geographical region. In addition to the archives of the Japanese Foreign Ministry and those of the Japanese Army, Navy, and other agencies (1868–1945) available in microfilm, I had gone through the extensive Chinese, Japanese, and Korean collections at Columbia University, the Hoover Institution of Stanford University, Harvard University, the Library of Congress, and the University of California, Berkeley. Although my primary interest was in the Korean movements, I had gotten into the habit of taking notes about the Chinese movements as well. I had been attracted to the various movements in Manchuria not only because they had not been subjected to scholarly research but because I had spent a good part of my childhood and adolescence there.

I was strongly encouraged in 1972, when I received a summer grant from the Joint Committee on Contemporary China of the Social Science Research Council and the American Council of Learned Societies. I had just completed a major book on Korean communism, and I was eager to go back to the Manchurian project. After going through the microfilm copy of the Shih Sou Collection at the University of Pennsylvania, I revisited the Chinese libraries in Berkeley (primarily at the Center for Chinese Studies) and the Hoover Institution. From there, I went to Taipei, Hong Kong, and Tokyo. This trip proved to be most profitable. A new batch of Chinese Communist Party (CCP) documents had just become available because the authorities in Taipei decided to allow foreign scholars access to their vast archives on Chinese communism. At Berkeley, I was generously assisted by Mr. Chi-ping Chen. At Stanford, Mr. David Tseng served as my guide in locating pertinent new materials. In Tokyo, Professor Etō Shinkichi's generous introduction enabled me to contact various persons with long experience in Manchuria, among them Mr. Hirano Hiroshi of Zenrin Kyōkai (Friendship Association) and Mr. Fujikawa Yūzō of the Editorial Committee of the History of Manchukuo. Professor Ichikawa Masaaki of Aomori University also led me to Mr. Inaba Masao of the War History Office of the Self-Defense Agency. All these individuals generously opened up their archival collections for my examination, and I am deeply grateful to them.

These new materials enabled me to put together the pieces of the jigsaw puzzle that I had been grappling with for years, and I began to see the outline of events. I was fortunate enough to receive another grant from the Joint Committee on Contemporary China that allowed me to take a sabbatical leave from my teaching duties during the academic year 1973–1974 and to devote myself to the project. Fortuitously, the Center for International Studies (Kokusai Mondai Kenkyūjo) in Tokyo began to publish the massive compendium of original CCP documents (*Chūgoku Kyōsantō-shi Shiryō-shū*) around that time, considerably lightening my task of placing the CCP policies toward Manchuria in the broad context of overall CCP strategies.

I was fortunate at this stage to receive a critical review from Professor Ezra Vogel who read the first several chapters of the draft and provided me with valuable ideas for improvement. The manuscript was then read by Dr. Ramon Myers of the Hoover Institution, one of the very few American scholars well versed with the situation in Manchuria, who suggested further improvement. I cannot say that all of the shortcomings indicated by these scholars have been corrected in the present version, but I am deeply grateful to them for their willingness to read the bulky manuscript and offer constructive criticism. I am, of course, solely responsible for the content of this book.

I was working on other books in the meantime, and had I not received continuing encouragement from the individuals mentioned above and other colleagues, this book would not have been completed. I owe special thanks to Philip E. Lilienthal of the University of California Press, whose involvement with this project dates back to 1966. His gentle reminders always rejuvenated and encouraged me "to return to Manchuria." Professors Marius Jansen and Allyn Rickett also read earlier drafts and continued to encourage me. Professor George Ginsburgs read a number of chapters and generously assisted me in locating and translating pertinent Russian sources.

I am grateful to Madame Li Sung-lan, Director of the Northeast Heroes Memorial Museum in Harbin, and her staff for their hospitality when I visited them in October 1981. I was very much enlightened and encouraged by them; the two books I received from them proved to be very valuable.

I am also indebted to numerous other scholars for their assistance. Professor Donald Klein was generous in answering my queries about Chinese leaders. I received other help from Mr. Fang Chun-kuei and his staff at the Institute for the Study of Chinese Communist Problems in Taipei, Dr. Bernadette Gentzler of New York, Mrs. Mōri Kazuko of the Center for International Studies in Tokyo, and Professors Chalmers Johnson, Dae-Sook Suh, Chae-Jin Lee, and Kim Chŏng-myŏng.

In addition, I must also register my debt to many other individuals. Mrs. Nancy Cheng, East Asian Bibliographer at the University of Pennsylvania, was tireless in obtaining the esoteric materials I needed. Messrs. Andrew Kuroda, Key Kobayashi, and Key P. Yang at the Library of Congress were always more than generous with their assistance. Jesse Phillips went through many versions of earlier drafts. Philip Robyn pored over the final draft with expert care; I am fortunate to have an editor who is equally at ease with the Chinese and English languages and who possesses a critical mind. Margaret Campbell and Kay Gadsby typed and retyped hundreds of pages. To all these individuals, I offer my heartfelt thanks.

More than a customary note of thanks is due to Dean Robert H. Dyson, Jr., and former Provost Vartan Gregorian of my university. I was surprised and deeply grateful when I learned that the University of Pennsylvania had provided a subsidy toward the publication of this book.

Some readers may object to my use of the term "Manchuria" in this book. The region, of course, is known today as *tung-pei* (*dong-bei* in *pinyin* romanization) or the "northeast." But during the period under study, the region was known throughout the world as Manchuria, and until the late 1930s the CCP officially referred to the region by that name. Thus, until it was abolished in 1936, the regional committee was known as the Man-chou Sheng Wei-yüan hui [Manchurian Province Committee]. (Manchuria, of course, is not a province, but the CCP designated the regionwide committee as the province committee.) Therefore, I decided to use contemporary appellations rather than following current usage. The same goes for Fengtien (Mukden), Dairen (Talien), and so forth.

Finally, I should like to be allowed a personal note to explain my dedication of this book to my old friends at Liaoyang Cotton Gin (Liao-yang Ya-hua ch'ang), now Liao-yang Cotton and Pulp Company (Liao-yang Mien-ma Kung-szu). It was during the dark days between 1946 and 1948 that I toiled with them. Although the circumstances were harsh for all of us, my Chinese friends treated the only alien youth among them with magnanimity and generosity that I cannot easily forget. I therefore wish to dedicate this book to those who provided me with work, learning, and friendship.

Berwyn, Pennsylvania
June 1982

Abbreviations

AJMFA	Archives of the Japanese Ministry of Foreign Affairs
CCP	Chinese Communist Party
CER	Chinese Eastern Railway
CPSU	Communist Party of the Soviet Union
CYC	Communist Youth Corps
ECCI	Executive Committee of the Communist International
KCP	Korean Communist Party
KMT	Kuomintang
MC	Manchurian Committee
NMR	North Manchuria Railway
NMSC	Northern Manchuria Special Committee
SMR	South Manchuria Railway
USNA	United States National Archives

Introduction

How did the Chinese Communist Party (CCP) manage to mobilize the masses in its struggle against the Nationalist Party (Kuomintang) and Japanese imperialism? Why did it fail in certain periods and regions but succeed in others? How appropriate were some of the tenets of Marxism-Leninism in the Chinese context, and what role, if any, did the policies of the Soviet Union and its creature the Communist International (Comintern) play in the Chinese Communists' successes and failures? What role did nationalism and socio-economic reform programs play in the Communist struggle for power? What were the strengths and weaknesses of certain strategies?

These are some of the principal questions that have absorbed scholars of Chinese communism for some time and undoubtedly will continue to occupy the minds of many others. Many outstanding works have already been published. Mao Tse-tung's emphasis on the peasant army as the principal instrument of revolutionary struggle is universally acknowledged as an outstanding feature of Chinese communism. Mao's use of the revolutionary bases and his employment of guerrilla tactics produced excellent results. The Chinese emphasis on the "mass line," the practice of linking party programs with the aspirations of the masses and mobilizing them for party programs, has been recognized as an important ingredient of the CCP's success. The CCP's call for land revolution and other socio-economic reforms also attracted much support for the party, and the CCP's call for a united front against Japan after 1936 had electrifying effects.

While a consensus exists on the principal factors that led to the CCP's success, some issues have aroused controversy among scholars. For example, Chalmers Johnson, in his seminal work *Peasant Nationalism and Communist Power*, argues that it was by successfully asserting their claim to leadership of the resistance movement against Japanese aggression that the Communists obtained a mass following. Other scholars, such as Donald Gillin and Mark Selden, have countered this by presenting evidence that it was the CCP's call for social and economic reforms rather than its nationalist appeals that enabled the CCP to mobilize the people.[1] James P. Harrison has concluded, on the other hand, that the "real key to Communist success was neither nationalism nor social revolution, or even both of them, but rather the Communists' ability to organize the Chinese people on the basis of both themes."[2] In his view, local conditions determined priorities and successes and failures. In some areas, the CCP stressed social revolution, but behind Japanese lines, the struggle against Japan was more important. But, one still wonders: would the CCP have been able to galvanize itself as a potent political and military force without the Japanese invasion?

This study of the Communist movement in Manchuria will show that the anti-Japanese theme played the most important role in the CCP's mobilization of the Chinese masses there. It was the devastation wrought by the Japanese army that led the Chinese peasants in Manchuria to the ranks of the Communist guerrillas. In contrast to the experience of the CCP in China proper, that is, the region south of the Great Wall, before 1927 the strategy of arousing the urban proletariat produced nothing but disasters. This was in spite of the presence of a large free-floating, rootless, male work force, experiencing anomie and feelings of relative deprivation. Also, the CCP's radical programs for social and economic revolution not only failed to mobilize the masses behind the party in the rural areas but had a long-lasting adverse impact on the party. On the other hand, the CCP's emphasis on anti-Japanese struggle and the call for a united front of all the patriotic people against Japan led to the CCP's ascendance.

"Local conditions" in Manchuria, of course, favored the anti-Japanese theme. The Japanese had dominated Manchuria's economy and politics since the turn of the century, and the cadres dis-

---

1. Chalmers Johnson, *Peasant Nationalism and Communist Power: The Emergence of Revolutionary China, 1937–1945* (Stanford, 1962), and "Peasant Nationalism Revisited: The Biography of a Book," *China Quarterly*, December 1977, pp. 766–785; Donald G. Gillin, "Peasant Nationalism in the History of Chinese Communism," *Journal of Asian Studies*, February 1966, pp. 269–289; Mark Selden, "The Guerrilla Movement in Northwest China: The Origins of the Shensi-Kansu-Ninghsia Border Region," *China Quarterly*, October–December 1966, pp. 63–81, and January–March 1967, pp. 61–81.

2. James Pinckney Harrison, *The Long March to Power: A History of the Chinese Communist Party, 1921–1972* (New York, 1972), p. 272.

patched to Manchuria had argued for the anti-Japanese struggle ever since the early 1920s. But, as will be shown, the party leadership rejected the recommendations and appeals of the local cadres time after time. Even after 1931, when the Japanese military was in complete control of Manchuria and thousands of Chinese were fighting against the Japanese aggressors, the CCP leadership was unwilling to permit the cadres in Manchuria to set the anti-Japanese struggle as its priority.

One of the theses of this study is that the CCP leadership was not at liberty to determine its priorities on the basis of its analysis of local conditions. Of course, when the CCP's revolutionary strategy did not affect the interest of the Soviet Union, the CCP leaders could debate the merits of various alternatives and adopt whichever strategy was most promising. But, on issues that concerned imperialism or the struggle against it, the CCP had to operate within the strict bounds established by the Communist International. This, of course, was an understandable stricture. Until the CCP leaders fled to the Kiangsi Soviet in the early 1930s, the CCP was effectively under the control of the Comintern, which was a creature of the Soviet leadership. While the Soviet leaders would have been interested in reinforcing the strength of the CCP, Soviet interest had to be given priority, and any CCP policy or action tending to jeopardize Soviet interest had to be prevented.

The Bolshevik leaders' proclivity toward sacrificing ideological principles in favor of the Soviet national interest was first shown in China by their 1920 reversal of their earlier renunciation in 1918 of all the special rights and interests acquired in China by the former Tsarist government, including control of the Chinese Eastern Railway. Isaac Deutscher has also lucidly expounded on the relationship between the Soviet "diplomatic interests" and its strategies toward the CCP, arguing that Stalin's "blunder" in forcing the CCP to enter into the united front in 1923, and ordering it to stay with it until the Kuomintang (KMT) decimated it in 1927, was motivated by his desire to maintain the Soviet alliance with the KMT. "The growth of Communist influence (in 1925) threatened to disrupt that alliance and so they were determined to keep the Chinese party in its place."[3]

With few exceptions,[4] however, scholars of the CCP's history

---

3. *Prophet Unarmed: Trotsky: 1921–1929* (Oxford and New York, 1959), pp. 319–338.
4. See, for example, Gregor Benton, "The 'Second Wang Ming Line' (1935–38)," *China Quarterly*, March 1975, pp. 62–65.

have tended to ignore the role played by Soviet interest in designing CCP strategy. For example, it is curious that the CCP did not espouse the anti-Japanese cause in 1928 even after the Tsinan incident of May greatly aroused the masses against Japan. The party's pronouncements of that era de-emphasizing the anti-imperial struggle do not sound very convincing. The party had gained greatly by stressing the anti-imperial theme in 1925 in the wake of the May 30th incident, and it would have been logical for the CCP to do so again. The reasons behind the party's decision not to pursue the anti-Japanese theme must be sought in the international context, and particularly in the relationship between the Soviet Union and Japan.

The Soviet Union, of course, had reason to be more concerned with the developments in Manchuria because this was one of the most likely places where a weak Soviet Union might come into conflict with a stronger Japan. Hence, we shall argue, the CCP cadres there were instructed via the central leaders not to take any action that could provoke the Japanese. Thus one may conclude that the situation in Manchuria was unique, but it should be remembered that the Soviet concern over the Japanese attitude in Manchuria directly affected the CCP's stance on the anti-imperial struggle not only in Manchuria but in China as a whole.

The Soviet national interest proscribed the CCP's anti-imperial struggle in the 1920s; but then, after 1933, a completely reversed situation emerged, when it became in the interest of the Soviet Union for the Chinese nation as a whole to struggle against Japan. The Soviet Union no longer needed to placate Japan, which was suffering from internal and external problems. As we shall see in chapter 6, in January 1933, the Comintern instructed the CCP cadres in Manchuria to pursue a new pan-national or broadly based united front policy. Ch'en Shao-yü (Wang Ming) was actively involved in this event. Some of the local cadres followed this policy, but the united front was far from what the CCP leaders in Shanghai could contemplate. The CCP headquarters there were being demolished by the KMT's police and the Kiangsi Soviet was being fiercely attacked. The CCP leaders, therefore, countermanded the Comintern's instructions. Some of the local cadres in Manchuria followed the line ordered by the Comintern, producing a favorable result. Others followed the central leaders' instructions, producing an entirely different result. In any event, in 1935, when the CCP's central leaders, engaged in the Long March, were no longer in a position to direct the Communist movement in Manchuria, the Chinese leaders in Moscow, Ch'en Shao-Yü and

K'ang Sheng, assumed command and ordered the cadres in Manchuria to implement the line first presented in January 1933. Subsequent debates among Chinese leaders on the issue of a second united front cannot be properly understood unless they are placed within the context of these events. The conflict between Ch'en Shao-yü and the CCP leaders did not originate in 1935; it had its beginning in 1933.

This study shows what effect the strategy of a broadly based united front had on the Communist-led guerrilla movement in Manchuria. As we indicated earlier, nationalism was the principal and dominant theme of the CCP when it was at its zenith, but by 1941 the Communist-led anti-Japanese guerrillas were totally decimated. Why were these guerrillas suffering a total loss when the CCP was so successful in northwest China? This question is examined in chapter 9.

The CCP strategists of the 1920s and 1930s tended—as have some latter-day social scientists—to overemphasize socio-economic conditions in their assessments of "revolutionary situations." Lenin had written in 1915, however, that a "crisis of the policy of the ruling class" was the first symptom of a revolutionary situation that would create a crack which the discontent of the oppressed classes could penetrate. The other two symptoms were an aggravation of the sufferings of the oppressed classes beyond the ordinary level, and a tendency of the oppressed classes, by virtue of the first two factors, to engage in mass revolutionary action.[5] In the hinterlands of Manchuria, the sufferings of the oppressed were indeed beyond the ordinary level. There were also many who engaged in mass revolutionary action. But in the 1930s the discontent of the oppressed could not "penetrate" the power of Japanese imperialism. The measures taken by the Japanese to eradicate the guerrillas, as well as the reasons behind their determination, therefore, are examined in this study.

5. V. I. Lenin, "Collapse of the Second International," *Sochineniya* [Works], (Moscow, 4th ed, 1955), vol. 21, pp. 189–199 (originally published in the journal *Kommunist*, no. 1–2 [1915]).

1 | Manchuria in the 1920s

THE CHINESE COMMUNIST PARTY (CCP) WAS ORGAnized in July 1921 in Shanghai by a small group of young intellectuals who had been attracted by the new ideology of Marxism-Leninism and hoped to create a new order in China. It was one of the outcomes of the intellectual, social, and political ferment that had stirred the young since the downfall of the Ch'ing dynasty in 1911. The party was dedicated to the cause of emancipating China from internal and external oppression through an immediate social revolution.

As we shall see in chapter 2, soon after the founding of the party, it dispatched a few agents to Manchuria, the vast territory lying outside, or in the northeast, of the Great Wall. Although Manchuria had not been the traditional habitat of the Han or Chinese race, it had become an integral part of China after the Manchus from that region overthrew the Ming dynasty (1368–1644) in 1644 and ruled over the territory both south and northeast of the Great Wall. The government established in Peking after the demise of the Ch'ing dynasty claimed authority over all the territory that the Ch'ing dynasty had ruled.

Before we trace the activities of these agents, however, we must examine the conditions in Manchuria. The efforts of the CCP cannot be evaluated without an understanding of the "revolutionary setting."

The Warlord Regime

The entire region of Manchuria was under the control of the warlord Chang Tso-lin. Chang, a man "from the green forest" (i.e., of bandit origin), had risen to prominence in 1911 when he was appointed director of the Fengtien Garrison Command (*ch'üan-sheng ying-wu-ch'u tsung-pan*) by the Ch'ing dynasty's last governor-general in Mukden. In this capacity, Chang squashed an attempt by the Revolutionary Party (Ko-ming-tang) to carry out a coup d'état in Manchuria.[1] After the dynasty disintegrated, he built a power base of his own and remained as the de facto ruler of Fengtien Province. In 1917, he succeeded in installing one of his followers as the governor of Heilungkiang Province in the north, and in 1919 Chang had himself appointed inspector-general for the Three Eastern Provinces in addition to being the civil and military governor of Fengtien Province.[2] In 1919, he brought Kirin Province under his control through maneuvers, intimidation, and diplomacy.[3] Ruthless against his opponents, Chang displayed considerable political acumen in cultivating support for his rule: he was scrupulous in having his conquests legitimized by the central government in Peking, which retained nominal control of the three provinces while he was their undisputed ruler.

Had Chang Tso-lin concentrated his efforts upon developing and consolidating his domain, the political and economic history of Manchuria might have taken quite a different course. But Chang Tso-lin had greater ambitions. He wished to become the leading figure in the political arena of all China, and he decided to join the "warlords' melee" that had developed after the death of Yüan Shih-k'ai in 1916. In 1918, when the "Peiyang clique" that had been headed by Yüan split into opposing groups in Anhwei and Chihli provinces, Chang led his troops into North China and sided with Tuan Ch'i-jui of the Anhwei group, enabling Tuan to become premier and winning for himself the aforementioned appointment as inspector-general. In 1920 Chang fought the Anh-

---

1. See a summary provided by Gavan McCormack, *Chang Tso-lin in Northeast China, 1911–1928: Japan and the Manchurian Idea* (Stanford, 1977), pp. 20–27. See also Ning Hai, "Brief Account of the Hsin-hai [1911] Revolution in the Northeast," in Chung-kuo Jen-min Cheng-chih Hsieh-shang Hui-i Ch'üan-kuo Wei-yüan-hui Wen-shih Tzu-liao Yen-chiu Wei-yüan-hui (Study Committee on Literary History Materials, Chinese People's Political Consultative Conference National Committee), ed., *Hsin-hai Ko-ming Hui-i-lu* [Recollections on the Hsin-hai Revolution] (Peking, 1963), vol. 5, pp. 544–549. Dugald Christie, who was in Mukden as a missionary at this time, recorded some of the events of 1911–12 in his *Thirty Years in the Manchu Capital* (New York, 1914), pp. 258–268. Appropriately enough, the chapter dealing with these events is entitled "Moukden and the Revolution."

2. Hayashi Masaaki, "The Formation Process of the Chang Tso-lin Military Clique and the Reaction of Japan," in Nihon Kokusai Seiji Gakkai (Japanese Association of International Politics), ed., *Nihon Gaikōshi Kenkyū* [Studies on Japanese Diplomatic History], *Kokusai seiji* [International Politics] no. 41 (Tokyo, 1970), p. 123. There were two other inspectors general (*hsün-yüeh-shih*) in China, one for the Yangtze region and one for Kwangtung and Kwangsi.

3. Ibid., pp. 122–131. For other details concerning Chang's career, see the excellent work by McCormack.

wei group, and in 1922 he ventured into North China once more, this time against the Chihli forces under Wu P'ei-fu, and suffered a decisive defeat. As a result, he was deprived of the post of inspector-general and the governorship of Fengtien. Declaring the independence of the Three Eastern Provinces on May 26, 1922, Chang defied Wu P'ei-fu, and in April 1924, he formed a tripartite alliance with Sun Yat-sen and Tuan Ch'i-jui to seek revenge for his defeat by the Chihli forces then in power in Peking. The ensuing battles were undecisive, but the Japanese persuaded (with cash, according to a Japanese source) Feng Yü-hsiang, one of the two pillars of Wu P'ei-fu, to mastermind a coup d'état against Wu, thereby aiding Chang Tso-lin.[4] In November, Chang entered Peking, and there Feng and Chang formed an alliance, becoming the uncontested bosses of northern China. In the South, however, the warlords in Chekiang Province and the Yangtse region soon launched a concerted attack against Chang's forces, and Feng Yü-hsiang broke the precarious alliance.[5]

Rebellion

Chang Tso-lin had to pay a heavy price for these ventures, both domestically and internationally. In November 1925, Kuo Sung-ling, one of Chang's commanders, launched a rebellion in collusion with Feng Yü-hsiang. Kuo attacked Chang's misgovernment and advocated reform measures of an enlightened nature.[6] Most of Chang's forces were in North China at this time, and had the Japanese Kwantung Army not intervened to prevent the movement of the rebel forces, Kuo Sung-ling would have succeeded in deposing his master.[7] Neither the Kuo rebellion nor the entreaties of his subordinates, nor his financial ruin in Manchuria could deter Chang Tso-lin from pursuing his grand dream. He took Peking

---

4. Hayashi, "Formation Process," pp. 134–142, and Ikei Masaru, "The First Fengtien-Chihli War and Japan" and the "Second Fengtien-Chihli War and Japan," in Kurihara Ken, ed., *Tai Man-Mō seisakushi no ichimen* [An Aspect of the History of Policies toward Manchuria and Mongolia] (Tokyo, 1966), pp. 163–224. Naturally concerned about the fate of their interests should Wu P'ei-fu triumph, the Japanese encouraged Feng's coup, confident that their interests would be safe under Chang.

5. Li Chien-nung, *The Political History of China, 1840–1928*, trans. Ssu-yu Teng and Jeremy Ingalls (Princeton, 1956), pp. 480–494.

6. Yanaihara Tadao, *Zenshū* [Complete Works] (Tokyo, 1963), vol. 2, p. 540. This portion of *Zenshū* (vol. 2, pp. 481–684) was published earlier as a monograph, *Manshū mondai* [The Manchurian Problem] (Tokyo, 1934). See also McCormack, chapter 5.

7. Shimada Toshihiko, *Kantōgun* [The Kwantung Army] (Tokyo, 1965), pp. 42–46.

again in April 1926 and, in alliance with Wu P'ei-fu, assumed leadership of the warlords in North China; subsequently Chang became commanding general of the National Peace Army (An-kuo Chün), which was established by the northern warlords to counter the threat of the Nationalist army under Chiang Kai-shek, whose "Northern Expedition" was launched in July 1926. In June 1927, Chang Tso-lin made himself the grand marshal of the Peking government. He was at the zenith of his career.

Relations with Russia

Chang's search for glory also produced serious international repercussions. Manchuria had been a scene of international rivalry since the 1890s, involving Japan, Russia, Germany, France, and the United States.[8] The Japanese won the Liaotung peninsula from China in the Sino-Japanese War of 1894–95, but the tripartite intervention of Russia, Germany, and France forced them to forfeit this prize. As a "reward" for intervention, in 1896 Russia was granted the right to build and operate the Chinese Eastern Railway across northern Manchuria, linking the Trans-Siberian line to Vladivostok; in 1898 Dairen (Talien) and Port Arthur (Lushun) at the southern tip of the peninsula were leased to Russia for twenty-five years. Liberally interpreting the provisions of treaties, and despite the repeated protests of China, the Russians began to take over large areas in northern Manchuria, to navigate the Manchurian rivers, to acquire mining and lumbering rights, and to establish municipal governments and para-military forces of railway guards.[9] Although at the end of the Russo-Japanese War of 1904–05 they turned over to Japan the southern extension of the railway below Changchun, together with the ports of Dairen and Port Arthur, the Russians continued to control the railway in the north.

Following the Bolshevik Revolution of 1917, the intervention of the Americans and British and the Japanese forces in Siberia created an opportunity—which Chang Tso-lin took—to wrest

8. Andrew Malozemoff, *Russian Far Eastern Policy, 1881–1904* (Berkeley, 1958); B. A. Romanov, *Russia in Manchuria (1892–1906)*, trans. Susan W. Jones (Ann Arbor, 1952); C. Walter Young, *The International Relations of Manchuria* (Chicago, 1929); Michael H. Hunt, *Frontier Defense and the Open Door: Manchuria in Chinese-American Relations, 1895–1911* (New Haven, 1973); and Akira Iriye, *Pacific Estrangement: Japanese and American Expansion, 1897–1911* (Cambridge, Mass., 1972).

9. Peter S. H. Tang, *Russian and Soviet Policy in Manchuria and Outer Mongolia, 1911–1931* (Durham, N.C., 1959), chapters 1–3.

control of the Chinese Eastern Railway from the Russians. This he did in 1920 while negotiations were continuing between the new Soviet government in Moscow and the authorities in Peking. Although the Bolsheviks had unilaterally signified their intention to renounce special rights and interests acquired in China by the former Tsarist government, including the railway (in declarations by Foreign Affairs Commissar Georgi Chicherin on July 4, 1918, and Deputy Commissar Leo M. Karakhan on July 25, 1919), they altered their stand in September 1920, when Karakhan proposed that the two countries negotiate a special treaty governing the future of the railway. On May 31, 1924, the Chinese government in Peking signed an agreement with Karakhan that provided for the reestablishment of diplomatic relations between China and Russia and joint administration of the railway. Chang Tso-lin at first refused to accede to this agreement, but he was not in a position to withstand Soviet pressure. On September 20 he signed a separate agreement with Karakhan, reiterating the substance of the Peking treaty. In effect, control of the railway reverted to the Russians in 1924. Chang was too deeply immersed in domestic struggles among the warlords to offer resistance.[10]

Relations with Japan

Chang Tso-lin's involvement in the warlords' melee also affected his amicable and partly dependent relationship with the Japanese. After defeating Tsarist Russia in 1905, Japan began to treat Manchuria as an area of special interest and made concentrated efforts to preserve and expand its influence there. Having obtained the Kwantung Leased Territory and the southern extension of the Chinese Eastern Railway between Dairen and Changchun by the victory of 1905, along with other rights the Russians had acquired over the "railway zone," the Japanese established the South Manchuria Railway Company in 1906, and the long and intensive process of colonizing Manchuria began. The Japanese kept a keen eye on politics in Manchuria, occasionally exerting strong and decisive impact. When Chang emerged as the ruler in 1919, the Japanese backed him as their man and provided him with support. Had they not intervened in the Kuo Sung-ling rebellion of 1925, certainly Chang would have lost power and slid into oblivion.

10. O. Edmund Clubb, *Twentieth-Century China* (New York, 1964), pp. 99–125.

As he acquired national stature, and as anti-Japanese movements mounted throughout China after the May 30 incident of 1925, Chang tended to assert himself more—to the point of betraying the expectations and subverting the interests of the Japanese. Over strong protests from the Japanese government, Chang built railroads between Changwu and Tungliao and between Hailun and Kirin that, according to the Japanese, ran parallel to the South Manchuria Railway and hence were in violation of the Sino-Japanese treaty. He denied the Japanese permission to establish branch consulates in Chientao, and he even ordered the closing of a Japanese-owned newspaper in Mukden. Meanwhile, Japanese protests against Chang's "encroachments on Japanese rights and interests" and their other demands only intensified the rising anti-Japanese sentiments in Manchuria and China proper.[11]

The Japanese found a direct threat to their interest in Chang's entanglement in Chinese politics. His active role in Peking created the possibility of a march into Manchuria by Nationalist forces under Chiang Kai-shek in pursuit of Chang's troops and hence threatened the Japanese scheme to separate Manchuria from China proper.[12] On May 16, 1928, the Japanese cabinet under Premier Tanaka decided on the policy of preventing an incursion of Nationalist forces and, if necessary, disarming the forces of Chang Tso-lin upon their return to Manchuria. Chang was notified of the decision and was urged to pull back to Mukden. The Japanese government declared in public that Japan would take

11. Nihon Kokusai Seiji Gakkai, *Taiheiyō sensō e no michi* [The Road to the Pacific War] (Tokyo, 1963), vol. 1, pp. 291–293 (hereafter cited as *Taiheiyō sensō*). In Mukden, students and merchants held mass demonstrations against Japan on September 4, 1927 that attracted some 20,000 people. See also Shimada, *Kantōgun*, p. 53.

12. Some of the Japanese army officers and *rōnin* (lumpen politicos) had advocated the independence of Manchuria and Mongolia as early as 1911. See Hayashi, "Formation Process," pp. 139–144. In 1916, while Yüan Shih-kai was attempting to enthrone himself as emperor in Peking, some highly placed Japanese officials urged Chang Tso-lin to declare the independence of Manchuria and Mongolia. This movement was spearheaded by the acting consul general in Mukden, Yada Shichitarō, but had the active support of Foreign Minister Ishii Kikujirō, Deputy Chief of Staff of the Army General Tanaka Giichi, and the Kwantung Army's chief of staff, Major-General Nishikawa Torajirō. Although this plot did not materialize, it aided Chang Tso-lin's ascendance in Manchuria in that Tuan Chih-kuei, the incumbent Fengtien General (*Feng-t'ien chiang-chün*) and the actual authority figure over all Manchuria, fled to Peking, yielding the post to Chang Tso-lin. Ibid., pp. 150–151, citing Archives of Japanese Ministry of Foreign Affairs, microfilmed for the Library of Congress, Washington, reel P23, pp. 6665–6915; hereafter cited as AJMFA. It is significant that in 1916 Tanaka had instructed Nishikawa to urge Chang to rise, and to promise him weapons and funds. Tanaka became the premier in 1925 and concurrently assumed the post of foreign minister.

"effective measures" in Manchuria in the event that the disturbance in North China spread there.[13]

Chang was finally persuaded to retreat from Peking in late May. By then, many Japanese officers in Manchuria, including the commander of the Kwantung Army, had come to regard Chang as a hindrance to the Japanese. In the early morning of June 4, when his private train neared the railroad station in Mukden, bombs planted by Japanese officers under the direction of Colonel Kōmoto Kaisaku, deputy chief of staff of the Kwantung Army, exploded, fatally wounding Chang Tso-lin.[14] The mantle of power in Manchuria fell to his son, Chang Hsüeh-liang, commonly known as the Young Marshal.

Even though Chang Hsüeh-liang succeeded to his father's position, he was by no means the sole master of Manchuria. In a sense, he did not fully inherit the mantle of his father. Many of the older military men closest to his father would not subordinate themselves to the young marshal. His power over Kirin and Heilungkiang provinces was tenuous.

Also, as we have noted, the Japanese were in control of the Kwantung Leased Territory at the western tip of the Liaotung Peninsula, an area of 3,462 square kilometers that included the Russian-built port city of Dairen and the naval base at Port Arthur. The Leased Territory was in fact a colony. The Japanese administration and its efficient police also had complete authority over the South Manchuria Railway zone, which traversed through 1,100 kilometers of the most fertile land in Manchuria, and they were permitted by treaties to station troops within the railway zone. Although the width of the zone was only 62 meters, there were a number of railway-annexed areas which blossomed into large commercial and industrial centers, thus becoming springboards for colonialism. The Japanese Kwantung Army, consisting of one division of garrison troops and six battalions of railway guards, was stationed at strategic locations.[15]

Thus the Japanese had overwhelming influence over Manchuria's politics. But this was not all. The Japanese controlled Manchuria's business, industry, and railroads. Before World War I, industry in Manchuria had been just as underdeveloped as in

13. *Taiheiyō sensō*, vol. 1, pp. 304–305.
14. Ibid., pp. 291–309; Shimada, *Kantōgun*, pp. 55–74; and Akira Iriye, *After Imperialism: The Search for a New Order in the Far East, 1921–1931* (Cambridge, Mass., 1965), p. 89.
15. F. C. Jones provides the general background of Japanese presence in Manchuria in his *Manchuria Since 1931* (Oxford and New York, 1939), pp. 13–17.

most other parts of China. But Chinese capital began to move into industries such as textiles, railroads, coal mining, and electric power generation after World War I. The first factory of some significance to be built by the Chinese was the Liaoning Textile Mill in Mukden, which began to operate in 1923 under joint government-civilian management and eventually employed 1,800 workers.[16] The Fengtien Arsenal, another major industry, was built in 1921; by 1930 it employed 18,000 workers.[17]

The Chinese investment, however, was meager in comparison with the large-scale penetration and industrialization by Japanese industries. The Japanese established the South Manchuria Railway Company in 1906 and set themselves the task of colonizing Manchuria. While the railway company maintained the structure of an independent private corporation, it was in fact an instrument of Japanese political power. Important political leaders of Japan, including the *genrō* (elder statesmen), the premier, and the army and navy ministers, participated in the planning of the company, and the incumbent deputy governor-general (*seimu sōkan*) of Taiwan (a Japanese colony since 1895) was appointed the first president.[18] The business of the company was, of course, not to be confined to railway transportation. The company played a major role in the development of mining, industry, and commerce in Manchuria.

Through their control of the railroad and energy resources, and their technology—in a land where natural resources were abundant, labor was cheap, and the native political regime was weak and divided—the Japanese were able to turn Manchuria into a colony within a relatively short time. Growth of the coal and iron industries in Fushun and Anshan, which laid the foundation for other industries in Manchuria, was phenomenal. In 1907, when the South Manchuria Railway took over the Fushun mines from the Japanese military (which had taken over from the fleeing Rus-

16. Man Shi Kai (Society for the History of Manchuria), *Manshū kaihatsu yonjūnen-shi* [Forty-Year History of Development in Manchuria] (Tokyo, 1964), vol. 2, p. 340. See also Ronald Suleski, "Regional Development in Manchuria: Immigrant Laborers and Provincial Officials in the 1920s," *Modern China*, vol. 4, no. 4 (October 1978), p. 428. Suleski refers to the mill as "the Textile Mill of the Three Eastern Provinces" (*Tung-san-sheng fang-sha-chang*); the Japanese source calls it the Liaoning Textile Mill.
17. Yanaihara Tadao, *Zenshū*, vol. 2, p. 663.
18. Gotō Shimpei, the first president, held this post until 1908, when he became minister of communications. Tsurumi Yūsuke, *Gotō Shimpei* (Tokyo, 1965), vol. 2, pp. 649–1060, tells of the colonization plan for Manchuria among high-level Japanese politicians around the time the South Manchuria Railway Company was established.

sian army, which had itself expropriated them from Chinese and Russian entrepreneurs), the Fushun mines produced only 230,000 tons of coal a year. Output increased to 1.5 million tons in 1912, 3 million tons in 1919, and more than 7 million tons in 1927.[19] The production of pig iron at the Anshan mines jumped from 36,000 tons in 1919 to 220,000 tons in 1928.[20] By 1930 the Japanese had invested 1.7 billion yen, which constituted more than 70 percent of total foreign investment in Manchuria.[21]

The Workers

These industries, of course, employed large numbers of workers, and a modern industrial labor force began to form in Manchuria. Some fragmentary data on the Manchurian labor force are available:[22]

South Manchuria Railway workers (as of 1923)		5,759
Anshan Iron Works (1925)		6,895
Regular workers	1,665	
Temporary workers	4,523	
Japanese workers	707	
Dairen docks (1925)		12,783
Yingkou docks (1925)		828
Szuping–Tiaoan Railway (Chinese operated)		2,934
Kirin–Changchun Railway (Chinese operated, Japanese financed)		1,575
Chinese Eastern Railway (joint Russo-Chinese operation; 2,446 Russian workers not included)		1,845

19. For further details on mineral production, see *Manshū kaihatsu yonjūnenshi*, vol. 2, p. 66.
20. Ibid., p. 342.
21. Ibid., vol. 1, p. 80 and vol. 2, p. 345; the figures on these pages differ slightly. According to the first, the investment percentages were: Japan, 72.3; USSR, 24.3; Great Britain, 1.4; and the United States and France, 1 each. According to the second, the percentages were: Japan, 76; USSR, 20; Great Britain, 2; and the United States and France, 1 each. Of the 1.7 billion yen which constituted Japan's total investment, the Japanese invested 526 million in transportation, 284 million in mining, 162 million in manufacturing, 117 million in trade, 204 million in banking, and 400 million for other enterprises.
22. "Study of the Treatment of the Workers in the South Manchuria Railway and its Competitors," in Itō Takeo, Ogiwara Kiwamu, and Fujii Masuo, eds., *Man Tetsu* [South Manchuria Railway], Vol. 33 of *Gendaishi shiryō* [Materials on Contemporary History] (Tokyo, 1967), pp. 595–737; hereafter cited as *Gendaishi shiryō*. Volumes 31–33 of this series contain documents of the railway company that were deposited at the home of Matsuoka Yōsuke, who served the company as trustee, vice-president, and president between 1921 and 1926. He later acquired international fame as Japan's foreign minister.

16 Revolutionary Struggle in Manchuria

As might be surmised, the wages were very low, barely enough for livelihood. When a family had a child, it was usually essential for both parents to work. Data provided by the South Manchuria Railway graphically illustrate these facts (see table 1).

A worker's wages often barely supported a family of two; some workers could support one but not two children. It should be recalled, too, that these are averages; a wide range of income existed among the workers. Furthermore, the Japanese firms paid three to four times more to Japanese employees than to Chinese engaged in the same type of work. This situation was one of the contributing factors that led to labor strikes. We shall refer to strikes further below.

Inflation

Chang Tso-lin's adventures had required great sums of money, and as a result, the entire region of Manchuria suffered from severe inflation. The annual cost of maintaining his army was reported to have been between 50 and 80 million *yüan*, which often

Table 1 Wages and Cost of Living of Manchurian Workers, 1925

	Average daily wage	Minimum daily cost of living per person	Number of persons supportable
	(Silver yüan)		
Ssuping–Tiaoan Railway	.43	.23	1.9
Kirin–Changchun Railway	.49	.17	3.2
Chinese Eastern Railway	.60*	.33	2.0
South Manchuria Railway	.46	—	—
Yingkou docks	.77	.28	3.8
Dairen docks	.67	.28	3.0
South Manchuria Railway Plants			
	(yen)		
Shahokou Plant	1.00	.34	3.2
Liaoyang Plant	1.11	.34	3.5
Dairen Machine Plant	.79	.34	2.5
Mukden Machine Plant	.70	.34	2.2
Fushun Repair Shop	.75	.34	2.6

*Highest daily wage.

Source: "Report of the Head of the Research Section, General Affairs Department, South Manchuria Railway, July 25, 1925, on repair plants in Shahokou, Liaoyang, Fushun, and elsewhere," in Ito Takeo, Ogiwara Kiwamu, and Fujii Masuo, eds., *Man Tetsu* [South Manchuria Railway], vol. 3, being vol. 33 of *Gendaishi shiryō* [Materials on Contemporary History] (Tokyo, 1967), pp. 659–660, 696.

Table 2 *Exchange Rate of Major Manchurian Currencies against Japanese Gold Yen, 1912–1931*

Year	Fengtien yüan Exchange rate	Fengtien yüan Annual depreciation (percent)	Kirin tiao Exchange rate	Kirin tiao Annual depreciation (percent)	Heilungkiang tiao Exchange rate	Heilungkiang tiao Annual depreciation (percent)
1912	1.20		5.50		6.10	
1914	1.39		14.80		16.50	
1918	.97		14.50		24.20	
1919	.97		25.10		38.00	
1921	1.39		92.40		65.90	
1925	1.68	5.2	136.00	11.8	160.60	35.9
1926	3.59	113.7	165.00	21.3	251.70	56.7
1927	9.57	166.6	180.60	9.5	132.60 [sic]	20.5
1928	25.10	162.3	180.00	.0	355.10	20.5
1929	56.83	126.4	207.40	15.2	437.60	23.2
1930	100.57	77.0	343.42	65.6	859.90	98.8
1931	134.83	34.1	776.18	126.0	3,050.20	254.7

Source: Manshū Chūō Ginkō (Manchurian Central Bank), *Manshū Chūō Ginkō Jūnenshi* [Ten-Year History of the Manchurian Central Bank] (n.p., 1942), p. 6.

exceeded the total revenue of the Fengtien government. By exporting soybeans, kaoliang, rice, and millet, Manchuria gained a trade surplus of 35 million *yüan* per annum between 1920 and 1927, but this was not adequate to cover the military expenditures. The deficit was covered by issuing paper currency, imposing heavy taxes, and manipulating the prices of goods.[23] Chang's search for glory gave rise to spiraling inflation after 1926, pressing the livelihood of the wage earners and the salaried, including soldiers, police, bureaucrats, and teachers. As can be seen from table 2, the Fengtien *yüan* depreciated precipitously between 1925 and 1929—at the rate of 113.7 percent in 1926, 166.6 percent in 1927, 162.3 percent in 1928, and 126.4 percent in 1929—while the Kirin and Heilungkiang *tiao* did not decline as rapidly. Since the Fengtien *yüan* was the most important medium of commerce in Manchuria and it circulated freely throughout the region, the effect of the fall of the Fengtien *yüan* was not confined to Fengtien Province. Depreciation of the major currency, of course, meant a high rate of inflation.[24]

---

23. McCormack discusses the details of economic dislocation caused by Chang's adventures in *Chang Tso-lin in Northeast China*, pp. 190–203. See also Shimada, *Kantōgun*, p. 52.

24. For a general discussion of the monetary and financial situation in Manchuria, see Kobayashi Hideo, "Manshū kinyū kōzō no saihensei katei" [The Pro-

Land Tenure and the Farmers

Although only 54 percent of the arable land in Manchuria was estimated to be under cultivation in 1926,[25] and many new immigrants headed for farms upon their arrival, they did not find the land unoccupied. After 1875, the Ch'ing dynasty publicly sold Manchurian acreage to Chinese farmers to meet the increasing expenses of the central and local governments, but this encouraged the development of large holdings by the warlords and commercial speculators.[26] Particularly in northern Manchuria, where most of the land remained uncultivated, transactions were in large units, with a square *li* (or 45 *hsiang*)[27] as the minimum. Such warlords as Chang Tso-lin, Pao Kuei-ch'ing, Feng Lin-ko, Wu Chün-sheng, and Yang Yü-t'ing acquired thousands of square *li* at nominal costs.[28] As a result, the new arrivals, most of whom were indigent, were obliged to begin their new lives as tenants or simply as farm laborers.

While details concerning landownership in early years are not available, the results of surveys conducted by the Manchukuo government between 1934 and 1935 are suggestive. Table 3 presents data concerning landholdings. Aside from the heavy concentration of ownership among a few large landowners in northern and southern Manchuria, the table also reveals substantial numbers of landless: 63.2 percent of the farmers in the north, 48.9 percent in the central region, and 32.5 percent in the south.

The pattern of landholdings is, of course, directly reflected by land tenure, shown in table 4. The owner-cultivator category indicates those who owned the land they tilled, having the status at

---

cess of Reconstituting the Manchurian Financial Structure], chapter 2 of Manshūshi Kenkyū-kai (Association for the Study of Manchurian History), ed., *Nihon teikoku shugi ka no Manshū* [Manchuria under Japanese Imperialism] (Tokyo, 1972); and Ronald Suleski, "The Rise and Fall of the Fengtien Dollar, 1917–1928: Currency Reform in Warlord China," *Modern Asian Studies*, 13:4 (1979), pp. 643–660.

25. South Manchuria Railway Company, *Manshū ni okeru nōgyō kinyū* [Agricultural Credit and Finance in Manchuria], Mantetsu Chōsa Siryō (SMR Research Series), No. 107 (Dairen, 1929), p. 126.

26. *Manshū kaihatsu yonjūnen-shi*, vol. 1, pp. 707–710; see also Kungtu C. Sun, *The Economic Development of Manchuria in the First Half of the Twentieth Century* (Cambridge, Mass., 1969), pp. 10–11.

27. The *hsiang* is a land measure in Manchuria equivalent to seven *mou*; it is also defined as the area of land that can be sown in one day. Since 6.6 *mou* are reckoned as equal to one acre, a *hsiang* can be regarded as approximately equal to one acre.

28. *Manshū kaihatsu yonjūnen-shi*, vol. 1, pp. 707–708.

Table 3 *Landholdings in Manchuria, 1934–1935*

	Northern Manchuria		Central Manchuria		Southern Manchuria	
	Households	Area	Households	Area	Households	Area
Large landowners (1)	2.9%	50.0%	—	—	—	—
Large landowners (2)	3.1	16.6	0.2%	3.2%	4.22%	40.42%
Middle landowners	8.1	21.3	17.6	69.0	14.76	35.88
Small landowners	10.5	10.0	17.5	22.3	15.47	13.71
Minute landowners	12.2	2.1	16.7	5.5	33.04	9.99
Landless	63.2	0	48.9 [sic]	0	32.51	0

Note: Definitions of categories of ownership, i.e., large, middle, and small, varied widely from region to region. In northern Manchuria, for example, the large landowners were (1) those with more than 100 *hsiang*, or (2) those with 50 to 100 *hsiang*. In central Manchuria, those with 500 *mou* or above (70 *hsiang* or above) were classified as large landowners. In some areas of southern Manchuria, those with 70 *mou* (10 *hsiang*) were classified as large landowners. Classification obviously depended much on the quality of the land and the climate. In northern Manchuria, where the harvest season is very short, one had to have a large area to qualify as a large landowner.
Source: Study by the Manchukuo government of 681 sample households in 16 *hsien* in northern Manchuria and 401 sample households in 10 *hsien* in central and southern Manchuria between 1934 and 1935. Cited in Man Shi Kai (Society for the History of Manchuria), *Manshū kaihatsu yonjūnen-shi* [Forty-Year History of Development in Manchuria] (Tokyo, 1964), vol. 1, p. 715.

Table 4 *Land Tenure in Manchuria, 1917 and 1926 (in percent of households)*

	Owner-Cultivator		Owner-Tenant		Tenant	
Province	1917	1926	1917	1926	1917	1926
Fengtien	40.6%	42.6%	29.6%	27.9%	29.8%	29.5%
Kirin	46.7	48.4	22.7	23.3	30.6	28.4
Heilungkiang	55.8	56.7	18.9	17.4	25.3	25.9
Average in Manchuria		49.2		23.2		27.9
Average in Japan		31.2		41.1		27.7

Sources: For 1917, South Manchuria Railway Company, *Man-Mō Zensho* [Complete Works on Manchuria and Mongolia] (Dairen, 1923), vol. 3, pp. 135–146 (based on Republic of China, *Statistics on Agriculture and Commerce* [*Nung-shang T'ung-chi*] for 1917); for 1926, South Manchuria Railway Company, *Man-shū ni okeru nogyō kinyū* [Agricultural Credit and Finance in Manchuria], Man-Tetsu Chōsa Shiryō [SMR Research Material], no. 107 (Dairen, 1929), pp. 126–127 (based on Republic of China, *Eighth [Set of] Statistics on Agriculture and Commerce* [*Ti-pa-ts'u Nung-shang T'ung-chi*], no other information provided).

least of middle farmers; the owner-tenants had small or miniscule landholdings insufficient for their livelihood. If the data in the table are accurate, no significant change took place in land tenure between 1917 and 1926. Close to half of the farming households tilled the land they owned, about a quarter supplemented their income by renting land from others, and the remaining quarter relied completely on rented land. Sample studies conducted by the Manchukuo government between 1933 and 1936 similarly revealed that 51 percent of the farmers cultivated the lands they owned, and 49 percent relied partly or completely on the rental of land owned by others.[29] Even though Manchuria is known for its fertile soil, most of the tenant farmers found it difficult to earn sufficient income to support themselves. A survey conducted by the South Manchuria Railway Company between September 1921 and March 1922 of 30 farming households in different areas revealed that five of the eight tenant farmers among the 30 households surveyed suffered losses in that farming year.[30] Presumably these farmers were forced to borrow at usurious rates to sustain life. Such debts, of course, are not easily repaid, and crop failures brought dire consequences.

A large proportion of farmers worked simply as hired hands, their tenure varying from a daily to yearly basis. According to a survey conducted by the Japanese between 1932 and 1935, 34.4 percent of the farmers in northern Manchuria were hired farm workers, as were 18 percent in the central region and 13.4 percent in the south.[31] In addition, 23.1 percent of the farmers in northern Manchuria belonged to the category of "semi-hired" workers (part tenant farmer and part hired farm laborer) and the extremely indigent. In the central region, 28.7 percent belonged to that category; in the south, 22 percent.[32] Those belonging to this category simply could not earn enough to sustain their livelihood and had to accumulate more debts.[33]

In connection with our discussion of the economic condition of the farmers, it is important to note the role played by the production and price fluctuation of soybeans. Manchuria was well

29. Ibid., p. 716.
30. South Manchuria Railway Company, *Manshū nōka no seisan to shōhi* [Production and Consumption of Manchurian Farming Households] (Dairen, 1922), pp. 90–93.
31. *Manshū kaihatsu yonjūnen-shi*, vol. 1, p. 719.
32. Ibid.
33. Ibid., p. 733. For further details on the farmers' livelihood in Manchuria, see ibid., pp. 717–758.

Table 5 *Wholesale Price Index of Soybeans in Manchuria, 1917–1934*

Year	Harbin	Dairen
1917	37.8	—
1921	—	70.5
1922	—	69.6
1923	—	69.2
1924	—	87.8
1925	—	100.0
1926	57.2	80.1
1927	98.4	71.8
1928	104.2	77.7
1929	97.1	73.8
1930	60.1	53.3
1931	59.4	33.0
1932	60.9	53.3
1933	42.2	58.1
1934	41.0	—

Note: The index for Harbin is the actual cash price in Harbin silver dollars (*ta-yang*); for Dairen, the price of 1925 is taken as 100.
Sources: For Harbin, Gunseibu, Komonbu (Advisors' Department, Ministry of Defense, Manchukuo), *Manshū kyōsanhi no kenkyū* [Study of Communist Bandits in Manchuria] (n.p., 1937), pp. 623–624; for Dairen, *Manshū keizai nempō* [Manchurian Economic Annual] (Dairen, 1936), pp. 288–289.

known for its export of soybeans and soybean byproducts, and, indeed, soybeans comprised one-third of the value of total agricultural production.[34] Soybeans constituted the principal cash crop of Manchurian farmers, more than 80 percent being sold for cash. Since soybeans were exported, the price was highly sensitive to fluctuations in the international market, and after 1929 the wholesale price of soybeans fell sharply, as table 5 clearly reveals.[35] Thus, the farmers in Manchuria directly felt the effect of the worldwide economic depression.

Population and Immigration

In spite of these conditions, a large number of impoverished farmers suffering from famine, floods, and political turmoil in northern China—mostly from Chihli (now Hopeh) and Shantung

---

34. Gunseibu, Komonbu (Advisors' Department, Ministry of Defense, Manchukuo), *Manshū kyosanhi no kenkyū* [A Study of Communist Bandits in Manchuria] (n.p., 1937), pp. 72–73.
35. Ibid., p. 73.

Table 6 *Estimates of the Chinese Population in Manchuria, 1860–1931 (x 1,000)*

	Total		Provinces[b]		
Years	Sun[a]	Amano[b]	Fengtien	Kirin	Heilungkiang
1860–70	3,000				
1896–1900	9,000				
1906	13,000				
1908		17,156	10,796	4,553	1,807
1916	20,000				
1918		21,569	12,527	6,180	2,862
1928		28,034	14,477	8,592	4,965
1930		29,575	15,152	9,192	5,231
1930–31	31,000				

Note: Taylor Meadow, British consul at Yingkou, and H. E. M. James traveled extensively in Manchuria in 1886, and calculated the population in that year to be between 20 and 23 million. James, *The Long White Mountain* (London, 1888), p. 3. In 1923, Li Chen-ying estimated the total population to be 29 million.

Sources: (a) Kungtu C. Sun, *Economic Development of Manchuria in the First Half of the Twentieth Century* (Cambridge, Mass., 1969), p. 21.; (b) Amano Motonosuke, *Manshū keizai no hattatsu* [Development of the Manchurian Economy] (Tokyo, 1932), p. 32.

provinces—continued to pour into Manchuria in search of employment.[36] Because the Ch'ing dynasty had forbidden immigration into Manchuria prior to 1887, the region had a relatively small population, approximately 25 million in the early 1920s, in an area as large as Germany and France combined. Since the railroads connecting the southern and northern parts of the region were opened only after the turn of the century, and because of the colder temperature in the north, Heilungkiang Province in the north was particularly underpopulated (see table 6). As the new industries, mines, and farms needed additional labor, many from northern China made their way to Manchuria by rail and ship.

As table 7 shows, most of the immigrants were transients, who stayed only for the warmer seasons or up to a year—until they earned some savings to take back to their homes. But many others settled in the cities, towns, and villages. While some of the men brought their families with them, most of the immigrants were male workers, free floating and rootless. Even those settling

36. On the impact of political instability, war, and natural calamities on the lives of the farmers in North China, where most of the immigrants of Manchuria originated, see Ramon H. Myers, *The Chinese Peasant Economy: Agricultural Development in Hopei and Shantung, 1890–1949* (Cambridge, Mass., 1972). See also Wang I-shou, "Chinese Migration and Population Change in Manchuria, 1900–1940" (Ph.D. dissertation, University of Minnesota, 1971).

in villages had only weak ties to their new homes and no claim to property rights.

It is reasonable to assume that the new immigrants constituted the most "exploited" elements in Manchuria, if one may use the much abused Marxist term. Although the warlord government did provide some subsidies to the immigrants between 1923 and 1928, the number of recipients was very small. It is, therefore, safe to assume that most of the new immigrants arriving year after year suffered from a sense of alienation, relative deprivation, and anomie. And yet, they may have been relieved by the prospect of employment not available at home and that of earning higher wages than in their home provinces. We have no concrete information to offer on the psychological state of the new arrivals. But many of them may well have been susceptible to Communist propaganda.

In addition to the Chinese majority, Manchuria also had minorities, such as the Manchus native to the region, Mongolians to the west, Koreans near the Korean border, and the newly arriving Japanese. Since the 1870s, the difficult political and economic conditions in Korea had prompted some Koreans to penetrate the

Table 7 *Migration of Chinese to and from Manchuria, 1923–1934 (x 1,000)*

Year	Source 1				Source 2			
	Number entering	Number leaving	Number staying	Percent staying	Number entering	Number leaving	Number staying	Percent staying
1923	392	286	105	26.9				
1924	429	232	196	45.8				
1925	490	214	275	56.2	479	193	286	59.7
1926	592	299	292	49.5	646	272	374	57.9
1927	1,050	341	709	67.5	1,043	281	762	73.1
1928	938	394	544	58.0	967	342	624	64.5
1929	1,046	621	424	40.5	941	541	400	42.5
1930	748	512	235	31.6	673	439	233	34.7
1931					416	402	14	3.4
1932					372	448	−76	
1933					568	447	121	21.3
1934					627	399	227	36.3

Source 1: Tō-a Keizai Chōsa-kyoku (East Asia Economic Research Bureau), *Man-Mō seiji keizai teiyō* [Synopsis of Politics and Economy in Manchuria and Mongolia], (Tokyo, 1932), p. 514.

Source 2: Tō-a Kaiun Kabushiki Kaisha (East Asia Maritime Transport Company), *Hoku-Shi nyū-Man kū-ri ni tsuite* [On Northern China Coolies Entering Manchuria] (n.p., February 1941), pp. 57–58.

mountains and rivers separating Manchuria and Korea, and by 1897, some 37,000 Koreans were reported to be in the "Eastern Border Region" (*Tung-pien-tao*) immediately north of the Yalu River. By 1903, another 30,000 were reported to be further east, across the Tumen River, in the region known as Chientao.[37] From these regions, the Koreans gradually spread northward; their number grew rapidly after 1910, when Korea was annexed by Japan. By the early 1920s, there were a half million Koreans throughout Manchuria, of whom approximately 350,000 were in the Chientao region.[38] Indeed, the Korean Communist Party had been active among these Koreans. Because of the strong anti-Japanese sentiment of the Korean immigrants and their poverty and destitution, the Korean Communists found a large number of sympathizers.[39]

Bandits and the Warlord Army

Deteriorating economic conditions vastly increased the number of bandits. Manchuria had long been known for rampant banditry,[40] but according to a Japanese estimate, the number rapidly increased after 1926. The number of bandits, estimated to be 20,000 in 1924–1925, rose to 28,000 in 1926, 50,000 in 1927–1928, and 58,000 in 1929.[41]

According to a Japanese study,[42] several factors encouraged the

37. Minseibu Sōmu-shi, Chōsaka (Research Section, General Affairs Division, Civil Government Department, Manchukuo), *Zaiman Chōsenjin jijō* [Condition of the Koreans in Manchuria] (Changchun, 1933), p. 222, in Archives of the Japanese Army, Navy, and other agencies, microfilmed for the Library of Congress, R110, F20437-670; see also *Manshū kyōsanhi no kenkyū*, pp. 487–489.
38. *Manshū kyōsanhi no kenkyū*, pp. 508–509, 543.
39. See Robert A. Scalapino and Chong-Sik Lee, "The Origins of the Korean Communist Movement," *Journal of Asian Studies*, vol. 20, no. 1 (November 1960), pp. 9–31, and no. 2 (February 1961), pp. 149–167.
40. We do not know how far the record of bandits in Manchuria can be traced back in history, but the Korean dynastic history for the year 1662 notes the arrival of a delegation from the Ch'ing court to discuss, among other things, the problem of bandits in the border regions endangering traffic between Liaotung and Korea as well as the tranquility of the two nations. Kim Kyu-hwan, *Hanguk Yu-i-min-sa* [A History of Korean Immigration] (Seoul, 1967), vol. 1, p. 130, quoting from *Hyŏnjong sillok* [Veritable Records of King Hyŏnjong], Vol. 5, 3rd Year of Hyŏnjong, Year of Jen-Yin (i.e., 1662).
41. Manshūkoku-shi Hensan Kankōkai (Editorial and Publication Committee of the History of Manchukuo), *Manshūkoku-shi* [History of Manchukuo] (Tokyo, 1971), vol. 2, p. 302.
42. Minami Manshū Tetsudō Kabushiki Kaisha, Harbin Jimusho-chō (Chief of the Harbin Office, South Manchuria Railway Company), "Manshū bazoku ni tsuite" [Concerning the Mounted Bandits in Manchuria] (December 20, 1924), in *Gendaishi shiryō*, vol. 32, pp. 795–805.

development of large groups of bandits in Manchuria. Gold discoveries attracted many immigrants from North China in the 1870s, despite the Ch'ing dynasty's prohibition of immigration. In order to defend themselves against the government and protect their gold mines from other intruders, the miners organized and armed themselves under various chieftains. Once the government authority became too strong for them to continue illegal mining, the miners grouped together and began to raid villages.

After the gold fever subsided, opium farming took its place as the major reason for the development of large armed groups. The government authorities often ignored the many immigrants cultivating opium poppies in the remote mountains until harvest time, when troops were sent to raid the fields and confiscate the crop. Losing a year's effort and having no means to support themselves, the farmers readily turned to banditry. Evidently some large farmers cultivating opium poppies enjoyed the protection of the bandits and, through bribes, the government troops.

Another contributing factor was the thriving lumber industry that provided work in the forested hinterlands. Unable to rely on government protection, businessmen involved in lumbering paid a share of their income to the bandits for protection. The forests, in turn, offered an ideal refuge for the bandits.[43]

Of course, had general economic conditions in Manchuria been more favorable, and had the government been determined and able to exterminate the bandits, the number of bandits would not have grown. But there was collusion between the government and the bandits at all levels. As in many parts of China, the government authorities resorted to accommodation rather than extermination as a means of pacifying bandits. When a bandit group became very powerful, the local governor or warlord would simply negotiate the enlistment of that group into the government army, granting the chieftain and all members of the group appropriate rank. Thus many ambitious young men regarded joining a bandit group as a means of sociopolitical advancement.[44] The most powerful Manchurian warlords, including Chang Tso-Lin and Wu Chün-sheng, were products of this system; General Ma Chan-shan, who later became a national hero, also had a bandit background.

The side effects of such a practice were obvious. Inevitably the quality of army officers and troops suffered, reinforcing the adage that good iron is not made into nails and good men do not become

43. Ibid., p. 797.
44. Ibid., pp. 798–799.

soldiers. The distinction between government troops and bandits was blurred, and the people could not feel safe, even when government troops were near them. The South Manchuria Railway Company reported that garrison commanders trod lightly against the bandits for fear that the bandit chieftains would be recruited into the army to outrank them and take revenge against overzealous enforcers of the law. It was, however, not fear of retaliation alone that kept the local commanders from annihilating the bandits: the presence of bandits was profitable. Often the bandits shared their spoils with the army units in return for making it possible for the bandits to engage in their pursuits. Army units would either look the other way in the presence of bandit groups or forewarn the bandits about planned attacks. The bandits also constituted an important source of income for the officers and troops of garrison units and local militia because the bandits paid cash for their weapons, ammunition, and supplies.[45] Further, authorities in the government were not punctual in the payment of military salaries, and this contributed to corruption at the lower levels and to the frequent desertion of members of local units, who quickly became bandits and devastated the local economy. Government finances were always on shaky ground, and the "return to the forests" existed as a possibility for officers and men: those contemplating such an alternative were not likely to enforce the law to the fullest extent.

The Russian Communists in Manchuria

Finally, we must briefly examine the Communist movement among the Russians in Manchuria. As we shall see, the Chinese Communist agents maintained some contacts with the Russian Communists.

The revolutionary activities among the Russians—the workers and railway guards along the Chinese Eastern Railway—can be traced back to 1905, the year in which the Tsarist regime began to disintegrate. During that year, the Russian army was routed in Manchuria, and the navy suffered a disaster in Tsushima Strait at the hands of the Japanese. Strikes, agrarian uprisings, national movements in border provinces, and mutinies in the army and navy characterized the Russian nation. In October, the whole country joined in a spontaneous general strike, in which inevitably the Russians in Manchuria were engulfed. By October 22, dec-

---

45. Ibid., pp. 797–798.

larations bearing the red flags symbolizing the revolution were being distributed in Harbin, and inflammatory meetings were being held at Russian clubs, halls, and other gathering places. On November 24, a strike committee was formed in Harbin, and the entire railway was struck for nine days (November 28–December 6). In February 1907, the Harbin branch of the Socialist Revolutionary Party was organized, primarily among the Russian workers and soldiers.[46] The Tsarist regime, however, gradually restored its authority, and by December 1910 most of the revolutionary leaders were in detention and the movement had been suppressed.

The fall of the Tsarist regime in 1917 revived the revolutionary movement among the Russians in Manchuria. In March, immediately after the abdication of Nicholas II, a worker-soldier soviet was organized in Harbin by a coalition of Bolsheviks, Mensheviks, and Social Revolutionaries, and it began to play a significant role in the governance of this largely Russian city. The soviet organized a May Day parade and sent representatives to the Provisional Executive Committee, which had been set up as the municipal governing organ.[47] On December 12 of the same year, the Bolsheviks took control of the soviet and declared that its decisions were to have the force of law.[48] On December 18, the Bolsheviks also attempted to take control of the Chinese Eastern Railway by issuing an order dismissing the Russian manager— General Dimitri L. Horvath—and appointing their men to key posts. When their order was not obeyed, the Bolsheviks attempted to enforce their demands by the use of arms, with the result that pro-Horvath forces and the Chinese army disarmed and deported 1,560 pro-Bolshevik troops.[49]

46. Kitakawa Shikazō, "Hokuman ni okeru ippan rōdō undō" [General Labor Movement in Northern Manchuria], Report of the Harbin Office of the South Manchuria Railway Company (September 1, 1925), in *Gendaishi shiryō*, vol. 33, p. 750. Hereafter cited as "General Labor Movement."

47. Frederick G. Gladeck, "The Peking Government and the Chinese Eastern Railway Question, 1917–1919," (Ph.D. dissertation, University of Pennsylvania, 1972), pp. 65–66. Seki Hiroharu analyzed the complicated relationship between the Worker-Soldier Soviet, the Provisional Executive Committee, the Railway Employees' Committee, and General Horvath between March and November 1917, in his "Harbin Revolution of 1917: A Study of International Politics Surrounding the Establishment of the Harbin Soviet," *Kokusaihō gaikō zasshi* [International Law and Diplomacy Magazine], vol. 57, no. 3 (August 20, 1958), pp. 37–83.

48. Gladeck, p. 156.

49. Ibid., p. 168. According to Seki Hiroharu (op. cit., p. 56), the population of Harbin in 1916 and 1918 was as follows:

	Chinese	Russian	Japanese	Total
1916	45,481	34,115	2,006	81,602
1918	94,000	60,200	2,768	156,968

The Bolsheviks were drastically weakened, but they did not abandon their efforts to organize the workers. For instance, according to a Soviet Russian author, V. Solomenik, who seems to be intimately acquainted with the situation at this time, an organizational conference of technical personnel and workers of the Chinese Eastern Railway was convened on February 15, 1918, at which the question of organizing the Chinese workers on the railway was discussed.[50] According to a Chinese Communist source, this conference of the representatives of the railway workers—both Chinese and Russian—was convened in Harbin on February 28, "under the leadership of the Bolsheviks," to discuss, among other matters, the organization of the Chinese railway workers, who, unlike the Russians, had not been organized. The alleged aim was to unite the Chinese and Russian workers to "oppose the enemies of the Soviet state and struggle against the common enemies of the Chinese and Russian peoples."[51] On April 4, workers at the Harbin Locomotive Yard struck against the Chinese government order to dissolve the Harbin Executive Committee and the Railway Workers' Union, but the strike was suppressed the same day.[52] On May 15, the Chinese and Russian workers carried out a one-day strike to protest the presence of the White Russian army.[53] The Bolshevik influence among the railway workers was thus substantial.

The Chinese workers began to be enlisted more frequently in this movement. On the morning of September 2, when the White Russian management ordered the dissolution of the Russian workers' organization, the Chinese workers joined the Russians' protest meeting. According to a Chinese source, when the management resorted to force by sending in the railway guards, all the workers took up arms to resist this attempt to break up the meeting.[54] On September 4, the workers struck again, shutting down the railroad until the 13th, when the management granted

---

50. V. Solomenik, "The Struggle for the Soviet Regime in the Chinese Eastern Railway Zone, 1917–1920," *Materialy po istorii revolyutsionnogo dvizhensya na Dalnem Vostoke* [Materials in the History of the Revolutionary Movement in the Far East], vol. 3 (Vladivostok, 1925), p. 65.

51. Chung-kuo K'o-hsüeh-yüan Chi-lin-sheng Fen-yüan, Li-shih Yen-chiu-so, and Chi-lin Shih-fan Ta-hsüeh Li-shih-hsi (Institute of Historical Research, Kirin Provincial Branch, Chinese Academy of Sciences, and Department of History, Kirin Normal University), eds., *Chin-tai tung-pei jen-min ko-ming yün-tung shih* [History of the People's Revolutionary Movement in Modern Manchuria] (Harbin, 1960), p. 295.

52. Kitakawa, "General Labor Movement," p. 751.

53. *Chin-tai tung-pei jen-min ko-ming yün-tung shih*, p. 293.

54. Ibid., pp. 294–295.

Table 8 *Workers' Strikes in Manchuria, 1905–1925*

Date	Description and Purpose
Early October, 1905	Russian employees of the Central Telegraphic Bureau of the Chinese Eastern Railway (CER); for higher wages.[a]
November 24, 1905, to February 1906	All Russian workers of the CER and some Russian soldiers (68 days); expressing sympathy with striking workers throughout Russia.[a]
1906	Chinese workers at a brewery in Changchun; against reduction of wages.[a]
January 9, 1907	Chinese workers at Harbin Machine Plant of CER joined the Russian workers' strike commemorating the anniversary of "Bloody Sunday" (the massacre of petitioners led by Father Gapon on January 22, 1905).[b]
February 1908	Chinese workers at oil presses and breweries in Tiehling; against reduction in wages.[b]
May 1, 1908	Chinese and Russian workers in Harbin; to celebrate May Day.[b]
July 1908	Chinese workers at oil presses in Mukden.[b]
November 1910	Dye workers at Yingkou; for increase of wages.[b]
May 6, 1915	Several hundred miners in Penhsihu; against Japanese management.[b]
May 1916	500 miners in Fushun (three days); demanding the release of a miner arrested by the management.[b]
March 4–20, 1917	All Russian workers of CER and other Russian workers in Harbin; demanding the turnover of the management of the CER to them.[a]
April 1917	1,000 basket weavers in Yingkou; demanding wage increase.[b]
June 1917	350 workers in Anshan Steel Mill; demanding wage increase.[b]
August 27, 1917	Chinese workers of CER at Harbin and at the stations along the CER line; for wage increase.[c]
August 27, 1917	Chinese waiters at Harbin restaurants; for wage increase. Prolonged for weeks.[c]

Table 8 *continued*

Date	Description and Purpose
January 1918	800 lathe operators in Shahokou plant of the South Manchuria Railway, joined by 1,000 other workers (nine days); for wage increase.[b]
April 4–5, 1918	Russian workers at the CER Locomotive Yard in Harbin; expressing opposition to the anti-Bolshevik Russian management.[a]
May 15, 1918	Chinese and Russian workers at CER (one day); expressing opposition to the Russian White Army.[b]
June 1918	Chinese workers in Anshan Steel Mill (two days); for wage increase.[a]
September 2–13, 1918	Chinese and Russian workers in the Harbin Machine Plant of the CER; expressing opposition to the White Army and the Chinese warlords.[b] Also for wage increase and the right to unionize.[a]
October 1918	2,062 workers at the Shahokou Plant of the SMR (seven days); for wage increase.[b]
April 30–May 10, 1919	Some Chinese workers of CER at Tsitsihar; for wage increase.[a]
May 2–10, 1919	Some Chinese workers of CER at Suifenho; for wage increase.[a]
May 4, 1919	Some Russian workers of CER at Hengtaohotzu; for wage increase.[a]
May 22–27, 1919	2,000 Chinese and 800 Russian workers at Harbin Locomotive Yard, CER; for wage increase.[a]
July 19, 1919	100 Chinese workers of CER at Manchouli and Hailar; for wage increase.[a]
July 19–August 15, 1919	500 Chinese and Russian workers of CER at Tsitsihar; for wage increase.[a]
July 25–August 15, 1919	General strike of Chinese and Russian workers of CER; for wage increase.[a]
March 13–17, 1920	General strike of CER; demanding the expulsion of General Horvath (Russian only?).[a]
May 20–June 20, 1922	1,000 Chinese and some Russian workers at Harbin Machine Plant of CER; against reduction in wage and discharge of workers.[a]
July to September, 1925	300 Chinese and some Russian miners at Chalainoerh mines; against reduction of wages.[a]

Table 8 *continued*

Note: Where the length of the strike is given in the source, it is reported here, by the inclusive dates or the number of days, or both; otherwise, it can be assumed that the work stoppage lasted for only a part of a day to a day or two. Similarly, when the purpose of the strike is given in the sources, it is reported here; in the absence of information, one may assume that wage rates were the issue.

Sources: (a) Harubin Jimusho (Harbin Office, South Manchuria Railway Company), "Hoku-Man ni okeru ippan rōdō undō" (General Labor Movement in Northern Manchuria), September 1, 1925, in Itō Takeo, Ogiwara Kiwamu, and Fujii Masuo, eds., *Man Tetsu* [South Manchuria Railway Company], vol. 3, being vol. 33 of *Gendaishi shiryo* [Materials on Contemporary History] (Tokyo, 1967), pp. 750–757.

(b) Chung-kuo K'o-hsüeh-yüan Chi-lin-sheng Fen-yüan, Li-shih Yen-chiu-so; Chi-lin Shih-fan Ta-hsüeh Li-shih-hsi (Institute of History, Kirin Provincial Branch of Chinese Academy of Sciences, and Department of History, Kirin Normal College), eds., *Chin-tai tung-pei jen-min ko-ming yün-tung-shih* [History of the Manchurian People's Revolutionary Movement in the Modern Era] (Harbin, 1960), pp. 308–316.

(c) Frederick Gladeck, "Peking Government and the Chinese Eastern Railway Question, 1917–1919," Ph.D. dissertation, University of Pennsylvania, 1972, pp. 67–68. Gladeck cites *North China Herald*, May–September 1917.

wage increases ranging from 75 to 366 percent. The workers participating in the ten-day strike demanded equal rights for the Russian and Chinese machinists and demanded the right to refuse the repair of armored trains for the White Army.[55]

The continuing decline of the Russian ruble kept the strike movements alive well into 1919. According to Solomenik, following the arrival in March 1919 of one Kiselev from Russia proper, the railway's Communist party branch vigorously developed its activity. Handbills and appeals to the entire working class were issued, explaining Japan's imperialist designs with respect to China and calling for active struggle and support of the proletarian revolution in Russia.[56] Evidently the party's efforts were successful. The Chinese workers in Tsitsihar, 170 miles northwest of Harbin, struck against the railroad on April 30, and another strike of Chinese workers occurred in Suifenho, at the southeastern end of the railroad, on May 2. Russian workers elsewhere went on strike in support of these workers. Some 2,000 Chinese and 800 Russian workers at the Harbin Locomotive Yard staged a strike on May 22–27.[57] In July, the movement spread the length of the railroad in a shutdown lasting from July 25 to August 15. The workers returned to work only after the White Army, under the management, arrested and executed some of the strik-

55. Ibid., and Kitakawa, "General Labor Movement," p. 751.
56. Solomenik, "The Struggle for the Soviet Regime," pp. 751–752.
57. Kitakawa, "General Labor Movement," pp. 751–752.

ing leaders. In most of these strikes, including the last prolonged one, the workers won considerable wage increases. It is significant that the initiative was increasingly taken by Chinese workers. The Chinese workers were becoming attuned to the use of strikes as a means of asserting their demands.[58] In addition to the strikes against the railroad, small-scale strikes took place among Russian and Chinese employees in other enterprises in northern Manchuria.[59]

A propaganda circular "circulated amongst the Chinese workmen and Coolie class" in Harbin and obtained by the American consulate reveals that the Bolsheviks were appealing to Chinese nationalism to influence and recruit the local population, presenting the Tsarist officials as oppressors of China and the Bolsheviks as liberators. The circular, discovered in late 1919,[60] alleged that "the corrupt Tsarist officials, availing themselves of the Boxer trouble, began their scheme of aggrandizement in China, encroaching upon the Chinese territory and infringing Chinese rights." These officials allegedly drove "one hundred thousand Chinese people into the river at Blagoveschensk and Khabarovsk." The main objective of Gondatti, the Russian governor of the territory, was "to persecute Chinese," and he took coercive measures, exacted heavy taxes, and finally evicted the Chinese from Vladivostok.

The circular also recounted alleged atrocities of "the present time." Many Chinese merchants going to Siberia allegedly went bankrupt because of frequent requisitions by Russian authorities. Many Chinese in Harbin and other cities also suffered because of the cancellation of the twenty- and forty-ruble notes accompanied by the issuance of the Siberian ruble notes.

According to the circular, the enemies of the Chinese people were Horvath and Gondatti and their party on the one hand and the Japanese on the other. It warned that the Japanese aggrandizement and development was "harmful to China." It then told of

58. Ibid., pp. 752–753. Some forty Chinese workers in the Manchouli yards and 50 Chinese laborers and other railroad employees in Tsitsihar started the strike on July 19.

59. Ibid., p. 753.

60. G. C. Hanson, American consul in Harbin, to C. D. Tenney, chargé d'affaires ad interim in Peking, January 12, 1920 (United States National Archives Document 893.00B/1 [Microfilm M329, Roll 71, frames 1–6], hereafter cited as USNA). The Bolshevik circular, discovered by the Chinese police and sent to the consulate by the *taoyin* (local prefect), was not dated; from the date of Hanson's letter we may infer that the circular was discovered sometime in late 1919. According to Hanson, the circular was first written in Russian and then translated into Chinese.

connections between Horvath and the Japanese, to whom Horvath "turned the Chinese Eastern Railway over"; the Japanese "wolves" had gobbled up all the rights in Siberia, Manchuria, and Mongolia and would become "the owners of China and Russia."

The Bolsheviks, on the other hand, were ready to turn the Chinese Eastern Railway over to the Chinese:

> Now the Moscow Bolshevik government has been established and it has declared to the Chinese government that should the old Russian officials be extinguished they would cede the Chinese Eastern Railway to China and cancel all the unjust treaties secured from China by the old Russian government, such as extra-territoriality and the sole employment of Russians on the railway, etc. . . . It is hoped that the whole Chinese people will wake up and expel the old Russian officials, Horvath and others, from the Chinese territory. Then the Japanese will not dare to despise China, and China and Russia will be able to go hand in hand both for existence and to promote and confirm the welfare in the Far East.

In March 1920, there occurred amid the political intrigues of both the Bolsheviks and the Chinese government a general strike, which provided an opportunity for the Chinese to take over the railway. By the spring of 1920, General Horvath's strength had plummeted because of the successive victories of the Bolshevik forces in Siberia over the White Russian Army under Admiral A. Kilchak and General G. Semenov. In April 1919, the Bolsheviks created a buffer state in eastern Siberia, known as the Far Eastern Republic, with its capital at Chita. In an apparent effort to bolster his position in Northern Manchuria, Horvath declared in January 1920 that thenceforth political power in the railway zone would be under his control. He was quickly challenged by the commander of the Chinese Railway Guards in Harbin, Pao Kuei-ch'ing who denounced him for infringing on Chinese sovereignty and demanded that he hand over all military and police power to the Chinese and reorganize the management of the railway. The Bolsheviks, on the other hand, infiltrated the ranks of the workers and instigated a workers' strike demanding the ouster of Horvath.[61] On March 12, the Central Railway Strike Committee under Bolshevik leadership issued an appeal to the railroad em-

---

61. Kitakawa, "General Labor Movement," pp. 754–755.

ployees, which explained the aims of the action and asked for their help and solidarity in gaining the objectives of the strike to begin the following day.[62] The Chinese commander, seeing advantage in worker agitation, encouraged the strikers. Horvath sought the support of the Chinese army in vain, while some of his own troops sided with the strikers. On May 15, the Chinese commander issued a proclamation denouncing both General Horvath and the strikers for infringing on Chinese sovereignty and for hampering the orderly operation of the railway. On the following day, the Chinese disarmed the Russian troops under Horvath, relieved Horvath of all power, forbade further political activities in the railway zone, and took full control of the railway.[63] Evidently the governor's actions subdued the local Bolsheviks. The American consul reported on November 5, 1920, that "while a large percentage of the Russian population undoubtedly sympathizes with the Moscow government, there has been no open and active Bolshevik propaganda in this district for several months, due, no doubt, to the presence of large numbers of Chinese troops and the supplanting of Russian governmental institutions in the Railway Zone by Chinese." He added, "The radical element here also is fully aware of the complicated political situation in an international sense and of the danger of stirring up disorder or trouble of any sort at this time."[64]

Thus the Russian Bolsheviks had sown the seed of the workers' movement in Manchuria, but it is not certain how many Chinese participants in the strike movement were enlisted into the Communist cause. There is no doubt, however, that some of the Chinese worked closely with the Russian Communists.[65] This was particularly so after 1924, when the Chinese warlords were busy fighting among themselves and Chang Tso-lin was not in a position to resist the Soviet government's pressure to yield control of the railway to them under a "joint management" formula. The Soviet management expelled all anti-Bolshevik Russians from the railway and implemented programs to propagandize communism among the Russian and Chinese employees. The Bolsheviks reportedly established the Northern Manchurian Prefectural Com-

62. Solomenik, "The Struggle for the Soviet Regime," pp. 75–76.
63. Kitakawa, "General Labor Movement," pp. 754–755.
64. Consul G. C. Jenkins to Charles R. Crane, U.S. Minister, Peking, November 5, 1920 (USNA, 893.001/12).
65. The American consul at Harbin had cabled the Department of State on May 22, 1920, to report that "I have to say that there are not many Bolsheviks among the Chinese workmen in this place. There are, however, some. I will continue the investigation and then report." (USNA, 893.001/1.)

mittee of the Russian Communist Party and the district and local organizations under it. The Japanese and Chinese authorities believed the Soviet consulate in Harbin to be the headquarters of Bolshevik operations and that the consulate was dispensing great sums of money to communize the Chinese employees.[66]

These conditions offered the CCP both challenges and opportunities. We shall now trace the activities of the CCP in Manchuria.

66. Manchukuo, Hsieh-ho-hui (Concordia Association), *Senmetsu kyōhi* [Annihilate Communist Bandits] (Changchun[?], 1934), pp. 44–48.

2 | The Chinese Communist Party among the Urban Workers

THE EARLY YEARS OF CHINESE COMMUNIST ACTIVIties in Manchuria are still shrouded in mystery. There are reports that the Fengtien branch of the Chinese Communist Party (CCP) was established between the first and second party congresses (July 1921 and July 1922), but no other information is available on that branch.¹ On the other hand, Chang Kuo-t'ao, one of the principal CCP leaders of this era, cites Ch'en Wei-jen as a delegate from Harbin in northern Kirin Province at the party's Third Congress held in Canton in June 1923.² According to Chang, Ch'en Wei-jen made an important contribution to the Third Congress by soothing the emotional encounter between Ch'en Tu-hsiu, the party secretary, and Chang Kuo-t'ao. Ch'en Wei-jen's sincere appeal to the congress for party unity and his advice to Ch'en Tu-hsiu to respect the views of the opposition changed the heated atmosphere at the congress, which had been split by a dispute on the question of whether to join the Kuomintang.³

One wishes to know more about the Fengtien branch and its possible ties with Ch'en Wei-jen. But, according to a recent biography of Ch'en, he arrived in Manchuria "sometime after the February 7 Massacre" of 1923.⁴ If this information is accurate, Ch'en had nothing to do with founding the Fengtien branch.

There is no doubt, in any event, that Ch'en Wei-jen was one of

    1. Ch'en Kung-po, *The Communist Movement in China* (edited with an introduction by C. Martin Wilbur) (New York, 1960), p. 83; Wang Chien-min, *Chung-kuo kung-ch'an-tang shih-kao* [Draft History of the Chinese Communist Party] (Taipei, 1965), vol. 1, p. 43.
    2. Chang Kuo-t'ao, *The Rise of the Chinese Communist Party, 1921–1927, Volume One of the Autobiography of Chang Kuo-t'ao* (Lawrence, Kansas, 1971), p. 311. (Volume two of Chang's autobiography bears the same title except the dates covered, that is, 1928–1938; hereafter cited as *Rise of the CCP*, followed by volume number.)
    3. Ibid.
    4. Chung-kung Liao-ning-sheng Tang-wei-hsiao Tang-shih chiao-yen-shih (Teaching and Research Office on Party History, Party School, Liaoning Province

the principal CCP leaders assigned to Manchuria. Ch'en, born in 1899, was of Hunan origin and was one of CCP's budding leaders. Since 1920, Ch'en had participated in the establishment of the Socialist Youth League in Shanghai and had been active among the small circle of Communists in Peking. He was sent to Moscow in 1921 along with Liu Shao-ch'i and Lo I-nung to attend the Communist University of the Toilers of the East for a brief period, returning to China with Liu in late 1921 or early 1922.[5] Ch'en was assigned to the Peking-Hankow Railway sometime after May as one of the secret inspectors on the railway,[6] and after the February 7 Massacre of 1923, in which troops of the warlord Wu P'ei-fu executed more than 40 Communists and labor leaders,[7] proceeded to Harbin.

In Harbin, Ch'en worked as a reporter for *Ch'en-kuang Pao* [Morning Light News], trying to inject revolutionary ideas into the newspaper, according to his biographers. Ch'en was forced to quit the paper because of the warlord regime's intimidation of the newspaper, and he then organized a news agency and a "youth institute." But Ch'en reportedly left the city for Dairen when his arrest became imminent.[8] In June 1923 he attended the Third Congress as a delegate from Harbin, as we noted earlier. Evidently he chose not to return to Harbin after the congress because he was too well known to the authorities; instead, he went to Dairen. But his stay in Dairen also did not last long. Since late 1923, Ch'en worked at the headquarters in Shanghai as a regular writer or possibly an editor of the party journal *Hsiang-tao Chou-pao* [Guide Weekly], which presented authoritative views of the party on diverse subjects.[9]

Ch'en Wei-jen's close collaborator was Li Chen-ying, a prolific writer and veteran labor organizer. Li had published numerous articles in such leftist magazines as *Hsin Ch'ing-nien* [New Youth], *Lao-tung-chieh* [Labor World], *Lao-tung Chou-k'an* [Labor

---

Party Committee, CCP) ed., *Manchou Sheng-wei Lieh-shih-chuan* [Biographies of Manchurian Provincial Committee Martyrs] (Shenyang, 1981), p. 3.

5. Ibid., p. 2.

6. Ibid., pp. 2–3; Donald W. Klein and Anne B. Clark, *Biographic Dictionary of Chinese Communism, 1921–1965* (Cambridge, Mass., 1971), vol. 1, p. 529, and vol. 2, p. 814.

7. For details, see James Pinckney Harrison, *The Long March to Power: A History of the Chinese Communist Party, 1921–1972* (New York, 1972), pp. 37–38.

8. *Manchou Sheng-wei Lieh-shih-chuan*, p. 3.

9. Ch'en Wei-jen contributed 25 articles and commentaries between no. 52 (January 20, 1924) and no. 79 (August 6, 1924) on a wide range of topics. Among the 208 signed articles and columns, 86 were written by Ch'en Tu-hsiu and 122 by others, including 25 by Ch'en Wei-jen. Mao Tse-tung, incidentally, contributed four articles, between nos. 31–32 (July 11, 1923) and 38 (August 29, 1923).

Weekly], and *Kung-ch'an-tang* [Communist Party].[10] Li had studied Russian at the Shanghai Foreign Language Institute with Ch'en Wei-jen, Liu Shao-chi, Lo I-nung, and others in 1920,[11] and he had been active in the trade union movements in Tientsin since early 1921.[12] Later, he was transferred to the Peking-Hankow Railway General Union, and like Ch'en Wei-jen, Li Chen-ying played a leading role in the union movement, having served as its secretary.[13] Li proceeded to Manchuria with Ch'en Wei-jen soon after the "February 7 Massacre."[14]

The January 20, 1924 issue of *Hsiang-tao Chou-pao* [Guide Weekly] printed Li Chen-ying's report entitled "An Analysis of the Situation in the Three Eastern Provinces."[15] Although it was published under Li's name alone, this may have been the joint product of Li and Ch'en Wei-jen. According to Ch'en's biography, Ch'en and Li were together in Dairen.[16] It may be that Ch'en carried the manuscript to Shanghai when he was reassigned to the headquarters, but since Ch'en was publishing another article in the same issue of the magazine, he may have considered it imprudent to list his name twice in the same issue. In any event, there is no doubt that the report had Ch'en's endorsement.

The report refers to various events in Dairen, Changchun, Harbin, Kirin, and other cities, showing evidence that Li Chen-ying (and Ch'en Wei-jen) travelled widely. He (or they) found that Chang Tso-lin and lesser warlords were completely in control of politics. The imperialists, particularly the Japanese imperialists, were in control of business, industry, and the railroads, and the Chinese merchants played an insignificant role. Public safety was poor; conditions tended to encourage banditry. Often residents suffered more from the government troops sent to wipe out the bandits than from the bandits themselves and thus were subject to double jeopardy. The chaotic financial and monetary system tended to favor the Japanese, who issued currency of their own, which was stable and trusted. The plight of the Chinese workers on the South Manchuria Railway was bad, but worse conditions prevailed among the miners. The farmers' livelihood was pre-

10. Chou Tse-tsung, *Research Guide to the May Fourth Movement* (Cambridge, Mass., 1963), p. 18, and the entries for the magazines just noted.
11. *Manchou Sheng-wei Lieh-shih-chuan*, p. 2.
12. See Chang Kuo-t'ao, *Rise of the CCP*, vol. 1, p. 128.
13. Ibid., vol. 1, pp. 278–279.
14. *Manchou Sheng-wei Lieh-shih-chuan*, p. 3.
15. [Li] Chen-ying, "Analysis of the Situation in the Three Eastern Provinces," *Hsiang-tao Chou-pao* [Guide Weekly], Shanghai, no. 52 (January 20, 1924), pp. 396–398, and nos. 53–54 (February 20), pp. 417–419.
16. *Manchou Sheng-wei Lieh-shih-chuan*, p. 3.

carious, and many farmers were tenants subject to high rents. Many workers on the Chinese Eastern Railway, both Russian and Chinese, were discharged, and unemployment caused serious problems, particularly for the Russians. Among the 11,000 Russian workers on the railway, 85 percent were members of the Russian Communist Party. They engaged in demonstrations against the White Russian management of the railway.[17]

Our analysis of the situation presented in chapter 1 supports much of what Li Chen-ying reported at the end of 1923, although he could not have anticipated some of the events that occurred after that year, such as the Bolshevik takeover of the Chinese Eastern Railway. In the course of travel and investigation in Manchuria and in the process of writing his long report, Li must have given much thought to the question of how the revolutionary movement could be organized and what strategies should be adopted.

> Under political conditions of this kind, the path of the future revolution cannot depart from the Chinese Eastern and the South Manchuria railways. The revolutionary masses will consist of a grand alliance of the Chinese, Japanese, and Russian workers along with the common people. The revolutionary tendency will be toward the formation of a united front of the oppressed Russians and Koreans, and the [Chinese] peasants, merchants, and workers, together with the outcast immigrants from other provinces. They will oppose Christianity and the illicit collusion of the British, American, French, and Japanese imperialists. They will also oppose the control of the [Chinese] Eastern Railway by either the old [White] Russian or the Japanese groups. They will demand a reduction in the circulation of Japanese gold currency, reduction of rents and taxes, and elimination of fees for cultivating virgin lands. They will . . . finally rally under the flag of the democratic revolution.[18]

Li Chen-ying thus saw hope in the grand alliance of all the oppressed elements in Manchuria against Japanese and Russian im-

---

17. The discharging of employees by the Chinese Eastern Railway mentioned by Li was caused by the stoppage of Bolshevik trade with China after 1920. The Chang Tso-lin government was in control of the railway at this time and its management was entrusted to the White Russians. The situation changed after 1923, as we shall note.

18. [Li] Chen-ying, "Analysis of the Situation in the Three Eastern Provinces," p. 417.

perialism. The alliance or united front was to consist not only of the workers and peasants but of the "common people" and people of other nationalities as well. He did include economic measures such as "reduction of rents and taxes and elimination of fees for cultivating virgin lands," but the main thrust of his argument was unmistakably the nationalist theme.

The grand alliance envisaged by Li Chen-ying was something the CCP should strive for in the future; its immediate task was to build a nucleus of dedicated revolutionaries who could identify potential followers, spread the revolutionary message, and provide training and direction to new recruits, molding them into an organization capable of concerted action. But where was the party to find these revolutionaries?

The doctrinaire answer to this question was among the workers, even though most, if not all, of the CCP leaders of this period had bourgeois intellectual backgrounds. Lenin had said in 1918 that the bourgeois intellectuals were the only carriers of proletarian class consciousness. According to Lenin, they become conscious of it by carrying the heritage of liberal thought to its logical conclusion. "Workers," on the other hand, "have to work in the factory as if on a chain gang, and neither time nor possibility remains for them to become socialist."[19] However, the CCP leaders had decided at the First Party Congress, held in July 1921, that the organization of labor was the "first aim of the party."[20] At the second congress, held in the early summer of 1922, they had decided further that the party was to be the vanguard of the proletariat, and the local cadres were to be drawn from the ranks of the workers. The CCP was to influence "such possible members of the labor unions as railway workers, seamen, metalworkers, textile workers, etc."[21] The labor union sponsored by the CCP, however, was not simply an organ for securing workers' benefits; it was to be a "fighting union" whose principal activity would be "to struggle against the capitalists and the oppressive government."[22] The labor movement, therefore, was a principal instrument for recruiting and training CCP members. In order to fulfill these aims, the CCP congress had ordered every union to "have a school in which to educate its members and to

19. Lenin's "Report on the Current Movement," made at the Fourth Conference of Trade-Union and Factory Committees, Moscow, June 27, 1918; in *Sochinenia* [Collected Works] (Moscow, 4th ed., 1952), vol. 27, pp. 421–438.
20. J. P. Harrison, *Long March*, p. 34.
21. Ch'en Kung-po, *The Communist Movement in China*, p. 89.
22. Ibid., p. 90.

develop the class consciousness of the workers." And the first step in organizing a union was to organize factory committees, "which should be groups of wage earners dependent upon a union."[23]

Furthermore, the CCP had been highly successful in organizing the workers in such places as Hong Kong, Shanghai, and Canton. Beginning with the strike of the Chinese Seamen's Union in Hong Kong in February 1922, the Communists were successfully directing strikes in various major cities and industries.[24]

Workers' Movements and the Communist Party

It comes as no surprise, therefore, to learn that Ch'en Wei-jen and Li Chen-ying worked among the workers. As we noted earlier, Ch'en Wei-jen moved from Harbin to Dairen after he participated in the Third CCP Congress held in June 1923. We do not know whether Li Chen-ying was in Harbin to work with Ch'en, but he is reported to have worked with Ch'en in Dairen.[25] Naturally enough, their work was centered on organizing and directing the workers. According to Ch'en Wei-jen's biography, Ch'en and Li "helped to streamline" the Dairen Chinese Workers' Study Association (Ta-lien Chung-hua Kung-hsüeh-hui).[26] The association was the first labor group of Communist leanings established in Manchuria at the end of 1923 among the Chinese workers at the Shahokou plant of the South Manchuria Railway Company (SMR). At that time, there were some 1,000 Chinese workers employed by that plant, which produced locomotives and other railroad vehicles. By 1925, it employed some 2,700 workers, of whom 1,374 were Chinese.[27]

In name, the group was innocuous enough, but the Japanese management was wary of what it might do. The manager of the railroad's Liaoyang Repair Plant southwest of Mukden reported in June 1925 that he had ordered all the foremen to search for members of the "Workers' Study Association, whose president was at the Shahokou plant." The blacklists maintained by the plant were consulted and all other leads were followed up, but he had not

23. Ibid.
24. For an overview, see J. P. Harrison, *Long March*, pp. 35–37.
25. *Manchou Sheng-wei Lieh-shih-chuan*, p. 3.
26. Ibid.
27. Report of the Head of the Research Section, General Affairs Department, South Manchuria Railway, July 25, 1925, on repair plants in Shahokou, Liaoyang, Fushun, and elsewhere, in Itō Takeo, Ogiwara Kiwamu, and Fujii Masuo, eds., *Man Tetsu* [South Manchuria Railway], vol. 3, being vol. 33 of *Gendaishi shiryō* [Materials on Contemporary History] (Tokyo, 1967), p. 654.

been able to uncover any members of the association in Liao-yang.[28] Evidently the movement had not spread to Liaoyang or some of the foremen concealed their knowledge; but there is no doubt that the railroad's management regarded the association as a radical group.

Ch'en's biography does not say that he and Li Chen-ying were instrumental in founding the association, but both of them were hard at work. They were the ones who drafted the charter of the association and gave it the mission of organizing a labor union. They instructed the association, along with the Chinese Youth Association and the Tseng-chih School, to hold meetings to report and discuss current affairs, propagate revolutionary ideology, and expand the party's influence. They also selected several better-educated elements among the members of the association and youth association along with employees of the T'ai-tung Daily News "to engage in passionate talks," and to introduce them to Marxism. Such journals as *Chung-kuo Ch'ing-nien* [Chinese Youth] and *Hsiang-tao Chou-pao* [Guide Weekly] were brought to them. According to Ch'en Wei-jen's biography, Ch'en and Li laid the foundation for party organization in Manchuria through these men.[29]

In spite of the Japanese watchfulness, the study association expanded with considerable dynamism. According to a report on Dairen by a CCP cadre, Shen Yin, in mid-1924, the association was the "general headquarters" (*ta-pen-ying*) of the railroad workers, and 700 of the 1,409 Chinese workers in 17 railroad plants had joined the association.[30] Out of the 700, more than 500 paid monthly dues. The association conducted classes in two night schools.

The study association leaders clearly regarded their organization as a labor union. The Second Congress of the National Railway Workers' Association, held in February 1925 at Chengchow, Honan Province, was attended by a delegate from Dairen representing the SMR workers.[31] It is very likely that the delegate was Fu Ching-yang, a worker at the Shahokou plant and the head of the Dairen Chinese Workers' Study Association.[32]

28. Ibid., p. 662.
29. *Manchou Sheng-wei Lieh-shih-chuan*, pp. 3–4.
30. *Hsiang-tao Chou-pao* [Guide Weekly], no. 68 (June 4, 1924), p. 545. There were probably more than 1,409 Chinese workers in 17 SMR plants in view of the fact that the Shahokou plant employed some 1,300.
31. *Hsiang-tao Chou-pao*, no. 145 (February 10, 1926), p. 1336.
32. According to a report by the railroad, Fu Ching-yang attended the congress

Nor was the study association the only labor group among the Chinese workers in Dairen. According to Shen Yin, the tram workers had organized the Electric Railway Youth Corps (Tien-t'ieh Ch'ing-nien-hui) and enrolled 400 members. This group conducted night classes for the study of English. Also, 250 of the 2,000 Chinese printers in Dairen had organized the Chinese Printing Workers' Comrade Association (Chung-hua Yin-kung T'ung-chih-hui).[33] Shen Yin did not specify whether these were legal groups.

Such organizations were evidently beginning to have some impact. Sometime in the early part of 1924, workers at the Tō-a (East Asian) Tobacco Company in Yingkou reportedly carried out a strike.[34] In May, some 600 workers of the Fengtien Hemp Company in Mukden, including 226 women, went on strike for a raise in wages and improvement of working conditions. The strike began as a result of a Japanese chief engineer's beating of Chinese workers suspected of theft, but inflation and the strike in Yingkou were cited as accompanying causes. The price of sorghum, a staple of the workers, had risen from 1.20 *yüan* per *tou* (a quarter of a bushel) in 1923 to 1.90 *yüan*, and hence the workers demanded a raise of 8 cents per day for child workers and 10 cents per day for adults. They also demanded rent subsidies. The company offered only a raise of 3 cents for child workers and 5 cents for adults, which was rejected. The child workers were receiving 25 to 40 cents per day and the adults 45 cents to 2 *yüan* (200 cents). The conflict was not resolved, and the company discharged all the workers and temporarily ceased operations.[35] Obviously the management was in an advantageous position because of the general weakness of the labor movement, the abundance of the labor supply, and the unskilled nature of the work.

In the early summer of 1925 some 300 workers of the Fukushima Spinning Mill near Dairen went on strike because a promised raise was not forthcoming. They were receiving a daily wage of only 28 cents. After deduction for meals eaten at the plant, they

---

in Chengchow held in February 1926 rather than 1925, but this could have been an error. South Manchuria Railway Company, Keizai Chōsakai (Economic Research Association), *Manshū kyōsantō undō gaikan* [A Survey of the Manchurian Communist Party Movement] (Dairen, 1935), p. 2.

33. *Hsiang-tao Chou-pao*, no. 68 (June 4, 1924), p. 545.

34. *Gendaishi shiryō*, vol. 32, p. 558. This source merely cites the strike as having influenced the hemp company strike (which we mention next), without providing details.

35. Ibid., pp. 558–559.

allegedly received only 7 or 8 cents, though they worked twelve hours a day with only 30 minutes' rest.[36] We do not know the outcome of the strike, but some of the strike leaders were arrested. The workers at the SMR's Shahokou plant reportedly struck again at this time, demanding supplementary pay because of inflation, free passes on the railroad, and the construction of dormitories for the workers.[37]

These examples clearly show that the workers in Manchuria were becoming accustomed to the use of strikes as a means of improving their wages and working conditions. The statistics compiled by the Japanese concerning the strikes reveal that not only did the incidence of strikes increase between 1924 and 1928, but also that the number of strikers grew significantly. Table 9 presents data compiled by one group of Japanese scholars.

The railroad authorities saw the hand of the Communists behind these strikes. The head of the Harbin office of the railroad reported on June 8, 1925:

> The strikes in China are not simply labor problems, but are antiforeign actions constituting an anti-imperialist movement. Since the damage to the Japanese is most extensive, it could be seen simply as an anti-Japanese action, but on the basis of observation of the situation in the Hankow area, this is not so. Judging from the activities of the anti-imperialist movement of the past, one cannot deny that the hand of the Russian Communist Party is behind them.
>
> While the surface cause of the strikes in Fengtien lies in the devaluation of the Fengtien currency, which led to the demand for increased wages, the strikes in Shanghai and Tsingtao were also influential.[38]

More specifically, the Harbin office reported the arrival in April 1925 of 26 students from Peking and Shanghai who were "officers" of the CCP-sponsored Chinese Labor Union. They recruited workers for the labor union in southern Manchuria, in and around Mukden, and then proceeded to Harbin, where they engaged in organizational activities in the Chinese section of the

---

36. Ibid., vol. 33, p. 160; also *Manshū kyōsantō undō gaikan*, p. 2. The latter gives the date of the strike as April 1926 and says that the existence of the study association became known because of this strike.
37. *Gendaishi shiryō*, vol. 33, p. 160. The report cited here is a summary of a news story in a Peking newspaper.
38. Ibid., p. 152.

Table 9 *Labor Strikes in Manchuria, 1916–1932*

Year	Number of strikes	Number of participants	Cumulative number of days
1916	5	1,290	—
1917	5	1,019	—
1918	20	5,970	—
1919	55	11,336	—
1920	18	3,694	—
1921	7	959	—
1922	25	4,021	—
1923	27	4,177	—
1924	29	5,256	—
1925	59	8,889	—
1926	67	12,642	325
1927	94	23,539	383
1928	79	17,606	356
1929	41	6,307	217
1930	35	2,785	114
1931	20	3,031	92
1932	8	3,134	23
1933	29	6,345	81
1934	11	836	52

Source: For 1916–1925, Manshūkokushi Hensan Kankōkai (Editorial and Publication Committee of the History of Manchukuo), *Manshūkokushi* [History of Manchukuo] (Tokyo, 1971), vol. 2, p. 1159. For 1926–1934, Gunseibu, Komonbu (Advisors' Department, Ministry of Defense, Manchukuo), *Manshū kyōsanhi no kenkyū* [Study of Communist Bandits in Manchuria] (n.p., 1937), p. 385, cited from *Manshū rōdō jijō sōran* [General Survey of Labor Conditions in Manchuria], no other data given.

city, among blacksmiths, brewery workers, and others. They distributed approximately 1,000 yüan for unspecified purposes, alleging that the funds were "to mourn the death of Sun Yat-sen" (Sun had died in March 1925). They reportedly returned to Tientsin and Shanghai via Vladivostok, using official passes issued by the Profintern (the Communist trade union international), presumably on a Russian ship. In late 1924, in connection with a report concerning the travels of the Japanese Communist Katayama Sen, the Harbin office stated: "Optimism is no longer permissable in Manchuria. . . . The communization movement in Manchuria must be closely watched."[39]

Aside from these organizations and movements, the overall attitude of the Chinese workers began to change. In 1925, for exam-

39. Ibid., pp. 152–153. Katayama allegedly passed through Harbin on his way from Moscow to Shanghai.

ple, the Mukden office of the Dairen Machine Works (Dairen Kikai Seisakusho), a South Manchuria Railway subsidiary, reported: "While the Chinese workers were very docile at the time of the founding of the company, they have gradually been aroused during the last two or three years and they are prone to resort to strikes. This tendency is likely to worsen."[40] A report about the Yingkou docks, where the Japanese employed some 800 laborers in 1925, stated:

> Since last year, the common sense of the coolies has increased, and they have been paying attention to social incidents. They now have some general ideas about socialism and strikes. This [new knowledge] is said to have been injected by the propagandists at public bath houses, barber shops, and other gathering places.[41]

Similarly, the manager of the Dairen docks, where 12,000 Chinese laborers were employed in 1925, stated:

> Some time ago, leading elements of the office personnel of the docks and permanent laborers of the company were planning to organize a mutual assistance society, but they were prevented from doing so. It is believed, however, that sooner or later the current of the time will lead them to unity. In that event, these elements will become the central force. They have all graduated from elementary-level schools and constitute the so-called intellectual class among the workers. We, the South Manchuria Railway Company, must watch where they are going, prevent [undesirable] happenings, and strive to provide proper guidance to their thoughts.[42]

Thus the union movement, if not the party organizational activities, was making considerable progress in Manchuria when the historic May 30 incident erupted in Shanghai. Dismissal of

40. Shomubu, Chōsaka (Research Section, General Affairs Department, SMR), "Man-tetsu sha-nai-gai kikai kigu kōjō rōdō jōtai hikakuhyō" [Comparative Tables on Working Conditions at Machines and Tool Factories in the SMR and others], July 9, 1925, in *Gendaishi shiryō*, Vol. 33, p. 659.

41. Shomubu, Chōsaka (Research Section, General Affairs Department, SMR), "Seitō, Tenshin, Shanghai, Eikō, Dairen futō rōdō jijyō hikaku" [Comparison of Working Conditions at the Docks of Tsingtao, Tientsin, Shangshai, Yingkou, and Dairen], July 3, 1925, in *Gendaishi shiryō*, vol. 33, pp. 697, 707.

42. Ibid., p. 716.

Chinese workers by a Japanese textile mill in February 1925 led to strikes and demonstrations, and then to the murder, in March, of a Chinese worker by a Japanese foreman. This precipitated further strikes and led to demonstrations and rallies by students and intellectuals in support of the workers. On the afternoon of May 30, British and Indian policemen of the British Concession in Shanghai fired on the demonstrators, killing 13 persons and wounding many others. A general strike was called in the city, and sympathy strikes broke out elsewhere. Anti-imperialist feeling was never stronger in China, and understandably, the British and Japanese were the primary targets.[43] The CCP, which had provided active leadership in the demonstrations, seized the opportunity to expand its forces among intellectuals, students, workers, and peasants.[44] Even the peasantry, which had not been affected by anti-Japanese movements before, became aroused and manifested intense hostility to foreigners.[45]

The news of the May 30 incident, which grew into a prolonged movement, naturally stirred the students, intellectuals, and workers in Manchuria. In the early morning of June 10, four to five hundred students, both men and women, from the Mukden Young Men's Christian Association School, Women's Normal School, South Manchuria Medical College, and other institutions gathered in front of the provincial government offices with placards and leaflets denouncing Japan and Great Britain and calling for a struggle for national salvation. While demonstrators and government officials were negotiating on the issuance of a permit to demonstrate in the streets, the ranks of the students grew to about a thousand. The permit eventually was refused, and the crowd was dispersed by police and troops.[46] In Harbin, Kirin, and other cities, strong editorials in the Chinese press denounced the

43. Detailed accounts are given in Wang Chien-min, *Chung-kuo Kung-ch'an-tang shih-kao* [Draft History of the Chinese Communist Party] (Taipei, 1965), vol. 1, pp. 168, 171; and in Jean Chesneaux, *The Chinese Labor Movement, 1919–1927*, trans. H. M. Wright (Stanford, 1968), pp. 262–289. A daily account of the events by Japanese agents and officials in China, including some perceptive analyses and forecasts of events to come, is found in *Gendaishi shiryō*, vol. 33, pp. 460–506.
44. The party membership increased from around 1,000 in early 1925 to 57,967 by April 1927. The rapid rise was attributed to the May 30 movement and the recruitment campaign that followed it. See Ho Kan-chih, *Chung-kuo Hsien-tai Ko-ming-shih* [A History of the Modern Chinese Revolution] (Hong Kong, 1958), p. 106.
45. See Stuart Schram, *Mao Tse-tung* (Baltimore and Harmondsworth, 1967), pp. 8–82.
46. *Gendaishi shiryō*, vol. 33, p. 154.

British and the Japanese, urged boycotts of their goods and newspapers, and called for strikes at factories and schools together with a general strike of all merchants and workers. On June 9, the "Harbin Comrades of the KMT"—presumably an affiliate of the KMT—distributed leaflets poignantly denouncing the imperialists and calling for the unity of all classes of people and assistance to the workers and students of Shanghai and Tsingtao.[47] Students in Port Arthur and Dairen, under Japanese jurisdiction, held memorial services, collected contributions for the workers, and went on strike at their schools.[48] According to news accounts published in Harbin, the Japanese police surrounded factories and schools where strikes were being planned or conducted, and forbade the singing of the Chinese national anthem at memorial services. Those engaging in strikes or collecting contributions were arrested.[49] The Chinese authorities elsewhere in Manchuria, though sympathetic, forbade public demonstrations against Japan and Great Britain lest these lead to riots that would provide an excuse for foreign intervention.[50]

Were the Communist cadres in Manchuria able to utilize this intensely patriotic atmosphere? Unfortunately, there is very little information from which to derive an adequate answer to this question. Indications are that the Communists were only partially successful. By the summer of 1927, the CCP had some 300 members in Dairen, 90 members in Mukden, and 130 in Harbin. While there were party organizations in Kirin and Changchun as well, details are not available.[51]

We do have some information concerning the most successful branch in Dairen, the bustling port city at the southern end of the Liaotung Peninsula. The Dairen Area Committee of the CCP was established in July 1926, and the committee's Youth Corps a few months later. The person responsible for founding these two organizations was Teng Ho-kao, a graduate of the Fine Arts College in Peking. Teng, a native of Paoting, Hopei Province, had studied Western painting, but became attracted to Sun's Three People's Principles and eventually to communism while he was still in the art school, and joined the KMT and the CCP. He was twenty-three years old and had recently graduated from the college when the

47. Ibid., pp. 153–154. 48. Ibid., pp. 159–160. 49. Ibid.
50. Ibid., p. 158.
51. "Report and Proposal of Comrade Wei-jen in Manchuria, December 22, 1927," in *Chung-yang cheng-chih t'ung-hsün* [Central Political Bulletin] (an organ of the CCP Central Committee), no. 16, pp. 70–80; hereafter cited as Ch'en Wei-jen Report. Specific page numbers cannot be provided here as the manuscript version consulted does not show the endings of pages within the article.

CCP leaders in Peking sent him to Dairen to investigate the workers' strike at the Fukushima Spinning Mill, to propagate communism, and to organize party branches. In Dairen, Teng persuaded Wang Shao-po and Yang Chih-yün to join him, and the three established the Dairen Area Committee, Teng becoming chairman and Yang heading the organization department. The propaganda department was also established. Wang at this time was an officer of the Dairen branch of the KMT, and Yang was secretary of the Chinese Youth Association (Chung-hua Ch'ing-nien-hui).[52]

Considering the large number of Chinese workers employed by the SMR, it was natural that the organizational efforts of the new committee be directed toward them, beginning with those at the giant Shahokou Rolling Stock Plant. Yang Chih-yün, who had been a teacher at the night school operated by the Dairen Chinese Workers' Study Association, was expelled from the Kwantung Leased Territory at the end of 1925 for his active role in the campaign to release the arrested leaders of the strike at the Fukushima Spinning Mill at Choushuitsu. Fu Ching-yang, the head of the association, was deeply involved in a strike that took place in Mukden in the early summer of 1925; he and eighteen others had been arrested. Yang evidently had slipped back into Dairen by the time Teng arrived. Yang's previous experience at the night school and as campaign organizer undoubtedly was useful in his current work. In early 1927 the Dairen committee established its workers' department, appointing Wang Li-kung, another Shahokou worker, as head. As the committee expanded, it added a youth corps to recruit and train sympathetic young men.[53] It is quite likely that the membership in the party and the youth corps overlapped. Teng Ho-kao headed both the committee and the corps.

By July the Dairen Area Committee had established 23 branches and had a membership of some 220, according to the Japanese,[54]

52. Ōsaka Tai-Shi Keizai Remmei (Osaka Economic Federation for China), ed., *Sa-Rempō to Shina Manshū no kyōsan undō* (The Soviet Union and the Communist Movement in China and Manchuria) (Tokyo, 1934), p. 548; hereafter cited as *Sa-Rempō to Shina Manshū*.
53. Ibid., p. 548. The committee recruited youth corps members from the Chinese Youth Association, a social and educational organization with 2,000 members headed by a rich merchant, Fu Li-yu, as of June 1924 (*Hsiang-tao Chou-pao*, no. 68 [June 4, 1924], p. 545). It is relevant to note here that the SMR officials obtained a copy of *Ju-tang hsü-chih* [Essential Knowledge for Joining the Party] at the Shahokou plant in the early summer of 1927. This short CCP document, prefaced by the Hymn of the Communist International, is preserved in Japanese translation in Man-tetsu Sha-chō-shitsu Jinjika, Rōmu-kakari (Subsection on Labor, Personnel Section, Office of the President, SMR), *Rōdō mondai shiryō* [Materials on Labor Problems] no. 5 (July 1, 1927), 12 pp.
54. *Sa-Rempō to Shina Manshū*, p. 548.

and more than 300 according to a CCP report.[55] Although the name "Dairen Area Committee" was kept, activities were extended to Mukden, where the party had 90 members.[56] Yang Chih-yün went to Mukden in February 1927 and instigated a workers' strike at the Mukden Hemp Company in May.[57] Organizational activities in Harbin were directed by an executive committee.[58] Since the party headquarters had called for 500 members by the Fifth Congress, to be held in the spring of 1927, one could say that the organizational work in Manchuria was progressing on schedule.[59]

In July, however, the activities of the Dairen Area Committee were brought to a complete halt by a mass arrest. The police later released full details of the "incident." According to an account published in the *Manchurian Daily News* (Dairen), the local (Japanese) police had "confiscated printed matter of communistic complexion here and there and could tell that the movement was far better organized than any labor agitation." The police learned that Teng Ho-kao was the local Communist leader.[60] But they would have to wait until they had arrested Yang Chih-yün in Mukden and another Communist, Wei Cheng-k'uei, in Dairen, to learn the details.

When about 600 Chinese workers at the Manchuria Hemp Company in Mukden went on strike early in May, the police decided that Yang Chih-yün was the principal instigator and went after him. Yang was arrested on June 29, and confessed that he had been converted to believe in the Three People's Principles about six years before and had been lecturing on these principles as teacher to the night classes of the "Chinese Labor Union, Dairen," which is known to us as the Dairen Chinese Workers' Study Association. He had been involved in the Fukushima Spinning Mill strike between April and June and had received frequent remittances from the south until told to quit the territory early in

55. Ch'en Wei-jen Report.
56. Ibid.
57. *Sa-Rempō to Shina Manshū*, pp. 547–548.
58. Wang Chien-min, *Chung-kuo Kung-ch'an-tang shih-kao*, vol. 1, pp. 357–358.
59. Ch'en Tu-hsiu, general secretary of the CCP, to "comrades in charge of various party branches," October 17, 1926. Ch'en's letter and other CCP documents were published in a pamphlet entitled *Chiao-yü tsa-chih* [Education Magazine], no. 3 (December 1, 1926). The cover and title were obviously intended to disguise the content. I have consulted a Japanese translation (undated) by the Shanghai Office of the South Manchuria Railway Company available at the Library of Congress.
60. *Manchuria Daily News* (Dairen), August 20, 1927.

the preceding January. He returned briefly to his native home near Yingkou but then came back to Manchuria, traveling between Dairen, Fushun, Mukden, and other places. He tried unsuccessfully to form a branch of the Chinese Labor Union in Fushun. At Mukden, he distributed money among the men in the hemp company and treated them to refreshments, thus managing to instigate them to strike. He hoped to spread the "strike mania" to the men of the Manchuria Woolen Manufacturing company, the Mukden plant of the Dairen Machinery Manufacturing Company, and even the Mukden Spinning Mill and Weaving Works.

In the meantime, the Shahokou police got wind of Wei Cheng-k'uei's propagating communism on the Dairen wharves, and on July 13, he was arrested at home. A large stack of "inflammatory printed matter" was discovered. Wei confessed that he received some money from Communist sources and engaged in propaganda work, but he revealed nothing more. It was Yang from whom the police obtained the most information. Since Yang had earlier been arrested and evicted from Dairen, the police had more reason to pressure him for information. In such instances, the Japanese police and military gendarmes did not hesitate to use extreme measures to squeeze information from suspects.

According to the news account, the Communists were planning to reorganize the local labor union into a Dairen branch of the CCP, recruiting men in the service of the bean mills, the Dairen Machinery Manufacturing Company, the Nakamura Foundry, the Changkuang Glass Factory, the Nishikawa Printing Office, the *Ta-tung Jih-pao* [Great East Daily], the East Asia Printing Company, the Onoda Cement Factory, the Wharf Laborers Company, the Dairen Ceramic Company, and other organizations. The leaders went under assumed names and, in spite of the close police vigilance, worked steadily toward consolidating a local party branch.[61] However, the arrest of some fifty members totally removed such a possibility.

Dedicated men such as Teng Ho-kao and Yang Chih-yün certainly did their best to propagate communism and organize workers. In the process, they undoubtedly went through much hardship. But their work had just begun when they were arrested, and the overall effect of their efforts on the labor scene in Manchuria was still insignificant. In this connection, an observation made by the American consul in Dairen in September 1927 is of particular interest:

61. Ibid.

Although the enclosed account of Communistic Activities [a clipping from the *Manchuria Daily News*] created the impression, to a certain degree, that those engaged in propaganda work had achieved considerable success until apprehended by the police, actually there were a few if any outward signs of it. In fact, the Chinese in the Kwantung Territory have generally given the appearance of being indifferent toward Communism. Their living conditions, compared with other [parts of] China, are good, and the administration of the Territory by the Japanese gives them small cause for complaint regarding their individual fortunes.

It is in fact common to hear travelers observe that the Chinese residents of the Kwantung Leased Territory appear to be considerably more prosperous than those in other provinces.[62]

Of course, the consul was speaking of the conditions in the Kwantung territory alone. But the CCP had not fared much better in other parts of Manchuria where the living conditions were considerably worse.

The Kuomintang in Manchuria

The slow growth of the CCP in Manchuria is sharply contrasted with its development in China proper and with the growth of Kuomintang (KMT) organizations in Manchuria. Some of the middle school students in Mukden who were aroused by the May 30 movement spontaneously formed a group and established contact with KMT headquarters in Canton. Students of Tungpei College and alumni of colleges and universities in Peking also gathered and established an organization of their own. When the two groups discovered each other, they held a conference of party members and established a temporary Fengtien provincial branch in October 1924.[63] By August 1926, the branch had 320 members, including 120 members in Mukden and 200 in outlying counties.[64] The branch actively recruited students, women, merchants, workers, and peasants, and by May 1927 its membership surpassed 2,000.[65] The Kirin branch of the KMT, established in April

---

62. Consul Leo D. Sturgron to the Secretary of State, September 3, 1927, USNA 893.00B/402.
63. *Rōdō mondai shiryō*, no. 4 (June 28, 1927), pp. 1–3.
64. Ibid.
65. Ibid., no. 3 (June 13, 1927), p. 6. This is a copy of a report prepared by the

1925 and comprised of 196 members by May 1926,[66] also actively engaged in propaganda and organizational activities. While we have no information concerning that branch after May 1926, it had held mass rallies and demonstrations and a memorial service for Sun Yat-sen before that date, gathering more than 10,000 persons on each occasion. All of the various public organizations in Kirin came out in support of the KMT-sponsored events, and even the army and police provided protection on these occasions.[67]

The KMT branch in Harbin, which was established in September 1925 and had 500 members by May 1926, was less successful in holding similar rallies because of police suppression, but propaganda materials were distributed and donations collected after the May 30 incident. However, the Harbin branch was permitted to hold a celebration of the Double-Ten holiday (October 10, commemorating the Wuhan revolution of 1911), at which the KMT members engaged in mass propaganda. Handbills attacking the Chang Tso-lin regime, imperialism, and the warlord regimes were printed in massive quantities (5,000 to 20,000 copies) and scattered on the streets. A newspaper, *Tung-pei Chao-pao* [Manchuria Morning News], was printed to propagate the cause of national revolution. The KMT party branch also actively supported the railway workers' union and other unions, establishing workers' schools and printing workers' newspapers.[68]

While the arrests of KMT members in Changchun and Mukden in March 1927[69] seem to have slowed the momentum of the KMT organizers, KMT activities in Manchuria seem to have been more dynamic than those of the CCP. Certainly the KMT organization in Mukden enjoyed a much more rapid expansion than the CCP could ever have hoped for, and it is quite likely that the KMT organizations in other areas attained similar results. Why was the KMT more successful than the CCP in recruiting members? Why did the workers in Manchuria not respond to the call of the CCP when their conditions seemed so favorable for the CCP organizers? Why did the CCP organizations in Manchuria fail to emulate the experience of the CCP in China proper?

A noticeable difference between the KMT and the CCP activities in Manchuria is the object of recruitment and the targets of operations. While the CCP did recruit a certain number of teach-

---

Police Bureau of the Kwantung Territorial Government (Kantō-chō Keimu-kyoku), dated May 20, 1927.
66. *Rōdō mondai shiryō*, no. 4 (June 28, 1927), p. 7.
67. Ibid., pp. 12–13.
68. Ibid., pp. 14–15.
69. Ibid., no. 3 (June 13, 1927), p. 1.

ers and students, its principal target was the workers. Although the KMT also paid considerable attention to the workers and indeed established a substantial number of labor unions in Mukden, Harbin, and elsewhere, its appeals were broader in nature than those of the CCP and its activities were aimed at the citizenry as a whole. Patriotic and humanitarian themes contained in Sun Yat-sen's Three People's Principles certainly appear to have had a wider appeal than did communism (although the CCP also subscribed to Sun's principles at this time).

What probably mattered more, however, is the nature of the leaderships. As we noted earlier, the CCP's leading cadres in Manchuria—Ch'en Wei-jen, Li Chen-ying, and Teng Ho-kao—were all non-natives, and they would not only have stood out among the native Manchurians in terms of accent and mannerisms but would also have lacked the intimate connections one develops through life. The KMT organizations, on the other hand, were all led by local men and women who had won the respect of others through various accomplishments. Chu Chi-ch'ing, the KMT leader in Harbin, was one of these. He had played a role in the establishment of the Fengtien branch of Sun Yat-sen's Chung-kuo T'ung-meng-hui (Chinese Covenant Society) as early as 1911 and began publishing the *P'ing-min Chou-pao* [Common People's Weekly] in Harbin in 1922.[70] Ch'ien Kung-lai, the leader of the KMT in Mukden, was a professor at the Mukden Shen-tao School,[71] also known as the Manchuria Christian College, and had a large following among the students and local intelligentsia. The students in Mukden were often from the surrounding countryside and were the most effective conveyers of new knowledge and revolutionary messages to their towns and villages. Being natives, they could select their comrades more carefully and easily, evade the authorities more effectively, and expand the network of organizations more rapidly. Of considerable importance to the

70. Li Chih, ed., *Tung-pei k'ang-pao lieh-chuan* [Biographies of Resisters of Tyranny in Manchuria] (Taichung, 1966), pp. 25–36. An interesting fact revealed by the biography is that after Kuo Sung-ling's rebellion erupted in 1925, Li Ta-chao of the CCP attempted to establish contact with some leading figure in Manchuria in order to gain a foothold there. Li allegedly offered three million *yüan* as expenses for mobilizing an army in Manchuria, presumably to destroy Chang Tso-lin and establish a Communist-led revolutionary army. When approached, Chu reportedly declined the money; he did organize a "General Headquarters of the National Revolutionary Army's Northeast Army," headquartered on the second floor of a Christian seminary in Mukden. This report is not corroborated by other sources.

71. *Rōdō mondai shiryō*, no. 3 (June 13, 1927), p. 1; Sturgron to the Secretary of State, September 3, 1927, USNA, 893.00B/402.

KMT in Manchuria was the fact that the local intelligentsia spontaneously rallied to the KMT cause, whereas the CCP was forced by circumstance to send outsiders into Manchuria to transplant a new and foreign ideology.

Was there any collaboration between the CCP and the KMT in Manchuria? This is indeed a tantalizing and important question, but the lack of information precludes a firm answer. According to Chu Chi-ch'ing's biographer, Chu dispatched five CCP members to Manchuria from Canton in 1926 while he was there to engage in youth activities.[72] A KMT manual discovered in Mukden also speaks of a united front with the CCP.[73] Ch'ien Kung-lai, the KMT leader in Mukden, was accused of being a Bolshevist agitator and propagandist when he was arrested in March 1927.[74] Therefore, it is possible that some collaboration existed; but Ch'en Wei-jen's report of December 1927 (to be discussed in chapter 3) makes no reference to either the result of past collaboration or the effect of the split with the KMT.[75] It may be that the cadres of both parties, who were operating under close police surveillance, failed to establish contact. And, since the Manchurian operation of the CCP was directed either from Peking or Shanghai, while that of the KMT was directed from Canton or Nanking, perhaps there was a lack of coordination at the higher level.

It is intriguing to speculate on what might have happened to the CCP in Manchuria had there been more collaboration before and after Chiang Kai-shek's coup against the CCP. Perhaps the CCP would have recruited more members, only to suffer a blow later; in any event, Chiang's coup of April 1927 and the final break between the CCP and the leftwing KMT in Wuhan a few months later ended the united front between the two parties.

Given the fact that the CCP dispatched a very limited number of trained cadres to Manchuria, their accomplishments among the workers were substantial. By 1927, the CCP had enlisted some five hundred workers, and, as Japanese reports attest, the workers as a whole were becoming more militant as a result of cadre propaganda efforts. In spite of this, however, the organization movement among the workers in Manchuria was not successful on the whole. Why was this so?

We have no adequate answer to this intriguing question. The

72. Li Chih, *Tung-pei k'ang-pao lieh-chuan*, p. 31.
73. *Rōdō mondai shiryō*, no. 3 (June 13, 1927), p. 45.
74. Samuel Sokobin, consul in Mukden, to J. V. A. MacMurray, U.S. Minister in Peking, March 15, 1927; USNA 893.00B/289.
75. Ch'en Wei-jen Report.

American consul's comment quoted earlier suggests that the living conditions among the Chinese population in the Kwantung Leased Territory were much better than those in China proper, and this was true throughout the region. Although a great proportion of the Manchurian population was by no means affluent, conditions in Manchuria compared favorably with those in northern China; otherwise, Manchuria would not have received so many new immigrants year after year. Also, the burgeoning industries and mines operated by the Japanese offered mobility to those seeking work. While many of the new immigrants would have suffered from feelings of relative deprivation, particularly in comparison with the established residents and the Japanese, many of them would have had fresh memories of the miseries suffered in their home provinces and they may not have compared their lot with the affluent elements. Banditry, of course, offered another, more immediate form of economic self-improvement to the radically disposed.

Lenin's statement quoted at the outset of this chapter also deserves serious attention. It is certainly extraordinary for the workers to possess "proletarian class consciousness"—let alone originate it. Unless their sufferings were beyond the normal level or unless there were good and immediate prospects of changing their lot by joining a movement, they could not easily be persuaded to join a venture that could adversely affect their livelihood. In the Manchurian context, participation in the Communist-led union movement presented high risks, but it was much more dangerous to join the Communist party.

Perhaps the most important distinction between China proper and Manchuria was the differing characters of their political regimes. As is well known, the CCP's organizational movements gathered momentum in China proper because of its initial successes in such cities as Shanghai and Canton, where the CCP took over the leadership of striking workers and students. The metropolis of Shanghai was ruled by a number of different governments in addition to that of the Chinese, such as the governments of British, Japanese, French, and German concessions. Canton, on the other hand, was under KMT control. In northern China, the presence of Feng Yü-hsiang, the "Christian General," also contributed to the initial success of the CCP because he had been very sympathetic to the CCP until the "February Massacre" of 1923. All in all, China proper had been ruled by many governments, both foreign and domestic, each of which held different perspectives on the "subversives," and coordination could not easily be established. Therefore, it was much easier for the Communists and KMT members to organize and direct various movements.

But the situation in Manchuria was totally different. Despite its weaknesses, the Chang Tso-lin regime was fully in control there, and Chang was determined to wipe out all revolutionaries, be they Communists or KMT. The Japanese, who exercised power over the South Manchuria Railway zone and the Kwantung territory, were equally determined and efficient in this regard. The Japanese army and police presented a special problem for the CCP because the Japanese were so efficient. They were well trained, well disciplined, and not susceptible to bribery. Shen Yin, who filed a report about Dairen for the CCP's *Hsiang-tao Chou-pao* [Guide Weekly] in June 1924, had this to say about the police:

> The police organization here is very thorough. The procedure for family registry investigation is very troublesome. If one's behavior receives the slightest attention or if his connections are not clear in the slightest, he cannot stay here even for a day.[76]

From a Japanese source we have a glimpse of the nature of the vigilance system maintained by the Japanese security establishment. The Japanese military police in Changchun, for example, maintained a card file of all suspicious persons. The cards recorded not only the suspects' biographical data, aliases, and physical features, but all relevant data about their families, livelihood, income, and friends. Membership lists of all socio-economic and political organizations within the jurisdiction were also maintained. The Japanese not only scrutinized the actions and movements of the people but kept a vigilant eye on rail shipments for possible clues about anti-Japanese activities. Needless to say, the Japanese government was inveterately opposed to communism.

The Japanese military and civilian police were not only thorough and efficient; they were also incorruptible. This could not be said, in general, of the Chinese police of Chang Tso-lin's government. A Japanese source alleged that many of the Chinese police in northern Manchuria, where the Russian Bolsheviks had been active for some time, were believed to have been bought off by the Bolsheviks. Perhaps such charges were true, for the Russians were relatively free to operate there. An interpreter in the Chinese police, for example, would inform the Bolsheviks of a forthcoming

76. *Hsiang-tao Chou-pao* (Shanghai), no. 68 (June 4, 1924), p. 545.

raid; or White Russian policemen in the Chinese service who were vigorous in pursuing the Bolsheviks would be summarily dismissed.[77]

These circumstances were of enormous significance because the CCP's strategy in the 1920s was directed toward urban workers; in Manchuria, this meant persons working and living under Japanese jurisdiction. It should be added that the South Manchuria Railway, which was under complete Japanese control, was the principal means of long-distance travel, although horse-drawn carriages were in very common use for intervillage or even intercity travel in most of Manchuria.

Even though some members of the police force under Chang Tso-lin might have been inefficient and corruptible, there was no question about the attitude of the Chang government toward the CCP. Even the Japanese admired the severity and resoluteness of the Chinese police toward the Communists. The treatment of the arrested Russian and Chinese Communists was brutal to a degree that, according to a Japanese source, could be tolerated only in China.[78] It can be concluded, therefore, that while the socio-economic conditions may have favored the CCP in Manchuria, the political superstructure was definitely adverse. The recruitment of party members and building of clandestine party organizations required much more than favorable socio-economic conditions.

Why did the CCP not dispatch more personnel and funds to Manchuria? Considering the geographic proximity of Manchuria to the Soviet Union and its strategic location, would it not have been advantageous for the CCP and the Soviet Union to have had a stronger and more vigorous Communist movement there? Were they not aware that more active support from Shanghai and Moscow would have made a critical difference to the incipient organizational movement in Manchuria?

The reason for the CCP's relative neglect of the Communist movement in Manchuria can be deduced from the membership quota contained in Ch'en Tu-hsiu's October 1926 directive. As we have noted earlier, Ch'en called for only 500 members (or 1.2 percent) in Manchuria by the time of the Fifth Congress, out of a 40,000 total projected membership for the party. Ch'en's estimate of the potentialities in Manchuria thus was very low when we

77. South Manchuria Railway Company, Research Section, General Affairs Department, *Manshū ni okeru sekka senden jijō gaiyō* [Summary of the Condition of Communist Propaganda in Manchuria] (Dairen, 1927), pp. 7–9.
78. Ibid., p. 9.

consider that he called for 10,000 members in Kwangtung and Kwangsi provinces, 7,000 in Kiangsu and Chekiang, 4,000 in Hupei, 3,000 in Hopeh and Shansi, 2,500 in Szechwan, and 2,000 in Shensi and Kansu. He had also called for 1,000 members each in Shantung and Honan provinces. Only in such smaller and rural provinces as Fukien and Anhwei had he called for 500 members each; in the most remote Chinese provinces, Kweichou and Yunnan, he called for 200 members each.[79] The size of the population in Manchuria, it should be added, was almost comparable to that of Kwangtung and Kwangsi provinces combined. As of 1931, Kwangtung Province contained an estimated 7.6 percent of China's total population and Kwangsi 2.5 percent, while Manchuria contained 9.9 percent. Fukien, on the other hand, contained only 3 percent and Anhwei 4.2 percent.[80]

Such a low assessment of the potential for organization in Manchuria obviously did not accurately reflect the socio-economic conditions in Manchuria and directly clashed with Li Chen-ying's observation of 1923 that Manchuria could become a new center of national revolution. Since the central leaders' estimate of the potentialities in Manchuria was so low, it is only natural that they did not assign the necessary personnel and funds.

Since we have no information concerning the way the central leaders arrived at decisions on Manchuria in this period, we can at best hazard a guess at why the central leaders discounted reports by Li Chen-ying and gave Manchuria such a low priority. It is possible, for instance, that the lack of familiarity with the region on the part of the central leaders played an important role: except for Chou En-lai, who had spent a few years of his childhood there, none of the Politburo members had ever been to Manchuria. It is significant that Honan, Fukien, Kweichou, and Yunnan provinces, as was the case with the Manchurian provinces, did not produce a single member of the Politburo between 1921 and 1945,[81] and that the party called for a membership of 1,000 or less in each of these provinces in 1926. It is probably not too far fetched to argue that the CCP leaders of the early 1920s did not consider Manchuria an integral part of China, or that they considered Manchuria a remote territory akin to Kweichou and Yunnan

---

79. *Chiao-yü tsa-chih*, no. 3 (December 1, 1926), pp. 33–34. The Fifth Congress was held in Wuhan, April–May, 1927.
80. *China Yearbook*, 1931, p. 2.
81. Robert C. North and Ithiel de Sola Pool, "Kuomintang and Chinese Communist Elites," in Harold D. Lasswell and Daniel Lerner, eds., *World Revolutionary Elites* (Cambridge, Mass., 1965), p. 403.

provinces in the southwest. Even though the central leaders did send Ch'en Wei-jen and Li Chen-ying to direct the organizational movement there, they were not willing or able to allocate massive resources. It is highly likely that the central leaders shared the stereotyped image of Manchuria held then by most Chinese, as characterized by Li Chen-ying in his 1923 report:

> When one mentions the Three Eastern Provinces, which are often forgotten by the people, one immediately conjures up an image of a vast, cold, and barren place. Even concretely, the most one's intuition can tell him is the actions of the Japanese, the Tatar bandits, and imperial Russia. Having been neglected for so long, these provinces developed into an area where culture is backward, and where industry and commerce developed in warped fashion by yielding to imperialism.[82]

In the meantime, the central leaders were obliged to contend with the movement in the vast territory within the Great Wall. The central leaders of this era were still novices in organizational movements, and many important problems in strategy and tactics needed to be ironed out. One wonders, therefore, whether the central leaders would have been able to devote much time to the situation in Manchuria. Indeed, as we have seen earlier, some of the cadres were dispatched from Peking, where the CCP's northern bureau was located. It is probable that, in spite of the vast size and large population of Manchuria, the central leaders may have delegated responsibility for Manchuria to the northern bureau. If this was the case, the party organization in Manchuria would have been treated as an appendage of the Communist movement in Hopeh and Shansi provinces. The first indication of regionwide organization in Manchuria was the establishment of the Temporary Committee of the Manchuria Provincial Committee in October 1927. It is quite possible that all organizational movement in Manchuria had been theretofore directed by the northern bureau, which was also responsible for Hopeh and Shansi provinces.

The central leaders' relative neglect of the situation in Manchuria also goes a long way toward explaining their ignoring the peculiar character of Manchuria's politics and economy. As had been stressed by Li Chen-ying, the Japanese were deeply entrenched in Manchuria's politics and economy by the early 1920s;

---

82. [Li] Chen-ying, "Analysis of the Situation in the Three Eastern Provinces," *Hsiang-tao Chou-pao* (Shanghai), no. 52 (January 20, 1924), p. 396.

this required a different set of strategies on the part of the CCP. Li correctly stressed the need to concentrate on the anti-Japanese sentiment among the Chinese populace and implicitly called for a broad-scale united front among diverse social strata. But as far as can be ascertained, the efforts of the CCP were directed toward organizing the proletariat on the basis of orthodox Communist slogans, and the anti-Japanese theme was not stressed.

But did the leaders assign low priority to Manchuria only because of their unfamiliarity with the region or their preoccupation with the movement elsewhere? Why did the Comintern or the Communist party of the Soviet Union not provide more active support to the movement in Manchuria? Why did the CCP cadres in Manchuria not establish a close working relationship with the Russian Communists operating in the Chinese Eastern Railway zone? Were there other considerations? We shall keep these questions in mind as we explore subsequent events.

3 | Fetters of Soviet National Interest

THE JULY 1927 ARREST OF THE CHINESE COMMUNIST Party (CCP) members in Dairen exposed the frailty of a subversive organization operating in a hostile environment. Although propaganda activities undertaken by party cadres had changed the mood of the workers and their attitude toward their employers, the number of those recruited into the party had been infinitesimal. Even those who had been admitted into the party were quickly demoralized once they came to be hunted by the Japanese military police, notorious for their severity toward the Chinese.

This situation caused the party leaders in Shanghai to engage in a heated debate with the cadres in Manchuria. How could the CCP overcome the obstacles in its way and organize and lead a viable mass movement? Should the CCP not adopt strategies and tactics that were more appropriate to local conditions? Should it not concentrate on mobilizing the masses against Japanese imperialism? Should it not establish alliances with various existing groups, such as bandits and other outlaw groups, in fomenting revolution? We shall trace the debate in this chapter.

An outstanding feature of this debate was the constraint placed upon the CCP leadership of this era by the requirements of Soviet national interest. This important factor, however, was unknown to the cadres in Manchuria; hence they passionately pleaded for the line of policy they felt most promising. They were not concerned that the success of their strategy would have hampered the current interest of the Soviet Union. The central leaders, however, were unable to articulate their primary concern in a straightforward manner and were thus obliged to accentuate the weaknesses in the strategy advocated by the Manchurian Committee and to ignore the plea for a clear-cut definition of the mission of that committee. But first we must review the condition of the party in Manchuria in 1927.

The CCP in Manchuria, 1927

Upon receiving the news of the arrests in Dairen, the CCP headquarters dispatched Ch'en Wei-jen, who, as we noted in chapter 2, was the first CCP cadre to be sent to Manchuria in 1923. In 1927, he was active in Peking as the head of the Organization Department of the Peking Area Committee (Pei-ching Ti-fang Wei-yüan-hui).[1] Ch'en arrived on the scene on October 14, 1927, and filed a detailed report on December 22.[2]

Ch'en found the situation in Manchuria dismal indeed. In Dairen, where there had been some 300 comrades, the party organization was completely demolished. In Mukden, only about 30 of the original 90 comrades remained. Various special branches in the vicinity had been out of contact with the party for nearly half a year. The organizations in Kirin and Changchun were stagnant. In Harbin, only about 30 of the original 130 members remained, and they were not taking any action; various branches had been out of contact with the party headquarters for nearly half a year and they had no liaison among themselves.

Ch'en Wei-jen immediately proceeded to reconstruct the party. On October 24, 1927, ten days after his arrival, Ch'en organized the Temporary Manchuria Provincial Committee (Manchou-sheng Lin-shih Wei-yüan-hui)[3] by convening a meeting of fourteen active elements from Harbin, Changchun, Kirin, Mukden, and Dairen. Ch'en does not say where the meeting was held, but it elected three members to the executive committee (himself, a man named "Ho Seng," and a printer), three control committee members (workers from Changchun, Harbin, and Dairen), two

---

1. Yüeh Sheng (Sheng Chung-liang), *Sun Yat-sen University in Moscow and the Chinese Revolution: A Personal Account* (Lawrence, Kansas, 1971), p. 23.
2. "Report and Proposal of Comrade Wei-jen in Manchuria, December 22, 1927," in *Chung-yang Cheng-chih T'ung-hsün* [Central Political Bulletin] (an organ of the CCP Central Committee), no. 16, pp. 70–80; hereafter cited as Ch'en Wei-jen Report. Specific page numbers cannot be provided here as the manuscript version consulted does not show the endings of pages within the article.
3. The system of temporary provincial executive committees had been instituted by the "Draft Plan of Party Activities in the Provinces" adopted by representatives of the party headquarters and others from Peking, Harbin, Hankow, and Shanghai, who met at an unspecified location to discuss organizational matters in February 1927. One or two agents were to be dispatched after the meeting to organize the provincial committees within a month of their arrival in the assigned area and then reorganize them into regular provincial committees within five months. The CCP therefore had no regular system of local organization. Each area had a special district committee (T'e-pieh Ch'ü Chih-hsing Pu). See Wang Chien-min, *Chung-kuo Kung-ch'an-tang shih-kao* [Draft History of the Chinese Communist Party] (Taipei, 1965), vol. 1, pp. 357–359.

candidate members of the executive committee and two candidate members of the control committee. The secretary for the temporary committee of the Communist Youth Corps was also elected.

The first task of the new executive committee was to revive the defunct organizations. Ch'en reported that agents were dispatched to Harbin, Changchun, Kirin, Fengtien, and Dairen for that purpose. The Harbin comrades had already established a city committee to organize workers along the Chinese Eastern Railway, and it had been able to gather 70 comrades, in about ten branches. On the anniversary of the October Revolution, they had carried out a propaganda activity that "shocked the enemy." The man assigned to take charge of operations at the railroad, however, was not able to accomplish much in organizing the workers because of the opposition of Russian comrades, according to Ch'en.[4]

District committees were organized in Changchun and Kirin, where, at the time of the report, there were 19 members, in four branches. They had instigated a workers' "economic strike" and won their demands, although Ch'en did not go into the details. He saw a "very good opportunity and possibility" for organizing secret labor unions among the workers of the Kirin–Changchun Railway and the Chinese Eastern Railway. "The comrade there is positive in attitude and action and can bear responsibilities; although only a very small number of comrades have been recruited, they have been effective."[5]

In Mukden, a district committee was established with 19 members, in ten branches. Presumably, the branches were scattered in various entrepreneurial or educational units. Ch'en was not very optimistic in his analysis of the comrades in Mukden. Except for one or two workers, they were all intelligentsia or shop employees, passive in orientation, short on courage, and rather ineffective. Ch'en had no great hopes for these members, although he thought that, with training, they might be used for some "internal technical work" (intelligence work?) and perhaps, on occasion, they might be given assignments dealing with workers' and farmers' movements. In the five *hsien* surrounding Mukden, Ch'en was able to bring together 28 comrades and reestablish branches. They were all primary school teachers and principals, rather than the workers and farmers desired by the party.

In Dairen, a municipal committee was established with 17

4. Ch'en Wei-jen Report.
5. Ibid.

members, in four branches, and seven of them were considered to be "energetic elements." Most of them were workers, the minority being shop employees. All were young. A branch was established in Lushun, and some comrades were found in nearby Chinchou.

Summing up the condition of the party in Manchuria as of December 1927, Ch'en said: "It is shameful to say in one breath that we have a party organization."[6] There were, all together, 173 comrades, of whom about half were intelligentsia and half workers and shop employees; there were no farmers. The comrades had no experience in party operations and very ambiguous notions about the party; some could not distinguish the CCP from the KMT. Therefore, the effectiveness of the party was unknown, and all that could be said was that the party had some links in northern and southern Manchuria for future operations.

Ch'en faced numerous problems in turning this amorphous body of men into a revolutionary group, expanding its numbers, and implementing the strategies handed down by the central leaders.

Ch'en sought help from the Russian Communists now operating the Chinese Eastern Railway but found them uncooperative. They had obviously received instructions from higher authorities not to lend a hand to the Chinese Communists, although Ch'en was not aware of it. The Russians refused to provide any funds, and they also refused to transmit coded messages for Ch'en, even though he bore introductions from Gregorii Voitinsky and M. N. Roy, the two Comintern representatives in China. "They only know how to obey the orders from Stalin and Bukharin and no one else," Ch'en bitterly complained.[7] He was pessimistic about the party's operation in northern Manchuria, which was very much in the Soviet domain.

Ch'en was bothered most, however, by the Russians' uncommunistic managerial practices and racial prejudice. The Russians, for example, could have ordered the railway to pay equal wages for equal work, but they had not done so. This, Ch'en argued, was not a matter to be solved by a workers' strike. (Indeed, how could the Chinese proletariat strike against a Bolshevik management?) Furthermore, the Russian workers and Russian party members brushed aside the suggestions of the Chinese workers and Chinese "worker comrades." Racial prejudice came out in the appointment of the secretary of the CCP's Harbin Municipal Committee, who

6. Ibid.
7. Ibid.

was originally a leader of the Chinese railway workers—and who had ability and was faithful to the party, Ch'en asserted. But a "Russian comrade" of lower rank spoke unfavorably of him and had him rejected. The Chinese proposed a joint investigation, that the Russian party send one investigator and the Chinese another, but the Russians refused, and in the end they "let him go the opposite direction" (presumably he turned to anti-party activity). Although Ch'en spoke of the need for having representatives from the Japanese and Korean Communist parties in Manchuria to facilitate cooperation among the Chinese, Japanese, and Korean workers, he was evidently having trouble mainly with the Russians because of their "obstinacy" and "unreasonableness."[8] We shall return to this issue later.

The published version of Ch'en's report omitted his discussion of the military and "economic" problems, but it sufficiently revealed the financial straits of the CCP in Manchuria.[9] The Russians' refusal of the Chinese Communists' requests for financial aid has been noted. Had the agents in Manchuria been sufficiently supported from Shanghai, there would have been no need to approach the Russians. Furthermore, in discussing the problem of the Chinese Communist Youth Corps operation in Manchuria, Ch'en indicated that the man dispatched from the Youth Corps' Northern (North China) Bureau, having received neither mail nor money, had, therefore, been forced to obtain a job as a proofreader, earning 18 *yüan* a month. Evidently, these agents were left to their own resources once the assignments were given. In fact, in discussing the problem of liaison, Ch'en said that "those in Manchuria felt like daughters sent off into marriage, about whom no one cared afterward."[10]

Ch'en called for assistance, and he was undoubtedly shorthanded. He requested the party headquarters to find comrades of Manchurian origin among the graduates of Whampoa Military Academy, Chungshan University (Sun Yat-sen University in Moscow), and the Farmers' Movement Institute and send them to him. Those of other provincial origins were not suitable because they would not be able to work among the people (owing to the difference in dialect) and also would be vulnerable to arrest.

A contemporary Japanese account supplements Ch'en's report with respect to the party's activities. From a resolution adopted by

8. Ibid.
9. The published version of Ch'en Wei-jen's report includes subheadings on the military and economic problems, but the content was not published.
10. Ch'en Wei-jen Report.

the Kwantung Prefectural Committee in Dairen on January 20, 1928, it appears that the lower echelons of the party in Manchuria strove to follow faithfully the instructions of the central leaders and that the local cadres approached their tasks with zeal. For example, the committee was determined to recruit 2,000 comrades into the dock workers' party branch and 2,000 into the pottery industry party branch within three months, and to establish unions with 5,000 members in both fields within the same period.[11] These goals would have been difficult to fulfill, even under optimal conditions.

The Kwantung Prefectural Committee noted that its activities during the previous two months had been confined to seeking out scattered former comrades. The organization had been completely demolished in July and had not yet recovered its strength and organizational momentum. The committee attributed past failures to errors in carrying out secret operations and called on party members to pay special attention to this problem. Further, without recruiting new members, the party could not find a new life. There was need also for the strengthening of discipline. Education and training of the party members were considered to be particularly important for overcoming the fears held by the comrades and improving their skill in conducting secret operations.[12]

The overall picture of the Kwantung Prefectural Committee that emerges from these documents is a dismal one. For all practical purposes, the farmers in the territory were out of reach because of their relative prosperity.[13] Creating disturbances and organizing the farmers through nationalistic appeals would have been difficult enough had the party possessed skilled veterans and the Japanese police been less efficient. A more important problem was the demoralized state of the old members, indicated by the reference to their fears. It would not be farfetched to think that the same fears restrained members in other parts of Manchuria.

The efficiency of the Japanese police was another problem to be reckoned with. In January 1928, the police in Dairen arrested Liu

11. Ōsaka Tai-shi Keizai Renmei (Osaka Economic Federation for China), ed., *Sa-Rempō to Shina Manshū no Kyōsan Undō* [The Soviet Union and the Communist Movement in China and Manchuria] (Tokyo, 1934), pp. 556–557.
12. Ibid., pp. 553–558.
13. A study of Ramon H. Myers and Thomas R. Ulie corroborates the party's prognosis. It conclusively shows that in the Liaotung Peninsula, which included the Kwantung territory, farm production increased at a more rapid rate than did the population, and crop yields rose impressively between 1906 and 1937. "Foreign Influence and Agricultural Development in Northeast China: A Case Study of the Liaotung Peninsula, 1906–42," *Journal of Asian Studies*, vol. 31, no. 2 (February 1972), pp. 329–350.

Li-ming, who reportedly had engaged in Communist activities in the Kirin and Changchun regions. In February, the police in Dairen arrested five CCP members who were on their way into Manchuria from North China. In March, the police rounded up five Communists, including Tu Chi-ts'eng, who had arrived in Dairen from Peking at the end of 1927 and played an active role in the Kwantung Prefectural Committee.[14]

The difficulty in conducting secret operations in Manchuria is amply displayed by Tu's career. Of Honan origin, he had been a teacher in North China after his graduation from the Peking Higher Normal School in 1925. He went to Kirin in 1926 and, while teaching at a middle school there, engaged in organizational activities for the KMT with a left-wing member of that party who was soon arrested by the local Chinese police. Tu fled to Harbin and then to Peking, where he joined the CCP. Sent back to Changchun, he succeeded in organizing the Kirin provincial branch of the KMT, but the police soon were pursuing him. He fled again to Peking and at the end of 1927 was back in Dairen, where he was finally arrested.

The arrests of these elements do not seem to have affected the operations of the Kwantung Prefectural Committee; but an action taken by the committee in late April 1928 had severe consequences. This was the distribution of a leaflet entitled "The May Day Declaration of the Kwantung Prefectural Committee of the Chinese Communist Party" on April 28.

What effect the leaflet had on the masses or how many persons actually read it is not known. But the cost of issuing the declaration was very high for the Communist movement in Manchuria. On April 29, the day after the leaflet was distributed, the police arrested Ch'ü Wen-hsiu, the secretary of the Kwantung Prefectural Committee, and seized the committee's files.[15] Shortly after that, 47 other party members were arrested in Yingkou, Mukden, Chinchou, and Dairen. The Communist movement in the Kwantung territory was thus wiped out. Although this was the most industrialized and most urbanized region in Manchuria, commu-

14. *Sa-Rempō to Shina Manshū*, pp. 549–550; Liu is not otherwise identified.
15. Ibid., p. 550. Chü was a young man of 23 when arrested. A native of Chinchou in western Manchuria, he went to Peking to study, where he joined the CCP in 1926, obviously influenced by the strong currents of nationalism and communism that swept the country after the May 30 Incident. He was with the Nationalist Army during the northern expedition, serving as a secretary, and later worked as a clerk in the Wuhan Labor Union. He returned home after the KMT-CCP split in 1927 and was solicited in January 1928 by one Chang Chih of the Fengtien Provincial Committee of the CCP to join the movement in Dairen.

nism was simply not to take root there. The many arrests, however, cannot be attributed primarily to the inexperience or ineptitude of the Chinese Communists; the efficiency of the Japanese police was responsible. Thousands of Korean Communists and nationalists, along with hundreds of Japanese Communists, had likewise been discovering that the Japanese police left them very little room to maneuver.

The arrests in the Kwantung territory must have weakened the entire movement in Manchuria, if only by adversely affecting the morale of the Communists in other areas. There are no records of arrests outside the Kwantung territory—indeed, no information on further party activities in Manchuria in 1928 is available.

All in all, Ch'en Wei-jen faced a formidable task in putting vitality into the Communist movement. In spite of Li Chen-ying's initial optimism that Manchuria could become a new center of national revolution, the movement was almost moribund at the end of the fifth year of its efforts.

The Strategy of Peasant Insurrections

Manchuria, of course, was not the only region where the CCP suffered a loss around this time. Indeed, 1927 was the worst year for the CCP since its founding in 1921, and the situation did not improve in 1928. Stalin's insistence on the CCP's continued subordination to the KMT had resulted in the Shanghai massacre of April, when tens of thousands of CCP members and CCP-affiliated workers were murdered by Chiang Kai-shek's troops. Stalin then pinned his hopes on the left wing of the KMT under Wang Ching-wei, but by July the breach between the left wing of the KMT and the CCP was complete, and Stalin's plan to maintain Soviet alliance with the KMT ended in complete failure.[16] It was necessary for Stalin to formulate a new China policy.

The new strategy, communicated through the two new agents from Moscow, Heinz Neumann and Besso Lominadze, was to call for massive uprisings throughout China. On August 7, three weeks after the leftwing KMT government in Wuhan expelled the CCP, a special conference of CCP leaders was held to endorse the new instructions. Ch'en Tu-hsiu, who had strenuously but unsuccessfully tried to extricate the CCP from KMT control, was made a scapegoat for the fiasco, and Ch'ü Ch'iu-pai was installed as the

---

16. James Pinckney Harrison, *The Long March to Power: A History of the Chinese Communist Party, 1921–72* (New York, 1972), pp. 112–117.

new leader. The conference then adopted a resolution calling for the "preparation of systematic, planned peasant insurrections, organized on as wide a scale as possible," and for taking advantage of the harvesting period that year to "intensify the class struggle in the villages." (Stalin had decided in Moscow that the agrarian movement in China would "grow into a mighty revolution embracing tens of millions of peasants" and that the tide of revolution was still rising.) The conference also called for the "arming of the workers" to "coordinate battles with peasant uprisings" to prepare for the overthrow of the counterrevolutionary movement.[17]

Ch'en Wei-jen in Manchuria received the text of the August 7 resolution and found the new instructions overwhelming.[18] He frankly admitted in his report that there was no possibility of bringing about a mass revolt in the immediate future. This was so, he declared, despite the fact that the objective conditions in Manchuria were highly favorable for revolution, for both political and economic reasons. Nonetheless, the Communist aim in Manchuria, according to Ch'en, was to instigate revolutionary riots and wage revolutionary war against Japan. The Chinese workers and farmers, the Korean farmers, and the Russians and Mongolians were to be brought together for this ultimate purpose. He argued that the workers' movement must be coordinated very closely with the farmers' movements, and that there should be meticulous preparation for the riots. Following the current party line, Ch'en stressed the need for collaboration between the workers and peasants.

Considering the anemic conditions of the CCP in Manchuria, Ch'en Wei-jen's remarks cannot be considered as anything more than rhetoric. But his call for "revolutionary riots" and "revolutionary war against Japan" was based on his analysis of the existing conditions in Manchuria. Ch'en was impressed—much more so than Li Chen-ying had been in 1924—by the extent of Japanese dominance in Manchuria. The Japanese controlled the press, the currency, and industry; Japanese soldiers and police operated freely everywhere; and the Fengtien Army was directed by Japanese advisers and staff officers. As soon as one crossed the border into Manchuria, Ch'en went on, one found the newspapers promoting Japanese policy, Japanese money in the markets, and triumphant Japanese soldiers and police committing "barbaric acts

17. Ibid., pp. 123–129.
18. Ch'en told of the efforts made in Manchuria according to the lines established in the resolution in Ch'en Wei-jen Report.

of aggression against China." In consequence, the peoples of Manchuria felt strong enmity and resentment toward the Japanese. Moreover, the economy was in ruin because of Chang Tso-lin's involvement in North China politics. The masses were exploited in hundreds of ways, and the value of the currency had plunged. Mukden was rather sparsely guarded, and Ch'en thought that one or two thousand rioters could take the city and hold it for at least a short period.

The events of subsequent years were to prove Ch'en's evaluation of the party's organizational potentialities in Manchuria too optimistic. Ch'en thought that the farmers and workers in Manchuria could be easily mobilized in support of the party's cause. The farmers had gone through an especially clear-cut process of class differentiation and were divided into a minority of landlords and a vast majority of landless. Many poor farmers were suffering severely. Hired farm laborers were striking because the money they received had little real value. The Chang government was imposing taxes and confiscating lands with little discretion because of its own growing needs. The farmers in various places were reacting against these policies by joining the "Poor People's Party" (i.e., bandit groups) or by engaging in petition movements.

The condition of the workers was also promising for the party, Ch'en reported, because those employed in Chinese and Japanese industries were faring little better than prisoners sentenced to hard labor. The miners were rising in spontaneous revolts, and the workers in Dairen had to be restrained from rioting by party comrades. The Chinese workers were severely discriminated against by both the Japanese- and Russian-operated industries, the pay of a Chinese worker being not more than one-tenth that of a Japanese. In short, Ch'en declared, "The worker's movement in Manchuria can be said to be completely a movement against Japan."

While Ch'en may have exaggerated the propensity of the workers and farmers to rise in revolt, there is no question that poverty and misery were widespread in Manchuria. Chang Tso-lin's political ambition was causing serious problems in Manchuria; it had also offered a golden opportunity for Japan to expand its already extensive influence in Manchuria. "Manchuria has all the objective conditions for a revolution," Ch'en went on. "It has a good operational environment for us. It has great possibilities for our implementation of new policies."[19] He had already dispatched a number of agents to various areas to locate former comrades and

19. Ch'en Wei-jen Report.

establish links with already existing farmers' and workers' movements, such as the "Poor People's Party" and the "Big Sword Society" (Ta-tao Hui). Efforts were being made to infiltrate the mines of Fushun, Penhsihu, and Anshan, and a Communist cell of seven persons had been established in Shahokou.

The Central Committee's response to Ch'en Wei-jen's report and proposal was generally favorable. In its "Resolution on the Plan of Activities in Manchuria," dated December 24,[20] the headquarters borrowed heavily from Ch'en's report in describing the conditions in Manchuria and formalized the bulk of his recommendations as official policy. It agreed with Ch'en that the Chinese and Korean farmers and industrial workers should establish close liaison for revolutionary purposes and that international cooperation should be effected. Commenting evidently on the "Poor People's Party" and the "Big Sword Society," the central leaders also encouraged the use of the bandits as a means of expanding the struggle in the villages. The only criticism in the Central Committee's resolution was directed toward the party members in Dairen who had erred in preventing the workers from rioting there, in clear conflict with the resolution of the Enlarged Conference of the Provisional Political Bureau of the Central Committee in November 1927, which had declared: "Even when the party considers it premature, the party must rise and provide guidance to all spontaneous struggles of the masses."[21] The rest of the Central Committee's instructions on the workers' and farmers' movements can hardly have been particularly new or surprising to Ch'en, who already had ample experience as an organizer.

On the issue of revolutionary war against Japan, however, the Central Committee was much more cautious than Ch'en Wei-jen. While the central leaders did stress the importance of the anti-Japanese movement,[22] they were not willing to direct the Man-

20. "Resolution on the Plan of Activities in Manchuria," dated December 24, 1927, *Chung-yang cheng-chih t'ung-hsün* [Central Political Bulletin], no. 16, pp. 60–70. A Japanese translation of this resolution is available in *Chūgoku kyōsantō-shi shiryō-shū* [Compendium of Materials on the History of the Chinese Communist Party], edited by the Chinese Department of the Nihon Kokusai Mondai Kenkyūjo (Japanese International Problems Research Center) (Tokyo, 1971), vol. 3, pp. 455–463. Hereafter cited as *Shiryō-shū*.

21. Text of the "Resolution Concerning the Present Situation in China and the Tasks of the Communist Party" in *Pu-erh-sai-wei-k'o* (Bolshevik), no. 6 (November 26, 1927), pp. 140–153. Japanese translation in *Shiryō-shū*, vol. 3, pp. 369–386. The quotation here is from ibid., p. 379.

22. The Central Committee's resolution stated "Opposing Japan is a natural, deep seated, and universal revolutionary action of the farmers in Manchuria. We must not avoid hardship and difficulty but seek them out everywhere and at all times.... In all operations, attention must be paid to propagating anti-Japanese operations." Propaganda addressed to workers was to call for equal pay for equal

churian cadres to move toward a revolutionary war against Japan. The resolution insisted that anti-Japanese activities would be carried on only through the "regular channel" of the workers' and farmers' movements and, moreover, that such activities must never count on the collaboration of the merchants and students in the cities. The party leaders held little hope that these elements would rise up, and they had all but abandoned operations to enlist them. The central leaders' clear intent was to subordinate the anti-Japanese struggle to the worker-farmer movement, which had not been progressing satisfactorily in either Manchuria or China proper; for reasons of their own, the central leaders were not willing to encourage Ch'en's hopes for a revolutionary war against Japan.

Bandits and Revolutionary War

One of the activities that Ch'en Wei-jen pursued—as he had reported to the party leaders in December—was the establishment of links with the "Poor People's Party" and the "Big Sword Society." For the Communist cadres in Manchuria, who hoped to achieve quick results in line with the party's instructions to prepare for "systematic, planned peasant insurrections," the presence of large numbers of bandits must have been tempting indeed. While it would be no simple task to organize the farmers and workers to engage in riots or guerrilla warfare, bandits might be easily persuaded to attack a weakly defended city. Many of these bandit groups were like private armies—some of them had thousands of men—with mobility, weapons, considerable discipline, and often connections with local military and political figures. As political and economic conditions deteriorated, the strength of the bandits grew in proportion, rising from an estimated 20,000 in 1924 to 28,000 in 1926, 50,000 in 1927, and 58,000 in 1929.[23]

---

work by Chinese, Russian, and Japanese workers, and they were to protest against physical punishment and abuse of the Chinese by Japanese soldiers, policemen, and others. The resolution contained a section listing five slogans on opposing Japanese imperialism. *Shiryō-shū*, vol. 3, p. 462.

23. Manshūkokushi Hensan Kankōkai (Editorial and Publication Committee of the History of Manchukuo), *Manshūkokushi* [History of Manchukuo] (Tokyo, 1971), vol. 2, p. 302. About the organization, operation and discipline of the bandit groups, see Chief of the Harbin Office, South Manchuria Railway Company, "Manshū bazoku ni tsuite" [Concerning the Mounted Bandits in Manchuria] (December 20, 1924), in Itō Takeo, Ogiwara Kiwamu, and Fujii Masuo, eds., *Man Tetsu* [South Manchuria Railway], vol. 2, being vol. 32 of *Gendaishi shiryō* [Materials on Contemporary History] (Tokyo, 1967), pp. 795–805; and Yen Ying, *Tung-pei I-yung-chün chan-shih* [Combat History of the Northeastern Volunteer Army] (Hong Kong, 1963), passim.

While the "Big Sword Society" differed from the ordinary bandits, it was also an outlaw group and hence amenable to proposals for collaboration in antigovernment actions. Since little is known about the Big Swords, a brief account of them would be useful here.

Although both the CCP Manchurian Committee and CCP Central Headquarters continually lumped the Big Sword Society of the Tung-pien-tao together with the bandits, the Big Swords were in fact a semi-religious, self-governing body, whose members were drawn from both the rural gentry and the peasants. Tung-pien-tao ("Eastern Border District") was the term applied to the mountainous region along the Korean border south of the Changpai Mountains, including Kuantien, Huanjen, Chian, Tunghwa, Linchiang, and Changpai *hsien*. This region had long been regarded as sacred by the Ch'ing dynasty, the Changpai Mountains in the northern part of the area being the homeland of the Manchu tribe, and the government had outlawed settlement in the entire region. But by the 1880s small communities of Chinese and Korean immigrants had sprung into existence there. These communities were governed by a guild which was not a part of the official government. In any event, because Tung-pien-tao was remote from the administrative centers in Kirin and Mukden, and because of its dense forests and steep ravines and ridges, the government had not extended protection to the residents by the 1920s; they were left to the mercy of bandits, who looted them at will.[24]

It was thus in the interest of self-protection that the residents introduced the Big Sword Society into the region. In the fall of 1927, some of the gentry in Tunghwa Prefecture invited Big Sword masters from Shantung Province to come and organize branches. The Big Swords, an offshoot of the Red Spear Society (Hung-ch'iang hui), which in turn had sprung from the famous Boxers, taught that those who drank water containing the ashes of paper amulets and uttered charms in prayer would become invulnerable to bullets and spears.[25] Thus fortified and armed with

24. Henry Evan M. James, *The Long White Mountain* (London, 1888), pp. 250–252. James traversed this region on foot in 1886 with Lieutenant (later Sir) Francis E. Younghusband. James presents a vivid account of the geography, climate, and inhabitants of the region. His companion wrote a shorter and equally interesting account in the *Heart of a Continent* (New York, 1896), pp. 1–15.

25. Tai Hsüan-chih, *Hung-ch'iang Hui, 1916–1949* [The Red Spear Society] (Taipei, 1973), p. 141. The author relies on information provided in Suematsu Takayoshi, *Shina no himitsu kessha to jizen kessha* [Secret Societies and Benevolent Societies in China] (Tokyo, n.d.), pp. 159–174. The process of indoctrinating

primitive weapons, members of the society offered stiff resistance to the bandits and succeeded in repelling their attacks. The influence of the society quickly spread to nearby areas, and within the same year, several tens of thousands were enrolled as members. Merchants, herb doctors, village chiefs, and landlords became the heads of local units, and Masters (*Lao-shih*) and Superior Masters (*Tsung Lao-shih*) toured the towns and villages to provide guidance and inspection.[26]

As the Big Swords expanded their power in the eastern border district, the government outlawed the society and attempted to suppress it. This led to an uprising and riot by members of the Tunghwa branch, who attacked government soldiers and destroyed telephone lines on January 2, 1928. Members of the society in nearby Linchiang, Chian, and Huanjen rallied in support of the Tunghwa branch, and on January 4, the town of Tunghwa fell to the Big Swords. But an army detachment quickly squashed the uprising. Many of the participants were massacred: in one village, every male above 12 years of age was executed. The soldiers then engaged in looting, rape, and arson throughout the region with a ferocity far exceeding that of any bandit group, and large rewards were offered for the arrest of the principal leaders of the society.[27] The brutal attempt at suppression, however, did not end the movement.

The Communist cadres in Manchuria quite naturally saw hope in the Big Sword Society. While the society was clearly a sectarian organization, it was also an organization of oppressed people harboring strong resentment toward the government. Far from being an ordinary bandit group, the society had its raison d'être in trying to protect its members from harm by both bandits and government agencies. The Manchurian leaders hoped that the Big Sword Society and the bandits could be used to create an upheaval, and that even if this did not lead to immediate success, it would create revolutionary excitement, thereby increasing the chance for further Communist recruitment. It is also possible that the Manchurian leaders sympathized with the leaders of the secret societies as well as the bandits, and—like Mao Tse-tung in the same period—regarded both as old-fashioned heroes who would come

---

invulnerability among the Big Swords was identical to that of the Red Spears in North China. See Roman Slawinski, "The Red Spears in the Late 1920s," in Jean Chesneaux, ed., *Popular Movements and Secret Societies in China, 1840–1950* (Stanford, 1972), p. 204.
26. Tai Hsüan-chih, *Hung-ch'iang Hui*, pp. 141–142.
27. Ibid., pp. 142–144.

to the aid of the masses in distress and restore justice.[28] The Manchurian cadres had more faith in the activities of these elements than in the day-to-day struggles of a more orthodox nature (in the Communist sense) ordered by the Central Committee.

As we have noted, the central leaders were favorably disposed to the suggestion that these groups might be used by the CCP. While the central leaders firmly warned against using "one or two bandit groups" or the Big Sword Society to lead farmers' uprisings, the use of bandits in the farmers' movement was not ruled out:

> In situations where the defense in the rear area has been weakened because of the Fengtien Army's involvement in the war in China proper, then in the districts where farmer masses are engaged in the struggles, it is possible to utilize the bandit masses and merge them with the farmers' guerrilla warfare to expand the village struggles and direct them toward riots. This is also an important operation. It is all the more necessary to lead the farmers to snatch away the warlords' weapons and incite the soldiers.[29]

The efforts of the Manchurian Committee were somewhat successful. In early 1928, the committee sent a representative to the central leaders reporting that the bandits in Tung-pien-tao wished to unite with the party for the purpose of engaging in riots. The representative was of the opinion that the party should utilize the power of the bandits to carry out riots in order to take over political power.[30]

Polemic Over Revolution in Manchuria

The Manchurian Committee's grand design for revolution, however, was not to be tested in action. Events in China and the reaction in Moscow compelled the CCP leadership to hold its rad-

---

28. On Mao Tse-tung's sympathy and relationship with bandit groups, see Stuart Schram, *Mao Tse-tung* (Baltimore and Harmondsworth, 1967), pp. 126–128. It is interesting that Alexander Ivin, a Soviet sinologist writing in 1927, argued that the Chinese revolution would profit from the Red Spears movement. "Red Spears," *Krestianskoe dvizhenie v Kitae* [Chinese Peasant Movements] (Moscow, 1927). Cited by Slawinski, "Red Spears," p. 201. Slawinski notes that the Communists in Loyang attempted to establish a cooperative relationship with the Red Spears in the 1920s, but the agents whom they sent to facilitate the relationship were either killed or wounded (op. cit., p. 208).

29. "Resolution on the Plan for Activities in Manchuria," December 24, 1927, *Chung-yang cheng-chih t'ung-hsün*, no. 16., pp. 60–70.

30. "Letter of the Central Headquarters to the Manchurian Temporary Com-

ical policy in abeyance. The CCP-directed uprisings in southern Chinese cities, including Nanchang, Swatow, Changsha, and Canton, between August and December had failed miserably, exposing the grievous errors of "putschism" beyond doubt. The Fifteenth Congress of the Communist Party of the Soviet Union had met in December 1927 to denounce the CCP's radical policies and call for more caution.[31]

For some reason, however, the central leaders were not willing to divulge to the Manchurian Committee that a change had taken place in the party's policies. Ch'ü Ch'iu-pai and Heinz Neumann did not give up their struggle to oppose the Comintern's new China policy until the Sixth World Congress of the Comintern was held between July and September of 1928,[32] and hence they may have been unwilling to announce the reversal of policy to a subordinate branch. But it was necessary to stop the Manchurian Committee from continuing the radical policy, and thus a rationale had to be offered.

The central leaders may not have anticipated it, but the rationale that they presented led to a serious polemic with the Manchurian Committee that was to last several months. A careless statement made by the central leaders in rationalizing their reversal of policy—undoubtedly reflecting their harried state of mind in this period—expanded the polemic far beyond the immediate issue of the use of bandits and eventually caused much damage to the morale of those operating in the hostile environment of Manchuria. The polemic is of special interest to us because it clearly reveals the primary concern of the CCP leaders in directing the movement in Manchuria, which was international in scope rather than limited to sole consideration of the fate of the Communist movement in Manchuria.

The rationale offered by the central leaders in halting the negotiations with the Big Swords and bandits was presented in their letter of February 20, 1928:

> The Manchurian Committee must prepare for the final greatest armed riot, but it is not to engage in rioting at the present time. This is because Manchuria is actually a Japanese imperialist colony, and riots in this region would give rise to serious international problems. Riots

---

mittee," dated May 1, 1928, *Chung-yang cheng-chih t'ung-hsün*, no. 30 (July 3, 1928), unpaginated.
    31. J. P. Harrison, *Long March*, p. 154.
    32. Richard C. Thornton, *The Comintern and the Chinese Communists, 1927–1931* (Seattle, 1969), pp. 4–22.

should be [carried out] only after the Chinese revolution has attained considerable success.[33]

The cadres in Manchuria were understandably baffled and even angered by this sudden reversal of policy. How could the central leaders, who had been urging them to organize riots, suddenly order them not to do so? They were perhaps all the more exasperated because negotiations with the Big Sword Society had progressed, and to break off the negotiations without offering a plausible explanation would mean a serious loss of face. The Manchurian Committee reacted to the new instructions with considerable asperity, declaring in its reply of March 21:

> We discussed [the letter] in detail, and as a result, we accept [your instructions] on the plan and methods concerning the party and the movements among the workers, bandits, farmers, and soldiers; but we disagree with respect to the Central Committee's estimate of the international situation in Manchuria and the question of riots in Manchuria.[34]

The committee affirmed that all its activities were preparatory to the "final greatest armed uprising" and the seizing of political power, but this final event must be based on the accumulated experience of incessant riots, starting with demands for reduced working hours and increased wages, demands for improved livelihood, movements against rent and taxes, and other clashes. Only through such a rallying of the rioting forces in various areas, the committee declared, could the "final greatest armed uprising" take place. Therefore, the Central Committee's instructions to prepare for the final uprising on the one hand and, on the other, not to conduct any riots at the present time were contradictory: "We are told to prepare for the great uprising but at the same time not to prepare for it." The language of the Manchurian Committee became more poignant:

> We also recognize that Manchuria is a Japanese colony and that it has a great importance to the existence as well as the rise and fall of Japanese imperialism; Japan will do everything possible to suppress the revolutionary forces of workers and farmers. Our party must, therefore, know its own strength as well as that of the

---

33. Quoted in the "Letter from the Manchurian Temporary Committee to the Central Headquarters," dated March 21, 1928. *Chung-yang cheng-chih t'ung-hsün*, no. 30 (July 3, 1928), unpaginated.
34. Ibid.

enemy. Only the strategy that takes these factors into consideration will be without error.³⁵

The committee then insinuated that knowing the enemy was quite different from fleeing the enemy: "To avoid the Japanese imperialist forces and not to carry out riots is like the strategy of the Second International during the World War." This was strong language indeed.

The Manchurian Committee was equally displeased by the idea that riots in Manchuria should wait for the success of revolution in China:

> The opinion of the Central Committee seems to be that riots should be carried out in Manchuria only after the revolution in China has achieved considerable success. Our observation is very much different from this. We see that the ruling class in Manchuria—the Fengtien warlords—have been able to rule the five northern provinces and the three special districts up to now exactly because there have not been any workers' and farmers' riots. Thus we see that workers' and farmers' riots in Manchuria should interact with workers' and farmers' riots in China proper, each influencing the other, in order to hasten the success of the Chinese revolution. According to the Central Committee's opinion, the revolution in Manchuria is only to be reflective [of events in China proper]. This is because the Central Committee greatly underestimates the significance of the worker-farmer revolution.³⁶

Having all but denounced the central leaders as right-wing opportunists, the Manchurian Committee called for an immediate action against Japanese imperialism and the forces of Chang Tso-lin. The extreme complexity of the international situation surrounding Manchuria was duly acknowledged, but the Manchurian Committee was not dissuaded. "Regardless of what the triangular relationship of Japan, Chang Tso-lin, and the Soviet Union might be," the committee insisted, "our party should unite with the revolutionary peoples of the Soviet Union, Korea, and Mongolia and, based on the main body of the Chinese worker-farmer masses, resist Japan, overthrow the Fengtien warlords, and clean out the bully gentry."³⁷ The committee was optimistic about the outcome: "Within the shortest period—especially because the Fengtien warlords are losing or have lost the war against

35. Ibid.   36. Ibid.   37. Ibid.

the new warlords under Feng Yü-hsiang and Chiang Kai-shek—our struggle against the warlords can be carried out."[38] The committee was doubtless encouraged by the resounding defeat of Chang Tso-lin's forces in North China by the nationalist army under Chiang Kai-shek.

Already having reported the propitious revolutionary environment in Manchuria (in Ch'en Wei-jen's letter of December 1927), the committee dismissed the environment as a problem. Their March 21 letter stated that the "objective conditions" no longer presented a question as to whether the uprising would come in due course; the question, rather, was whether the party in Manchuria was healthy, whether it could lead the worker masses in daily struggles, and, during the course of these struggles, intensify the faith of the masses in the Communist Party, and whether it could arouse the farmers and lead them to destroy the gentry and the officials. If it could perform these tasks successfully, then riots should be fomented immediately; if not, more effort should be exerted to prepare for them. Whatever the result, the Manchurian Committee wished to proceed.

The central leaders' reply to the strong challenge from Manchuria was feeble at best. Their letter of May 1 dismissed the Manchurian Committee's protest of the injunction against riots by saying that this did not extend to small struggles or farmers' riots, that it applied only to the notion of general rioting. Hedging on the charge that they were in effect avoiding or running away from the Japanese imperialists, they stated that the passage in question was meant to indicate the difficulties involved in carrying out riots, particularly when these could succeed only with the use of bandits. They skirted the protest that the significance of the revolution in Manchuria had been underestimated and that it had not been assigned a role in the Chinese revolution as a whole, commenting that the worker-farmer movement there had yet established no deep foundation and that no broad struggle of the masses had taken place.

Confronted with the direct challenge that they had ignored the role of the worker-farmer revolution in Manchuria as part of the total picture, one might suppose that the central leaders would attempt to provide some kind of definition. Certainly the claim of the Manchurian Committee that an upheaval in Manchuria would substantially weaken Chang Tso-lin's forces and thereby significantly affect the course of Chinese revolution rings true. But, as of May 1928, the leaders in central China were more con-

38. Ibid.

cerned with the party's current weaknesses in Manchuria than its potentialities. To the suggestion that the Manchurian Communists could make a positive contribution by destroying Chang Tso-lin, they replied that the ruling class in Manchuria had not reached the "final stage of collapse." To the proposal that the CCP should oppose Japan, they retorted that Japanese imperialism was becoming steadily stronger in that area. There was a curious divergence of basic views: the Manchurian Committee was seeking guidance on long-range goals while the central leadership was absorbed in immediate problems; hence one interpreted the objective conditions for revolution as being favorable while the other painted a dark picture, citing the viability of the warlord government, the increased Japanese control, and the lack of class consciousness among the workers and farmers. We shall return to this matter at a later point.

Partly as a defense against this unmitigated attack by the Manchurian Committee in general, and also perhaps in an attempt to destroy the premises of the committee's call for a more aggressive attack on Japanese imperialism, the central leadership lashed out against the committee's preoccupation with the bandits. In the opinion of the central leaders, the Manchurian Committee had not grasped the true nature of the bandits, and hence their plan was unrealistic. Detailing their criticism, the central leaders noted a "Plan for Operation of the Southeastern Special Committee" adopted by the Manchurian Committee (and in doing so revealed the existence of the party's Southeastern Special Committee for the first time). According to the central leaders, the plan included the following passage:

> Our important duty is to go into the ranks of the armed bandits, change their character, and hasten their dissolution. With regard to bandits under our influence as well as other bandits and the Big Sword Society, we should follow the links already established or the new links [to be established], conduct divisive propaganda, and absorb the bandits into [our own] organizations.[39]

The central leaders found this plan unrealistic; in their opinion, elements such as these, owing to their composition and motives, would not be amenable to such handling. In evidence, a paragraph from a report from the Southeastern Special Committee

---

39. "Letter of the Central Headquarters to the Manchurian Temporary Committee," dated May 1, 1928, *Chung-yang cheng-chih t'ung-hsün*, no. 30 (July 3, 1928), unpaginated.

was cited. This committee had reported that 80 percent of the lower elements of the bandits and Big Swords were poor farmers and the remainder were vagrants. Their leaders were bully gentry or fallen officials whose main aim was either to acquire wealth for their own well-being or to become officials again. The only aim of the lower elements was to acquire wealth and escape from suffering. They could be utilized to destroy officials, powerful families, and bully gentry because of their desire to seize the property of those persons, but they were no different from the soldiers, whose sole interest lay in plundering the rich and poor alike. Hence, all were hated by the farmers. Therefore, the Southeastern Committee concluded (and the central leaders concurred), it would be impossible to bring all these elements into the farmers' organizations. The best of them might join the farmers' organizations, but they would have to turn over a new leaf. The central leaders' conclusion was explicit:

> We can clearly see from this that the Red Beards and Big Swords in Manchuria in no way differ from ordinary bandits. We cannot hang high hopes on them. Particularly, it is impossible to dream of using the Red Beards to seize political power.[40]

The danger in using the bandits would be that of failing in the intended purpose and being used by the bandits. The central leaders declared: "In seeking to use the Red Beards, the result may be that, instead of using them, we may end up being the tail of the bandits."[41] Therefore, policy toward the bandits should be to destroy—that is, disband—them. The party should infiltrate the bandit groups and arouse the "masses" among them to oppose their leaders, thereby bringing about the collapse of the bandit groups. This was the so-called "united front from below" strategy that was to become the predominant theme of the CCP. In any event, the party was to veer away from work with the bandits and concentrate upon the "basic operation" of organizing the worker-farmer movement. Through "leading the small daily struggles of the workers and farmers," the party was to "create the foundation of the worker-farmer movement"[42] and expand the party organization. Only thus could the operation in Manchuria make headway; otherwise, the party would only shout about riots and none would ever take place.

It should be noted that the central leaders distinguished the

40. Ibid.　　41. Ibid.　　42. Ibid.

Red Beards (*hung hu-tzu*) from other bandits (*t'u-fei*). The term *hung hu-tzu* was used in Manchuria to refer to all bandits, and we are at a loss to distinguish the difference.[43]

Had the committee been allowed a rebuttal, it might have retorted that the policy of destroying the bandits was practically the same as the "dissolution" operation that it proposed. While the Central Committee was interested in destroying the bandits, the Manchurian Committee wished to recruit sympathetic elements among them who would help launch a mass movement. This was the only difference. The fact that the bandit groups consisted of poor farmers and the dispossessed would be a distinct advantage to the party.

The central leaders' position prevailed, and the party in Manchuria abandoned the project. The local leaders must have been chagrined at the loss of a good opportunity to display the potentiality and might of the Communist Party and to launch a mass recruitment program due to the central leadership's adherence to the narrowly defined, orthodox Marxist view. The Manchurian Committee, however, was too frail at this point to defy the central leaders and pursue its own policies.

While the central leaders' counterattack against the Manchurian Committee was focused on the use of the bandits and the Big Sword Society, their thrust was not on the bandit issue but on that of riots. We have already alluded to the decision of the Fifteenth Congress of the Communist Party of the Soviet Union. The Ninth Plenum of the Executive Committee of the Comintern was also highly critical of the uprisings. In its February 25, 1928, resolution—submitted by Stalin, Bukharin, and the two Chinese delegates to the meeting, Li Li-san and Hsiang Chung-fa—the CCP was accused of insufficient preliminary work among workers and peasants and insufficient subversion of enemy forces; there had been a faulty appraisal of the loyalties of workers belonging to "yel-

43. Harvey J. Howard, an American missionary who was kidnapped by a bandit group in northern Manchuria in 1925 and held for ten arduous weeks, had the following to say about the Red Beards: "During the eighteenth and nineteenth centuries roving bands of unshaven, red-bearded Russians preyed upon the Chinese who had settled in Siberia north of the Amur River and even now and then upon those who lived in Manchuria just south of the river. The Chinese name for these foreign brigands was *hung hu-tzu*, which, literally translated, means 'red-beards.' But Russian bandits gradually disappeared from this region, and their place was more and more taken by Chinese. Therefore, the term *hung hu-tzu*, which formerly referred to Russian bandits only, came to be applied to Chinese bandits as well, even though the latter, with but a rare exception, have no beards." Howard received this information from the Chinese captain of a steamboat on the Sungari River. *Ten Weeks with Chinese Bandits* (New York, 1930), pp. 2–3.

low" (i.e., non-Communist) unions; the party and Young Communist Corps had not organized themselves properly; there had been insufficient preparation for strikes; the soviet in Canton had been appointed, not elected. The CCP was directed "resolutely to oppose dabbling with insurrection" and to refrain from engaging in "unprepared and disorganized actions."[44] In the face of these directives, the Manchurian Committee's insistence on riots must have appeared infantile.

Soviet Interest and the Chinese Revolution

But why was the Central Committee so hesitant, indeed unwilling, to define the role of the Manchurian Committee in the Chinese revolution or to encourage its proposal for a more intensive campaign against Japan? Certainly the allegations that the worker-farmer movement in Manchuria had no foundation and that Japanese control was tightening did not provide adequate answers to the questions posed and were too negative to serve as guidelines for the nascent party branch. The Manchurian leaders could well have characterized the response from the central leaders as defeatist.

Three possible explanations can be offered. One was given by the party itself, a second has been proposed by a veteran Communist leader of this era, and the third may be inferred from circumstances confronting the Soviet Union at the time. The party's resolution of August 1927 declared that premature provocation of imperialists was damaging to the revolution:

> If there is a possibility of coming into direct contact with foreign capitalism in the area where mass revolt has succeeded (in such places as Canton and in other port cities), our party must possess a strategy for anti-imperialist struggle but must not arouse premature armed conflict against imperialism. Our party must incessantly intensify anti-imperialist political propaganda and, when necessary, even lead economic struggles (such as boycotts of foreign goods). At the same time, when direct conflict may endanger the newly rising revolutionary regime from its foundation—when the democratic dictatorship of the worker-farmer class

44. "Resolution on the Chinese Question," *International Press Correspondence*, vol. 8, no. 16 (March 15, 1928), pp. 321–322.

has only a small base—our party must for the time being avoid direct conflict with imperialism (such as the takeover of the concessions or the confiscation and nationalization of foreign industry).

It must be remembered that imperialism will always provoke actions, commit murder under pretenses, and suppress the truly revolutionary and truly anti-imperialist people's regime in collusion with various reactionary forces of China (such as Chang Tso-lin and Wang Ching-wei). Our party must see through these dangers and, when it is disadvantageous to the new revolutionary regime, must evade imperialist provocations. The CCP must guide the Chinese worker-farmer masses and engage in direct struggle against imperialism under the support of the international revolutionary proletariat and under the most advantageous conditions for the revolution.[45]

Readers of this resolution certainly could not fault the logic behind the decision of the central leadership that the party should not engage in premature actions against imperialism. From the viewpoint of those in China proper who were completely absorbed in the anti-KMT struggles, the anti-imperialist struggle would have been an added burden, and it would certainly have been naïve to open another front. But the warlord Chang Tso-lin was a domestic enemy against whom the CCP in China proper was engaged in a war. Why should the CCP cadres in Manchuria not be assigned a role in this struggle?

The second explanation was offered by Chang Kuo-t'ao, a founder of the CCP and a top-ranking party leader during much of this period. According to Chang, Ch'ü Ch'iu-pai was reluctant to engage in an anti-Japanese campaign because he believed that it would benefit the KMT and Chiang Kai-shek. After the Tsinan Incident of May 1928 aroused a nationwide anti-Japanese tide, Chang and others saw a great opportunity for the party and urged the party to lead the mass movement, but Ch'ü and other leaders continued to oppose the idea. In Chang's opinion,

> this was a downright sacrifice of an opportunity to win over the masses. The Central Committee apparently

---

45. Ibid., pp. 274–275. According to the editors of *Shiryō-shū*, this resolution followed the policy lines decided upon by the August 7, 1927, Emergency Conference of the CCP, but the date of its adoption is not known.

thought that the revolution to carry out land reform was the main task, and it refused to take anti-Japanese, anti-imperialist principles seriously.[46]

Chang thought that "being anti-Japanese by no means helped Chiang Kai-shek"; on the contrary, "not only could the masses rally around the anti-imperialist banner of the CCP, but they could also strike a blow at Chiang Kai-shek, the represser of the anti-imperialist campaign."[47]

But the central leaders' allusion to the "serious international problems" in their February 20 letter leaves little doubt that the matter of greater concern to them was the impact of riots and other revolutionary movements on the Soviet Union. They were concerned that a show of force by the Communists in Manchuria would adversely affect the interest of the Soviet Union in Manchuria and might provoke Japan to commit aggressive acts against the Soviet territory along the Manchurian border. This is why the central leaders discouraged the cadres in Manchuria from preparing for riots and told them to wait until the Chinese revolution had attained considerable success. It should be recalled that the central leaders' interdiction was not confined to anti-Japanese struggle. The Manchurian Committee was not to play a role even in the struggle against the warlord regime of Chang Tso-lin.

How would Communist-led riots in Manchuria have adversely affected the Soviet interest? If riots would indeed have been damaging to the Soviet interest, would the Soviet Union have found other forms of Communist movements there desirable? Were there some reasons behind the refusal of the Soviet agents in Harbin to aid the Chinese Communists in Manchuria? These questions call for a brief survey of international relations surrounding Manchuria.

Ever since December 1, 1917, less than a month after the Bolshevik coup d'état, and despite Japanese intervention in Siberia between 1919 and 1922, the Bolsheviks had vigorously pursued a policy of establishing new diplomatic, commercial, and economic relations with Japan.[48] Partly because of deep-seated distrust of So-

46. Chang Kuo-t'ao, *The Rise of the Chinese Communist Party, 1928–1938, Volume Two of the Autobiography of Chang Kuo-t'ao* (Lawrence, Kansas, 1971), pp. 72–73.
47. Ibid.
48. George Alexander Lensen, *Japanese Recognition of the USSR: Soviet-Japanese Relations, 1921–1930* (Tokyo and Tallahassee, Florida, 1970), provides a meticulously detailed account of the Soviet-Japanese negotiations.

viet motives and partly because of the scorn in which many Japanese leaders held the weaknesses of the new regime, the negotiations dragged on until 1925, but the patient efforts of the Soviet diplomats finally resulted in the "Convention Embodying Basic Rules of the Relations," signed in January of that year.[49] The importance attached by the Bolsheviks to their relationship with Japan can be seen from remarks by G. U. Chicherin and L. M. Karakhan, the commissar and deputy commissar for foreign affairs. Chicherin said:

> The signing of the Soviet-Japanese Treaty in Peking on January 20 is much more significant than a mere recognition of the USSR by still another government; it is even more significant than the settlement of the points in dispute between the two governments. . . .
> For us, the treaty means the end of the whole period of intervention, civil war, and unregulated relations; it is the culmination of the continually progressing general development of our political relations in the Far East. . . . The treaty marks a new indisputable consolidation of our position in the Far East.[50]

Karakhan was more specific:

> The agreement with Japan, which has strengthened our position in the Pacific, serves as a warning to America, which, by refraining from concluding a treaty with us, only makes her own position worse. This agreement, which strengthens us in the Far East, secures at the same time the conditions for our further consolidation on the Pacific and the economic development of our territories in the Far East. *Without the establishment of normal relations with Japan it would have been impossible to hope for a complete restoration of our rights to the Chinese Eastern Railway.*[51]

49. Text of the convention is in ibid., pp. 177–181, and in Leonard Shapiro, ed., *Soviet Treaty Series: A Collection of Bilateral Treaties, Agreements and Conventions . . . Concluded Between the Soviet Union and Foreign Powers*, vol. 1: 1917–1928 (Washington, D.C., 1950), pp. 283–285.

50. *Pravda*, no. 18 (January 22, 1925), p. 3, quoted in Xenia Joukoff Eudin and Robert C. North, *Soviet Russia and the East, 1920–1927: A Documentary Survey* (Stanford, 1957), p. 319.

51. *Izvestiya*, no. 20 (January 25, 1925), p. 1; also published in *International Press Correspondence*, no. 12 (February 6, 1925), p. 148. Quoted in Eudin and North, *Soviet Russia and the East*, p. 322 (emphasis added).

The close link between Soviet-Japanese relations and the protection of the Soviet interest in the Chinese Eastern Railway was further substantiated by a statement made by Stalin in his "Political Report of the Central Committee of the Communist Party of the Soviet Union" at the Fourteenth Congress of the CPSU on December 19, 1925. He said:

> But [Chang Tso-lin] is ruined also because he built his entire policy on quarrels between us [the USSR] and Japan. Any general or governor of Manchuria who builds his policy on quarrels between us and Japan, on a worsening of relations between us and Japan, will certainly come to grief. Only he will keep his position who builds his policy on the improvement of our relations with Japan and on a rapprochement between us and Japan; only such a general and such a leader can keep his position in Manchuria secure, for we have no interests which would lead to a worsening of our relations with Japan. Our interests point to a rapprochement between our country and Japan.[52]

The Soviet effort to maintain amicable relations did not stop with the normalization of diplomatic relations. In August 1926, the Soviet Union proposed a neutrality pact; in May 1927, the Soviets also proposed a non-aggression pact.[53] The Japanese government, however, was not interested in either of the proposals.

The Soviet leaders did their best to placate the Japanese and thus protect the Soviet interest in the Chinese Eastern Railway and prevent Japanese expansion into the maritime provinces. The Japanese attitude was of particular importance because the Bolsheviks were experiencing considerable difficulty with the Chinese government in Peking currently under the control of the Manchurian warlord Chang Tso-lin. Under a general agreement signed in Peking in May 1924, the Soviet side appointed a new general manager, A. N. Ivanov, but some of his actions quickly aroused controversies, and Sino-Soviet relations rapidly deteriorated. Ivanov's dismissal of White Russian school officials in the railway zone, his assistance to Soviet organizations such as trade unions, and some other actions were interpreted by the Chinese

---

52. Jane Degras, ed., *Soviet Documents on Foreign Policy* (London, 1951), vol. 2, p. 75.

53. Hosoya Chihiro, "Japan's Policies Toward Russia," in James William Morley, ed., *Japan's Foreign Policy, 1868–1941: A Research Guide* (New York, 1974), pp. 395–396.

as an attempt to Bolshevize the railway.[54] When Ivanov refused to transport Chinese troops on credit after November 1925, the simmering conflict boiled over into open struggle. The Chinese arrested Ivanov and three Soviet directors of the railway on January 22, 1926, causing Chicherin to issue an ultimatum on the same day. Tension subsided temporarily in the spring when a new agreement was signed to solve immediate problems, but the Chinese efforts to eliminate Soviet domination of the railway persisted. On September 2, the Chinese authorities in Harbin seized eleven steamers and thirty barges of the Sungari River fleet operated by the railway company, and its wharves, warehouses, and machinery. On September 4, the Chinese threatened to proclaim martial law, abolish the board of directors, and take over the railway.[55] The Russian side was compelled to accede to the Chinese demands.

The Bolsheviks evidently considered the option of using force against Chang Tso-lin, but this option was not taken. Reportedly, the Russians sounded out the Japanese about their attitude concerning the possible dispatch of Soviet troops to North Manchuria, but the Japanese general staff voiced strong objections.[56] British diplomats at this time conjectured that the Soviet Union was reluctant to resort to force, partly because of the fear that Chang might receive foreign backing and partly in expectation that a more indirect approach would prove more effective in the long run.[57]

Even in 1927 the trouble over the railway had not ceased. A Soviet scholar, V. Avarin, has alleged that the Chang regime was intent on finding an excuse to break off diplomatic relations in order to take over the railway. According to Avarin, Chang Tso-lin had carried out many small-scale and experimental provocations since early 1927 to fulfill his aim. In January, for example, the head of the Soviet-supported labor union in Harbin was arrested without a warrant and the office of the Railway Employees' Union was searched. A White Russian policeman in the Chinese employ stopped the automobile of the Soviet consul-general in Harbin and demanded the removal of the Soviet flag from it. In February, the Chinese seized a Soviet steamship and its crew "with a firm resolve to break off diplomatic ties." In March, the Soviet trade representative's office in Harbin was searched. The Chinese police also demanded the removal of Lenin's portrait and the Soviet

54. George Alexander Lensen, *The Damned Inheritance: The Soviet Union and the Manchurian Crises, 1924–1935* (Tallahassee, Florida, 1974), pp. 17–18.
55. Ibid., pp. 22–25.   56. Ibid., p. 86.   57. Ibid., p. 89.

emblem from a gathering of Soviet citizens celebrating the February Revolution. These minor provocations continued until April 6, when the Soviet Embassy in Peking was raided by the Chinese police. This raid, according to Avarin, was the final act designed to bring about the diplomatic break, and it was in accord with the wishes of the imperialist powers. The only reason that the Chinese did not take over the railway at this time, according to Avarin, was that this action would have exposed too clearly their true intent. Allegedly, the warlords in Manchuria had made preparation for the takeover at this time: White Russians had been selected to replace the Soviet personnel on the railway, army units were assigned to key positions, and the police were placed in combat readiness.

All these maneuvers were in vain, according to the Soviet expert, because the Soviet government persisted in its "peace policy" and did not fall into the trap. Only this policy, he declared, had halted Chang Tso-lin. Until the Manchurian warlord's passion for control of the railway was cooled by his defeat in North China in the early part of 1928, however, he continued to engage in provocation by other means, such as demanding a change in the accounting system of the railway whereby the local Chinese currency would replace the more stable gold ruble as the basic monetary unit—which would have brought financial ruin to the railway and provided Chang with an excuse for assuming management of it. Chinese soldiers and policemen allegedly assaulted innocent Soviet personnel, arresting and even torturing them. Attacks on Soviet citizens by White Russians were ignored by the Chinese police. Labor unions of Soviet citizens were suppressed.[58]

For our purposes here, it is unimportant whether the charges against the Chang Tso-lin regime were justified or not. Indeed, the Chinese side presented many countercharges against the Soviet management, citing alleged violations of Chinese sovereignty and mutual agreements.[59] It is clear, however, that the Soviet Union gave priority to protecting its interest in the Chinese Eastern Railway and therefore was willing to endure many insults and abuses.

Of course, the Soviet Union could easily have subdued the Manchurian warlord but for international repercussions. But, according to Avarin, the Soviet Union unfortunately found it neces-

58. V. Avarin, *Imperialism v. Manchzhurii* [Imperialism and Manchuria] (Moscow, 1934), pp. 238–243.
59. See Peter S. H. Tang, *Russian and Soviet Policy in Manchuria and Outer Mongolia* (Durham, N.C., 1959), pp. 194–198.

sary to foil Chang's scheme because it had the support of all the imperialists, that is, the American, British, French, and Japanese imperialists, who allegedly saw a golden opportunity to wrest control of the railway from the Soviet Union. Not all of these fears were unfounded.

The Soviet Union was in a particularly sensitive position between 1927 and 1928 because of other developments in China and the Soviet Union. The Nanking incident of March 1927—when troops of the Revolutionary Army attacked foreign residents and consular offices in that city—had the effect of turning many of the foreign powers against the Communist radicals and, by implication, the Soviet Union. Japanese officials placed the blame on the Communist elements in the Revolutionary Army, distinguishing them from the moderate Nationalists under Chiang Kai-shek. An American official flatly declared that the Nanking incident had been created by the Russian advisers. Documents seized at the Soviet Embassy in Peking on April 6 by Chang Tso-lin's police proved that Soviet officials were in contact with the Chinese Communists, which intensified Western distrust of the Soviet Union. Incidentally, the diplomatic corps in Peking reacted favorably toward the raid on the embassy, reflecting their general attitude toward the Soviet Union.[60] On May 26, the British government, which had been among the first of the European powers to recognize the Soviet Union, severed relations with it, and in July the KMT left wing in Wuhan expelled its Soviet advisers. Domestically, the Soviet Union was just concluding its New Economic Policy phase and was moving into the New Socialist Offensive of five-year plans; it was scarcely in a position to further antagonize Japan and the other imperialist powers. Widespread agitation or rioting in Manchuria would be certain to exacerbate tension, and, as in the Nanking incident, the Soviet Union would be blamed for bad faith.

For the Soviet Union, of course, the attitude of Japan was most critical. In April 1927, the Wakatsuki cabinet, with its moderate foreign minister, Shidehara Kijurō, was replaced by the Tanaka cabinet, General Tanaka Giichi concurrently assuming the post of foreign minister. These developments gave no cause for joy in the Soviet Union. Bessedovskii, the acting Soviet ambassador to Japan, called on Vice-Minister of Foreign Affairs Deguchi Katsuji on April 22 to say that the Soviet Union feared that Japan might pro-

---

60. Akira Iriye, *After Imperialism: The Search for a New Order in the Far East, 1921–1931* (Cambridge, Mass., 1965), pp. 125–135.

vide support to Chang Tso-lin to exert pressure against the Soviet position in northern Manchuria.[61] Indeed, as was learned later, some of the Japanese high officials were contemplating actions against the Soviet Union and the CCP should the situation deteriorate—that is, should communism make inroads into Manchuria. In private conversation, War Minister Ugaki Issei had told Premier Wakatsuki on April 8, 1927, that since it was only a matter of time until the Chinese Communist movement expanded into northern China, Manchuria, and Mongolia, Japan should forewarn the Soviet Union about such an outcome and denounce the CCP's activities. Ugaki was particularly concerned about the use of Siberia as a staging area of Communist expansion. For this reason, he suggested the possibility of using the Japanese army to "seal off" China proper, primarily to prevent an influx of Soviet military supplies and to assist the moderate elements in northern and southern China in suppressing and annihilating the Chinese Communists.[62]

We do not know how accurately the Soviet leaders perceived the current thinking of their Japanese counterparts. But, as Bessedovskii's message indicates, the Soviet leaders were definitely wary of provoking the Japanese. In this situation, it was unthinkable for the Comintern representatives in the CCP to abet or even encourage Communist activities in Manchuria. If the Manchurian Committee had succeeded in organizing or precipitating riots, the Manchurian warlords and Japan would certainly have blamed the Soviet Union, and Japan might have been roused to take preventive measures. Not only would Soviet control over the railway have been jeopardized, but the carefully cultivated friendship with Japan would also have been damaged.

Thus, it is beyond doubt that the root of the problem for the Communist cadres in Manchuria lay in the broader concerns of the Soviet Union. The Soviet concern over the railway as well as the future of Soviet-Japanese relations made it necessary for the CCP to steer the Manchurian Committee away from struggle against Japanese imperialism. Even an attack against the warlords was to be avoided lest they seize the railway. In short, the Manchurian Committee was not to engage in any activities that would destabilize the delicate international balance in Manchuria.

In some ways, the dispute between Ch'en Wei-jen and the CCP

61. Nihon Kokusai Seiji Gakkai (Japanese Association of International Politics), *Taiheiyō sensō e no michi* [The Road to the Pacific War] (Tokyo, 1963), vol. 1, p. 280.
62. Ibid., p. 278.

headquarters is reminiscent of at least one aspect of the struggle between Stalin and Trotsky, although there appears to be no direct connection between the two disputes. Stalin called for "socialism in one country"—that is, the Russian Bolsheviks should build the Soviet Union as a general headquarters and powerful base for world revolutionary activities before diverting too much energy abroad. This was akin to the arguments of the CCP headquarters. Trotsky, on the other hand, demanded an immediate overthrow of capitalism everywhere,[63] a line of argument Ch'en would have favored within the Chinese context. Ch'en's position was that the revolution in Manchuria should be promoted simultaneously with that in southern China. In this connection, it is interesting to note that the CCP's policy on riots changed between December 1927 and February 1928, just as Trotsky was being drummed out of the Communist Party of the Soviet Union and the Comintern.

In any event, imposing these restrictions on the Manchurian Committee was tantamount to saying that the committee should do nothing. For there were in fact no other means whereby the committee could arouse and organize the masses, lift the spirits of old members, and attract new recruits. The central leaders' directive that the committee should build the foundation of the worker-peasant movement through its guidance of the daily struggle of the workers and peasants had been proven ineffective by the experience of the previous six or seven years.

A British diplomat, Sir John Pratt, remarked in 1932 that the Chinese Eastern Railway was a "damnosa hereditas" that had come down to the Soviets from Tsarist Russia, a "wild and reckless military adventure that never brought any additional strength or profit to Russia but was, on the contrary, a running sore and a source of weakness."[64] Had the Communist cadres in Manchuria been apprised of the overall situation in 1928, they would have heartily agreed.

But were they fully informed of these complexities? When the Manchurian Committee retorted to the central leaders that "regardless of what the triangular relationship between Japan, Chang Tso-lin, and the Soviet Union might be, our party should . . . resist Japan, overthrow the Fengtien warlords, and clean out the bully gentry," were they aware of all the implications? If not, why were they not informed of the Soviet desires? If they were, why were they less prone than the central leaders to accept the thesis?

63. Robert C. North, *Moscow and Chinese Communists*, rev. ed. (Stanford, 1963), p. 79.
64. As quoted, without source, in G. A. Lensen, *The Damned Inheritance*, p. 1.

These are intriguing questions for which, regrettably, no firm answers can be provided. Judging from the tone of the argument presented by the Manchurian cadres, they were not fully informed of the thought behind the central leaders when the latter too briefly referred to international ramifications of the policies advocated in Manchuria. Perhaps the central leaders found it too embarrassing to spell out the problems in detail because they were reversing their previous directives, in effect calling for the sacrifice—or at least the delay—of the Chinese revolution for the sake of protecting the national interest of the Soviet Union. On the other hand, the cadres in Manchuria were probably too agitated by the refusal of the Soviet cadres in Harbin to extend support to the Chinese party and the sudden reversal of the central leaders' directive to think for themselves in terms of the long range. Having worked diligently to establish contact and negotiate with the Big Swords and some of the other bandits, the Manchurian cadres were not only placed in the uncomfortable position of losing face with their potential allies, but saw the hope of carrying out a revolution also fade away. Therefore, the Manchurian cadres demanded a more convincing answer from the central leaders, who were in no position to provide one.

Whatever the case may have been, the Manchurian cadres had no choice but to obey. Unlike Mao, who in the hinterland of Kiangsi Province could circumvent the instructions from the central leaders and follow his own course, the Manchurian Committee did not have an independent base. The effect of these developments on the morale of the cadres in Manchuria can be easily surmised.

4 | Sino-Soviet Conflict of 1929 and the Li Li-san Line

THE POLEMIC BETWEEN THE MANCHURIAN PROVINcial Committee and the Chinese Communist Party (CCP) headquarters in 1927 and 1928 clearly showed that, in order to protect the Soviet interest over the Chinese Eastern Railway, the leaders of the CCP had decided to hold the revolutionary movement in Manchuria in abeyance. Its organizational movements being in the doldrums, the party also decided to tone down its attack against imperialism. Provocations from imperialism were to be evaded until the party could receive the support of the international revolutionary proletariat (i.e., the Soviet Union) under conditions most advantageous to the revolution.

It was natural, therefore, that the CCP's policies toward Manchuria would change when the Soviet perspective on Manchuria changed. The Soviet policy toward Manchuria did change in 1929 because of Chang Hsüeh-liang's attempt to take over the Chinese Eastern Railway (CER). Indeed, the conflict over the CER and the corollary shift in the Soviet policy toward China was to affect the CCP's development throughout China between 1929 and 1931. The events in Manchuria precipitated the emergence of radical strategies under Li Li-san, which came to be known as the Li Li-san line.

The Conflict over the Railway

As we have seen in the previous chapter, there had been numerous points of friction between the Fengtien government and the Soviet Union since 1924 over the question of joint management of the railway, which was supposed to be run by both Chinese and Russian officials. The Young Marshal, who had taken over the reins in Manchuria and established liaison with the Kuomintang only in December 1928, evidently decided to tackle the thorny issue at once. If he succeeded in "recovering" the railway from the Soviet Union, his status was sure to rise, not only in Manchuria but also throughout China.

Thus, Chang Hsüeh-liang took over the communication facilities of the CER at the end of 1928.[1] On January 24, 1929, the Chinese police raided the Russan railroad offices in Harbin, arresting several "trade-union officials." During the next week more arrests were made, but all suspects were released by early March.[2] Tensions, however, were not reduced. On May 27, the police raided the Soviet consulate-general in Harbin, arresting 48 Soviet citizens and confiscating alleged Communist propaganda materials. Soviet consulates along the railway at Manchouli, Tsitsihar, and Suifenho were similarly raided. On July 10, Chang Hsüeh-liang went a step further by dismissing the Russian officials from the directorate of the railway and closing all Soviet commercial establishments in Manchuria.[3]

These actions naturally led to a rupture in diplomatic relations between the Soviet Union and China, and military skirmishes began in August. But Chang's troops proved no match for the Soviet forces, and the Nationalist government was not able to render any assistance during the crucial months of November and December, being fully occupied in putting down rebellions in central and northwestern China. The Japanese, on the other hand, were willing to let the Chinese and the Russians settle the score among themselves. Being concerned with the possibility of the victorious Chinese clamoring for the return of the South Manchuria Railway and other concessions in China, the Japanese government was more in sympathy with the Russians than with the Chinese. At the end of the year, the Chinese estimated that they had suffered in excess of 10,000 civilian and military casualties and that their property losses amounted to 500 million United States dollars.[4] Routed and humiliated, they signed a peace protocol at Khabarovsk on December 22, restoring Russian dominance over the railway.

Little imagination is needed to see the impact of the Chinese Eastern Railway incident on the nationalist sentiment of the Chinese people. It was certainly imprudent of Chang to oppose both

1. David J. Dallin, *Rise of Russia in Asia* (New Haven, 1949), p. 258.
2. Richard C. Thornton, *The Comintern and the Chinese Communists, 1928–1931* (Seattle, 1969), p. 93.
3. Peter S. H. Tang, *Russian and Soviet Policy in Manchuria and Outer Mongolia* (Durham, N.C., 1959), pp. 193–267.
4. *New York Times*, December 28, 1929, p. 4.

the Japanese and the Russian imperialists, but there was no doubt about the popularity of his actions among the Chinese. The railway, the Young Marshal, and Manchuria won attention not only in China but throughout the world. In the eyes of the Chinese, the Soviet attitude and actions could be regarded only as those of an imperialist power.

Indeed, the Soviet actions disgusted many Russian Bolsheviks who were repulsed by the thought of Russian Communists having to fight a weak nation for the privilege of operating a railroad on its territory. Some of them argued that the railway should be relinquished to China. Socialist parties of Europe also severely censured the Soviet Union's policy of imposing its will on China and its control over the railway by means of armed might. "What was the difference," the critics asked, "between the classical and the Soviet patterns of imperialism and aggression?"[5] The Russians defended their action as a means of "preventing the transfer of the railroad into the hands of the imperialists subjugating China," and as an action taken "in the interest of an easier transfer of the railroad into the hands of the Chinese people after the victory of the national revolution" and "in the interest of the defense of the Soviet Union itself from the threat of invasions on the part of hostile capitalist countries."[6]

Thus the railway incident placed the CCP in a dire predicament, particularly in Manchuria. The party was in no position to support Chang Hsüeh-liang or to cease denouncing the warlord as an agent of foreign capitalism. On the other hand, it was impossible even to conceive of the thought that the CCP should denounce the Soviet Union.

Facing this predicament, the party simply decided to harp on the themes stressed by the Soviet Union: the world imperialists were ganging up to attack the Soviet Union, which must be protected by all means. The Second Plenum of the Sixth Central Committee, meeting in Shanghai in June 1929, adopted a political resolution in which it criticized itself for not having paid sufficient attention to the matter of propagandizing against the imminent world war and calling for the protection of the Soviet Union.[7]

---

5. Dallin, *Rise of Russia in Asia*, pp. 261–262.
6. Ibid., p. 262, quoting *Communist International*, Russian ed., August 31, 1929, p. 46.
7. The text of the resolution is in *Kung-ch'an-tang erh-chung-ch'üan-hui chüeh-i-an* [Draft Resolution of the Second Plenum of the Central Committee of the Communist Party], n.p., mimeographed, 1929. I have relied on the Japanese translation in *Chūgoku kyōsantō-shi shiryō-shū* [Compendium of Materials on

Elsewhere in the resolution, the Central Committee declared that the Soviet Union, through the strengthening and development of its economy, had become the general headquarters of anti-imperialist struggle in the world, and that, fearing it, the imperialists were bringing ever closer to reality the plot to attack the Soviet Union. As a part of this general scheme, the imperialists were supposed to have directed the Kuomintang (KMT) government to search the Soviet consulate and find a pretext for taking over the railway, thus fulfilling the aim of an armed attack on the Soviet Union.[8] The struggle against imperialism, therefore, was to be closely tied to the campaign and the movement to protect the Soviet Union. This was, in fact, the line that the Comintern took in its "appeal" of July 18, reconfirmed by the CCP in its appeal of August.[9]

To call for the protection of the Soviet Union was, under the circumstances, to call for the defeat of the Chinese and to oppose frontally the strong popular current of nationalism and anti-Soviet feeling. Obviously, as Ch'en Tu-hsiu, the deposed former leader, argued repeatedly in his letters to the Central Committee, such appeals "could not mobilize the broad masses."[10] Indeed, they made it easy for the KMT and Chang Hsüeh-liang to portray the CCP as the enemy of China and traitors to the Chinese people. But the Central Committee was—despite Ch'en Tu-hsiu's prolonged criticisms—committed to these propaganda strategies, and it could not extricate itself from the situation unscathed.

As the military conflict dragged on, and as the Soviet army decided to penetrate further into Chinese territory, the Russians evidently began to concern themselves with the possibility of Chinese retaliatory capabilities.[11] If Chang Hsüeh-liang were to muster more of his forces from various parts of Manchuria and if the KMT government were to dispatch its forces from China proper, the conflict could be prolonged and the chances of the Soviet Union restoring its control over the CER would be substantially

---

the History of the Chinese Communist Party], edited by the Chinese Department of the Nihon Kokusai Mondai Kenkyūjo (Japanese International Problems Research Center) (Tokyo, 1971), vol. 4, pp. 354–378, hereafter cited as *Shiryō-shū*. The self-criticism noted here is from p. 364.

8. *Shiryō-shū*, vol. 4, p. 355.

9. See "The Appeal of the Communist International," *International Press Correspondence*, vol. 9, no. 36 (July 26, 1929), pp. 773–774, and "Appeal of the C.C. of the C.P. of China Regarding the Chinese Eastern Railway Conflict," ibid., no. 42 (August 23), p. 894.

10. *Shiryō-shū*, vol. 4, p. 447.

11. Thornton, *Comintern and Chinese Communists*, pp. 96–97.

reduced. The Soviet Union obviously needed to prevent these possible outcomes. The CCP, therefore, was ordered to cause as much havoc as possible in the rear in order to tie down the Nationalists and Chang Hsüeh-liang's troops elsewhere.

The Political Secretariat of the Executive Committee of the Communist International (ECCI) stated in a letter to the CCP on October 26 that China had "entered a period of deep national crisis," and ordered the CCP to "prepare the masses to carry out a revolutionary overthrow of the political power of the landlord-capitalist bloc and establish a soviet dictatorship of the workers and peasants."[12] The CCP was to destroy the warlord regimes, including that of Chang Hsüeh-liang, and promote the movement concerning the Eastern Railway problem and the conflict in Manchuria "through the slogan of directly protecting the Soviet Union." At the same time, the CCP was told to "strengthen and expand guerrilla warfare." Particularly "in Manchuria and in the operational areas of Chu Teh and Mao Tse-tung," the CCP was to "oppose resolutely the tendency within the party to underestimate the revolutionary significance of the farmers' struggle, especially guerrilla warfare."[13]

The CCP leadership under Li Li-san quickly responded to the Comintern directive. In its "Central Circular No. 60," issued in early December, the Central Committee led the party further toward a radical policy.[14] In the circular, the leadership asserted that an imperialist attack against the Soviet Union was imminent and hence the protection of the Soviet Union was no longer a matter for propaganda alone. The time had come for the party to mobilize the masses. "In general," the Central Committee argued, "this duty [the protection of the Soviet Union] and our party's duty to win over the masses to oppose the wars among the warlords and to prepare for armed uprisings have become inseparable, and the preparation for armed uprisings has increased in importance."[15] For these reasons, the Central Committee had directed the party to organize strikes among the workers and lead them

---

12. The text of the October 26 letter can be found in either *International Press Correspondence*, vol. 10, no. 2, or in *Hung-ch'i* [Red Flag], no. 76 (February 15, 1930), pp. 1–2. I have relied on the Japanese translation in *Shiryō-shū*, vol. 4, pp. 505–513.

13. The *International Press Correspondence* text mentioned Ho Lung instead of Chu Teh. See Thornton, *Comintern and Chinese Communists*, p. 100.

14. Printed in *Hung-ch'i*, no. 60 (December 7, 1929), p. 4. Japanese translation in *Shiryō-shū*, vol. 4, pp. 525–531. For a detailed discussion of the Li Li-san line, see Thornton, *Comintern and Chinese Communists*, pp. 103–186.

15. *Shiryō-shū*, vol. 4, p. 525.

toward general strikes, emphasize the need for armed uprisings among the workers, guide the general armed struggles and the guerrilla warfare among the farmers to bring about general local uprisings, raise the daily struggles among the farmers to level of agrarian revolution, and instigate and organize soldiers' revolts. The Red Army was also to be expanded, and it should engage in large-scale attacks against major cities and occupy them. Even if the occupation of the cities was of short duration, it still would have extremely great political influence. "If the Red Army implements these tactics and merges with struggle of the workers, farmers, and soldiers throughout the nation, the great revolutionary tide will be accelerated."[16] Even after the Chinese Eastern Railway incident ended in favor of the Soviet Union, the CCP was to continue the policy set forth in the circular.[17]

The CCP in Manchuria, 1928

In the meantime, there were apparently some changes in the leadership of the Manchurian Committee. There is no record as to whether Ch'en Wei-jen remained in Manchuria, returned to China, or became a victim of the police. A Japanese source lists T'ang Hung-ching and Wang Li-kung as the leaders of the Manchurian Committee in September 1928, when the committee was believed to have become a permanent committee, shedding the "temporary" title.[18] T'ang had been a laborer at Shahokou; Wang had been the head of the Workers' Department of the Dairen Area Committee and, before that, a member of the Dairen Workers' Study Association. In June 1929, however, the new secretary of the committee, Liu Shao-ch'i, arrived in Manchuria.[19] He was to

---

16. Ibid., p. 528.
17. See, for example, "The Resolution of the Central Political Bureau of the CCP in Accepting the Resolution of the Tenth Plenum of the ECCI" (Executive Committee of the Communist International) (adopted December 20, 1929), *Pu-erh-sai-wei-k'o* [Bolshevik], vol. 3, no. 1 (January 15, 1930), pp. 139–147 (Japanese translation in *Shiryō-shū*, vol. 4, pp. 551–558). The Chang Hsüeh-liang regime signed a truce with the Soviet forces on December 3.
18. South Manchuria Railway Company, Keizai Chōsakai (Economic Research Association) *Manshū kyōsantō undō gaikan* [A Survey of the Manchurian Communist Party Movement] (Dairen, 1935), p. 3.
19. Chung-Kung Yen-chiu Tsa-chih-she (Institute for the Study of Chinese Communist Problems), ed., *Liu Shao-ch'i wen-t'i tzu-liao chuan-chi* [Special Collection of Materials on the Liu Shao-chi Question] (Taipei, 1970), p. 698 (hereafter cited as *Liu Shao-ch'i wen-t'i*). Another Communist writer noted the presence of Liu in Manchuria in the spring of 1929, but June is accepted by the CCP as the correct month of Liu's arrival. Ho Ch'eng-hsiang, "Three Meetings with Comrade

stay in that post until March 1930, when he was transferred to Shanghai.[20]

Two letters exchanged between the Manchurian Committee and the Central Committee reveal some aspects of the organization and activities in Manchuria. On September 27, 1929, the Central Committee sent a list of appointees to the committee as follows:

> Liu Shao-ch'i, secretary, propaganda chief; Meng [Yung-] chien, organization; [T'ang] Hung-ching, workers; [?] Kuo-chen, candidate member of the Standing Committee, to Fushun; [Ting] Chün-yang, candidate member of the Standing Committee, to Harbin; [Wang] Li-kung, a committee member, to Harbin; the secretary of the Communist Youth League will join the party's provincial committee. These seven persons shall form the Temporary Provincial Committee.[21]

The Manchurian Committee replied on October 19 that because some actions had already been taken, it was necessary to alter some of the assignments. Meng and "Kuo-chen" were already in Harbin, and they could not be transferred at once to Mukden; Meng had been arrested once in Mukden and was rather well known near the cotton mill and at the Police Bureau, and hence he could not work there. As concerns the movement in Fushun, all those who had worked in the organization there had been arrested or had fled; the organization had disintegrated completely, and there was a need to establish new connections. A comrade had been dispatched recently to work among the workers, but so far there had not been much effect. The committee also reported that it was in the process of searching for a comrade who had fled from Shantung and was thought to be better suited than Meng for directing activities in Mukden. Therefore, the commit-

---

Yang Ching-yü," *Hung-ch'i P'iao-p'iao* [The Red Flag Waves], vol. 5 (December 15, 1957), p. 119.

20. *Liu Shao-ch'i wen-t'i*, p. 696. A Japanese writer, writing in January 1937, placed Liu in Manchuria between the end of 1930 and February 1932, but he is evidently in error. Interpreter Maruta, "Kahoku kyōsan undō-shi" [History of the Communist Movement in Northern China] in Hatano Kenichi, ed., *Chūgoku kyōsantō-shi* [History of the Chinese Communist Party] (Tokyo, 1961), vol. 7, p. 853. Just prior to his assignment to Manchuria, Liu was the secretary of the Hopei Provincial Committee.

21. The letters were printed in *Liu Shao-ch'i wen-t'i*, p. 705. As we noted earlier, the Manchurian Committee was given permanent status, but this letter still refers to it as the "Temporary Committee." I am unable to explain the discrepancy.

tee had decided that Liu Shao-ch'i should concurrently head the Propaganda Department, Ting should head the Organization Department and concurrently direct activities in Mukden, T'ang should head the Workers' Department, and the trio should form the Standing Committee; Meng should be the secretary and the head of the Organization Department in Harbin, "Kuo Chen" should be head of the Propaganda Department in Harbin, and the secretary of the Communist Youth League should also join the Standing Committee in Mukden. Although T'ang Hung-ch'ing had proposed one Hsi P'ing as a committee member, there were bad feelings among the comrades toward this person; because he had "errors in his concepts (*kuan-nien*)," they were unwilling to have him on the committee.[22]

We do not have detailed information concerning these individuals, but there is no doubt that some of them were veteran organizers of some importance. Ting Chün-yang and Meng Chien, for example, had participated in the Sixth CCP Congress in Moscow in the summer of 1928 as full delegates.[23] Before arriving in Manchuria, Ting Chün-yang allegedly participated in killing wealthy gentry in Tsinan, served as a liaison officer with Moscow for the CCP Central Committee, and had also traveled to Nanking, Hankow, and elsewhere to supervise party activities.[24] While Meng Chien's earlier background is unknown, he was to rise in the CCP hierarchy in later years.[25] Liu Shao-ch'i, of course, needs no introduction. Thus the lineup of the leaders of the Manchurian Committee in 1929 leaves no doubt that the CCP headquarters attached special importance to the situation in Manchuria.

These experienced cadres, however, had great difficulty in making progress. Ever since the Sixth Congress, the party had been emphasizing ever more strongly the agrarian revolution while at the same time directing the revival of the destroyed party cells and headquarters on all levels by paying special attention to the "establishment and development of party cells in big industrial

22. *Liu Shao-ch'i wen-t'i*, pp. 706–707.
23. Yüeh Sheng (Sheng Chung-liang), *Sun Yat-sen University in Moscow and the Chinese Revolution: A Personal Account* (Lawrence, Kansas, 1971), p. 187.
24. Naimushō, Keihokyoku (Bureau of Police and Security, Ministry of Home Affairs), *Gaiji keisatsu-hō* [External Police News] no. 96 (July, 1930), pp. 117–118.
25. Meng Chien (Meng Yung-ch'ien) survived the Manchurian ordeal and, during the Sino-Japanese War, became a senior official in the Chinese Industrial Cooperative. In 1950 he was appointed a Chinese delegate to the Trusteeship Council and served as a member of the Chinese delegation to the United Nations. Later, he served as director of the International Relations Research Institute, Academy of Sciences. See Donald W. Klein and Anne B. Clark, *Biographic Dictionary of Chinese Communism, 1921–1965* (Cambridge, Mass., 1971), vol. 2, pp. 690–692.

establishments and factories"[26] and the active recruitment of party members among workers. It was, therefore, incumbent upon the Manchurian Committee to engage in recruitment work among both workers and farmers. Priority had to be given to the recruitment of workers because only they, according to the Sixth Congress resolutions, could provide the needed leadership.

The scanty information available on the Communist movement in Manchuria between 1928 and 1929 indicates that the party members faced great difficulties in implementing the resolutions of the Sixth Congress and suffered gravely from these and other strategies advanced by the party leadership in China proper. The cadres dispatched to recruit workers were quickly arrested, and even the top cadres of the Manchurian Committee had difficulty staying out of the hands of the police. The odds against the Manchurian Committee seem to have been too formidable. Certainly, the pro-Russian stance of the CCP with respect to the Chinese Eastern Railway incident could not have endeared the party to the local Chinese masses. Its radical policies against the landlords and the bourgeoisie would have alienated most of the well-to-do elements, and the very idea of analyzing the society in economic and class terms would have been too alien and too far removed from the illiterate masses. At any rate, these foreign and radical ideas were not worthy of the high personal risks that accompanied membership in the CCP or any of its ancillary organizations. The brutal and efficient police of both the Chang Hsüeh-liang regime and the Japanese forces were nearly impossible to elude. If anything is surprising about these years, it is that the Chinese Communist movement continued at all rather than the fact that so little progress was made by the CCP organizations. Let us, in any event, trace the activities of the Manchurian Committee.

In March 1929, the committee dispatched three party members to Fushun to organize the tens of thousands of miners and industrial workers in the burgeoning mining-industrial complex there. Fushun, an ancient town 30 miles east of Mukden, was an obvious target of the CCP. The rich bituminous coalfields surrounding the city had attracted the attention of peoples of all nationalities from the ancient period (Korean potters of the Koryŏ era [A.D. 932–1392], for example), and the Japanese had turned it into a major mining and industrial complex that included a sprawling

26. Conrad Brandt, Benjamin Schwartz, and John K. Fairbank, *A Documentary History of Chinese Communism* (Cambridge, Mass., 1952), p. 149.

network of strip mines, thermal power plants, machine production plants, steel mills, and cement factories. The Japanese had also built a new city and a new railroad complex between 1920 and 1924. All these projects, of course, employed large numbers of Chinese workers. The three CCP agents established the Fushun Labor Union (Fushun Kung-hui) with seven committeemen, and beneath it subunions (*hsiao kung-hui*) appropriate to the various enterprises, such as the mines and factories, or oriented toward particular professions, such as painters. The leaders solicited workers both through direct contacts and through plainly written mimeographed materials emphasizing slogans such as those calling for increased wages and shortened working hours. By late August, the union had established at least six subunions or branches, but the number of workers enlisted does not appear to have been very large. In describing the status of the union movement as of August, the Japanese Ministry of Foreign Affairs said that the "movement has not yet gained momentum and has not engaged in detailed activities."[27] There is no indication that any of these union members were recruited into the party.

On July 26, the Japanese had discovered propaganda materials posted on the walls in Fushun; they had also found handbills bearing similar Communist propaganda.[28] On August 1, "Red International Day," the Japanese also discovered posters, leaflets, and pamphlets bearing two messages or declarations issued by the CCP Manchurian Committee, namely, "To the Masses in Manchuria on Red International Day" and "On the Sudden Outbreak of the Chinese Eastern Railway Incident." These were found not only in various parts of the Fushun mining and industrial complex but also in Mukden.[29]

While Japanese officials doubted the effectiveness of these messages in view of the widespread, intense anti-Russian feeling among the Chinese in Manchuria at this time,[30] the Chinese and Japanese police moved swiftly to apprehend the culprits. Events again proved the absurdity of passing out propaganda in the streets without laying the proper foundation: by August 2, some twenty

27. Chief of the Asia Bureau, Japanese Ministry of Foreign Affairs, to related agencies, "Concerning the Actions of the Chinese Communist Party in Southern Manchuria," September 30, 1929, Archives of the Japanese Ministry of Foreign Affairs (1868–1945), microfilmed for the Library of Congress (hereafter cited as AJMFA), reel S373, file S9452-5, pp. 290–295.
28. Osaka Tai-Shi Keizai Remmei (Osaka Economic Federation for China), ed., *Sa-Rempō to Shina Manshū no kyōsan undō* [The Soviet Union and the Communist Movement in China and Manchuria] (Tokyo, 1934), p. 562.
29. Ibid.
30. Ibid.

suspects had been arrested in Mukden by the Chinese police.[31] On August 30, the Japanese police apprehended another fifteen suspects in Fushun, including Chang Kuan-i, who was to become a revolutionary hero in later years under the name of Yang Ching-yü.[32] The police confiscated a number of very important CCP documents, including the operations plan of the Manchurian Committee, reports on the status of operations in Fushun, instructions from the provincial party to the Fushun branch, outlines of propaganda activities to be conducted on May Day and on the anniversary of the May 30th Movement, the operational plan for Red International Day, conclusions of the First Plenum of the Manchurian Provincial Committee, the Central Committee's instructions on secret operations, an outline of the report of the Labor Union Congress, and a letter from the Comintern to the CCP.[33] Even without confessions from the arrested, the Japanese and the Chinese police would have gained very extensive knowledge about the Communist movement in Manchuria.

The plan of operation adopted by the Manchurian Committee sometime before August shows the party's emphasis on urban operations. The operational plan confiscated by the Japanese police at Fushun read as follows:

> *Outline of Operational Plan of the Manchurian Committee (1929)*
> 1. *Workers' Movement*
>   a. Target cities: Harbin, Changchun, Kirin, Anshan, Mukden, Fushun, Penhsihu, Yingkou, Dairen, Antung.
>   b. Special target areas: South Manchuria Railway, Chinese Eastern Railway, and Peking–Mukden Railway.

---

31. Report from Consul-General Hayashi in Mukden to Foreign Minister Shidehara, August 2, 1929, AJMFA, reel S373, file S9452-5, pp. 286–287.

32. Chang Lin, "The Story of General Yang Ching-yü," *Hung-ch'i P'iao-p'iao*, no. 8 (July 1958), pp. 62–63, says that Yang Ching-yü, who used the alias Chang Kuan-i at this time, was repeatedly tortured by the Japanese police in Fushun and that he did not divulge any information. Chang Lin evidently compiled data about Yang from interviews. Some of the information published by the Chinese Communists about Yang Ching-yü is in error. For example, Chang says that Yang was arrested in early 1929, and Ho Ch'eng-hsiang says that Yang had been sent to Fushun in the spring and was arrested in the winter of 1929. See "Three Meetings with Comrade Yang Ching-yü," *Hung-ch'i P'iao-p'iao*, no. 5 (December 15, 1957), p. 119. As related above, Yang and others were arrested on August 30. See Hayashi to Shidehara, AJMFA, reel S373, file S9452-5, p. 288, and "Actions of Chinese Communist Party in Southern Manchuria" (September 30, 1929), loc. cit., pp. 290–295.

33. "Actions of Chinese Communist Party in Southern Manchuria," p. 295.

c. Method of operation: Establishment of organizations to approach the workers; investigation of the workers' living conditions and their demands; expansion of economic struggles; publication of printed materials; penetration of "yellow labor unions."

2. *Farmers' Movement*
   a. Investigate the condition of farmers in Peichiao [outskirts of Mukden], Taian, Yenchi, Harbin, Acheng, Changchun, Fushun, and the Kwantung territory.
   b. Establish party platforms for operational areas.
   c. Guide the farmers to engage in struggles on their own volition.
   d. Establish close liaison with the Korean Communist Party.

3. *Soldiers' Movement*
   a. Assign one specialist to the Provincial Committee and one to the Harbin City Committee to be responsible for operations.
   b. Pay special attention to the propaganda addressed to the Japanese soldiers.

4. *Student Movement*
   a. Arouse the students to win the right of freedom.
   b. Encourage the students to struggle for the right to participate in [decision making on] school affairs.
   c. Establish student associations and study groups in the schools in Mukden and Harbin for the anti-imperialist movement and for other purposes.

5. *Proletarian [Publication] Movement*
   a. Publish materials openly to instigate ideological struggles and to accelerate the establishment of anti-imperialist organizations.
   b. In the above publications, emphasize the fact that the anti-imperial leagues are to consist of the poor masses.

6. *Women's Movement*
   a. Establish plans for relief activities [on behalf] of those sacrificed in various movements.
   b. Advocate the liberation of women through publications.
   c. Arouse women to present their demands.

7. Anti-Imperialist Movement and Anti-Kuomintang Movement
   a. Publish materials against the war and against imperialism.
   b. Strive especially to expose the intrigues of Japanese imperialism and stimulate anti-Japanese sentiments.
   c. Expose the false masks of various policies of the Kuomintang and the Diplomatic Association (Wai-chiao Hsieh-hui) as well as the antirevolutionary crimes of the KMT in the name of the "Three People's Principles."[34]

The impression one receives from the operational plan is that the party had not made much progress in winning mass support. Plans for both the workers' and farmers' movements speak of the need to "investigate" the conditions of the workers and farmers, and plans for all other movements are also of a preparatory nature rather than being aimed at the redirection, change or expansion of ongoing movements.

Before making substantial progress, however, the Manchurian Committee needed to overcome the continuing problem of police detection. The incident of August 21, 1929, was particularly important because it involved the committee's new secretary, Liu Shao-ch'i, and the head of the Organization Department, Meng Yung-ch'ien.

According to information gathered by an ad hoc group of the CCP Central Committee between 1967 and 1968, Liu's arrest was triggered by the discovery of propaganda leaflets outside the gates of the Mukden Spinning Mill between July and August of 1929. An investigation was ordered, and one of the workers who had been suspected of being a Communist was bought off by the management. This worker provided a list of party members in the factory, and the head of the party cell was arrested. Using him, the police laid a trap on the following day, when a meeting about a strike had been scheduled. Liu and Meng were the victims of this trap.[35]

Liu and Meng were released some twenty days later, and Liu allegedly told his comrades that the release came about because

34. Sa-Rempo to Shina Manshū, pp. 563–564; also in Gunseibu, Komonbu (Advisors' Department, Ministry of Defense, Manchukuo), Manshū kyōsanhi no kenkyū [Study of Communist Bandits in Manchuria] (n.p., 1937), pp. 6–7.
35. Liu Shao-ch'i wen-t'i, pp. 698–699.

he and Meng had been suspected only of organizing a workers' strike—for which evidence was lacking—rather than for being Communists.[36] But this explanation does sound a little incongruous, since the local Japanese newspaper, *Manshū Nippō* [Manchuria Daily], reported on August 25 that the Chinese authorities had been on the alert because of indications that many Communist Party members had infiltrated the spinning mill and that several mill workers were arrested in the late afternoon of August 21 while meeting with a worker who appeared to be of South Chinese origin and who handed them Communist leaflets and funds for other materials. The only worker named in the article was one Wang Sheng-i, who had reportedly been at the mill for three years and had attempted at every opportunity to propagandize for the Communist cause.[37] The report did not say why he had not been arrested before or whether he had succeeded in his attempts.

In any event, Liu's former colleagues referred to some of the subordinate organizations in Manchuria, providing a glimpse of party activities during this period. Meng Yung-ch'ien, for example, named three special committees (*t'e-wei*)—those in northern Manchuria, eastern Manchuria, and the Kwantung Leased Territory.[38] It is probable that the movement in southern Manchuria was placed directly under the Manchurian Provincial Committee. When we group the cities named in the statements, it appears that the party organizers were established as follows:[39]

Northern Manchuria: Harbin (later Acheng, Chuho, Mutanchiang, Tungning, and Mishan)

36. Ibid., p. 696. During the Great Cultural Revolution in 1967, Red Guards obtained a confession from Meng Yung-ch'ien to the effect that he and Liu Shao-ch'i quickly confessed their status in the party after the first round of torture and promised to provide information on future activities of the CCP in Manchuria in exchange for their release. This confession was used as one of the grounds to discredit Liu, and Meng was sentenced to life imprisonment. But in June 1979 Meng was released from jail, where he had feigned insanity, and retracted his signed testimony, which he said had been written under coercion. Richard S. Ehrlich, "Liu Accuser Retracts 'Confession,'" (UPI, Hong Kong) in *Korea Herald*, June 5, 1979. For the CCP's official comment on this episode, see "Comrade Liu Shaoqi in 1925, 1927, and 1929," *Beijing Review*, March 31, 1980, pp. 14–18. This report unfortunately reveals no information concerning Liu's activities in Manchuria.

37. The *Manshū Nippō* article is reprinted in *Liu Shao-ch'i wen-t'i*, p. 692.

38. Meng was sent to Harbin after his release. When Liu went to Harbin in November or December, he allegedly told Meng that he was in communication with the Mukden police and that he needed materials on northern Manchuria which he was expected to submit, whereupon Meng allegedly provided information concerning the movement in Acheng, Chuho, Mutanchiang, Tungning, and Mishan *hsien*, along with a list of officers and statistics on membership. Ibid., pp. 695–696.

39. Ibid.

Eastern Manchuria: Yenchi
Kwantung Leased Territory: Dairen, Yingkou
Southern Manchuria: Mukden, Liaochung, Liaoyang, Fushun, and Penhsihu

Unfortunately, none of the statements released in 1968 reveals the number of party members or supporters recruited by the party into various peripheral organizations. But the places named confirm the suspicion that the party at this time was still largely urban-centered, in that all but Yenchi and Liaochung were major industrial, mining, or shipping centers. Only after the arrest and release of Liu Shao-chi does the party seem to have made some progress in smaller towns east of Harbin, such as Acheng, Chuho, and Mutanchiang.

The provincial committee did report that struggle among the laborers of the Chinese Eastern Railway had recently been fomented. The committee enclosed a report from Harbin and the resolution of the committee on the activities at the railway, and expressed hope for instructions from the Central Committee. Because the members of the provincial committee were too busy to compose another set of instructions on this matter for transmittal to Harbin, the Central Committee was requested to publish its instructions either in *Hung-ch'i* (Red Flag), the official organ of the CCP, or in a publication of the All-China Federation of Labor. Because the provincial committee was attempting to invigorate the movement on the railway, Liu Shao-ch'i himself was proceeding to Harbin.[40]

While the Manchurian Committee was undergoing these trials, the Central Committee continued to dispatch directives to Manchuria reinforcing some of the earlier ones. In June 1929, the Second Plenum of the Central Committee stated in its political resolution that there had been eight or nine labor struggles (presumably strikes) in Manchuria during the preceding several months.[41] It instructed the committee, in the resolution on the labor movement, to actively expand the organizational movement among the railroad, mine, metal, and textile workers, and among seamen, in the major industrial areas.[42] Manchuria was cited along with Shanghai, Hong Kong, Canton, Tientsin, and Tsingtao as one of the six major industrial centers of China where the red labor union movement was to be emphasized.[43] The resolution

40. Ibid., pp. 706–707. 41. *Shiryō-shū*, vol. 4, p. 361.
42. Ibid., p. 419.
43. Ibid., p. 430. While all the industrial centers other than Manchuria are cities, the CCP Central Committee referred to Manchuria as a whole.

also noted the success of daily newspapers in Shanghai as a means of propaganda, and instructed the Communists in Manchurian and other industrial centers to publish similar papers on a daily basis or every three days to disseminate propaganda intended to arouse the workers.[44]

In August the Central Committee issued a directive on the farmers' movement, in the form of a resolution, after receiving a letter from the Comintern (dated June 7) which sharply criticized the "right-wing error" of the Sixth Congress of the CCP in 1928 with respect to the rich peasants.[45] The "Resolution Accepting the Instruction of the Comintern concerning the Peasant Question" dealt with the overall status of Chinese agriculture, the party's past errors with regard to the peasantry, and its future policies.[46] A considerable portion was devoted to the situation in Manchuria. This was the first resolution adopted by the Central Committee on all-party affairs which referred to the situation in Manchuria at length; in dealing with matters of general concern, the Central Committee had theretofore made only passing reference to Manchuria. In essence, the Communists in Manchuria were instructed to pursue a policy line of opposition to exploitation by the warlords, landlords, capitalists, and imperialists. Specifically, they were to relate the anti-imperialist slogans to all other slogans and use anti-imperialism as the principal theme in the village struggles. The party was to build a foundation among the farm workers and poor farmers and enlist the support of middle-level farmers in order to establish a solid revolutionary front.[47] Farmers' associations (*nung-min hsieh-hui*) were to be established and used as a vehicle for organizing the masses. Presumably, the peasants would join these associations because the slogans advanced by the CCP would appeal to them.

44. Ibid., p. 426.
45. The Sixth Congress had decided that the rich peasantry as a class was differentiable into "reactionary" and "progressive" elements and that the former were to be opposed and the latter supported. It was considered unnecessary to antagonize the rich peasants needlessly at the time. Although the Comintern changed its policy toward the rich peasantry in its letter of June 7, the CCP did not change its policy until August. For details, see Thornton, *Comintern and Chinese Communists*, pp. 87–93. The June 7 letter is reprinted in *Kung-ch'an-tang erh-chung ch'üan-hui chüeh-i-an* [Resolutions of the Second Plenum of the Central Committee of the Communist Party] (n.p., 1929), pp. 1–5. *Shiryō-shū*, vol. 4, pp. 431–441, contains a Japanese translation.
46. In *Kung-ch'an-tang erh-chung ch'üan-hui chüeh-i-an*, pp. 1–5. I have used the Japanese text in *Shiryō-shū*, vol. 4, p. 470.
47. *Shiryō-shū*, vol. 4, p. 474. The rich farmers were to be rejected because "they would undoubtedly run toward the counterrevolutionary side."

In short, despite the dispatch of experienced and presumably dedicated cadres to Manchuria, the CCP had not made any significant progress, and the Manchurian Provincial Committee was hardly in a position to destroy the Chang Hsüeh-liang regime, promote the movement concerning the Chinese Eastern Railway, or strengthen and expand guerrilla warfare.

CCP Admission of Korean Communists

It was at this juncture that the Comintern and the CCP leadership turned to the 400,000 Koreans living in the Chientao region in the southeastern corner of Manchuria, on the Russo-Korean border, which included such counties as Yenchi, Holung, and Wangching. Because of the large number of political refugees among them, the Koreans in Chientao were more politicized than the population in general, and Korean Communists had been active among them since 1920, when Korean nationalists had established contact with the Bolsheviks in eastern Siberia. After the founding of the Korean Communist Party in Seoul in 1925, the Manchurian General Bureau of the Korean Communist Party (KCP) was set up to continue and direct organizational activities in Manchuria. Although the Korean Communists were plagued by frequent arrests and internal strife, the strength and influence of the KCP in Manchuria far surpassed that of the CCP.[48] In September 1930, the Japanese estimated the Communist Party membership in the Chientao region to be 3,800 Koreans and 150 Chinese.[49]

Added to the strong anti-Japanese feelings held by many of the Korean immigrants were other socio-economic and political reasons that tended to draw them to communism. Foremost among these were issues concerning land. Under the Chientao Treaty, signed by the governments of China and Japan in 1910, Koreans were permitted equal rights with Chinese with respect to owning land in Chientao. In other parts of Manchuria, however, Koreans could not own land unless they were naturalized citizens. In 1930, even in Chientao, 56.6 percent of all Koreans worked entirely or partly as tenants, while only 23.7 percent of the Chinese

---

48. See Robert A. Scalapino and Chong-Sik Lee, *Communism in Korea* (Berkeley and Los Angeles, 1972), vol. 1, pp. 138–151.

49. "The Process of Admission of the Korean Communist Party in Manchuria to the Chinese Communist Party and the Present Condition of the Korean and Chinese Communists in the Yenpien Area," Report of the consul-general in Chientao to the foreign minister, September 18, 1930, AJMFA, reel SP102, file SP205-5, p. 6550; hereafter cited as "Process of Admission."

fell into this category.[50] In sum, poverty was widespread among the Koreans living in Manchuria. Aside from the economic destitution that made them more susceptible to Communist propaganda, they also harbored strong resentment against the warlord regime because they suffered severely at the hands of the Chinese authorities. Before 1925, this situation had not existed; indeed, Korean immigration had been encouraged, since it meant the opening up of wasteland and its conversion to productive land. For a time, moreover, the Chinese authorities had supported the Korean nationalists and provided active assistance to some. Gradually this amicable relationship had changed, partly because Koreans increasingly became linked with the Japanese, who actively used the pretext of protecting the abused Koreans to establish consular branches and otherwise intrude on Chinese authority.[51]

In 1925 an agreement was signed by Chang Tso-lin's government and the Japanese governor-general of Korea, relating to the control of so-called recalcitrant Koreans in Manchuria. This provided for the active cooperation of the Mukden government with the Japanese; there was to be a monetary reward for each arrest. The Korean nationalist and Communist movements suffered heavily as a result of this agreement, and so did nonpolitical Koreans. In many cases, the order to suppress "recalcitrant" or anti-Japanese Koreans became a license for local officials to abuse their authority. Under the pretext of suppressing radicals, Chinese officials and even residents sometimes molested or arrested innocent farmers, extracted large sums of money in "fines," drove them off their land, or killed them. Such outrages, increasingly frequent after 1927,[52] naturally drove many Koreans to desperation, and many of them turned toward the Communist movement. In 1930, the Japanese consul-general in Chientao reported that a tenth of the adult Korean population in Manchuria could be accounted "Communist or sympathetic to the Communists."[53]

50. In Chientao, 31.2 percent of all Korean farmers were tenants who possessed no land; 13.7 percent of the Chinese farmers were in that category. *Manshū kyōsanhi no kenkyū*, p. 554.
51. Manshū-shi Kenkyū-kai (Association for the Study of Manchurian History), *Nihon teikoku shugi ka no Manshū* [Manchuria under Japanese Imperialism] (Tokyo, 1972), pp. 345–350.
52. Yi Hun-gu, *Manju wa Chosŏnin* [Manchuria and the Koreans] (Pyongyang, 1932), pp. 239–263; see also Scalapino and Lee, *Communism in Korea*, vol. 1, pp. 140–141.
53. Report of Consul-General Okada to Foreign Minister Shidehara, "The Recent Condition of Various Factions of the Korean Communist Party in East Manchuria," March 4, 1930, AJMFA, reel SP102, file SP205-5, pp. 6179-98. For "Statistics Concerning the Communist Movement in Chientao and Hunchun Areas,"

This was what led CCP cadres such as Ch'en Wei-jen to advocate a united front of Chinese and Korean workers and farmers and the CCP's Manchurian Committee to include in its August 1929 plan the need to "establish close liaison with the KCP." But in late 1929 the Comintern decided on another approach, that of placing the Korean Communists in Manchuria under the CCP. This, of course, was in accord with the Comintern's long-standing "one country, one party" principle, although with respect to the Korean and Russian movement in Manchuria it had never been enforced. In practical terms, it was hoped that the annexation of the Koreans by the CCP would considerably ameliorate the langorous condition of the CCP in Manchuria, and that, in particular, a more positive campaign could be launched with respect to the railway.

In November 1929, according to a Japanese report, the Comintern dispatched two agents—a Korean, Han Pin, and a Chinese, Li Ch'un-shan—to Shanghai for conferences with the CCP leaders, after which the agents and Su Wen, a representative of the CCP headquarters, went on to Harbin in January 1930. There they met with fourteen Chinese officers of the Manchurian Province Committee, still under Liu Shao-ch'i, and a dozen or so Korean Communists. Although a minority of the Koreans objected to the idea of dissolving all KCP groups in Manchuria, it was agreed that the Koreans should join the CCP.[54]

It was not easy for Communists of this era to disagree with the decisions made in Moscow. Furthermore, the Korean Communists were at a disadvantage, having been severely criticized in the Comintern's December 1928 theses for their continuing inner quarrels, ineffectiveness in providing leadership for revolutionary struggle, and "lack of contact with the workers."[55] When the Comintern evoked the "one country, one party" principle and reminded them of their failure to obey the theses, few Koreans could offer effective argument against the new instructions.

The Li Li-san Line

Meanwhile, under the impetus of such Comintern letters as that of October 26 and driven by his own political motivations, Li Li-san rapidly led the CCP toward a more radical course of ac-

---

which covers the years 1923–1927, see AJMFA, reel S722 (no pagination), or Scalapino and Lee, *Communism in Korea*, vol. 1, p. 139.
54. "Process of Admission," pp. 6537–6550.
55. "Resolution of the ECCI on the Korean Question," in *International Press*

tion.⁵⁶ Although the Sixth Congress (June–July 1928) had cited the uneven development of labor and peasant movements and uneven development of different geographic areas (the "developed South" vs. the "underdeveloped North") as two of the primary causes of the failure of the 1928 uprisings and had decided that the revolutionary situation would not reach a high tide until these disparities had been removed, Li Li-san was impatient. By February 26, 1930, when he issued Central Circular No. 70, Li had decided that the uneven situation had been satisfactorily resolved and that a new revolutionary high tide was at hand. In the circular, Li asserted: "The present nationwide crisis is deepening daily and the new revolutionary wave is developing forward." The warlord war had continued to expand and had affected every facet of Chinese life, thus helping to create the objective basis for the maturation of a "new revolutionary high tide." According to the circular, the intense activity among the workers, the deepening of the peasant struggle, the victories of the Red Army and the expansion of soviet areas confirmed that the "nationwide mass struggle" was developing "evenly."⁵⁷ Those in Manchuria would have noted with particular interest that the progress made in Harbin was cited as one of the evidences of this "high tide." Urban work was said not only to have revived from its previous ebb, but especially in key cities like Wuhan, Canton, and Harbin, to have made great strides forward.⁵⁸ Thus, long before June 11, 1930, when the CCP Politburo called for the takeover of political power in one or more provinces, Li Li-san was steering the party in a radical direction.

Given the weakness of the CCP in Manchuria, it was natural that the Korean Communists in Chientao should be given the task of putting the Li Li-san line into action. The Korean Communists were eager to accept the assignment not only because they wished to display their loyalty to their new superiors but also because they had already formed similar plans of their own. Koreans generally, both in and out of Korea, had been greatly agitated by the Kwangju incident of late 1929, which touched off student strikes and demonstrations throughout Korea for five months. A

Correspondence, vol. 9, no. 8 (February 15, 1929), pp. 130–133; reprinted in Dae-Sook Suh, ed., *Documents of Korean Communism* (Princeton, 1970), pp. 243–256.

56. Thornton presents a convincing argument that Li Li-san took to the putschist line for his own reasons rather than because of instructions from the Comintern. *Comintern and Chinese Communists*, pp. 103–186.

57. Ibid., p. 111.

58. Ibid., p. 112.

clash between Korean and Japanese students in the south Korean town on October 30 had brought to the surface the intense anti-Japanese feeling among the Koreans engendered by the discriminatory manner in which the authorities handled the minor flare-up among the students. Between February 28 and March 1, 1930, some of the Korean Communists in Yenchi organized hundreds of farmers in different localities and carried out mass demonstrations, in which banners saying "Destroy Japanese Imperialism" or "Long Live Korean Independence" were displayed and hundreds of thousands of leaflets were distributed. The demonstrations were scheduled for these dates to coincide with the anniversary of the March First movement of 1919. Emboldened by their success, those who took the leadership in these demonstrations met on March 5 and formed the "All East Manchuria Riot Committee" to continue their activities.[59] There is little surprise in the fact that the Korean Communists were turning to a radical line.

To absorb the Koreans and to carry out the new instructions, the Manchurian Committee created the Yenpien branch in the spring of 1930 by enrolling local Chinese teachers and Korean Communists, and charged it with the task of organizing uprisings on the fifth anniversary of the May 30 Incident "for the purpose of driving out Japanese imperialism, destroying the KMT warlords, and completing the Communist revolution in Manchuria."[60] It was agreed that riots should be carried out at Lungching village, the village of Toutaokou, and in the vicinity of the Tienpaoshan–Tumen railroad. Buildings and other facilities belonging to the Japanese and the KMT warlords were to be set on fire, and Japanese or Chinese policemen preventing rioting were to be killed. A Korean Communist, Kim Ch'ŏl, was placed in charge of the operation, and a representative from the Manchurian Committee, Pak Yun-sŏ, also a Korean, provided funds and guidance.

The activists recruited for the May 30 riots consisted of no more than 150 to 200 individuals, but, according to the official Japanese accounts, the damage they did or incited was quite extensive. Vandalism spread throughout the Chientao area. Using guns, gasoline-filled bottles, and ordinary matches, the rioters attacked, and in many instances set fire to, the Japanese consulate,

---

59. The Japanese arrested 172 Koreans as a result of the February 28–March 1 demonstrations, whose leaders were members of the so-called "Tuesday group." See "The Preliminary Trial for the Chientao May 30 Incident Concluded," Kōtō Hōin, Kenjikyoku (Government General of Korea, High Court, Prosecutor's Bureau), *Shisō geppō* [Thought Monthly], vol. 1, no. 4 (July 15, 1931), pp. 177–178. This issue is in AJMFA, reel S355.

60. Ibid., p. 187.

the East Asian Colonial Company office, electric power facilities, railroad bridges, the printing house, schools, and the homes of certain police informers, pro-Japanese individuals, and wealthy bourgeoisie. The riots were conducted during the night between May 29 and May 31, and "supporting units" exploded firecrackers and shouted slogans to distract the police from the main units engaged in arson and other destructive activities.[61] These were only the first in a series of terrorist actions undertaken by Korean radicals during this period. On August 1 (Red International Day) and again on August 29 (National Humiliation Day for the Koreans, the date of Korea's annexation to Japan in 1910), Koreans in the area along the Kirin–Tunhua railroad carried out numerous acts of sabotage and violence.

The Central Committee in Shanghai not only approved these radical actions in Chientao but strongly urged the Manchurian Committee to expand the movement throughout Manchuria. In an article entitled "The Farmers' Movement Operation in Manchuria," which was published in the August 29 issue of *Hung-ch'i Jih-pao* [Red Flag Daily], the Central Committee argued that the situation in Manchuria was ripe for pushing forward the agrarian revolution with full force.[62] According to the Central Committee, the agrarian economy in Manchuria was controlled by Japanese imperialists, and the people were severely oppressed by the Kuomintang warlords, who had become huge landowners and were the "running dogs of imperialism." More than 70 percent of the farmers were said to be either indigents or tenants; in particular, the "1,300,000 Korean farmers" in Manchuria who owned no land were "suffering from the cruelty and inordinate exploitation of landlords and usurers." The Central Committee saw only two possibilities for the agrarian economy in Manchuria: either there would be a complete victory of the imperialists, or the workers and farmers would "confiscate all land, eradicate the existing system, establish a soviet regime, and progress toward socialism." The task of the Communists was to promote the second course and thereby "guarantee the victory of revolution."

In pointing out the past mistakes of the Communists in Manchuria, the Central Committee also indicated the appropriate future course of action. First, the Communists in Manchuria had

61. Ibid., pp. 194–200.
62. The discussion here is based on a commentary on the article by Ōtsuka Reizō, "Manshū no nōmin undō" [Farmers' Movement in Manchuria], *Mantetsu Shina Gesshi* [South Manchuria Railway Company China Monthly], Shanghai, vol. 7, no. 11 (January 15, 1931), pp. 97–107.

mistakenly believed that it was impossible to organize local riots and arouse partisan warfare so long as Manchuria was under the control of Japanese imperialism and the rule of the warlords was moderate. They had also believed that revolution would come in Manchuria only at the last stage of victory throughout China. "This was because," according to the Central Committee, "they did not understand the revolutionary situation in Manchuria, the sharpening conflict between imperialism and the warlords, or the life of the masses."[63] Their attitude was criticized as negating the revolution in Manchuria.

Although the Central Committee ostensibly criticized the Communists in Manchuria for their "erroneous views," the article in *Hung-ch'i Jih-pao* actually amounted to a vindication of the Manchurian leaders. In the exchanges of 1928, the "mistaken" views clearly were those of the central leadership, not of the cadres in Manchuria. Had any of the latter from 1928 still remained on the Manchurian Committee in 1930, they would have been pleased to see the new leadership finally come round to the position that they had so ardently advocated earlier. But the other criticisms and directives in the article would have quickly quelled any surge of enthusiasm: "Through failing to comprehend the revolutionary situation properly," they were said to have assumed incorrectly that partisan warfare could be carried out only in the mountainous region of eastern Manchuria and along the Heilungkiang–Kirin border. They were told that it was incorrect to believe that the warlords with the support of imperialism would easily suppress the revolutionary uprising. Moreover, the Communists in Manchuria, particularly the Korean Communists, were told that it was incorrect to oppose the merging of the struggle of the Korean farmers with that of the Chinese farmers on the ground that the Korean farmers had considerable experience while the Chinese did not. The Central Committee denounced all these beliefs and attitudes as right-wing deviation.[64]

The central leaders, on the other hand, continued the position of their predecessors with respect to the use of bandits: to argue for an alliance with the bandit leaders in order to carry out thorough land reform was to engage in extreme opportunism. This argument, in the view of the central leaders, ignored the class background of the bandit leaders, which was the same as that of the landlords and the gentry.[65] In conclusion, the Central Committee instructed the party in Manchuria to win the support of the Chi-

63. Ibid., p. 106.   64. Ibid., pp. 106–107.   65. Ibid., p. 107.

nese farmers, to center activities around the farm workers and poor farmers, and to organize local riots, arouse partisan warfare, thoroughly implement land reform, and establish a "Red Army" and a soviet regime.[66]

As is well known, Li Li-san exaggerated the revolutionary tide in China as a whole, but the situation in Manchuria was so remote from some of Li's assumptions that the new instructions could not have sounded more hollow. For one thing, the party had not been able to build a foothold from which to launch the organizational movement among the farmers or to expand the partisan movement outside of eastern Manchuria; for another, the Manchurian Committee was going through another serious crisis when the *Hung-ch'i* article was published and many other instructions from Li Li-san were dispatched. As will be noted shortly, the mass arrests of April 1930 had nearly demolished the Manchurian Committee. In June, some who had escaped the dragnet of April and attempted to revive the organization were arrested.[67] The police were relentless in pursuit of the Communists, and it is not clear how many of the committee members managed to stay out of their hands.

According to a Japanese source, however, the Manchurian Committee met in September and adopted a resolution on "The Political Situation in Manchuria and the Party's Tasks and Operational Line." The text of this resolution has not been discovered, but, according to the same source, the committee defined its tasks as (1) the organization of political (or general) strikes; (2) the organization of local guerrillas, which would lead to the establishment of soviet governments; (3) the organization of riots among soldiers; and (4) the establishment of a Red Army.[68] It is reasonable to assume that the Manchurian Committee mimicked the numerous directives being issued from the Central Committee regarding demonstrations (Central Committee Notice No. 136, July 3, 1930), on the establishment of the soviet regimes (Central Committee Circular No. 83, July 18), and on preparation

66. Ibid.
67. South Manchuria Railway Company, Keizai Chōsakai (Economic Research Association), *Manshū kyōsantō undō gaikan* [A Survey of the Manchurian Communist Party Movement] (Dairen, 1935), p. 4.
68. Ibid. The author of this volume, Ōtsuka Reizō, says in a footnote that he discussed this resolution in detail in his previous work "Manshū ni okeru kyōsantō undō" [The Communist Party Movement in Manchuria], *Tōhō pamfuretto tsūshin* [Eastern Pamphlet Communication], vol. 1, no. 9 (August 1, 1931). Extensive search for this work both in the United States and Japan, however, has not yielded a copy.

for armed riots and general strikes (Central Committee Circular No. 84, July 21).[69] When Li Li-san reorganized the party machinery into the Central General Action Committee on August 6, the Manchurian Committee followed his example and reorganized itself as the Manchurian Provincial General Action Committee in September.[70] But for all practical purposes, the new committee was powerless to implement the new directives.

Nonetheless, the Central Committee's directive for more radical action seems to have given impetus to the Korean Communists in eastern Manchuria. A "guerrilla unit" was organized within the Yenpien branch under the command of Pak Yun-sŏ to carry out radical activities. According to a Japanese report of September 1930, the unit consisted of approximately 80 members, each equipped with a pistol and bombs. The plan was to deploy a guerrilla unit of 30 to 50 members under each district committee in various prefectures. It was rumored that the Manchurian Provincial Committee was planning to smuggle in 1,000 Mauser pistols and 500 bombs from the Soviet Union in order that the guerrillas could conduct riots during the harvest season, plunder farm products from the landlords, and carry out arson.[71] Regardless of whether the guerrillas received new supplies of weapons, they were busy. The Japanese authorities recorded 690 appearances of guerrillas during 1930, and the reported cumulative number of guerrillas reached 15,810.[72] The guerrillas reportedly terrorized villages and demanded the free distribution of lands, declared the abolition of all tenant fees, burned loan documents, and denounced all debts. Sometimes the guerrillas killed the rich and those designated as pro-Japanese elements. They also burned crops and destroyed the property of landlords. When the order to abandon the Li Li-san line finally reached the Manchurian Communists in the spring of 1931, some 190 persons had been killed or injured and damage to property had been extensive.[73]

69. Texts of these documents are in *Shiryō-shū*, vol. 5, pp. 18–28.
70. *Sa-Rempō to Shina Manshu*, p. 566; also Chūō Keimu Tōsei Iinkai (Central Police Affairs Control Committee, Manchukuo), *Manshū ni okeru kyōsan undō no suii gaikyō* [Summary Survey of the Changes in the Communist Movement in Manchuria] (n.p., 1937), appendix (chronology). Hereafter cited as *Suii gaikyō*.
71. Okada to Shidehara, "The Recent Condition of Various Factions," March 4, 1930, AJMFA, reel SP102, file SP205-5, pp. 6545–6546.
72. AJMFA, reel SP103, file SP205-5, p. 6878–81.
73. *Suii gaikyō*, p. 21; also Naimushō, Keihokyoku (Bureau of Police and Security, Ministry of Home Affairs, Japan), *Chūka minkoku ni okeru kyōsan shugi undō no genkyō* [Present Condition of the Communist Movement in the Republic of China] (Tokyo, 1931), p. 30. According to the latter source, the Communists burned the harvested crops of 26 (presumably landlord) families in two commu-

It must be remembered that this was a period in which similar events were taking place in China proper on a much more massive scale. On July 28, 1930, the Fifth Red Army under P'eng Teh-huai had attacked Changsha, holding it for a few days before being driven out with heavy casualties. Mao Tse-tung's forces also had attacked the city of Nanchang but without success. These failures sealed the doom of Li Li-san, although he managed to hold on for a few more months. In mid-November the Comintern issued a letter criticizing Li's "adventurism" and "putschism" in devastating terms.

But what were the results of the frenzied activities in eastern Manchuria? Did these actions contribute to the consolidation of the party or to the cause of Communist revolution? At least one effect of the riotous actions was highly visible: the Japanese consular police retaliated with vigor, arresting a total of 13,168 persons by April 1931,[74] and many of the leaders were sent to Korea for trial. On the other hand, according to a document issued by either the Manchurian Committee or the East Manchurian Special Committee in February 1931, the guerrilla units that sprang up in the fall of 1930 did not last long.[75] The guerrillas that were organized for the May 30 riot (presumably those led by Pak Yun-sŏ) met with defeat at Taomukou and completely disappeared. The guerrilla unit that had sprung up on the occasion of the August riot in Tunhua disintegrated naturally after several days. Although the masses who engaged in guerrilla activities during the autumn had "killed numerous running dogs and confiscated much property," a more enduring guerrilla unit did not emerge from these activities, which had ended tamely, according to the CCP document. All this was quite harmful to the CCP in that the "comrades in general" had "come to be dominated by incorrect notions about guerrilla activity" and their confidence in it had greatly diminished.

In analyzing the causes of the failure of the guerrilla movement in eastern Manchuria, the document revealed the character of that movement. It stated that the guerrilla units had not engaged

---

nities in Yenchi *Hsien* in October–November and inflicted more than 100,000 *yüan* in damage. The armed men moved about in small groups of five to ten, making them very difficult to apprehend. For a similar account, see also *Manshū kyō-santō undō gaikan*, p. 4.

74. *Manshū Kyōsanhi no Kenkyū*, p. 69.

75. "Principles of Guerrilla Unit Operations in Eastern Manchuria" (Tung-Man yu-chi-tui kung-tso ta-kang), dated February 15, 1931, in AJMFA, reel S373, file 9452-6, pp. 89–116. The Yenpien branch had been reorganized into the East Manchurian Special Committee in August 1930. *Manshū kyōsanhi no kenkyū*, p. 69.

in political activities. They had not fostered contacts with the people and had not merged with the struggle of the masses. The party had not provided systematic and planned leadership. The guerrillas did not have a proper command system. Instead of striving to expand their ranks, they had engaged in adventuristic actions without any ties with the masses. Their indulgence in "military opportunism" had caused the masses to respect the weapons of the guerrillas rather than develop awareness of their own might. In short, it was nothing more than the prolongation of a disorganized riot. Therefore, when the guerrillas left an area or suffered a defeat, the masses ceased to support them. The indiscriminate and aimless burning of schools and harvests, the wanton burning to death of entire families including the aged and young, and the damage inflicted on the small Chinese merchants and middle-class farmers had aroused negative emotions. This drove the petty bourgeoisie and the middle-class and poor farmers away from the Communist camp. The excesses of the guerrillas led the "feudalistic farmers and those elements with nationalistic notions to support the counter-revolutionary movement and actively engage in the destruction of the guerrilla units, having been deceived by the landlords, rich farmers, and the ruling class."[76] The greatest excess seems to have been committed in a place called Wengshenglatzu, where the guerrillas, relying on their weapons, had evidently engaged in indiscriminate killing and destruction, which caused the local Chinese to rise in retaliation.[77] All in all, the so-called guerrilla activities directed by the Manchurian Committee turned most of the population against the Communist party and drove a deep wedge between the Koreans and the Chinese.

These were exactly the dangers that the Sixth Congress had warned against in 1928. In commenting on the "many weaknesses" in past guerrilla operations, the congress had noted:

> First, the conduct of guerrilla warfare separated from the masses has the effect of making them misunderstand the meaning of guerrilla warfare, or even respond to the propaganda of the landlords that guerrilla warfare is banditry. . . . Second, the tendency to destroy cities and kill, burn, and rob purposelessly: this tendency is only a reflection of a lumpen-proletariat, peasant mentality that may hamper the development of the

---

76. "Principles of Guerrilla Unit Operations in Eastern Manchuria," p. 99.
77. Ibid., pp. 96–99.

party among the peasant masses or even among the proletariat.[78]

These, one might add, were the same kind of criticisms lodged against the guerrillas in Kiangsi under Mao Tse-Tung by the Central Committee in late 1927.[79]

Even though the riots in Chientao produced adverse results for the CCP in the long run, the absorption of the Korean Communists into the party was a boon to the Manchurian Committee. Not only were the Korean Communists numerous, but their influence extended over a wide territory ranging from Chientao in the southeast to Ilan and Mulan in the southern part of Heilungkiang Province, where the Koreans had formed communities of their own. Beginning in early 1929, each group of Korean Communists had its farmers' league (*nongmin tongmaeng*), which for all practical purposes had served as a self-governing unit among the Korean farmers in the vicinity; thus it was relatively easy for the Korean Communists to select potential party recruits from among the farmers. After the Korean Communists joined the CCP, many members of the farmers' leagues were enrolled in the CCP's Farmers' Association (Nung-min Hsieh-hui) and in the party itself.[80] The Japanese estimate of 3,800 Korean and 150 Chinese party members in September 1930 may have been inflated, but it needs to be added that the estimate included only those in the Yenpien party branch, which was limited to the Chientao area (Yenchi, Holung, and Wangching *hsien*).

A case in point is the Yen-Ho (Yenchi-Holung) *Hsien* Committee in April 1931. This committee was under the East Manchurian Special Committee, which had jurisdiction over ten *hsien* (Yenchi, Holung, Wangching, Hunchun, Tunhua, Omu, Huatien, Antu, Changpai, and Fusung). Under the Yen-Ho committee were eight district committees which had a total of more than 110 branches. In November 1930, the Japanese and Chinese police carried out mop-up campaigns in the Yen-Ho area,[81] but the strength

---

78. "Resolution on the Peasant Movement," in C. Brandt, et al., *A Documentary History of Chinese Communism*, p. 162.

79. See CCP Central Committee to "Brother [Chu] Teh and the Comrades in the Army," December 21, 1927, *Chung-yang cheng-chih t'ung-hsün*, no. 16 (December 1927). Japanese translation in *Shiryō-shū*, vol. 3, pp. 444–450.

80. Director, Police Affairs Bureau, Government-General of Korea, "Present Condition of the Communist Movement in Manchuria and Plan for Riots on the Forthcoming May Day" (March 17, 1931), AJMFA, reel S374, file S9452-7, pp. 367–377. This report is based on the interrogation of five Koreans who had been involved in the organizational movement among Koreans in Manchuria.

81. The consular police arrested 134 Korean Communists between November

of the *hsien* committee as of April 1931 was still considerable, according to a Japanese estimate:

Party members	331
Communist Youth Corps members	484
Members of farmers' leagues, anti-imperial student associations, etc.	16,000[82]

In submitting these figures, the Japanese consul indicated that those affected by communism represented one in 17 of the entire Korean population (297,916 as of December 1930) in these *hsien* and attributed this to the adroitness and persistence of those engaged in the movement. If we consider the fact that women were largely excluded and take into account the aged and the young, approximately one out of five adult males had either a direct or an indirect tie with the Communists.[83]

Thus, in spite of the severe damage inflicted by the reckless policy of Li Li-san, the Korean Communists in eastern Manchuria displayed considerable resilience and had a strong potential for development. We can feel sure that—unlike the Chinese masses, whose natural sympathy inclined toward Chang Hsüeh-liang rather than the Russians—the Koreans found it easy to accept the CCP's anti-warlord slogans, and the slogans against imperialism also appealed to their nationalist sentiment against Japan. Further, the radical economic slogans of the CCP would have appealed to the Koreans in Chientao in view of the fact that a majority lived in poverty under landlords. The Korean community in Chientao and elsewhere in Manchuria thus presented what could be characterized as a revolutionary situation.

This situation among the Koreans, however, was hardly to be found among the Chinese in Manchuria. The Manchurian Committee continued to suffer from the ubiquitous police, and the movement among the workers made little headway. After Liu Shao-ch'i left for Shanghai in March 1930, the committee suffered severely at the hands of the police in April, following the arrest of

---

6 and 19 in Lungching village. In the Yenchi district some 40 officers of the party were arrested between November 6 and 7. *Chūka minkoku ni okeru kyōsan shugi undō no genkyō*, p. 30.

82. "Condition of the Communist Movement in Yenchi and Holung *Hsien* and Translated Secret Party Documents," prepared by the Police Department of the Chü-chih-chieh branch consulate, May 1931, in AJMFA, reel S373, file 9542-6, p. 4, to reel S374, p. 424. This report and the documents were prepared after the arrest of Kim Sang-sŏn (alias Ch'en Kung-mu), head of the Yen-Ho *Hsien* Committee, and seventeen others on April 8, 1930.

83. Ibid.

Tu Lan-t'ing, the head of the Anti-Imperial League in Mukden. The police interrogation of Tu and others revealed the existence of the league as well as details of the CCP organization in Mukden. Students and teachers from various middle schools were arrested along with party cadres; documents and mimeograph machines were confiscated; and at the homes of party leaders and in other suspicious places the police discovered important party files. Within a few days, 32 persons had been arrested, and at least eight others were being sought. The Manchurian Committee and the party structure in Mukden were in a shambles.[84] To aggravate the situation for the Manchurian Committee, Tu Lan-t'ing, whose arrest had triggered the havoc, defected to the government and became an informer for the gendarmerie of the Mukden government. One of his first deeds in his new capacity was to reveal the identity of one of the arrested as Ting Chün-yang. After verifying his identity and learning of his status within the CCP and his past activities in Tsinan and elsewhere, Marshal Chang Hsüeh-liang personally ordered Ting's interrogation, which began with bloody tortures.[85]

Some of the confiscated materials are preserved in Japanese translation, but their context is obscure. It is clear, however, that the party had established three branches or cells in Harbin, three branches in Mukden, and a branch in Fushun, and that agents were sent to such places as Dairen, Liaoyang, and Antung. Within Mukden, serious efforts had been made to penetrate the arsenal, a cement plant, a spinning mill and a number of factories, Tungpei College, South Manchuria Medical College, and a number of secondary educational institutions. It does not appear, however, that the party had been able to build a large following. In Fushun, only twelve persons had been recruited, and their quality as revolutionary cadres was very low.[86]

84. Information on the arrests and subsequent discoveries is from Naimushō, Keihokyoku (Bureau of Police and Security, Ministry of Home Affairs, Japan), *Gaiji keisatsu-hō* [External Police News], no. 95 (May–June, 1930), pp. 104–114. Meng Yung-ch'ien stated in his December 1967 confession that Liu Shao-ch'i left the Manchurian Committee in March 1930 and that in April the Manchurian Committee "suffered severe destruction." *Liu Shao-ch'i Wen-t'i*, p. 696.

85. *Gaiji keisatsu-hō*, no. 96 (July, 1930), pp. 117–118. Ting told the interrogators that he had arrived in Mukden in October 1929 and that Liu Shao-ch'i had appointed him head of the organization department. He worked at first as a laborer in an iron workshop and then became a teacher at P'ing-tan Middle School while issuing propaganda materials which were printed at the home of Tu Lan-ting, who eventually betrayed him. He revealed also that a "Chen-hua" was head of the local Communist Youth Corps branch. Ting and four others were executed and eight were given prison sentences.

86. Ibid., no. 95, pp. 107–115.

In late April, even as the Mukden police interrogated the arrested and followed new leads to arrest others, some of the Communists appeared on the streets to distribute a CCP document, Central Circular No. 72. The police arrested thirty-seven suspects between April 23 and May Day, and foiled any attempt to conduct demonstrations on the latter day.[87] Organizational work at the Fushun mines continued until October, when the arrest of Ch'en Tzu-chen, the "central figure in the Manchurian General Action Committee in Mukden," led to the arrest by Japanese police of 26 persons in Fushun, including the head of the Fushun party branch. Ch'en was arrested on the train while he was returning from a meeting with the party cadres in Fushun.[88] As before, the police collected many party documents at the time of the arrest and acquired detailed knowledge of the organizational efforts of the party branch. It was discovered that the Fushun Mining Workers' Union and the Fushun branch of the CCP had been established in August, and that the party had planned to arouse the workers to strike and riot. There were also plans to destroy factories, government buildings, and communications facilities in Fushun, murder influential figures in the city, and eventually occupy the entire *hsien* and establish a local soviet. These actions were to be coordinated with similar riot plans for Harbin, Mukden, and Dairen that the Manchurian Committee had drawn up for the occasion of the All-China Congress of the Soviets, scheduled to be held at Juichin on December 11.[89]

Thus, in spite of optimistic forecasts for Communist revolution in Manchuria and the dedication of numerous cadres, the CCP was still without much of a foothold. Earnest efforts to recruit the workers in such industrial centers as Dairen, Fushun, and Mukden proved unrewarding. Some workers had been recruited and cells organized, but none of them was able to remain free from police attention for very long. Party operations became increasingly difficult in Manchuria as the Chinese and Japanese police accumulated experience in detecting the Communist organizers and became familiar with the strategies and plans of the party. Only in Harbin did the situation look a little more promising, this perhaps because the Chang Hsüeh-liang regime had only

---

87. Asia Bureau, Ministry of Foreign Affairs, *Shōwa gonen Shina ni okeru mē-dē gaikyō* [Summary of May Day Activities in China, 1930], May 7, 1930, Archives of the Japanese Army, Navy, and Other Agencies (1868–1945), reel 25, p. 34420.

88. *Chūka Minkoku ni okeru kyōsan shugi undō no genkyō*, p. 30.

89. *Suii gaikyō*, p. 22. This source says that the arrest of a Chinese suspect came on November 11 and that the total number of the arrested in Fushun was 24. This congress did not take place until November 1931.

recently established its rule there and because the city had known communism for a longer period under the Russians.

Of course, the Manchurian Communists were not alone in having difficulties in organizing the workers. The CCP had been facing the same problem throughout China since 1927. After the May 30 incident of 1925, the future of the labor movement appeared to be very promising. The All-China General Union claimed a membership of 540,000 at its founding in May 1925, 1,240,000 members in May 1926, and 2,800,000 in June 1927.[90] But when the united front with the KMT broke up and the political climate became unfavorable, the movement was decimated. A labor movement, particularly the kind supported by the CCP, could not thrive in a hostile political environment. It was simply impossible to recruit any large number of workers into the Communist party when membership often meant risking arrest, undergoing tortures, and several years of imprisonment.

90. Jean Chesneaux, *The Chinese Labor Movement, 1919–1927*, trans. H. M. Wright (Stanford, 1968), p. 395.

5 | Japanese Takeover of Manchuria and the Chinese Communist Party

THE BOLD MOVE OF THE JAPANESE KWANTUNG ARMY to take effective control of all Manchuria in September 1931 was well calculated. Having been routed by the Soviet army only shortly before, the Young Marshal's Manchurian forces could not possibly present an effective resistance against the modern Japanese army that had been stationed on Manchurian soil for over a quarter of a century. The Kuomintang (KMT) government army had its hands full in southern China, being absorbed in campaigns to exterminate the Communist guerrillas. The Western powers, on the other hand, had yet to recover from the Great Depression, and there was no prospect of any Western power applying sanctions against the Japanese takeover of a territory remotely located in the northeastern corner of Asia.

The Soviet Union was in no better position in 1931 vis-à-vis Japan than it had been in 1925 or 1928. Maintenance of "normal relations" with Japan was still the essential ingredient for protection of the Soviet interest in the Chinese Eastern Railway. In fact, as the Japanese proceeded to take over all Manchuria, there was a danger that the momentum of military adventurism might be directed against the Soviet Far East as well as the Soviet satellite, Outer Mongolia. There was a clear need for the Soviet Union to deter such a course of action, and the Soviet Union therefore began a crash program to store emergency food supplies in eastern Siberia and to redeploy its armed forces to bolster its defenses.[1] On the diplomatic front, the Soviet Union strictly adhered to a neutralist policy. While *Pravda* and *Izvestiya* issued editorials

1. *Documents on British Foreign Policy, 1919–1939*, second series, vol. 8, pp. 763–765. An interesting account of the food supplies stored in the vicinity of Tomsk in 1932 is provided by a Korean leader of the anti-Japanese armed group who had fought in Manchuria and retreated to the Soviet Far East in October 1932, along with some 20,000 Chinese fighters. These men and women spent eight months in Tomsk. Yi Pŏm-sŏk, *Wu-tung-pul* [Bonfire] (Seoul, 1971), p. 263.

critical of Japanese imperialism and concluded that "the only power that would end imperialist oppression of Chinese workers ... is the victory of the Chinese worker-peasant revolution led by the CCP,"[2] the Soviet government was not willing to take any action which might aggravate the situation. Indeed, Soviet Foreign Commissar Maksim Litvinov proposed on December 31, 1931, to the Japanese foreign minister-designate, Yoshizawa Kenkichi, that the two countries conclude a non-aggression pact.[3]

The Chinese Communist Party (CCP) in central and southern China was also hard pressed; the Kuomintang authorities relentlessly pursued the Communists and nearly succeeded in eradicating the Communist movement in the urban centers. The CCP, in turn, all but gave up the hope of organizing workers in the "white areas." Only the rural soviets in Kiangsi and a few other enclaves offered the CCP a ray of hope, and these areas were also under constant threat of KMT attack.

The CCP leadership was also in disarray at this time. The Fourth Plenum of the Central Committee, held in January 1931, finally repudiated the Li Li-san line and removed Li from his top leadership position; but internecine struggles involving the twenty-eight "returned students" from the Soviet Union, who constituted the main group of leaders, and such veterans as Ho Meng-hsiung and Lo Chang-lung, among others, continued to plague the party.[4] Ku Shun-chang, the head of the Secret Service of the Central Committee, who had overall control over the party's communications and traffic, was arrested in April by the KMT, to which he subsequently defected. Hsiang Chung-fa, the general secretary of the CCP, was arrested and executed by the KMT government in June, and the others were exposed to the constant danger of arrest. For the first time since its founding in 1921, the CCP's central leaders found it necessary to abandon Shanghai as the party's headquarters. During August and September of 1931, many central leaders, including Chou En-lai, fled to Juichin, the seat of the Kiangsi soviet base under Chu Teh and Mao Tse-tung.[5]

2. *Pravda*, September 25, 1931, and *Izvestiya*, September 26, 1931; as quoted in Nihon Kokusai Seiji Gakkai (Japanese Association of International Politics), *Taiheiyō sensō e no michi* [The Road to the Pacific War] (Tokyo, 1963), vol. 2, p. 319.
3. Ibid., p. 326.
4. For a very lively discussion of the factional struggles of this era, see Chang Kuo-t'ao, *The Rise of the Chinese Communist Party, 1928–1938, Volume Two of the Autobiography of Chang Kuo-t'ao* (Lawrence, Kansas, 1971), chapter 3.
5. Ibid., p. 262. Kai-yu Hsü, *Chou En-lai: China's Gray Eminence* (New York, 1968), pp. 97–105, says that Chou En-lai left for Kiangsi with his wife in September. Hsü cites Kung Ch'u, *Wo yü hung chün* [I and the Red Army] (Hong Kong, 1955), p. 256. Kung was active in the Kiangsi soviet at this time.

Some other important figures left earlier. Pavel Mif, the Comintern representative in China, and Ch'en Shao-yü (Wang Ming), Mif's protégé and the ringleader of the "returned students," went to Moscow soon after the Fourth Plenum.[6] Chang Kou-t'ao, who returned to Shanghai from Moscow in late January and participated in important decisions of the party, left for the Oyüwan soviet area (i.e., the Hunan-Hupeh-Anhwei border area) in April. Only Chang Wen-t'ien and Ch'in Pang-hsien appear to have stayed in Shanghai, where they maintained the "Provisional Central Political Bureau" until 1933.[7] The twenty-four-year-old Ch'in, known in the party as Po Ku, headed the bureau.

The situation in Manchuria, in the meantime, was becoming more conducive to revolutionary action. While neither the KMT nor the Chang Hsüeh-liang regime offered any resistance to Japanese aggression, substantial numbers of soldiers, farmers, and bandits organized bands of resistance and stiffly countered the Japanese army and the pro-Japanese forces.[8] According to one estimate, as of June, 1932, there were 122,000 resistants in Liaoning Province, 70,000 in Heilungkiang Province, and some 107,000 in Kirin Province, a total of nearly 300,000 men.[9] The intensity of struggle in Manchuria can be seen from the statistics compiled by the Japanese authorities on the resistants' appearances and the casualties they suffered. They are presented in tables 10 and 11.

Not only had the political environment become favorable, but

6. Chang Kuo-t'ao, *Rise of the CCP*, p. 145. James Pinckney Harrison, in his excellent work, *The Long March to Power: A History of the Chinese Communist Party, 1921–1972* (New York, 1972), says that Ch'en Shao-yü left for Moscow in September (p. 218), but Chang Kuo-t'ao appears to have a vivid memory of the situation in Shanghai at this time.

7. Donald W. Klein and Anne B. Clark, *Biographic Dictionary of Chinese Communism, 1921–1965* (Cambridge, Mass., 1971), vol. 1, pp. 63 and 197. Chang Kuo-t'ao heard in the Oyüwan soviet that Chin Pang-hsien and Chang Wen-t'ien had also fled to Juichin in August 1931, but Chang Wen-t'ien (Lo Fu) told Nym Wales in 1937 that he had remained in Shanghai until 1933. See Wales, *Inside Red China* (New York, 1939), p. 228.

8. For details, see Chong-Sik Lee, "The Chinese Communist Party and the Anti-Japanese Movements in Manchuria," Alvin Coox and Hilary Conroy, eds., *Chinese-Japanese Relations: The Search for Balance* (Santa Barbara, 1976), pp. 141–172.

9. Kwangtung Fu-yüan Tung-pei I-yung-t'uan (The Kwangtung Volunteer Corps to Aid Manchuria), *Tung-pei chin-ch'ing pao-kao* [Report on Recent Conditions in Manchuria] (n.p., 1932), pp. 20–26. The Japanese estimate of the anti-Japanese fighters was as follows: 1931, 60,000 (including 14,000 in Jehol Province, which is not included in the above Chinese estimate); 1932, 360,000; 1933, 52,000; 1934, 40,000; 1935, 21,000. See Ranseikai (Orchid Star Society), *Manshūkokugun* [The Manchukuo Army] (Tokyo, 1970), pp. 270–271, and Manshūkokushi Hensan Kankōkai (Editorial and Publication Committee of the History of Manchukuo), *Manshūkokushi* [History of Manchukuo] (Tokyo, 1971), vol. 2, pp. 302–303.

Table 10 Appearances of Anti-Japanese Forces in
Manchuria, 1932–1934

Year	Number of times reported	Cumulative number of resistants reported
1932	3,816	3,774,184
1933	13,072	2,668,633
1934	13,395	900,204

Source: Manshūkokushi Hensan Kankōkai (Editorial and Publication Committee of the History of Manchukuo), *Manshūkokushi* [History of Manchukuo] (Tokyo, 1971), vol. 2, p. 312.

Table 11 Losses Suffered by Anti-Japanese Forces in
Manchuria, 1932–1934

Year	Killed	Wounded	Captured	Rifles captured	Ammunition captured (rounds)	Horses captured
1932	7,591	5,160	831	3,642	8,238	1,588
1933	8,728	2,381	1,461	5,970	174,288	2,731
1934	8,909	4,264	1,435	3,153	36,107	2,889

Source: Manshūkokushi Hensan Kankōkai (Editorial and Publication Committee of the History of Manchukuo), *Manshūkokushi* [History of Manchukuo] (Tokyo, 1971), vol. 2, p. 312.

the economic situation also offered ample grounds for Communist exploitation. As immigration data for 1931 and 1932 indicate, the situation of the workers and farmers in Manchuria was at its worst since the early 1920s.[10] Worldwide depression severely affected the farmers, particularly because soybeans raised mostly for export comprised a large share of their crops. The ravages of war and floods had also wrought economic havoc.

These new developments clearly called for a bold revision of the CCP's Manchuria policy. If Ch'en Wei-jen had been premature in advocating concerted efforts against Japanese imperialism in 1928, there was no doubt that the time had now arrived for such a course of action. But the CCP faced the task of devising a strategy that would promote the cause of Chinese revolution while protecting the interest of the Soviet Union. Needless to say, this was a Herculean task; but the future of the CCP in Manchuria depended on it.

There is no doubt that the central leaders closely watched developments in Manchuria and that a number of them were actively engaged in devising appropriate strategies. It is clear also,

10. See table 7, above.

however, that the central leaders disagreed among themselves on what should be the party's policy. Eventually, the party leaders decided not to make any changes in the party's strategy toward Manchuria.

The first response of the CCP Central Committee was issued in the form of a resolution of September 22, four days after the Japanese onslaught began, and it contained no surprises; perhaps the central leaders had had no time for deliberation. The resolution simply reiterated the line of CCP policies of earlier years. After denouncing the Manchurian incident as a "product of the Japanese imperialists' colonial policy" and an attempt to turn Manchuria into a military base for attacking the Soviet Union, the central leaders exhorted the party branches "to arm and protect the Soviet Union, to oppose the imperialist robbers' war, to oppose Japanese colonial butchery policy, to annihilate . . . the reactionary Kuomintang government, to carry out anti-imperialist land reform," and so on.[11] This long and repetitious document offered no precise formula for opposing the Japanese; in fact, the resolution prescribed more anti-Kuomintang than anti-Japanese actions, declaring that "only by overthrowing the Kuomintang government, which is that of the landlord-bourgeois class, is it possible to wage a war of national revolution." The position of the central leaders, in short, was that (1) the struggle against Japanese imperialism was only an aspect—albeit a major one—of the struggle against all imperialists; (2) the KMT was the puppet of imperialism, and the overthrow of the KMT was a precondition for anti-Japanese and anti-imperialist struggle; and (3) the Chinese Soviet government and the Red Army were the basic leading forces of the war of national revolution, and only the workers and farmers constituted the revolutionary core. The national bourgeoisie was regarded in general as the enemy of the revolution.[12]

The November 20, 1931 issue of the party organ *Hung-ch'i Chou-pao* [Red Flag Weekly], however, carried an article on Manchuria that appeared to enunciate a strategy significantly divergent from the one set forth in the September 22 declaration. In the article, entitled "The Central Task of the Manchurian Party Headquarters in the Struggle against the Japanese Imperialist Occupa-

11. Text of the resolution is in *Hung-ch'i Chou-pao* [Red Flag Weekly], no. 19 (October 18, 1931), and Wang Chien-min, *Chung-kuo Kung-ch'an-tang shih-kao* [Draft History of the Chinese Communist Party] (Taipei, 1965), vol. 3, pp. 12–16.
12. An excellent statement of the anti-Japanese and anti-imperialist line of the CCP between 1931 and 1935 is to be found in Ishikawa Tadao, *Chūgoku kyōsantō-shi kenkyū* [A Study of the History of the Chinese Communist Party] (Tokyo, 1959), chapter 4.

tion of Manchuria,"[13] Su Kuang criticized the Manchurian Committee for failing to stress the "central task of fighting Japanese imperialism." In his article (which bears the date of October 25), Su accused the committee of not having properly evaluated the heightening of the anti-Japanese movement among the oppressed masses of the entire nation. While the committee properly attacked the KMT for having suppressed the anti-imperial movement, it failed to observe the great discontent and resistance of the oppressed masses. Because the anti-Japanese movement among the masses was underestimated, the committee failed to present a single slogan summing up the central task of the moment, according to Su. Instead of presenting abstract slogans, such as "Strike against Imperialist Occupation of Manchuria," "Drive Out the Japanese Army and Navy and All Other Imperialists," or "Establish a National Soviet Regime," the committee "must more properly grasp the central point and call on the masses in Manchuria to arm themselves, drive out Japanese imperialism, and establish their own government." Although the committee was correct in presenting numerous "partial demands" of the masses, such as opposing unemployment, it failed to lead them from the struggle for partial demands to the struggle for seizing weapons and fighting to establish a soviet regime. Also, by vague appeals for opposition to Japanese imperialism and connecting Japanese imperialism with other imperialisms in the same slogan, the foremost task in Manchuria—to oppose Japan—had been slighted. Su Kuang then presented a number of specific slogans centered on the task of fighting against Japan.

While approving the Manchurian Committee's propaganda work regarding the Chinese soviet, Su Kuang also called on the committee to intensify uprisings and guerrilla wars of the masses so as to encircle and harass the cities and key transportation points. The party should also lead a rebellion among the soldiers, who were engaged in movements against surrender or disarmament; the rebellious soldiers should be led to the villages with their rifles in order that they might join the farmers' war, implement land reform, and establish new soviet districts.

The Manchurian Committee was also directed to mobilize the workers, indigents, revolutionary students, and all oppressed masses in the cities and towns of Manchuria as well as the farmers in the suburbs to form revolutionary anti-Japanese societies and organizations of their own, such as labor unions, farmers'

13. *Hung-ch'i Chou-pao*, no. 23 (November 20, 1931), pp. 9–16.

associations, associations of the poor, or revolutionary student associations. These revolutionary organizations were then to form a representatives' congress to counter all the governmental organizations in Manchuria set up by the Japanese imperialists. The oppressed masses were also to organize their own armed self-defense corps to protect themselves. The Manchurian Committee was warned, however, that the landlords, bourgeoisie, and any persons who had surrendered to imperialism should never be allowed to join any of the revolutionary organizations or the representatives' congresses. These organizations should become genuine agencies of the masses, managing their own affairs, taking over the arms of the enemy, and establishing a soviet regime. Su Kuang expected the Japanese to prohibit these organizations, but he saw clear possibilities for them where the Japanese had not yet entrenched themselves and where the old regime had lost all effective control. In areas under strong Japanese control, organizational movements should be conducted in secret. In Northern Manchuria, which the Japanese had not yet occupied, a broad movement should be carried out to link the anti-Japanese movement with the struggle against the Chang Hsüeh-liang regime.

Finally, Su Kuang directed the Manchurian Committee to emphasize the unity of the oppressed masses of China and Korea and make every effort to arouse the Japanese workers and the soldiers in Manchuria to overthrow the Japanese imperialist rule.

It is likely that the cadres in Manchuria reacted to Su's article with enthusiasm. This was the first time that the Manchurian Committee had been told in unequivocal terms to fight against the Japanese. Although Su's directive still insisted on opposing the KMT, the Chang Hsüeh-liang regime, the landlords, and the bourgeoisie, the emphasis was shifted from fighting the KMT and Chang Hsüeh-liang forces in Manchuria to the struggle against the Japanese. Devoid of the heavy ideological overtones that had characterized earlier directives, Su's article set forth strategies, tactics, and slogans that appealed predominantly to the anti-Japanese feelings among the masses in Manchuria.

Who was this Su Kuang who stressed the need to mobilize "all the oppressed masses," excluding only the landlords, bourgeoisie, and any persons who had surrendered to imperialism? According to Feng Chung-yün, a veteran of this era, Lo Teng-hsien, who was soon to assume the leadership in Manchuria, returned to Harbin from Mukden in the spring of 1932 with an issue of *Hung-ch'i Pao* [Red Flag] that carried an article by Chou En-lai instructing the Manchurian Committee to direct a national revolutionary war in Manchuria against the Japanese and drive them out.[14] Presumably Feng was referring to Su Kuang's article. Was Su Kuang a pseudonym of Chou En-lai? Tantalizing as this conjecture is, we have not been able to identify the person behind the pseudonym.

The Northern Conference

It soon became clear, however, that the strategy favored by Su Kuang was not to be the official policy of the CCP leadership. By June 1932, those in control of the party decided to hold a major conference, a joint conference of the representatives of the provincial committees in the north (*Pei-fang Ko Sheng Wei tai-piao lien-hsi hui-i*) to enunciate the official line.

Judging from the texts of various resolutions adopted by the conference, representatives from Shensi, Hopei, Honan, Shantung, and Manchuria were present at the conference. According to a Japanese source, Chang Wen-t'ien, the stalwart of the returned students' groups and one of the two central leaders remaining in Shanghai, and Nieh Jung-chen, one of the military leaders of the CCP, were at the conference to provide guidance.[15] This source also asserts that the conference was held in Tientsin.[16]

The three resolutions adopted by the conference leave little doubt that there had been no change in the basic strategies. The main concern of the party was still with the national revolutionary war based on the organization of the urban proletariat. On June 24, the conference adopted a resolution on "The Heightening of the Revolutionary Crisis and the Tasks of the Northern Party";

14. Feng Chung-yün, "Remembering Comrade Lo Teng-hsien," in Hua Ying-shen, ed., *Chung-kuo kung-ch'an-tang lieh-shih-chuan* [Biographies of Chinese Communist Party Martyrs] (Hong Kong, 1949), p. 198.
15. South Manchuria Railway Company, Keizai Chōsakai (Economic Research Association), *Manshū kyōsantō undō gaikan* [A Survey of the Manchurian Communist Party Movement] (Dairen, 1935), p. 21. *Chūgoku kyōsantō-shi shiryō-shū* [Compendium of Materials on the History of the Chinese Communist Party], edited by the Chinese Department of the Nihon Kokusai Mondai Kenkyūjo (Japanese International Problems Research Center) (Tokyo, 1971), vol. 6, p. 68, agrees on the presence of Chang Wen-t'ien and Nieh Jung-chen without citing any source. Donald W. Klein and Anne B. Clark, in their *Biographic Dictionary of Chinese Communism, 1921–1965* (Cambridge, Mass., 1971), vol. 1, p. 63, also state that Chang was at the conference, and again no source is provided. It appears that both of these works depend on *Manshū kyōsantō undō gaikan*; yet the author of *Manshū kyōsantō undō gaikan* does not appear to have had access to the resolutions adopted by the conference, as he dates the conference as either February or March 1932. Gunseibu, Komonbu (Advisors' Department, Ministry of Defense, Manchukuo), *Manshū kyōsanhi no kenkyū* [Study of the Communist Bandits in Manchuria] (n.p., 1937), p. 21, also relied on *Manshū kyōsantō undō gaikan*.
16. *Manshū kyōsantō undō gaikan*, p. 14.

on the 25th, it adopted a resolution on "Some Major Tasks in the Workers' Movement in the Northern Provinces"; and on the last day, it adopted a resolution on the "Development of the Guerrilla Movement and the Creation of Northern Soviet Districts." The unusual length of the resolutions—about 12,000 characters in the first, 16,000 in the second, and 8,000 in the third—suggests that the central leadership had previously decided upon the contents and the phrasing.[17] If the conference lasted only three days (or four, as one source suggests),[18] there is little likelihood that full-scale discussion took place. The conference apparently was very much a one-sided affair.

The general tone of the conference was set by the first resolution, which was predicated on the assumption that an imperialist attack against the Soviet Union was imminent, that the KMT had sold out to the imperialists, and that the principal task confronting the CCP was to organize the working masses of China, expand the struggle against imperialism and the KMT, and destroy the rule of the landlords and bourgeoisie. The "Northern Party"— the party branches in North China and Manchuria—was attacked for slighting the danger of an anti-Soviet war and also for slighting the struggle to lead the national revolutionary war. These were not simple errors to be corrected: the party branches in the north were charged with having been influenced by imperialists and "social-fascists" to engage in opportunism.

If the specific criticisms lodged against the Manchurian Committee were familiar ones, they were also very pointed. The resolution declared that the scanty results of the workers' strikes were due to the "opportunistic guidance" of the committee. While many party members were commended for positively and heroically engaging in the struggle against Japanese imperialism, the results were nevertheless unsatisfactory. The party's operations, which had not kept pace with the intensifying activism among the masses, were found to have manifested "many grave defects, errors, and opportunistic vacillations." In leading the anti-imperialist struggle, clear-cut class position had been lacking, and the party's slogans and principles had often been "modified or twisted."

17. The resolutions were published in *Chung-kung chung-yang wen-chien* [Chinese Communist Party Central (Committee) Documents], 1932–1933, edited by the Organization Department of the CCP Central Committee (Chung-kung Chung-yang Tsu-chih-pu). I have consulted the hand-copied texts held by the Hoover Institution Library. The first resolution is available in Japanese translation in *Shiryō-shū*, vol. 6, pp. 68–82. My references to the resolutions, unless otherwise noted, are from the hand-copied, unpaginated texts.
18. *Shiryō-shū*, vol. 6, p. 68.

(This was so in Honan and Shensi as well as in Manchuria.) The party organizations had not, in general, become the organizers and leaders of strike movements, and they had been passive and ineffective in organizing guerrilla warfare and soldiers' revolts. The struggle against the antirevolutionary groups had been extremely inadequate, the style of leadership had been poor and clumsy and the training and selection of the cadres insufficient, and party organizations had manifested the grave error of factionalism. In short, the party in Manchuria had totally failed to satisfy the central leadership.

The Manchurian Committee was instructed to strengthen the organization of workers' strikes against the march of capitalism and imperialist aggression, deliver merciless blows against opportunism in the labor movement, develop the daily struggle of the farmers and the calamity-stricken people to instigate a revolutionary guerrilla war, and, through the positive actions of the guerrillas, establish the new Red Army and the soviet districts. In organizing and leading the farmers' struggles, the party must not harbor illusions about the rich farmers and must not compromise with them. The party was also to infiltrate the Big Sword Society and all other secret societies of the farmers, win over the masses at the lower levels, and expose the antirevolutionary character of their leaders. In organizing the soldiers' revolts, the onerous task of gaining the support of the soldiers must not be replaced by the opportunistic line of linking up with the officers. In other words, a "united front from below" was to be formed among members of the secret societies and the soldiers. Further, the Manchurian Committee was to pay special attention to the minority peoples, particularly the Koreans, and lead them to join in the revolution.

The second (and longest) resolution, on the workers' movement, discussed in detail the need for and the means of (1) firmly providing independent leadership to the economic struggle of the working class, (2) arousing and intensifying the anti-imperial struggle by the organizing of strikes against Japan and against imperialism, (3) organizing the struggle of the unemployed workers, (4) destroying the "yellow" (i.e., KMT-supported) unions and winning over the masses in those unions, (5) solidifying and expanding the Red Labor Union Movement, (6) intensifying activities in the factories, (7) fulfilling common tasks among the railroad and marine workers, and (8) organizing the farm workers, coolies, and handicraft workers.

Certain remarks in the second resolution were interestingly revealing as to the condition of the workers' movement in the parts of Manchuria that were "under CCP influence." The rising tendency of the workers to engage in strikes was cited to refute all the defeatist arguments of the "opportunists" and also as evidence of the opportunity for the party to provide positive and independent leadership. Favorable notice was given to the remarkable victories of certain strikes led by the party (particularly at the Mukden Tobacco Factory), but this was followed by criticism of the party for lagging behind the workers. The party was said to have underestimated the workers' propensity for struggle (in Manchuria and Honan), to have abandoned leadership of strikes (also in Manchuria and Honan), and to have slighted day-to-day economic struggle and shouted empty slogans calling for political strikes. For systematic strike organizing the party had substituted propaganda and agitation, and it had failed to join in spontaneous workers' strikes. Besides neglecting the organization of red labor unions, the party had failed to win over the masses in the "yellow" unions and had not established revolutionary opposition to those unions. The party had failed to perceive the demands of the masses and had tried to "ascertain them through discussions with the masses." In spite of the directives of the Sixth Congress, the northern party had also failed to mobilize and organize the workers, and some of the strike committees were established with an extremely small number of persons (such as the one at the Manchurian-British-American Tobacco Factory, which consisted of only seven persons).

The fact that the Red Labor Union in Harbin had only 71 members as of the end of 1931 received special mention as deplorable. The Manchurian Committee was again criticized for opportunist passivism in having failed to take up the organization of red labor unions as a major task. This was unforgivable particularly because of the favorable atmosphere of the rising tide of strikes and also because of the presence in Manchuria of great numbers of industrial workers. Even in enterprises where the party and the youth corps had branches, there were no Red Labor Union sections. Citing a report of the representative of the Manchurian Committee, the resolution commented that ineffectual individuals had been selected to lead the unions, and that the cadres had merely created upper-level organizations that failed to enlist the masses. The party was separated from the workers, and its empty slogans produced no effect. The party in Manchuria was therefore instructed to admit its errors openly before the comrades and the masses and to mobilize the workers to actively participate in the anti-imperial struggle and enlist in the volunteer army.

In many ways, the last resolution, on the guerrilla movement and creation of northern soviets, was similar in tone. In Manchuria, the resolution noted, numerous small volunteer army units had very rapidly brought together the spontaneously rising broad masses of workers, farmers, rebellious soldiers, and policemen, creating an "extremely great force" (*chi-ta te li-liang*). The leadership of the greater part of the volunteer units had fallen into the hands of the KMT, the warlords, the bully gentry, the rich farmers, and the bandits, but even so, because of the vehement and intense anti-Japanese emotions of the broad masses, their activities were spreading over all of Manchuria.

While the resolution thus reacted favorably to the anti-Japanese struggles in Manchuria, it sharply criticized the inability—or indeed the unwillingness—of the Manchurian Committee to capitalize on the situation. The cadres were attacked as being passive toward the volunteer armies, which they allegedly regarded simply as gatherings of bandits. Some cadres had attempted to establish links with the higher echelons of these armies instead of working with the toiling masses, or they had shouted empty slogans while refusing to heed the call of the broad masses for their leadership and abandoning all opportunities for breaking into the volunteer armies. As a result, according to the resolution, the "glorious volunteer army movement" continued to lack correct leadership and the party was unable to engage fully in either antiimperial activity or land reform.

Even more damaging to the Manchurian Committee, according to the third resolution, was certain information gathered by inspectors from the party headquarters. Many instances were found where dissatisfied troops of the volunteer armies passionately and urgently demanded the party's leadership. Some units put up the CCP's banner on their own initiative. In a number of areas, the resolution conceded that the volunteer movement was actually initiated under the leadership or influence of "individual comrades" and the "red masses." Yet the party had not taken the necessary steps or measures to develop its operations or to establish its leadership. As a result, up to the time of the Northern Conference, there was not one unit in Manchuria that was under the direct leadership of the party. Even in areas where the party had its greatest strength, no significant results had been obtained. Why the "inspectors" themselves did not provide the needed leadership on the scene is not explained. Nor did the resolution indicate where the party had its "greatest strength."

It may be observed that, even though the CCP had repudiated

the Li Li-san line as putschist in January 1931, the instructions embodied in the resolution on the guerrilla movement were very much reminiscent of the putschist line. The Manchurian Committee was told that, in areas where the party was relatively strong, as in Yenpien and Panshih, it should "boycott" goods (i.e., goods produced by the Japanese and other imperialists), beat up traitors (*han-chien*), and extend the movement to confiscate stores and enterprises of the Japanese and all other imperialists, confiscating the lands and properties of all bureaucrats, bully gentry, and landlords and distributing them to the peasants, calamity-stricken people, and unemployed workers, and also using them to meet the expenses of the volunteer armies. The cadres in the north would have been hard put to distinguish these instructions from those promulgated by the Li Li-san leadership. The CCP had already tried these measures in Chientao—now under the Yenpien Hsien Committee—with disastrous results. Various other instructions, on the workers', farmers', and soldiers' movements and the anti-Japanese societies, would have been long familiar. There were also paragraphs dealing at tedious length with the urgency of exposing the deceitfulness of the reactionary leaders of the volunteer armies, the need to assume leadership of the masses, and the opportunity provided by the anti-Japanese war to volunteer armies for carrying out "land reform."

Why did the central leaders reject the strategy of uniting with all the anti-imperialist masses excluding the landlords and bourgeoisie? Why did they insist on organizing the proletarian workers' strikes, class differentiation, and rejecting the rich peasantry? Why did they continue to equate the struggle against imperialism with that against the KMT?

It can be argued that, as far as the leaders of the CCP were concerned, the Japanese takeover of Manchuria did not warrant a major revision of party strategy. Harried by the KMT nearly to extinction, the CCP was naturally absorbed with the problem of countering the KMT and the goal of overthrowing the rule of the KMT. The "Statement of the CCP on the Current Situation," issued on January 1, 1932, reflects this.[19] In the minds of such leaders as Ch'en Shao-yü, the principal leader of the "internationalist" or the returned student group, the leading role in the Chinese revolution was to be played by the proletariat, whose recruitment was of the greatest importance.[20] As the resolution issued on Janu-

19. See Hsiao Tso-liang, *Power Relations within the Chinese Communist Movement, 1930–1934: A Study of Documents* (Seattle, 1961), p. 200.
20. Ibid., pp. 204–205.

ary 9 indicated, taking key cities for the purpose of achieving preliminary successes in one or more provinces[21] was still considered to be the only sure way. Without these basic foundations, the CCP leaders were arguing, the Japanese imperialists could not be countered.

Since the Japanese takeover of Manchuria had turned that region into a genuine Japanese colony separate from the remainder of China, and since many Chinese in that region were actively engaged in anti-Japanese operations, the CCP could, as Su Kuang proposed, adopt a different strategy for the Manchurian region alone. But this would have led to the loss of effective control by the party headquarters of the party branch in Manchuria, since that branch would have become more or less independent as soon as it was allowed to pursue a fundamentally different strategy. As we shall see presently, this was something that the party leaders could not permit.

There was also the possibility that the nascent CCP might be swallowed up by the more powerful anti-Japanese groups led by non-Communists, making the Communist party the tail of the movement. Hence, the party cadres must organize anti-Japanese guerrillas of their own, which could effectively lead the entire movement.

It is also possible that the CCP leaders of this period were concerned about the possible adverse impact of a new strategy in Manchuria upon Soviet-Japanese relations. As we have indicated in chapter 3 and earlier in this chapter, the Soviet Union was in no position to antagonize Japan. The Japanese had struck a few years too soon as far as the Soviet Union was concerned. Such being the case, the Comintern, as an instrument of the Communist Party of the Soviet Union, would not have encouraged the CCP to change its strategy either in 1931 or 1932.

In any event, it is highly unlikely that the resolutions of the Northern Conference bolstered the morale of the northern cadres. Previously, Li Li-san's blaming the "rightist elements" within the party's Northern Bureau for the bad situation had led to arguments on several occasions between the Central Committee and the Northern Bureau. In February 1931, when Chang Kuo-t'ao (then one of the three members of the Standing Committee of the Politburo)[22] visited Tientsin and called an emergency meeting of the Northern Bureau, he found the cadres of the branches in Pe-

21. Ibid., pp. 200–201.
22. Chang Kuo-t'ao, *Rise of the CCP*, vol. 2, p. 149. The other two were Hsiang Chung-fa and Chou En-lai.

king, Tientsin, Taiyuan, and Kaifeng demoralized, resentful, and discouraged.[23] The participants at the meeting related stories of suffering, intra-party quarrels, and dissatisfaction among the comrades, expressed their fury at the way the Central Committee had discriminated against the Northern Bureau after the August 7 Emergency Conference (1927), and criticized Li Li-san, who had issued orders at random, completely disregarding the actual conditions in North China. Objections to Li's unreasonable orders had been overruled as right-wing opportunism, and the local cadres were forced to endure the destruction of the organization and the arrest of its members. As a result, some of the members became passive, others disobeyed orders, and still others refused to attend meetings. Party discipline became lax. According to Chang, a question often asked by the comrades in the North was: "If the party does not love its members, then why should we obey the party?" They implored Chang to find a way to improve the work style of the Central Committee and to grant them greater autonomy. Chang found them still doubtful whether the Fourth Plenum of the Central Committee, held in January, had succeeded in blocking the Li Li-san line and deeply concerned over Ch'en Shao-yü's leadership.[24]

According to Chang Kuo-t'ao's account, he was able to revive the spirits of the northern cadres by reassuring them that decisions about work procedures in the North would be reached on the basis of objective conditions in the North, with the Central Committee respecting the opinions of the Northern Bureau, and that the committee would take into account the comrades' wishes and their safety in assigning work and would expand democratic procedures within the party. But the Northern Conference revealed that all the complaints and Chang Kuo-t'ao's promise were of no avail. Other central leaders obviously did not share Chang's conciliatory attitude.

The Party in 1931

It should be recalled that Liu Shao-ch'i left for Shanghai in March 1930 and the Manchurian Committee was decimated by mass arrests in April. In June 1931 the Chinese police again arrested some of the officers of the committee in Mukden and, according to a Japanese source, the committee's activities declined.

---
23. The Northern Bureau had branches also in Tsinan and Sian, but these did not send delegates to the meeting.
24. Chang Kuo-t'ao, *Rise of the CCP*, vol. 2, pp. 160–161.

The central leaders reportedly dispatched a Chang Meng-k'uan, who, along with two survivors from the previous committee, Li Ch'eng-hsiang and Liu I-ch'eng, reconstructed the group.[25] According to the same source, Chang became the chairman, Li the head of the organization department, and Liu the head of the propaganda department.[26] At the headquarters in Mukden, committees were established to deal with specific targets: the workers, the "oppressed minority nationalities," the commercial district, and the Japanese soldiers. By September the Manchurian Committee had reestablished connections with the special committee for southern, northern and eastern Manchuria, and for the Liaohsi and Jehol regions.[27]

Details are not available, but the East Manchurian Special Committee still appears to have had the largest number of party members and followers because of the legacy of the Korean Communists in that area.[28] A report filed by the Japanese consulgeneral in Chientao on June 2, 1931, cited CCP *hsien* committees in Mengchiang, Omu, Changpai, Fusung, Yenho (Yenchi and Holung), Tunhua, Antu, Wangching, and Hunchun, a total of nine, and provided figures on membership in the party and auxiliary organizations (see table 12).

Because, as noted earlier, Chientao was a stronghold of the Korean nationalist and Communist movements, being adjacent to Korea and populated predominantly by Koreans for several decades, the CCP strength in these *hsien* was atypical. It is evident that the Anti-Imperial League and farmers' associations enlisted very substantial numbers of the Korean farmers in the region. Recruits from these organizations were highly important when the Communist movement entered the guerrilla phase later on.[29]

25. Sasaki Hideo, "Manshūkoku o shisatsu shite" [Having Observed Manchuria], in Chōsen Sōtokufu, Kōtō Hōin, Kenjikyoku (Prosecutor's Bureau, High Court, Government-General of Korea), *Shisō ihō* [Thought Report], no. 3 (June 1935), p. 130; hereafter cited as *Shisō ihō*.
26. Ibid.
27. Ibid. The Liaohsi and Jehol special committees apparently were new creations; an account of the party organization as of June 1930 mentions only the special committees for northern, southern, and eastern Manchuria. Chūō Keimu Tōsei Iinkai (Central Police Affairs Control Committee, Manchukuo), *Manshū ni okeru kyōsan undō no suii gaikyō* [Summary Survey of the Changes in the Communist Movement in Manchuria] (n.p., 1937), p. 16. Hereafter cited as *Suii gaikyō*.
28. As of 1931, there were 395,847 Koreans and 120,394 Chinese in the Chientao area. Because the area was separated from the other regions by mountains and forests, which made travel very arduous, and since land was abundant elsewhere in Manchuria, relatively few Chinese had been attracted to it until the Kirin–Tunhua Railway was opened in 1929. Thus, in 1926, there were 356,016 Koreans and 86,347 Chinese. *Manshū kyōsanhi no kenkyō*, p. 544.
29. The consular police raided the Yen-Ho *Hsien* Committee on May 28, 1931,

Table 12   Communist Strength in Chientao, June 1931

	Party members	Youth Corps	Red Militia[a]	Anti-Imperial League or Farmers' Association	Total
East Manchurian Special Committee	7 (5)[b]	3			10 (5)
Yen-Ho Hsien Committee	2	2			4
Laotaokou District	70 (1)	75	200	2,500	2,845 (1)
Wengshenglatzu District	30	25	70	300	425
Shantaokou District	40	130	150	2,400	2,720
Pingkang District	80	215	40	2,000 (6)	2,335 (6)
Lungching District	13	15	35	117	180
Yenchi District	45 (5)	80 (10)	300	800	1,225 (15)
Kaishantun District	50	80	250	1,300	1,680
Talatzu District	30	60	55	—	145
Wangching Hsien Committee	200	1,100	600	2,600	4,500
Hunchun Hsien Committee	20	50	30	50	150
Total	587 (11)	1,835 (10)	1,730	12,067 (6)	16,219 (27)

[a] Red Militia refers to members of the party or its auxiliary organizations who were either armed or given military training.
[b] Figures in parentheses indicate the Chinese members. The remainder are Korean.
Source: Report of Consul-General Okada Kenichi to Foreign Minister Shidahara Kijūrō, June 2, 1931. AJMFA, reel S374, file S9452-6, pp. 428–429.

As was to be expected, the Manchurian Provincial Committee and the subordinate organizations that had eluded the authorities promptly reacted against the Japanese invasion by distributing leaflets bearing the Communist declaration and slogans. Table 13 summarizes these activities.

These leaflets, issued in the name of the CCP's Manchurian Committee, Northern Manchurian Special Committee, and other auxiliary organizations such as the anti-Japanese societies, seem to have been printed in considerable quantities at Mukden and transported to the areas where the party had branches. The Jap-

---

and arrested 78 members, including Yu Chi-won (Liu Chih-yüan, if Chinese), the new head of the committee. As a result, some of the district committees disbanded, but the Communists soon began to regroup. The district committees in Pingkang, Laotoukou, Talatzu and Kaishantun were reported to have held meetings of branch chiefs and decided on mobilizing new members of revolutionary character, "guiding the masses with earnestness instead of resorting to deceitful means as in the past," and collecting revolutionary funds on a large scale through the guerrilla units. Members of guerrilla units under the military departments in each district were reported to be staying in the forests during the day and with the local people at nights. They were also reported to be collecting funds from the rich through intimidation and threats. AJMFA, reel S374, file 9452-6, pp. 452–455.

Table 13 *Declarations and Leaflets Issued by Communist Organizations in Manchuria after the Japanese Invasion, 1931*

Date	Place	Issuing organization	Groups addressed or theme of material
September 20	Mukden	MC/CCP-CYC	To Korean workers, farmers, students, and all working masses
September 21	Harbin	NMSC/CCP	All citizens—arm and demonstrate
September 23	Mukden	MC/CCP	To Japanese soldiers
September 23	Harbin	NMSC/CCP	To workers in Harbin
September 23	Harbin		Slogans for revolution
September 25	Harbin	NMSC/CCP	To working masses in Harbin
September 25	Mukden	Mukden Anti-Japanese Society	Destroy Kuomintang
September 26	Harbin	Harbin Anti-Japanese Society	Citizens: rise, advance
September 26	Harbin	NMSC/CCP	Oppose massacre of Chinese masses
September 30	Dairen	Dairen Branch, CCP	To workers of Dairen
Early October	Mukden	MC/CYC	To Chinese and Korean workers, farmers, soldiers
October 10	Kirin	MC/CCP	To Japanese soldiers
October 25	Harbin	NMSC/CCP	To soldiers on 14th anniversary of Soviet Revolution
October 27	Harbin	NMSC/CCP	October Revolution Pictorial: "Imperialism and the Soviet Red Army"
October 27	Harbin	NMSC/CYC	To young students in northern Manchuria
October 28	Hailung	Hailung *Hsien* Committee	To soldiers in the Chinese Manchurian Army
November 7	Harbin	NMSC/CCP	October Revolution Pictorial: "Workers' Conditions"
November 7	Mukden	Mukden Commercial District Committee	Commemorating Russian Revolution and establishment of Chinese Soviet Republic

Table 13 *continued*

Date	Place	Issuing organization	Groups addressed or theme of material
Early November	Dairen	Dairen Branch, CCP	To Japanese seamen
Late November	?	CCP	To the people—by the Chinese Soviet Government
December	?	MC/CCP-CYC	To Kuomintang soldiers

MC = Manchurian Committee; CCP = Chinese Communist Party; CYC = Communist Youth Corps; NMSC = Northern Manchurian Special Committee.
Source: Selected from Osaka Taishi Keizai Remmei, *Sa-Rempō to Shina Manshū no kyōsa undō* [The Soviet Union and the Communist Movements in China and Manchuria] (Tokyo 1935), pp. 578–584. The original source refers to Fuchiatien rather than Harbin in some entries Fuchiatien is the Chinese section of Harbin.

anese Consulates at Chientao (in Yenchi) and Kirin and their branch consulates collected some of these and sent copies to the Foreign Ministry in Tokyo.[30] The position taken by the Communists in Manchuria, therefore, can be easily determined.

In general, the Manchurian organizations simply reiterated the themes stressed by the central headquarters: Japanese imperialism must be opposed; the KMT must be destroyed; soviets must be established; the Soviet Union must be defended.

These materials are quite consistent with the Central Committee's resolution of September 22, though some were issued before that date. Faithfully reflecting the attitude of the central leaders, the Manchurian leadership focused primarily on fighting the KMT and protecting the Soviet Union. Although in its September 20 declaration the Manchurian Committee analyzed the motives of Japanese aggression in detail, it was not ready to call for a concerted attack against the Japanese.

The Japanese action in Manchuria obviously required further strengthening of the leadership in Manchuria, and the Central Committee dispatched a party cadre of some prominence, Lo Teng-hsien. Lo, a hero of the Hong Kong strike of 1925 and the

---

30. Many of the leaflets listed in table 13 are in AJMFA, reel S374, file S9452-6. The Manchurian Committee's declaration of September 20 (see table 13) is on pp. 506–513; "To the Chinese and Korean Workers, Farmers, and Revolutionary Soldiers," pp. 513–515; "Slogans of the Central Executive Committee of the CCP," dated October, 1931, pp. 526–530; "Appeal of the Eastern Manchurian Committee on the Anniversary of the October Revolution," pp. 542–548; Northern Manchurian Committee's September 25 declaration, pp. 492–495; slogans for the same anniversary by the Panshih Special Committee, reel S382, file S9452-12, pp. 843–845; and "Joint Declaration of the Chinese and Japanese Communist Parties to the Chinese and Japanese Masses" (n.d.), reel S374, file S9452-7, pp. 9–33.

Canton uprising of 1927, was elected, according to some CCP accounts, a member of the Politburo of the Central Committee of the CCP at the Sixth Congress.[31] In January 1931, he was also appointed chairman of the All-China Federation of Labor. Evidently Lo was dispatched soon after the Manchurian Incident erupted, because Feng Chung-yün, a cadre in Harbin during this period, says that Lo was in Harbin a few days after September 18, when the Japanese action began. Another cadre of this period, Hsüeh Wen, has recollected that Lo arrived in Harbin in early fall of that year.[32] It is curious that Lo Teng-hsien decided to work in Harbin even though the Manchurian Provincial Committee was still located in Mukden. It is possible that the leaders in Manchuria were making preparations to relocate the committee to Harbin. Lo, however, does not appear to have taken over the command of the Manchurian Committee until November, when some leaders were arrested.[33]

The Japanese takeover of Manchuria, while thrusting new responsibilities and challenges upon the committee, also heightened the risk of police suppression. The takeover of Mukden in September particularly made the Communists' operations there more dangerous. While the Chang Hsüeh-liang regime was neither less severe nor less efficient in its pursuit of Communists (local authorities in other areas, of course, were another matter), the previous existence of different authorities with different jurisdictions (the Japanese police in the South Manchuria Railway zone and the Chinese police in the Chinese section of the city) had offered distinct advantages to the Communists. There were the usual jurisdictional rivalries and lack of cooperation and coordination.[34] These propensities naturally had become more intensified when anti-Japanese sentiment among the Chinese became

---

31. Feng Chung-yün, "Remembering Comrade Lo Teng-hsien," in Hua Ying-shen, ed., *Chung-kuo kung-ch'an-tang lieh-shih-chuan*, pp. 189–197; Hsüeh Wen, "Remembering Comrade Lo Teng-hsien," *Hung-ch'i P'iao-p'iao*, vol. 1, pp. 93–94; Klein and Clark, *Biographic Dictionary*, vol. 2, p. 655, citing Wang Ming in *Lieh-shih-chuan* [Biographies of Martyrs] (Moscow[?], 1936), pp. 154–161. Chang Kuo-t'ao says, on the other hand, that Lo was elected an alternate member of the Central Executive Committee at the sixth congress, but not to the Politburo. Op. cit., vol. 2, p. 82.

32. See above articles by Feng and Hsüeh.

33. *Suii gaikyō*, p. 39. This Japanese source says that Chang Meng-k'uan was in command of the Manchurian Committee until he was arrested in November.

34. Some cooperation did exist between the Japanese and the Chang Hsüeh-liang regime, but some of the Japanese writers complained of the lack of it. See, for example, South Manchuria Railway Company, Research Section, General Affairs Department, *Manshū ni okeru sekka senden jijō gaiyō* [Summary of the Condition of Communist Propaganda in Manchuria] (Dairen, 1927), p. 8. When the Chinese police arrested the Communist leaders in April 1930, the Japanese were

more pronounced; but the Japanese takeover had totally eliminated this state of affairs, and the Communists were placed in much greater jeopardy. In late September 1931, the Japanese military police appear to have arrested some of the Communist leaders in Mukden, Dairen, and Fushun.[35] Another roundup took place on November 21, which netted Chang Meng-k'uan, Liu I-ch'eng, and Huang Yün-t'eng, the principal leaders of the Manchurian Committee.[36] The committee therefore decided to move to safer ground in Harbin. The Japanese were hesitant to send their forces to Harbin because of Russian sensitivities, and not until February 1932 did they dispatch a division there to fight against Ma Chan-shan's forces. Until the summer of that year, various forces vied for control of the city and the vicinity.[37]

Before moving to Harbin, the Manchurian Committee directed the Northern Manchuria Special Committee in December 1931 to establish a soviet district in Tumuho, Hulin Hsien, near the Russo-Manchurian border, and relocated the special committee officers there. The preparations being completed, the Manchurian committees of the CCP and the CYC were moved to Harbin. The Harbin City Committee and 14 hsien committees and 12 branches that had been under the special committee were now placed directly under the Manchurian Committee headed by Lo Teng-hsien,[38] thus in effect abolishing the special committee. In addition to the two other special committees—those for southern Manchuria (in Huangkutun near Mukden) and eastern Manchuria (near Yenchi)—a new committee was created in Taian, west of the Liao River (Liaohsi), in January 1932. The city committee in Dairen was still operating.[39]

The relocation of the committee headquarters and minor reorganization of the party structure did not cure the problems that the Manchurian Provincial Committee faced. Further reorganizations between March and July, 1932, suggest that the committee was struggling with internal problems. According to one

---

forced to wait for the release of details. See Naimushō, Keihokyoku (Bureau of Police and Security, Ministry of Home Affairs), *Gaiji keisatsuhō* [External Police Report], no. 95 (May–June 1930), p. 105.

35. Sasaki, "Manshūkoku o shisatsu shite," *Shisō ihō*, no. 3 (June 1935), p. 130.
36. *Suii gaikyō*, p. 39.
37. *Manshūkokugun*, pp. 86–103.
38. Sasaki, "Manshūkoku o shisatsu shite," p. 131. The Japanese sources, incidentally, never cite Lo Teng-hsien by name or by his pseudonym, Ta P'ing. Evidently the true identity of the man who headed the operation in Manchuria at this time was not known to the Japanese. The locations of hsien committees and branches (in actuality, cell-type organizations in Harbin) are recorded in *Suii gaikyō*, p. 39.
39. *Suii gaikyō*, p. 40.

source, an inspector from the Central Committee arrived in Manchuria in March and reestablished the Northern Manchuria Special Committee. Then, according to the same source, the party suffered a "major blow" from the Japanese army. Presumably another round of arrests took place. Meanwhile, the inspector discovered many "antiparty and impure elements" among the party ranks and judged that party activities in Manchuria were in error in many aspects. The party work, therefore, was held in abeyance.[40] The party in Manchuria was obviously due for a purge and reorganization.

Agents were dispatched again after the Northern Conference to implement the resolutions adopted by the conference. According to a Japanese source published in 1933, "distinguished cadres" of the Third International Line (the returned students?), including T'ai I,[41] T'ang Yü-shan, and Ch'u Chün-feng, arrived in Manchuria in July 1932 and, "in accordance with the decision of the Northern Conference," purged the party and implemented another reorganization.[42] Judging from the fact that the names of the new cadres appear in a Japanese report of June 1932,[43] agents are likely to have reached Manchuria in late June, but the substance of information concerning subsequent events appears to be accurate. One wonders how the new agents were able to reach Manchuria so quickly and how their names became known to the Japanese within a matter of a few days. It cannot be doubted that the Japanese had reliable informers in the CCP organization. But the fact that the Japanese obtained the names of agents within the month of June also indicates the possibility that the agents had been selected, instructed, and dispatched to Manchuria before the Northern Conference convened. If this was indeed the case, the conference would have been a mere ritual to legitimize what the CCP leaders had already decided upon and done. In any event, the reorganization involved the abolition of the Northern Manchuria

40. Manchukuo, Hsieh-ho-hui (Concordia Association), *Senmetsu kyōhi* [Annihilate Communist Bandits] (Changchun[?], 1934), p. 8.

41. A certain T'ai I, whose name is almost identical to the writer referred to here, contributed an article to *Min-chung* ["The People's Bell"] magazine, which was an anarchistic Communist magazine, published between 1922 and 1927. It is very likely that the two are the same person. Incidentally, Li Chen-ying, whose activities are discussed in chapter 2, also contributed one or more articles to the same magazine. See Chow Tse-tsung, *Research Guide to the May Fourth Movement* (Cambridge, Mass., 1963), p. 112.

42. *Senmetsu kyōhi*, p. 8.

43. Police Department, Consulate-General in Harbin, "Present Condition of the Situation in Northern Manchuria," dated June 1932, in AJMFA, reel S386, file 9452, p. 16. Unfortunately, the report does not provide the specific date of the month. This source names five Chinese and two Koreans and describes them as graduates of the Toilers' University in Moscow dispatched by the Third International.

Special Committee, the redesignation of the Southern Manchurian Special Committee as the Fengtien Special Committee, the abolition of the Liaohsi Special Committee, and the classification of various cities and *hsien* as "central cities" (*chung-hsin ch'eng-tzu*), "special industrial areas," and "outer *hsien*." Harbin, Mukden, Changchun, and Dairen were the central cities; the Hulan–Hailun Railway, Chinese Eastern Railway, South Manchuria Railway, and Mukden–Shanhaikuan Railway zones were the special industrial areas; and the Eastern Manchurian Special Committee and various *hsien* committees were the outer *hsien*.[44] The Chuho, Suining (Suifenho and Ningan), and Jaoho *Hsien* committees in southern Manchuria were elevated to the status of "central *hsien*" committees, with jurisdiction over one or more *hsien*. Unlike the ordinary *hsien* committees, which were subordinate to the special committees, the central *hsien* committees were placed directly under the provincial committees.

The purged cadres were charged variously with supporting the Li Li-san line, right-wing opportunism, anti-internationalism, and anti-Bolshevism. T'ang Hung-ching, prominent in the CCP movement in Manchuria since the 1920s, was considered one of the anti-international elements opposed to the line handed down by the returned students because he allegedly criticized the "Moscow line" as a continuation of the Li Li-san line.[45] Oddly, Ting Chün-yang is mentioned as one of the "impure elements" purged at this time;[46] he reportedly was executed by the Chang Hsüeh-liang regime in 1930.[47] According to at least one Chinese source hostile to the CCP, the purging and punishment of party and youth corps cadres in Kwangtung, Hopei, Honan, and Manchuria at this time were simply selfish actions by the Moscow faction to eliminate the old cadres.[48] Obviously a wave of purges was under way. In December, Lo Teng-hsien, the erstwhile secretary of the Manchurian Committee, was recalled to Shanghai. His former colleague alleged that he was recalled because the central leaders feared for his safety,[49] but the situation in Manchuria around the time of his recall puts this point in doubt.

The resolutions of the Northern Conference, the purges, and

---

44. *Senmetsu kyōhi*, p. 8.
45. Ibid., p. 30; *Manshū kyōsantō undō gaikan*, p. 22; and Hatano Kenichi, ed., *Chūgoku kyōsantō-shi* [History of the Chinese Communist Party] (Tokyo, 1965), vol. 1, pp. 561–563.
46. *Senmetsu kyōhi*, p. 20.
47. See chapter 4, p. 124, above.
48. Hatano, *Chūgoku kyōsantō-shi*, vol. 2, p. 130.
49. Hsüeh Wen, "Remembering Comrade Lo Teng-hsien," *Hung-ch'i P'iao-p'iao*, vol. 1, p. 94.

the reorganization did not yield immediate results. Probably the turnover at the provincial headquarters impeded the CCP's operations in Manchuria. The fragmentary information available suggests that the party was still struggling to build a base in many areas.

Ho Ch'eng-hsiang, who was active in Harbin in 1931, later described the accomplishments of the cadres and the problems that they faced.[50] Ho's account was presented in an effort to extol Yang Ching-yü, the greatest of the CCP heroes in Manchuria, and this fact should be kept in mind. Yang Ching-yü, known at this time as Chang Kuan-i, was, according to Ho, the party secretary in charge of the All-Manchuria Anti-Japanese Society. This organization was formed in Harbin and gradually expanded into the surrounding villages, thereby encompassing the "broad masses." Because of the vigilance of the Japanese imperialists, says Ho, the work was extremely difficult, but members were recruited in Harbin at the factories, the railroad, the post office, the schools, and even among the police. Anti-Japanese leaflets were distributed at night on the streets and left at residences, and on the desks of the "puppet government offices." One daring youth corps member painted the slogan "Destroy Japanese Imperialism" on a stone column in front of the railroad bureau. Yang later became secretary of the CCP's Harbin City Committee, whose activities were also hampered by the Japanese *T'e-wu* (*Tokumu*), or counterintelligence agency. But, according to Ho, the party in Harbin grew daily, and members were recruited among persons in the same categories as those who joined the Anti-Japanese Society. In order not to reveal the whereabouts of the cadres, meetings were held in streets or parks. In February 1932, when the party was planning to induce the Harbin Guard Unit (*ching-pei-tui*) of the warlord army to engage in guerrilla operations, through some of the Anti-Japanese Society members recruited from the unit, the Japanese Army entered Harbin and disbanded the guard unit.

The Japanese consulate in Harbin had a more detailed knowledge of the activities of the Manchurian Provincial Committee than the bare outline provided by Ho Ch'eng-hsiang. An intelligence report of June 1932[51] indicates that someone with access

50. Ho Ch'eng-hsiang, "Three Meetings with Comrade Yang Ching-yü," *Hung-ch'i P'iao-p'iao*, vol. 5 (December 15, 1957), pp. 120–121. Ho speaks of the "puppet Manchukuo regime" in connection with this period, but Manchukuo was not established until March 1, 1932, and the Japanese Army did not move into Harbin until February 1932.

51. "Present Condition of the Situation in Northern Manchuria," AJMFA, reel S386, file 9452, pp. 21–31.

to party documents was regularly reporting to the consular police, placing the party members in great jeopardy. The Japanese consular police and army gendarmes were constantly monitoring party activities and were in a position to arrest the major leaders at critical moments. The following is a summary of parts of the June report.

1. In order to direct the guerrilla activities of the special [or regional] and *hsien* committees under it, the Provincial Committee in early June dispatched eight party members to eastern, southern, and northern Manchuria. In Panshih *Hsien* in southern Manchuria, the area committee already has a guerrilla unit with 150 members. The unit has already inflicted damage of several hundred thousand *yen* to Japanese and Chinese property.
2. In Harbin
   a. Eight comrades are working among seamen, but aside from distributing leaflets, no other action has been taken.
   b. A branch of the Mass Mutual Aid Society has been established in the electric power company and is being expanded.
   c. Since the secretary in charge of the Workers' Committee in the Chinese Eastern Railway has been arrested, not much has been accomplished on the railway. The party's liaison with the "mass branch" is being improved.
   d. Soldiers' Committee members instigated a revolt in the old Harbin barracks. A few comrades enlisted in the security unit (*pao-an tui*) in Wenmiao. There are revolutionary soldiers in the 3rd company of the 3rd battalion of the guard unit (*ching-pei-tui*), and they are planning a revolt.
3. The Volunteer Army
   a. Battalions are to consist of 60 troops, with 5 companies in a battalion, 4 platoons in a company, and 3 troops in a platoon.
   b. Anyone opposing Japanese imperialism and having previous military training may be admitted.
4. Anti-Japanese Society
   a. The Fourth Representatives' Conference was held on May 24. In the General Association [headquarters] there are two party members and one

youth corps member; in the branches, one each of party and youth corps members.
b. The Student Anti-Japanese Society has a medical college branch, workers' branch, hospital branch, and Fulun City [sic] branch.
c. The Workers' Anti-Japanese Society has three branches in the Chinese Eastern Railway and three branches elsewhere.
d. The General Mass Anti-Japanese Society has a "street branch," a teachers' branch, and two other branches.

5. Fengtien Special Committee
   a. There are some sixty comrades in Liaohsi who are directly connected with guerrilla war, utilizing the Kuomintang, the Volunteer Army, and the numerous masses.
   b. The Korean guerrilla unit in Panshih consists of one unit of 100-plus members in five platoons of twenty members each and possesses 120 rifles. Numerous masses support the unit.
   c. There is no direct struggle among the workers of the Peking–Mukden Railway and South Manchuria Railway, but mass branches exist in Mukden, five of them among the students, six in the power plant, and three among other employees [in other places of work].
   d. Three soldiers' revolts, in Antung, Yingkou, and Dairen, have occurred as a result of party operations.
   e. There are five local branches under the Fengtien Special Committee in Hailung *Hsien*, six in Liaohsi *Hsien*, and eight in the city of Mukden. There are student associations, anti-Japanese associations, soldiers' associations, unemployed associations, and workers' associations.

6. Northern Manchurian Special Committee
   a. No report from the Jaoho and Ningan *hsien* committees.
   b. According to the report from the Tangyuan *Hsien* committee on May 1, there has been a demonstration by Koreans; a volunteer army has been organized by the Farmers' Association; and the Hokang mine workers have been incited to strike for increased wages.

c. Hailun local committee: a representative of the Anti-Japanese Society from Harbin attempted to utilize the Ma Chan-shan army, but the latter withdrew to the mountains. Approximately 200 troops of the Volunteer Army are active in the Chingcheng area.

7. Officers of the CCP provincial committee and youth corps moved across the Sungari River to Sungpuchen on June 15 because of the danger of arrest caused by the tightening investigation by Japanese and Manchukuo authorities. They took with them all documents and printing (mimeographing) machines.

This situation would have given no cause for the central leaders to rejoice. They might have been encouraged that the Manchurian cadres had finally begun to organize some guerrillas, but the activities among the urban workers were simply making no headway.

The situation in Manchuria, however, did not improve. In fact, the Communist cadres in the industrialized southern and central regions of Manchuria were constantly being arrested, whereby some of the party branches were completely destroyed. In October 1932, the Japanese military police in Mukden, evidently well informed about the activities of the major leaders there, arrested a number of CCP cadres. A meeting of six cadres was raided on October 6, and tens of thousands of printed leaflets and 82 documents were confiscated. Other leaders not present at the meeting, including the acting chairman of the Fengtien Special Committee, were also rounded up.[52] The documents revealed that the party had approximately 60 members in Mukden and had been operating in industrial establishments and in schools.[53] These arrests, of course, shut down the Fengtien committee.

On the same day, the police in Harbin raided the printing department of the Manchurian Provincial Committee, arresting those in charge of printing and confiscating documents and propaganda materials. The printing department of the Communist Youth Corps suffered the same fate on November 24. Mimeograph machines and offset printing presses were confiscated along with supplies.[54]

The Manchurian Committee was not only plagued by the police but also by the difficulty of maintaining liaison with the Cen-

52. Ōsaka Tai-Shi Keizai Renmei (Osaka Economic Federation for China), ed., *Sa-Rempō to Shina Manshū no kyōsan undō* [The Soviet Union and the Communist Movement in China and Manchuria] (Tokyo, 1934), pp. 572–575.
53. *Manshū kyōsantō undō gaikan*, p. 6.
54. *Senmetsu kyōhi*, p. 18.

tral Committee and the other party branches. About this time, according to a Japanese source, the committee lost contact with the East Manchurian Special Committee for about a year, and in effect the latter became an independent body. The Manchurian Committee was also short of money because the subsidy received from the Central Committee had been reduced.[55]

Such weaknesses, along with the consolidation of the puppet regime of Manchukuo, reportedly led to a movement among some of the "Li Li-san line cadres" within the Manchurian Provincial Committee to separate the committee from the CCP central headquarters and establish an independent Communist party in Manchuria. Given the difficulty of maintaining liaison with Shanghai and Kiangsi, and considering the difficulties that the CCP was facing in China proper, as well as the fact that Manchuria had actually become a Japanese colony, the argument for an independent party did have some merit. But, in January 1933 the Central Committee denounced this separatist movement as a policy of cowards who had lost all revolutionary character, and dispatched an inspector who charged the party cadres in Manchuria with being dispirited by the white terror and having lost the will to engage in revolutionary struggle. Further, the cadres were criticized for having been misled by right-wing tendencies.[56] The inspector instituted a purge and replaced the officers of the Harbin City Committee with new appointees.[57]

It is quite obvious, however, that purges and reorganizations could not revitalize cadres "dispirited by the white terror" and suffering from a lack of funds and party support in general. Indeed, the gravest problem of the party cadres in Manchuria was that presented by the unreasonable and radical policies set forth by the central leadership. By 1932, the CCP had been in operation in Manchuria nearly a decade, and the Central Committee had sent some of its better-known men to guide operations there, though to little avail. This situation obviously called for a review of not only the attitudes and skills of men at the front line but also the strategies and tactics devised by the central leaders. But, for whatever reasons of their own, those leaders were not willing to concede the possibility that the party strategies were inappropriate. The local cadres must be held responsible for all failures regardless of the situation.

The cure prescribed by the central leaders for the dismal situation in Manchuria was more of the same medicine that they had dispensed at the Northern Conference in June 1932. On Decem-

55. Ibid., p. 20.   56. Ibid., pp. 20–21.   57. Ibid., pp. 21–22.

ber 7 the Central Committee sent a letter to the Manchurian Committee denouncing it in the most stringent terms.[58] The letter revealed that a new slate of officers had been appointed to the committee and that the organizational structure of the committee had been changed. The new committee had held an enlarged conference and accepted the instructions of the Northern Conference and those of the Central Committee, called a conference of the outer *hsien*, and established relationships with a few other outer *hsien* that presumably were either new or were not able to send delegates to the conference. Some of the operations had begun to change in style and some results had been attained, according to the letter, which referred to "Panshih, Payen, and Tangyuan, where volunteer armies were developed and established," and to the printers' strike and the struggle of the calamity-stricken people, the connections established in the Harbin Telephone Company and the Chinese Eastern Railway, and the development of "farmers' and soldiers' branches." Still, according to the central leaders, even the new provincial committee "did not have an adequate understanding of the correct line in the transformation of the operations in Manchuria," and many important problems were "not yet thoroughly solved."[59]

The basic complaint of the central leaders was that the new provincial committee was too much like the old one, which had committed both left-wing and right-wing errors of criminal proportions. In the opinion of the central leadership, the committee's most important error had been its failure to expose errors thoroughly. The Northern Conference for that reason had cited the serious errors of the past, but the enlarged conference of the new provincial committee had not adequately treated the points stressed by the Northern Conference.

The central leaders' disappointment—indeed, anger—at the new provincial committee was not confined to the committee's failure in the operational sphere. The central leaders also found the state of the party in Manchuria totally shameful and directed the new committee to redouble its efforts to expand its membership:

> The foundation of the party at present is confined to the Korean comrades. Eighty percent of party members today are Korean comrades. Even though the environment in Manchuria is very conducive to the absorbing

58. "Letter of the Central Committee to the Manchurian Provincial Committee," December 7, 1932 (*Chung-kung chung-yang wen-chien*, item 24).
59. Unfortunately, we have no information concerning the activities referred to in the letter.

of new members by the party, in the context of development of the anti-Japanese war and the revolutionary struggle of the broad masses, it has not, throughout its entire operation, exerted the effort to double party membership. Especially, it has not engaged in a resolute operation [for membership expansion] among the Chinese revolutionary worker-farmer masses. Exclusivism has been a very serious phenomenon in the organization of the Manchurian party. Thorough reform in the party ranks and strengthening of the foundation of the proletarian class are tasks of paramount importance facing the Manchurian party at the moment.[60]

In order to rectify this abominable state of affairs, the central leaders instructed that the party in Manchuria

> expend the utmost effort to consolidate those industrial branches that the party already had, improve relations between the leadership organs and the branches, deeply inculcate the resolutions of the Northern Conference among the branches, greatly stimulate the positive character and creativity of the comrades, intensify the training of the cadres in the party branches, and establish the viability and operations of the branches.[61]

The central leaders' assessment of the leadership qualities of the Manchurian Committee was very harsh indeed. The December 7 letter said, without qualification, "The leadership style of the Manchurian Provincial Committee can be said to be the worst among all the party branches of the nation." Self-criticisms had been ineffectual; documents from the Central Committee had been held at the provincial committee as reference materials instead of being transmitted to the comrades at the lower levels for practical implementation; operational errors were blamed on the comrades at the lower levels; the positive character of the lower-level masses was obstructed; operations were in disorder; "universalism" (*p'u-pien chu-i*) was practiced and there was no clear-cut focus on operations; and collective leadership was not exercised. The situation was bad indeed.

How could such a deplorable situation be improved? The central leaders provided an answer: the separation of the party from

60. "Letter of the Central Committee to the Manchurian Provincial Committee, December 7, 1932," unpaginated.
61. Ibid.

the masses and the comrades should be corrected. A two-pronged struggle (against left- and right-wing errors) should be carried out thoroughly at the branch level; the cadres should listen to the opinions of lower-level comrades; enthusiasm and creativity should be encouraged among the lower-level comrades and the masses; many new operational methods should be implemented; truly Bolshevik self-criticisms should be developed; and the party's resolutions should really be put into action.

Finally, in order to overcome the difficulties in communication, the Central Committee had decided to place the special committee—not further identified, but surely the Fengtien Special Committee—under its direct command. The special committee, however, was to maintain horizontal relations—relationship of equal rank—and continue to report to the Manchurian Provincial Committee, which was to continue to transmit instructions to the special committee. Notwithstanding the reason given, it would seem that the central leadership had decided to place the Mukden committee under its direct command as an experiment to see whether activities in Manchuria as a whole could be saved from the blundering leadership of the provincial committee.

We can conclude, in any event, that the response of the CCP headquarters and the Manchurian Committee to such momentous events as the open aggression of Japan and the mounting resistance movement in wide segments of society was very anemic. Up to the end of 1932, the CCP played virtually no role in the spontaneous rise of anti-Japanese struggles and remained in the role of a bystander. While various agencies of the CCP distributed anti-Japanese declarations and slogans, the efforts of the CCP were of no consequence. Instead of arousing, organizing, and leading the masses, the CCP cadres in Manchuria were forced to deal with managing their own survival, moving the regional headquarters from Mukden to Harbin, and shuffling the organizational tables of the various agencies under their jurisdiction. The few thousand Communists commanded by the Manchurian Committee were all Koreans living and operating in the hinterlands of Chientao. The urban-centered movement simply could not gather momentum. Obviously, a change in strategy beyond the ritualistic denunciations from the center leaders was needed.

6 | The Comintern versus the Chinese Communist Party on United Front, 1933

WHILE THE OVERALL WEAKNESS OF THE SOVIET UNION forced it to acquiesce in the Japanese takeover of Manchuria and continue to placate Japan, there is no doubt that the Soviet leaders perceived the Japanese action in Manchuria as a threat to Soviet national interest. Given the fact that Japan had extended its power over all of Manchuria and had established the puppet regime of Manchukuo in March 1932, it was only a matter of time until the Japanese would have designs on the Chinese Eastern Railway, and it would have been futile for the Soviet Union to hold onto the railway. The Soviet Union, therefore, yielded to all the Japanese demands upon the railway, including the appointment of a Chinese manager designated by Manchukuo and the changing of the railway's name to the North Manchuria Railway, and in September 1932, the Soviet Union agreed to the Japanese idea of selling the railway to Manchukuo. The negotiation for the sale, however, was to drag on until March 1935.[1]

A more serious problem for the Soviet Union was the possibility of Japanese military encroachment upon the Soviet Far Eastern territory. The young officers of the Japanese Kwantung Army had already defied the political leadership in Tokyo by taking over Manchuria, and, indeed, the military officers were taking over political power in Japan. Would the Japanese military stop at Manchuria? Would they not direct their expansionist attention toward Siberia, to which Japan had dispatched two divisions during the Russian Civil War?

In late 1932, the Soviet leaders began to harden their attitude toward Japan. For example, the Soviet Union refused the Japanese request for the return of anti-Japanese troops from the Soviet ter-

1. Hirai Tomoyoshi, "The Trend in the Soviet Union," in Nihon Kokusai Seiji Gakkai (Japanese Association of International Politics), *Taiheiyō sensō e no michi* [The Road to the Pacific War] (Tokyo, 1963), vol. 4, pp. 259, 272.

158

ritory, where they had fled from Manchuria in December 1932. In spite of Japanese warnings that the permission granted for their leaders' departure to Europe constituted an "unfriendly act against the Japanese government," the Soviet Union adhered to its decision. The Soviet leaders ignored and, indeed, ridiculed Japanese displeasure at the resumption of relations between the Soviet and Chinese governments in December 1932. On the other hand, the Soviet Union accelerated military production, increased its armaments in the Far East, stockpiled large quantities of food, and began to denounce Japanese bellicosity in public.[2] The successful completion of the first five-year economic plan (1928–1932), which, among other things, emphasized military production, and the gradual improvement of Soviet foreign relations evidently bolstered the confidence of Soviet leaders. In any event, since the Soviet leaders had already decided to abandon the Chinese Eastern Railway and preparations were being made to counter a possible attack from Manchuria, the Soviet Union no longer needed to be circumspect toward the Japanese.

In the meantime, the Soviet Union had reasons to cultivate Sino-Japanese hostility, which would absorb Japanese energy that might otherwise be directed against the Soviet Union. It was in the Soviet interest, therefore, to prevent the Kuomintang (KMT) government under Chiang Kai-shek from surrendering to the Japanese or reaching a modus vivendi vis-à-vis Manchuria. But none of the Western powers showed any inclination to buttress Chinese efforts against Japan, and the KMT government needed allies with definite military capabilities. These practical considerations led the Soviet Union to renew its diplomatic relations with China in December 1932, even while the KMT government was engaged in the fiercest campaign against the Chinese Red Army in the central and southern part of the country. The Russian willingness to restore diplomatic ties with the archenemy of the CCP may have been demoralizing to the Chinese Communists engaged in battle against the KMT, but the Soviet Union had to take a "broader" perspective of international relations in the region.

It would not be too farfetched to assume that during the course of negotiations the Soviet leaders attempted to persuade Chiang Kai-shek to terminate the costly encirclement campaigns against the Red Army in southern China. It was argued by numerous Chinese that a united China would offer much more formidable opposition to Japan than a country engaged in internecine struggles;

2. Ibid., vol. 2, pp. 327–338.

this, however, did not dissuade Chiang Kai-shek from launching the Fifth Encirclement Campaign in early 1933, with the result that the Red Army was forced to abandon the Kiangsi soviet districts in the summer of 1934.

Manchuria was another matter. There is no indication that the Soviet Union offered active assistance to the various anti-Japanese groups operating there after 1931, but there was no doubt that the Soviet Union was sympathetic to their cause. The defeated "generals" of the anti-Japanese groups, including Ma Chan-shan, Li Tu, Su Ping-wen, and Wang Te-lin, escaped the clutches of the pursuing Japanese in late 1932 and emerged in Berlin in April 1933.[3] As we noted earlier, the Soviet Union denied the Japanese request for the return of these leaders and their men.

A strong indigenous anti-Japanese movement would have been in the interest of the Soviet Union. Such a movement had come into existence, but the situation was turning rapidly against it. The Japanese Kwantung Army along with the puppet army of Manchukuo frontally attacked the major elements of the anti-Japanese forces in various parts of Manchuria and succeeded in destroying large-scale organized resistance by November 1933. The number of resistance fighters killed between 1932 and 1933 was over 16,000 and the wounded exceeded 7,000. By the spring of 1933 many of the principal leaders of the resistance had fallen in battle, surrendered, or fled to China or Siberia. The KMT government was then still absorbed in its efforts to exterminate the Communist forces in Kiangsi Province. After the Japanese conquered Jehol and marched into North China, Chiang Kai-shek concluded a truce with them at Tangku on May 31 to stave off their further advance. The elimination of the internal enemy was of utmost concern to Chiang, and the KMT had little desire to engage the Japanese in battle or come to the aid of the anti-Japanese forces in Manchuria. The latter dwindled in number from a maximum of some 300,000 men in 1932 to between 45,000 and 52,000 in the latter part of 1933.[4]

The Comintern's New Strategy

The problem of injecting vitality into the anti-Japanese movement in Manchuria must have aroused the concern of the Soviet

3. *New York Times*, April 21, 1933.
4. Manshūkokushi Hensan Kankōkai (Editorial and Publication Committee of the History of Manchukuo), *Manshūkokushi* [History of Manchukuo] (Tokyo, 1971), vol. 2, pp. 302–303.

leaders, particularly in the wake of the retreat of the Manchurian commanders. Presumably the Soviet officials discussed the problem with the routed commanders, seeking to assess the situation in Manchuria. In any event, evidence indicates that the Comintern leaders in Moscow actively discussed Manchuria in late 1932 and in 1933 and decided that the narrowly fixed policy of the "united front from below" should be abandoned and that the Chinese Communist Party (CCP) ought to join with any group that was willing to participate in the common struggle against Japanese imperialism.

The change in the united front strategy would have been very palatable to the CCP cadres in Manchuria; we need only recall the debate between Ch'en Wei-jen and the central leaders.[5] The local leadership in Manchuria would have welcomed a change in party policy that would treat Japanese imperialism as the principal foe. But the difficulty both for the Comintern and the Manchurian Provincial Committee was that the CCP leadership—located thousands of miles away—did not see fit to change its strategy. As a result, the Comintern leadership, through Ch'en Shao-yü (better known by his alias, Wang Ming), engaged in a heated polemic with the CCP leaders on the issue of a united front in Manchuria. An irony here is that the CCP in this period was still under the leadership of the returnees from Russia.

The Comintern's adoption of a new strategy toward Manchuria can be ascertained from a variety of sources. The first evidence is the testimony of Li Yao-k'uei, who served as acting secretary of the Manchurian Committee between May and October 1933. Li, a graduate of the Sun Yat-sen University in Moscow[6] and already slated for assignment to Manchuria, attended a meeting of the Chinese section of the Comintern in Moscow in February 1933. According to a Japanese report of an interrogation of Li in 1934, other participants in the meeting were Pavel Mif, the head of the Chinese section, "Shao Hsing [Ch'en Shao-yü?], the CCP representative in Moscow," and five Chinese students. At the meeting it was reportedly decided that the CCP's policy of applying a uniform strategy in North and South China "on the basis of the Comintern's Eastern Conference of 1932" was in error. Under the new

---

5. See chapter 3, pp. 76–84, above.
6. Yüeh Sheng (Sheng Chung-liang), one of the "28 Bolsheviks" or "returned students," mentions Li Yao-k'uei as one of the graduates of Sun Yat-sen University. Sheng, Li, and some twenty others were sent in 1929, after the Chinese Eastern Railway Incident, to the Soviet Far East to engage in propaganda work. See Yüeh's *Sun Yat-sen University in Moscow and the Chinese Revolution: A Personal Account* (Lawrence, Kansas, 1971), p. 237.

policy, the party in Manchuria would (1) win over the masses by stressing patriotism and agitate for struggle against foreign oppression, monopoly capitalism, and the warlords; (2) infiltrate cadres among the "bandits" (the anti-Japanese groups) in order to expand and strengthen the revolutionary forces; and (3) postpone the establishment of the soviet republic until the completion of the communization of Manchuria.[7]

Another evidence is the Manchurian Committee's June 1933 directive to its subordinate organizations and its membership on the "National Anti-Japanese and Anti-Imperial United Front." Unfortunately, the text of this important directive cannot be located, but the CCP's central leaders criticized the Manchurian Committee in February 1934 for issuing the directive, which called for the broadest possible united front of the people of Manchuria. As reasons for such a measure, the committee reportedly cited the Manchurian masses' political immaturity, their lack of experience with the great revolution of 1925–1927 (in southern China), their lack of direct experience with Soviet revolution, and the fact that they had just been awakened politically. The committee was quoted as stating that the "entire masses" were "anti-Japanese" and that the CCP in Manchuria was at the time frail, both politically and as an organization.[8]

We also know from surrendered Communists of this period that a man named P'an of the Manchurian Provincial Committee and Chang Jung of the East Manchurian Special Committee convened an enlarged *hsien* committee conference at Tahuangkou, in Chientao, in July 1933, to reveal the new directives from the Comintern and the Central Committee of the CCP. They criticized the line of policy implemented since the Japanese takeover of Manchuria as "left-wing opportunism." Because the property of all the landlords and rich farmers was confiscated under that line, those with anti-Japanese thoughts had been driven from the anti-Japanese front and the strength of the anti-Japanese movement had been reduced, according to the cadres. The killing of the worker-farmer masses under the slogan of destroying running dogs was criticized as a grave error. The conference was told in no

7. A summary of Li Yao-k'uei's interrogation is presented in a report of the Japanese ambassador to Manchukuo in Changchun to the foreign minister, May 22, 1934, in the Archives of the Japanese Ministry of Foreign Affairs (1868–1945) (hereafter cited as AJMFA), microfilmed for the Library of Congress, Washington, D.C., reel S386, file S9452-15, pp. 188–195.

8. Gunseibu, Komonbu (Advisors' Department, Ministry of Defense, Manchukuo), *Manshū kyōsanhi no kenkyū* [Study of Communist Bandits in Manchuria] (n.p., 1937), p. 430; based on information provided by a surrendered Communist.

uncertain terms that the revolution in Manchuria was now at the stage of national revolution and that there were anti-Japanese elements even among the landlord-capitalist classes. The slogan of the Central Committee was now to confiscate the property of national traitors only, according to P'an and Chang. The soviet governments were to be replaced by people's revolutionary governments, and the farmers' associations by farmers' committees. The workers' guerrilla units, on the other hand, were to be reorganized into a people's revolutionary army, and the Red Militia and the pioneer units were to be brought into the anti-Japanese volunteer army.[9] Obviously, these cadres were attempting to translate the June directive into action.

Ch'en Shao-yü versus the CCP Leadership

Another evidence of the Comintern's shift in policy is a long article written by Ch'en Shao-yü in January 1933,[10] which will be discussed below. Ch'en's article accurately reflected the Comintern's new line. The fact that the CCP leaders quoted a large part of Ch'en's article verbatim in their letter of January 26, 1933,[11] addressed to the Manchurian Committee, indicates that Ch'en's article reached not only the cadres in Manchuria but the central leaders in southern China as well. However, the CCP leaders found the main thrust of Ch'en's article—the Comintern's new strategy—unacceptable, and they proceeded to alter it to suit their own strategy. In doing so, the CCP leaders clearly indicated

9. Ibid., p. 87. Information given by Pak Tu-nam, a surrendered Communist, to the Advisors' Department of the Chientao District Command, Manchukuo Army, on August 30, 1934. In fact, the CCP's policy on the landlords was to liquidate them, as was reaffirmed by the eight-*hsien* land survey conference held in the Kiangsi Soviet district, June 17–21, 1933. The conference stipulated: "The landlord class is the principal enemy of land reform. The policy of the Soviets toward the landlords is to confiscate all their land and [other] property and to annihilate the landlord class." The rich farmers, on the other hand, were to be deprived of their land but would be allowed to continue farming. See Hsiao Tso-liang, *The Land Revolution in China, 1930–1934* (Seattle, 1969), pp. 103–105, 254–309.

10. Ch'en Shao-yü, "Tung-pei ch'ing-hsing yü K'ang-Jih t'ung-i chan-hsien t'se-liao" [The Situation in Manchuria and the Anti-Japanese United Front Strategy], *Ch'en Shao-yü (Wang Ming) chiu-kuo yen-lun hsüan-chi* [Selected Works of Ch'en Shao-yü (Wang Ming) on National Salvation] (Hankow, 1938; reprint edition, Tokyo, 1970), vol. 1, pp. 293–312. Hereafter cited as *Ch'en Shao-yü hsüan-chi*.

11. The text of the January 26 letter of the CCP Central Committee, "Manchou te chuang-k'uang ho wo-men tang te jen-wu: Chung-yang chih Manchou tang ho chüan-t'i tang-yüan te hsin" [The Situation in Manchuria and Our Party's Mission: Letter of the Central Committee to the Manchurian Party and All Party Members], is in *Tou-cheng* [Struggle], Shanghai edition (mimeographed), no. 44 (June 10, 1933), pp. 11–18, and Juichin edition (printed) no. 18 (June 19, 1933), pp. 1–5, no. 19 (July 25), pp. 14–16, and no. 20 (August 5), pp. 14–16.

their points of disagreement with the Comintern. We shall, therefore, compare the text of Ch'en's letter with the CCP Central Committee's letter of January.

Before comparing Ch'en's article with the January 1933 letter of the CCP, we must offer a caveat. The text makes it clear that the article was written in January 1933 ("one year and four months after the armed occupation of the Three Eastern Provinces by Japanese imperialism"), but the only version available to us appears in a selection of Ch'en's writings published in Hankow in 1938. The year of publication (or republication) is important because after 1937 the CCP was in alliance again with the KMT in the anti-Japanese struggle; also, Hankow happened to be a city under the rule of the KMT. Therefore, one cannot rule out the possibility that Ch'en edited the text before republishing it in 1938 and may have deleted portions of the earlier (1933) version critical of the KMT. This is a point of some interest for historians of the CCP simply because the absence of anti-KMT remarks in 1933 would constitute a marked departure from the practices of the CCP at that time. It is relevant to point out that the Manchurian Committee was unequivocal in its attack on the KMT in November 1933, when it issued two statements commemorating the sixth anniversary of the Canton revolt of December 1927.[12]

Yet it is possible that Ch'en refrained from attacking the KMT in 1933 because the Soviet Union had just restored diplomatic relations with the KMT in December 1932. The Comintern may have tried through Ch'en to concentrate the efforts of the CCP in Manchuria on the fight against Japan and avoid their being sidetracked by anti-KMT operations. Also, in contrast with the situation in central and southern China, the KMT played a relatively minor role in Manchuria, and it would not have been necessary for Ch'en to criticize the KMT to advance his points. In any event, the possibility that Ch'en revised his original text on matters dealing with the KMT does not detract from the value of his article for our study of the situation in Manchuria. What is more important is that Ch'en's arguments clearly parallel those presented by Li Yao-k'uei and others on behalf of the united front strategy.

On the Bourgeoisie and Landlords

Ch'en Shao-yü not only seemingly refrained from attacking the KMT but departed from the current policy to the extent of suggesting the possibility of forming alliances with the bourgeoisie

12. Manchukuo, Hsieh-ho-hui (Concordia Association), Senmetsu kyōhi [Annihilate Communist Bandits] (Changchun[?], 1934), pp. 117–121.

and even the landlords in Manchuria. He stated that the bourgeoisie were unhappy with Japanese imperialism and that they, along with some of the landlords, held anti-Japanese feelings. This, according to Ch'en, was because both the bourgeoisie and the landlords had suffered considerably under the rule of Japanese imperialism. Some of them were struggling against Japanese imperialism and the puppet regime of Manchukuo and even provided leadership to the working masses. Ch'en added that if this situation were not properly taken into account, the party would be isolated from the masses and would not be able to develop a large-scale anti-Japanese movement.[13] The general strategy of the CCP in Manchuria, according to Ch'en, should take into account the special circumstances at the time and establish a general national anti-Japanese united front with "the very broad masses, all of whom hold anti-Japanese feelings": the political slogans in Manchuria should call for confiscation of the property of Japanese imperialists and traitors, opposition to the oppressive rule of Japanese imperialism and the Manchukuo government, the development of a broad anti-Japanese movement, and the establishment of an elected people's revolutionary government.

Ch'en claimed that the basic weakness of the CCP organization in Manchuria was that it did not understand and therefore did not correctly implement the strategy of the anti-Japanese united front. Nevertheless, the strategy was appropriate: Manchuria was occupied by Japan and the people were suffering the fate of persons without a country, and the broad masses longed for an anti-Japanese united front.[14]

On the Aims of the United Front

Thus, for Ch'en Shao-yü, the most important task before the CCP in Manchuria was to form a broad anti-Japanese united front. He did stress the importance of having the "backbone of the proletariat" in the anti-Japanese movement; otherwise, it would be impossible to establish a true revolutionary unity and a united front beneficial to the proletariat. But the struggle against the bourgeoisie was not included in this strategy.

With this the CCP leaders could not agree. According to the January 26 letter, there was another—and more important—aim in forming the anti-Japanese united front:

> When the proletariat, under certain definite conditions and circumstances, forms a united front with part

13. Ch'en Shao-yü hsüan-chi, pp. 306–307.
14. Ibid., p. 306.

of the national bourgeoisie to wage an armed struggle against imperialism, the purpose is not confined to the joint struggle against imperialism; it also lies in bringing the peasants and the petty bourgeoisie under the leadership of the proletariat. It also signifies that a struggle is being waged against the bourgeoisie in a special way.... Therefore, every effort must be made to expand the proletariat, the peasants, and the petty bourgeoisie (especially the laborers), and we must rely on the progress of their politico-economic struggle. This is the foremost and basic mission of our party in Manchuria at this time.[15]

On this premise the CCP leaders included in the January letter many instructions that could be categorized as narrowly class-oriented carryovers from the past. To the task of establishing a general national anti-Japanese front, the Central Committee added the task of "preparing for struggle within the united front and preparing for the future victory of soviet revolution in Manchuria." Unlike Ch'en Shao-yü, the central leaders linked the struggle of the revolutionary masses in Manchuria with the attainment of national liberation, protection of Chinese soviets, and the armed protection of the Soviet Union. The Central Committee's policies stressed the promotion of strikes, the absorption by the CCP of "yellow" unions and the unorganized workers, and the transformation of the red labor unions into organizations of the broad masses. While defining the winning of hegemony in the anti-Japanese mass struggle as one of the fundamental duties of the party, it also enumerated other tasks, such as the "development and merging of soviet districts, consolidation of the Red Army, the overthrow of the KMT, and the expansion of mass revolutionary struggle." It criticized the underestimation of the extent of the "land reform movement" already attained and stressed the importance of the movement of the farmers to oppose the Chinese landlords and usurers. In addition to repeating Ch'en's politically oriented slogans, the central leaders urged the Manchurian cadres to call for economic struggles among the farmers, for example, by advocating the reduction of rent to 20 percent of the crop.[16] To various slogans proposed by Ch'en for the students and intelligentsia, the central leaders added their own, calling for opposition to "Sun Yatsen-ism," which was defined as the banner of

15. *Tou-cheng* (Juichin), no. 19 (July 25, 1933), pp. 15–16.
16. Ibid.

Map 2. Provinces of Manchukuo, 1932–1945
(Courtesy U.S. Department of the Army,
Office of the Chief of Military History)

"white terrorism" and "national betrayal." In short, while Ch'en argued for a united front appealing more to the anti-Japanese sentiment among the masses in Manchuria and including some of the landlords and bourgeoisie, the central leaders stressed ideologically oriented programs in addition to nationalistic appeals. While Ch'en emphasized the situation in Manchuria, the CCP leaders in China, mindful also of China as a whole, were willing to go only halfway in changing their views.

On the Analysis of Guerrilla Groups

The differing views of Ch'en Shao-yü and the CCP central leaders can also be seen in their characterizations of the various guerrilla groups in Manchuria and their policies concerning them. Ch'en divided the guerrillas into four groups and recommended policies for each. The CCP leaders used Ch'en's classifications and some of his terminology in characterizing the guerrilla groups, but the January letter expanded on some of Ch'en's comments in ways that contradicted his analysis. While Ch'en's emphasis was on collaboration to bring about an effective united front incorporating all anti-Japanese guerrilla groups, the central leaders' emphasis was on struggling against most of the guerrilla leaders.

Ch'en's basic point was that the guerrilla groups could be categorized according to the composition and the attitudes of the leaders and members of each group, and that for each category a different kind of united front strategy was required. Ch'en divided the groups into (1) those consisting mostly of former soldiers of Chang Hsüeh-liang's old Kirin Army, (2) those composed of a combination of army troops and armed civilians, (3) those composed of farmers, who were in some instances also members of secret societies, and (4) those under the direction of the CCP.

According to Ch'en, all of the former Kirin Army groups were commanded by officers who had served under Chang Hsüeh-liang, such as Ma Chan-shan, Li Tu, and Su Ping-wen. The influence of the KMT among them was considerable. Although now engaged in armed struggle against Japan, they still were not inclined toward forming a united front with the masses and relying on them. At times, they reverted to their old habits and opposed and even oppressed the revolutionary movement of the workers, farmers, and students. Thus, although they had more and better weapons, they had already suffered severe losses, and they faced the danger of failure through lack of popular support. Their situation, however, did not mean that the anti-Japanese guerrilla movement as a whole was doomed. It only highlighted the fact that anti-imperial national liberation could not succeed unless the soldiers and the masses were united.[17] What should be the CCP's policy toward these guerrilla groups? According to Ch'en, their leaders still opposed the united front strategy. Therefore, the

17. Ch'en Shao-yü hsüan-chi, pp. 303–304.

CCP should strive to build a united front from below while gradually moving toward the goal of establishing a united front from above.[18]

In contrast to Ch'en's rather patronizing attitude, the central leaders were violently hostile toward guerrillas of this category. The January letter stated:

> They obey the orders of the KMT and depend upon [the support of] the landlords, bourgeoisie, and rich farmers. These few people, while under the influence of [American] imperialism, fight against Japan because of the heightened movement of the broad masses against imperialism and for the national revolution, because of the threat of anti-Japanese emotions among the officers and many of the soldiers under them, and for their own profit as exploiters. However, they view the revolutionary movement of the workers and farmers and all others of mass nature with absolute enmity. They shot to death revolutionary workers, farmers, soldiers, and students. They disarmed the anti-Japanese volunteer army. They oppressed the workers. They are undependable and vacillating. When expedient or necessary, they commit treason and surrender to Japanese imperialism. They have already obstructed the development of a true mass guerrilla movement. Their low combat strength, failure, and surrender are due mainly to their enmity for the workers.[19]

What should be the policy toward these scoundrels? The January letter said: "Mainly the united front with the soldiers should be established from the lower level. When there is need for joint operations against Japan, detailed operational agreements should be drawn up."[20]

Thus the central leaders viewed the leaders of the guerrilla groups in the first category with total hostility and utter contempt, and they did not foresee any possibility of forming a united front from above with them. The only concession made to Ch'en's view was that it was permissible for the cadres in Manchuria to engage in joint operations with these groups under strict contractual terms. This totally clashed with Ch'en's view that the united

18. Ibid., p. 308.
19. *Tou-cheng* (Juichin), no. 18 (July 19, 1933), p. 3. Unfortunately, we do not have any information to corroborate these charges.
20. Ibid., no. 19 (July 25, 1933), p. 14.

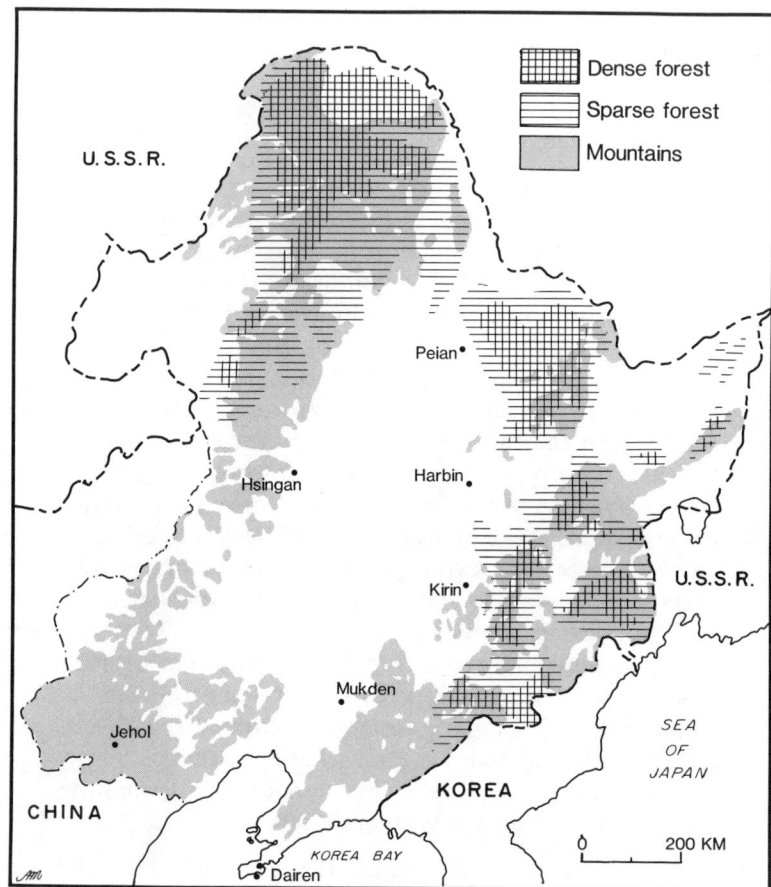

Map 3. Mountain and Forest Terrain in Manchuria

front from above should be established when the guerrilla leaders agreed to such a strategy. It should be noted that the central leaders' prescription severely restricted the options of the local cadres, whereas Ch'en would have allowed them considerable freedom of action.

With regard to the three other categories of guerrillas, the central leaders agreed completely with Ch'en's analysis and policy recommendations. The second category of Manchurian guerrillas included some of the former Kirin Army troops, but the CCP leaders saw a significant difference in the social composition of the rank and file. The only commander named in this category was Wang Te-lin, who had been a battalion commander in Yenchi.

The central leaders stated in the January letter: "Most of these anti-Japanese volunteer army groups come from the peasantry, petty bourgeoisie, and laborers, rather than soldiers. The Kuomintang's influence over them is relatively small, and at one time they acknowledged to a certain degree the CCP's right to agitate for anti-imperialism and revolution." The Manchurian Committee was told: "There is a possibility for forming a united front not only with men of the lower level but, to a certain limited extent, with the upper ranks as well."

Included in the third category were the Big Sword Society, Red Spear Society, and Self-Defense Society (Tzu-wei Hui). As we have seen, the question of cooperation with such groups had been a source of friction between the cadres in Manchuria and the central leaders for some time. The central leaders' analysis in 1933 was as follows:

> Some laborers, petty bourgeoisie, and intelligentsia can be found among [these groups], but the majority are farmers. Because of their weaknesses in political maturity and in knowledge of military techniques, some of them—and still the majority—are under the command and influence of the landlords, rich farmers, and old Kirin Army officers. For these reasons, they are not only unable to put their movement on a truly revolutionary course but are at times selfishly exploited by leaders of reactionary groups. Some other guerrillas of this category are under the influence and guidance of the revolutionary elements. Although they show an extremely favorable attitude toward the comrades of the [proletarian] class, they have not yet found the correct and thoroughgoing course of revolutionary struggle.[21]

Thus the central leaders' attitudes toward these groups were mixed, and hence the Manchurian Committee was instructed to "determine the scope and extent of a united front [with them] in accordance with the extent of their opposition to their reactionary leadership and the magnitude of our revolutionary political influence within the group." The leaders saw the possibility of "some kind of an arrangement with them," in the form of an "anti-imperial alliance" or (as proposed by Ch'en) an anti-Japanese political alliance.[22]

21. Ibid., and *Ch'en Shao-yü hsüan-chi*, p. 304.
22. *Tou-cheng*, no. 19 (July 25, 1933), p. 14; *Ch'en Shao-yü hsüan-chi*, p. 308.

The fourth category—the guerrillas under the CCP, or "red guerrillas"—was cited in both documents as the most advanced and most revolutionary, and as having the most powerful combat capabilities. These groups could become the core of the broad masses and mobilize and unite the millions of masses around them in the struggle to oppose Japan and its running dogs. But the leaders admitted that, because of the weakness of the party's organization and influence, the red guerrillas had not yet become the leaders of the anti-Japanese guerrilla movement in Manchuria.[23]

What, then, were the immediate tasks of the CCP members in Manchuria? Ch'en emphasized the following requirements:

(1) The political and organizational independence of the Communist party must be absolutely maintained.
(2) In applying the united front strategy, the true conditions (among the guerrillas) must be taken into account.
(3) The education and organization of the workers must be intensified.
(4) Since the anti-Japanese struggle in the Three Eastern Provinces must mobilize the ever broader worker-farmer masses, the CCP must protect the farmers' struggle against the forcible occupation of land by Japanese imperialism and must assist the demands of the farmers.[24]

In their January 26 letter, the central leaders agreed with the first two requirements presented by Ch'en but replaced the last two with requirements of their own. Instead of mentioning the education and organization of the workers, the central leaders instructed members to "remember that the united front from below is the foundation of our activities. The united front from above can be established only when there is a solid base of the united front from below and when the bosses are threatened by the revolutionary emotions of the lower level." Ch'en's fourth point was replaced with an exhortation, as noted earlier, that the united front, including certain elements of the bourgeoisie, should not only engage in anti-imperial struggles but win over the farmers and the petty bourgeoisie to acceptance of the leadership of the proletariat. This was a "special method of fighting the bourgeoisie."[25]

Thus, while Ch'en Shao-yü was attempting to steer the move-

23. *Tou-cheng*, no. 18 (July 19, 1933), p. 4 and *Ch'en Shao-yü hsüan-chi*, p. 305.
24. *Ch'en Shao-yü hsüan-chi*, pp. 307–309.
25. *Tou-cheng*, no. 19 (July 25, 1933), p. 14.

ment in Manchuria away from past errors by redirecting the party toward a strategy of a broad-scale united front, the leaders in China—who seemed to be jealously guarding their prerogatives—insisted that the past policies should be continued to a large extent.

The Reaction of the Manchurian Committee

As we have seen earlier, the Manchurian Committee followed the Comintern's directive. This was only natural in that the committee was headed by Li Yao-k'uei, who received his appointment in Moscow rather than in Shanghai or Peking. As we shall see in the next chapter, the guerrillas organized by the Manchurian Committee in Panshih in South Manchuria also began to follow Ch'en's directive on forming a united front with other anti-Japanese groups, producing favorable results. But the cadres in Manchuria were aware of the sharp criticism of the Comintern line by the central leadership. The party branch in eastern Manchuria followed the January letter of the central leadership more faithfully. The environment and the backgrounds of the regional parties obviously affected their choice of strategies.

The Manchurian Committee's proclamation of November 15–16, 1933, reflects the attempt of the Manchurian Committee to reconcile the two contrasting, if not contradictory, directives from above. In its "Declaration of the CCP's Manchuria Provincial Committee on the Occasion of the Sixth Anniversary of the Canton Revolt" (December 11–14, 1927) and "Letter to the People on the Occasion of the Anniversary of the Canton Revolt," the committee launched a sharp attack against the KMT, likening the KMT's Fifth Encirclement Campaign against the Chinese soviet to the Japanese attack against the anti-Japanese forces in Manchuria, and denounced the KMT for having sold out the nation. The KMT was also accused of having betrayed two anti-Japanese guerrilla leaders in Manchuria, Tien Ch'en and Sun Ch'ao-yang, to the Japanese. The people were urged to join the People's Revolutionary Army and the Volunteer Army and take part in the true anti-Japanese struggle. The committee then presented fourteen slogans dealing with such subjects as the increase of wages, reduction of farm rent to 20 percent, support of the Red Army and the soviets, and opposition to the threatened war against the Soviet Union. But there was no mention of land reform or the confiscation of lands belonging to the landlords; only the property owned by Japanese and by traitors was to be confiscated and distributed to the worker-farmer masses.[26] Thus, the Manchurian Committee persisted in following the Moscow line—although by attacking the KMT the committee acknowledged its support for the central leadership.

The Party Leaders' Reactions

The central leaders, however, found this compromise formula unacceptable. The Manchurian Committee was to come under sharp criticism. The earliest reaction of the central leaders that we can find is in an article by Li Wei-han (alias Lo Mai), published in the Juichin edition of *Tou-cheng* [Struggle], on the situation in Manchuria on the second anniversary of the Manchurian Incident.[27] Li, one of the key members of the Ch'ü Ch'iu-pai faction, was again in the top echelon of the party as the director of the Organization Department of the Central Committee, dispensing authoritative party views.

In general, Li Wei-han was pleased by the accomplishments of the Manchurian Committee after the January letter was issued. Li's overall tone could be characterized as buoyant, particularly in contrast with the severe tone of previous resolutions and directives. But Li cited a number of shortcomings that needed to be corrected. The first of these was the "right-wing opportunist distortion" of the united front strategy by some of the cadres. They distorted the strategy to mean "collusion" (*kou-chieh*) with non-Communist groups at the upper level and thus taking the "chieftain line" (*kuan-chang lu-hsien*). Referring to the January letter, Li said: "They have not understood that the united front from below must be the foundation of the party's activity, and that the united front from above should be applied only when the party has firmly established the united front from below and the upper strata feel threatened by the revolutionary emotions of the lower strata." According to Li, the party had already suffered numerous defeats through indiscriminate collusion with the upper echelons. The best examples of this were the failure of the Payen guerrillas and the mutiny in Weiho. In the latter case, the party's

26. *Senmetsu kyōhi*, pp. 117–121.
27. Lo Mai, "The National Revolutionary War in Manchuria at the Second Anniversary of the Manchurian Incident," *Tou-cheng* (Juichin), no. 26 (September 15, 1933), pp. 3–11. For Li Wei-han's career see Donald W. Klein and Anne B. Clark, *Biographic Dictionary of Chinese Communism, 1921–1965* (Cambridge, Mass., 1971), pp. 534–540. For Li's position after 1933 see also Kuo Hua-lun, *Chung-kung shih-lun* [History of the Chinese Communist Party] (Taipei, 1969), vol. 2, p. 377.

agent among the anti-Japanese soldiers was completely detached from the masses; he depended solely on collusion with the reactionary leaders, thereby becoming their prisoner. In spite of numerous such incidents, many cadres in the Manchurian branch of the party had not learned their lesson and repeated this error time and time again.[28]

The other error, according to Li Wei-han, was left-wing "exclusionism" (*kuan-men chu-i*): "Our leading comrades proffered slogans about the establishment of soviets and the Red Army and the confiscation and equal distribution of landlords' lands too early." They organized red armies with very small bodies of red guerrillas and shouted empty slogans of protecting the Soviet Union with arms and of protecting the Red Army and the soviets while abandoning the task of organizing the anti-Japanese movement of the broad masses. They also called out for attacks against the Japanese but neglected the urgent task of providing leadership in the daily economic and political struggles of the workers. They clamored for land reform but failed to provide leadership in the farmers' struggle to divide the crops and to oppose taxes. While everywhere the workers, farmers, students, volunteer army soldiers, and the bandit masses were looking toward the Communist party, each of the anti-Japanese societies had only a few members—ten or, at most, forty to fifty members. In some extreme cases, these societies operated in secret.[29]

It is highly significant that Li Wei-han chose to criticize the "left-wing errors" of the Manchurian Communists and that he included in this category the call for the confiscation of lands and the establishment of the Red Army and the soviets. We know that these very points had been strongly emphasized by the central leaders at the Northern Conference of June 1932. The Manchurian cadres, along with those from other provinces in northern China, had been denounced for delaying the implementation of land reform and for their inability and unwillingness to organize the Red Army and the soviets. The January letter also had criticized the Manchurian Committee for underestimating the land problem and the "level of the movement for land reform." But in September 1933, efforts at meeting these criticisms were criticized as a "left-wing error." Were the central leaders perhaps beginning to bend toward Ch'en Shao-yü's line of thought? Or were the central leaders divided among themselves?

28. Lo Mai, "National Revolutionary War," p. 7.
29. Ibid., p. 8.

Following the line of argument presented in the January letter, Li Wei-han also stressed the party's failure to organize the urban workers. Even though many spontaneous strikes of workers had taken place since the Manchurian Incident, the party's operations among the workers had failed to make progress and were in some areas weaker than before. The weakness in Dairen was quite astonishing to Li: "At present, one cannot even find a branch with ten members!" The membership of the Red Labor Union was even smaller, and the Anti-Japanese Association also had a very narrow base. The party was preoccupied with the volunteer armies and the guerrilla war and was dispatching all the cadres to the villages. The Manchurian Committee was therefore urged to train its members and dispatch them to such major cities as Mukden, Fushun, Dairen, and Harbin to work among the workers of the railroad and other major industries; it was also urged to increase its efforts at organizing the farm laborers.[30]

The February 1934 Letter

Li Wei-han's preliminary analysis of September 1933 was followed by an official letter from the Central Committee to the Manchurian Provincial committee, dated February 22, 1934, and entitled, "The Immediate Tasks of the Party in the Anti-Japanese War in Manchuria."[31] The party headquarters in Shanghai had moved to the Kiangsi soviet area,[32] where the Central Committee had its Fifth Plenum in January. The plenum reconfirmed the leadership of the returned student faction and issued a number of directives on various facets of party activities, including the Second All-China Soviet Congress, held in Juichin from January 22 to February 7.[33] The February letter to the Manchurian Committee was an outgrowth of these developments.

30. Ibid., p. 10.
31. *Tou-cheng* (Juichin), no. 60 (May 19, 1934), pp. 9–16.
32. Most of the top CCP leaders moved to Juichin between 1932 and early 1933, and according to at least one source, the central headquarters was officially operating there by January 1933. See Kuo Hua-lun, *Chung-kung shih-lun*, vol. 2, p. 374. The CCP, however, maintained the Shanghai Bureau to "direct its work in the KMT-controlled areas" until the middle of 1934. See Yüeh Sheng, *Sun Yat-sen University*, pp. 250–255. According to *Chūgoku kyōsantō-shi shiryō-shū* [Compendium of Materials on the History of the Chinese Communist Party] edited by the Chinese Department of the Nihon Kokusai Mondai Kenkyūjo (Japanese International Problems Research Center) (Tokyo, 1971), vol. 7, bibliography, p. 29, the Shanghai edition of *Tou-cheng* was published until May 8, 1934 (through no. 72).
33. The Second Soviet Congress concerned itself mostly with problems of the soviets in southern China, but Manchuria received some attention. Among the

The Fifth Plenum's resolution on "The Current Situation and the Tasks of the Party,"[34] adopted on January 18, contained a section on anti-imperial struggle and the movements in Manchuria. It stressed the importance of struggling for the formation of a united front from below, strengthening of the leadership of the proletariat within the united front, propagation of the three-point declaration of the soviet government issued on January 10, exposure of the true nature of the KMT, and expansion of mass organizations for anti-imperial and anti-Japanese struggles. More specifically, the Communists in Manchuria were told to actively participate in the volunteer armies, to dispatch trustworthy comrades and "labor elements" to strengthen them, and to conclude agreements on joint operations with various anti-Japanese groups "based on clear revolutionary principles." The anti-Japanese struggle, furthermore, was to be tied closely with the movement for land reform and the overthrow of the gentry and landlords; people's regimes were to be established, campaigns for withholding payment of taxes were to be organized in Japanese-occupied areas, and the masses were to be encouraged to ignore all orders issued by Manchukuo and the Japanese authorities.[35] Sharp-eyed cadres in Manchuria would have noticed that the Fifth Plenum's directives on land reform continued the Central Committee's previous policies, which varied significantly from Li Wei-han's criticisms. The January 18 resolution called for determined struggle against rich farmers and for confiscation and redistribution of lands belonging to the landlords and gentry. Only the middle farmers and poor farmers were to be rallied around the party.[36] Prudent cadres

---

700 delegates at the congress was one Ho Te from Manchuria, who was elected to the 57-member presidium of the congress. Like many others, Ho delivered a short speech in support of Mao Tse-tung's main address; he also appealed for the soviets' support of the struggle in Manchuria. On the fourth day of the congress, January 26, delegates from the "white area" (enemy-occupied territory) held a meeting, dealing particularly with guerrilla warfare. Here, Ho raised some practical questions that had arisen in Manchuria, such as that of the relationship between the Northeastern Volunteer Army and the workers. The February letter also indicates that discussions took place between the central leaders and the delegates. At the end of the congress, Yang Ching-yü of Panshih was elected a full member of the Central Executive Committee of the Chinese Soviet Republic (ranking 86th of 175), the highest political organ of the republic of Juichin. (Yang was mentioned under his earlier alias, Chang Kuan-i, which he evidently was still using at this time.) Hatano Kenichi, *Chūgoku kyōsantō-shi* [History of the Chinese Communist Party] (Tokyo, 1961), vol. 4, pp. 71–72, 91, 98–99; Klein and Clark, *Biographic Dictionary*, vol. 2, p. 1075.

34. The resolution was published in *Tou-cheng* (Juichin), no. 47 (February 16, 1934), pp. 1–6. A Japanese translation is available in *Shiryō-shū*, vol. 7, pp. 12–30.
35. *Shiryō-shū*, vol. 7, pp. 27–28.
36. Ibid., pp. 25–27.

would have hesitated to vigorously implement these directives under such conditions.

These points were naturally incorporated into the February letter, and it is possible to argue that the CCP leaders did not show marked change in their attitude. The letter again stressed the need to build a strong base among the urban workers, the need for very broad mass support of the anti-Japanese front, and the importance of adhering to the basic strategy for a united front from below. The CCP leaders were still against the KMT and all the counterrevolutionary groups, and they saw the purpose of the struggle in Manchuria as being the isolation of the bourgeoisie. They again criticized the Manchurian cadres for minimizing the importance of land reform and for their neglect of the "daily economic struggles" of the workers and farmers.

Nevertheless, the February letter betrays a subtle shift in the central leaders' priority, from a class-oriented movement to an anti-Japanese movement that would encompass broader segments of the population. For instance, the February letter emphasized the failure of the Manchurian Committee to expand the organization of the anti-Japanese masses. The Manchurian Committee was accused of committing the grave error of engaging in "exclusionism" and narrowly limiting participation in party activities to a few relatively progressive workers, farmers, and petty bourgeoisie in the cities. Contrary to their earlier instructions, the central leaders criticized the committee for using such a slogan as "Protection of the (Chinese) Soviet and Red Army, and Unity with the Soviet Union" in its anti-Japanese propaganda. The Panshih People's Revolutionary Army was criticized for including in its platform a call for "Protection of the CCP, Organizer and Leader of the People's Revolutionary Army." These slogans obviously would not have appealed to the non-Communist masses.[37]

Another evidence of exclusionism cited by the February letter was the failure of the Manchurian Committee to expand the anti-Japanese societies, which, according to the central leaders, had in fact become copies of the party. As a result, they still had only a few thousand members in all of Manchuria. The committee was told not to stand "outside the masses" and shout at them, but to join in their movement and become one with the masses. Only when the masses believed that the party was in fact fighting alongside them against the Japanese bandits, the February letter said, could the mass movement be expanded and the claims of the

37. *Tou-cheng* (Juichin), no. 60 (May 19, 1934), pp. 9–10.

party be accepted. It would have been highly appropriate at this point for the central leaders to recall a paragraph from their letter of June 8, 1933, on the united front, which had said that "Our slogans are understood and supported by only a small number of vanguard units; [we] have not learned how to speak to the millions of masses."[38]

It is also interesting that the February letter directed the Manchurian Committee to explain and win support for the "Basic Platform of the Chinese People in the Anti-Japanese War," as proclaimed by the "All-China People's Armed Self-Defense Committee" (Tsung-Chung-kuo Min-tzu Wu-chuang Tzu-wei Wei-yüan-hui), and to propagandize for this new organization, which the Central Committee was now trying to establish.[39] These operations were to be directed toward the workers, farmers, guerrillas, soldiers, students, petty bourgeoisie, poor people, and merchants. Those supporting the self-defense committee and its basic platform were to be mobilized to undertake joint operations against Japan.

It is significant that the February letter of the CCP headquarters mentioned the basic platform, which was not officially adopted by the self-defense committee until nearly three months later, on May 3, and that all the pronouncements of the self-defense committee were carried in the CCP organ *Hung-se Chung-hua* [Red China]. These facts leave no doubt that the self-defense committee was an organization closely associated with the CCP, although publicly it was not to be linked with the party. The self-defense committee was headed by Madame Sun Yat-sen (Sung Ch'ing-ling), and signers of the basic platform were well-known non-Communist leaders in political, military, and intellectual circles, including such figures as Ho Hsiang-ning (Madame Liao Chung-k'ai), Hu Han-min, Li Ta, and Pai Yün-t'i. It is noteworthy that Li Tu, the commander-in-chief of the Volunteer Army in Manchuria, often castigated by the CCP as in the January 1933 letter, was one of them.[40] Although the self-defense committee did not progress beyond the preparatory stage, its principles illuminate the current strategy of the CCP on the united front.[41]

From the names of the signers, it is understandable that the

38. *Tou-cheng* (Shanghai), no. 44 (June 10, 1933), p. 3.
39. *Tou-cheng* (Juichin), no. 60 (May 19, 1934), p. 15.
40. *Shiryō-shū*, vol. 7, p. 288; Wang Chien-min, *Chung-kuo kung-ch'an-tang shih-kao* [Draft History of the Chinese Communist Party] (Taipei, 1965), vol. 3, pp. 33–34.
41. *Shiryō-shū*, vol. 7, p. 288.

basic platform would not overtly advocate Communist programs. Its six-point program announced these objectives.

- To mobilize the armed forces against Japan;
- To mobilize the entire population;
- To arm the entire population;
- To collect funds to meet military expenditures against Japan;
- To organize the All-China People's Armed Self-Defense Committee, elected by the representatives of the workers, farmers, students, and merchants;
- To form an alliance with all enemies of Japanese imperialism.[42]

The central leaders' emphasis on the basic platform and the self-defense committee and the inclusion of Li Tu as a signer raises the question of how much the leaders were willing to modify the policy of a united front from below in Manchuria: in particular, would they permit the Manchurian cadres to form alliances with all anti-Japanese guerrillas who were willing to accept the basic platform? More to the point, could the Manchurian cadres establish a united front from above with groups not associated with the KMT and the national traitors? If so, the Manchurian Committee had acted correctly in following the line of Ch'en Shao-yü and issuing its June directive.

Had the leaders of the Manchurian Committee entertained the hope of such a relaxation of policy, they were destined to be sorely disappointed. The idea of establishing a united front of all the people in Manchuria, which had been presented in Ch'en Shao-yü's article and in the Manchurian Committee's directive of June 1933, was severely criticized from various angles. The directive was criticized, first of all, for saying that "the masses were entirely anti-Japanese." Such a statement, according to the February letter of the central leaders, indicated that the Manchurian cadres had forgotten the Central Committee's analysis, which found that only part of the bourgeoisie in Manchuria was hostile to the aggressors, and that this hostility was based only on self-interest; they were always ready to surrender to the enemy and betray the cause.

The cadres in Manchuria, along with Ch'en Shao-yü, were also accused of underestimating the strength of counterrevolutionary groups in Manchuria and denying their deceitfulness. The Man-

42. *Hung-se Chung-hua* [Red China], no. 236 (September 21, 1934), pp. 1–2.

churian cadres allegedly had said that the KMT had lost all influence among the masses and that other counterrevolutionary groups had not been active. They had falsely stated that the "yellow" unions had been dissolved and that "Japanese imperialism and Manchukuo are not deceitful." In the opinion of the central leaders, this kind of analysis had misled the cadres in Manchuria into slighting and even denying the need for a united front, particularly a united front from below. The central leaders emphatically denied that the influence of the KMT had disappeared among the masses and the anti-Japanese forces in Manchuria, although its influence had considerably diminished during the preceding year. This influence would not disappear completely until the party's "Bolshevik operations toward the masses" had succeeded. While the Communists' influence extended over many of the anti-Japanese groups, the KMT's influence was still strong, particularly among the leaders. The Manchurian cadres were told, therefore, to isolate all counterrevolutionary groups and intensify the struggle against them.

All these arguments, of course, led the central leaders to the conclusion that the party must continue to emphasize the strategy of a united front from below. Their basic aim was to engage in class struggle within the united front. The party must openly organize anti-Japanese societies and conferences of soldiers' representatives within the anti-Japanese units and build up solid party organizations. The party must pay special attention to the guerrillas of working-class origin. Only through a strong political and organizational base could the party achieve independent leadership of the guerrilla war; only when such a base had been built in the lower echelons of a guerrilla group was the party to form a united front with the top level of that group.

The central leaders not only criticized the erroneous analysis, timidity, and blunders of the Manchurian Committee but also instructed it to take bold steps to advance concurrently the cause of the anti-Japanese struggle and socialist revolution. The Manchurian Committee was instructed to organize or expand the people's revolutionary armies, which would be under Communist leadership and would be able to provide both political and military leadership to all anti-Japanese guerrilla units. Within the People's Revolutionary Army, political operations must be carried out to the maximum extent, and "healthy and active party organizations must be built." Also, in areas where the party was able to stabilize its military influence (i.e., in areas where either riots had succeeded or in which guerrillas had won victory), the Manchurian

Committee was instructed to establish revolutionary bases and revolutionary regimes. While the party should not push for the bases to the extent of hindering the development of guerrilla forces, there was no justifiable reason for opposing them. When the bases and regimes were established, however, revolutionary political platforms and laws must be promulgated immediately, the worker-farmer masses must be immediately armed and the counterrevolutionary elements suppressed, and all struggles of the workers and farmers, along with all anti-Japanese action, must be coordinated and protected. Within the guerrilla districts, the land and other property of the "lackeys of Japanese imperialism" must be confiscated to pay for the anti-Japanese war and to win the support of the people. "As the anti-Japanese struggle mobilizes more and more worker-farmer masses," said the central leaders, "it will correspondingly intensify the 'land movement' of the farmers against the Chinese landlords and usurers." In this connection, the party in Manchuria was again criticized for its underestimation of the land problem. The guerrilla movement was definitely to be linked with and raised to the level of land reform. That is to say, when the worker-farmer masses were sufficiently mobilized during the course of anti-Japanese struggles, they should be led to the socialist-revolutionary process of confiscating landholdings and redistributing them to the worker-farmer masses. Slogans calling for confiscation of all property of the "counterrevolutionary and traitorous elements" and refusal to pay taxes imposed by the Manchukuo government should be presented, whereby the anti-Japanese struggles would be directed toward land reform.

The central leaders were evidently concerned that their emphasis on class struggle would be criticized for weakening the anti-Japanese cause. Thus the committee was instructed to take countermeasures against the "nationalistic demagoguery" of the argument that class struggle should be modified for the sake of the anti-Japanese cause. The enemy was attempting to estrange the masses from the party by saying that the Communist party was destroying the anti-Japanese struggle, and this must be opposed.

Finally, the central leaders criticized the Manchurian Committee's failure to establish viable local party committees that could act on their own. Such committees were not yet established in major cities, and the leadership organs in guerrilla districts were very weak. The leaders in various places were of the intelligentsia and were therefore not only incapable of acting independently and spontaneously, but their link with the masses was also very weak. A certain comrade was quoted as having reported that "not even the minimum number of [capable] cadres could be found in Manchuria."[43] Citing the strikes, soldiers' revolts, and farmers' riots, and the mass nature of the anti-Japanese struggle in Manchuria, the central leaders dismissed the comrade's report as an outright fabrication but urged the committee to absorb the progressive workers in the factories and volunteer armies and enlist them into the party leadership. All the cadres in Manchuria were urged to engage in "Bolshevik self-criticism" in order to eliminate their negative attitude and positively implement the directives of the Central Committee.[44]

Thus the cadres in Manchuria were left with contradictory instructions. While the basic platform was supposedly addressed to all the people of China regardless of social or economic position, the Manchurian Committee was specifically told to approach only certain segments of the population—the workers, farmers, students, soldiers, petty bourgeoisie, and small merchants. In spite of the fact that such a "reactionary" leader as Li Tu had signed the basic platform, the committee was still enjoined from forming a united front with the non-Communist guerrillas, who were an important part of the anti-Japanese movement in Manchuria. Even before the Communist guerrillas established a solid foundation, they were to begin the work of subverting the non-Communist guerrillas. The cadres were in effect told to engage in class struggle within the united front before establishing a united front.

Why did the central leaders introduce these changes in their policy vis-à-vis Manchuria at this time? Although the CCP leadership underwent some reorganization at the Fifth Plenum of the Central Committee, there was no major change in top-level personalities,[45] and since the policy preferences of the individual leaders are not sufficiently known, we cannot attribute the change in policy to internal politics. But the leaders are likely to have been affected at this time by the continuing Japanese aggression in northern China. In April 1933, the Japanese forces penetrated the Great Wall and entered Hopei Province. The KMT government, in turn, met the current Japanese threat by accepting, in

43. "The Immediate Tasks of the Party in the Anti-Japanese War in Manchuria" (February 22, 1934), in *Shiryō-shū*, vol. 7, p. 193.
44. Ibid., p. 194.
45. James Pinckney Harrison, *The Long March to Power: A History of the Chinese Communist Party, 1921–1972* (New York, 1972), pp. 234–235.

the Tangku Truce of May 31, the Japanese demand for demilitarization of a part of Hopei Province. The Japanese appetite for conquest, however, was not assuaged. They demanded other rights and concessions in North China, and in October the KMT assigned generals Huang Fu and Ho Ying-ch'in to engage in negotiations with the Japanese Kwantung Army officers.[46]

These developments were of obvious concern to the CCP. Its agencies issued denunciatory statements on November 11 and 20,[47] and on April 10, 1934, the Central Committee issued a statement: "On the Japanese Imperialists' Invasion of North China and Their Threat of Conquest of the Entire Nation."[48] Thus, in spite of their preoccupation with the KMT's encirclement campaigns, the CCP leaders became more attuned to the need to focus their attention on the anti-Japanese struggle. They may also have been influenced by the initial success of the Communist guerrillas in Panshih and elsewhere to expand their forces by appealing to Chinese nationalism. Whatever it was that caused the central leaders to modify their policies, it was not strong enough to swing them completely toward the line of policy advocated by Ch'en Shao-yü in Moscow.

Ch'en Shao-yü's Rebuttal

What was Ch'en Shao-yü's reaction to the central leaders' January 1933 and February 1934 letters? Was he in any way critical of the central leaders? In December 1933, Ch'en delivered a speech at the Thirteenth Plenum of the Executive Committee of the Comintern and, in reviewing the achievements and problems of the CCP, touched on the situation in Manchuria.

While his speech is carefully worded so as not to criticize the CCP leadership openly, it is easy to see that he was annoyed by their recalcitrance. Ch'en said:

> In its *anti-imperialist* national revolutionary struggle the C.C. [Central Committee] waged and is still waging a struggle throughout the whole country, especially in Manchuria and North China, *against the views which express distrust in the ability of the broad armed masses of the people to carry to a victorious conclu-*

---

46. For details, see T. A. Bisson, *Japan in China* (New York, 1938), pp. 40–77.
47. *Shiryō-shū*, vol. 6, pp. 671–682.
48. The text of this statement was published in *Tou-cheng* (Juichin), no. 59, (May 15, 1934) and ibid. (Shanghai), no. 71 (April 23, 1934).

sion the national revolutionary war against Japanese and other imperialists. On the other hand, the Party fought against the unwillingness and the failure to understand, and the inability to create and strengthen the united anti-imperialist front of all forces fighting under the banner, under the leadership, of the proletariat in accordance with the concrete conditions of any given place. . . .[49]

Despite the tremendous successes achieved by the Party and the revolutionary movement, still if one compares the strength of the subjective factor with the demands and possibilities of the objective situation, the relative lagging of the first behind the second becomes clearly apparent. The objective situation in present-day China is such that if the Party intensified its work we would have every possibility of winning over all who may be called honest "defenders of the nation" who are unwilling to be the slaves of the Japanese or other imperialists and who are ready to sacrifice their lives to save their native land and their people.[50]

Thus, Ch'en found the party's efforts to win over the "honest 'defenders of the nation'" insufficient. Of particular interest is his definition of the "defenders of the nation" as all those "unwilling to be the slaves of the Japanese or other imperialists" and "ready to sacrifice their lives to save their native land and their people." This definition would include the bourgeoisie and the bourgeoisie-supported guerrilla leaders, and even the leaders of those guerrillas classified in the "first category," the former Kirin Army groups, distrusted by the central leaders.

Ch'en's discussion of the "new tasks—working under new conditions in a new way" is also suggestive. Among the immediate tasks was the "all-around development of the anti-Japanese mass partisan movement (especially in Manchuria and North China)"[51] and the control of the leadership of this movement. Elaborating on this point, Ch'en said:

Today we have every possibility legally and semi-legally, whenever the opportunity presents itself, to

49. Wang Ming [Ch'en Shao-yü] and Kan Sing [K'ang Sheng], *Revolutionary China Today* (Moscow and Leningrad, 1934), p. 65 (emphasis in the original).
50. Ibid., p. 67 (emphasis in the original).
51. Ibid., p. 75.

bring up and discuss this question of the way out of the national crisis, to *discuss it among all strata of the nation and all mass organizations*, to prove to the masses the correctness of our revolutionary slogans and to lead them to decisive action.[52]

However, Ch'en did not openly attack the CCP leaders in the published version of his speech. At least his comrades in Juichin had accepted his advice to abandon their exclusive reliance on a united front from below. Perhaps Ch'en and the Comintern leaders were not ready to push the Chinese leaders too far, too fast. After all, the comrades in Juichin were confronted by more urgent and desperate problems. It may have been thought prudent to allow the central leaders more time to bring about the required change.

Conclusion

Why were the central leaders so slow to change their policies toward Manchuria? Was not the situation in Manchuria sufficiently different—as Ch'en Shao-yü and the Manchurian cadres repeatedly argued—to warrant a different strategy?

As suggested earlier, the needs and premises of the central leaders were very different from those of either the Comintern (Ch'en Shao-yü) or the Manchurian cadres. To those in Juichin, no task was more urgent and sacred than that of the destruction of class enemies. From their perspective, the survival of the entire Communist movement in China depended on this task. To be sure, the Japanese aggressors needed to be repelled; but, for the central leaders, confronted by tight rings of KMT encirclement, the principal enemy was the domestic counterrevolutionary forces and not Japanese imperialism. Only when the Japanese began to engulf all of northern China did the central leaders begin to reassess their position. In this sense, the CCP leaders in Juichin agreed with Chiang Kai-shek and the KMT government that the destruction of internal enemies was more necessary than the defense of China against the Japanese invasion. The assessment and needs of the Manchurian cadres and the Comintern, on the other hand, were exactly the reverse. The differences shown between Li Weihan's article and the Central Committee's February letter also suggest that the central leaders were also divided among themselves on the Manchurian issue.

52. Ibid. (emphasis in the original).

It is, of course, possible that the central leaders, or at least the majority of them, were genuinely concerned that the nascent Communist movement in Manchuria might be smothered by much stronger nationalist forces with or without connections with the KMT and Chang Hsüeh-liang's forces; the CCP in Manchuria, in other words, might end up playing the role of the tail rather than the head of the anti-Japanese movement. Between 1933 and 1934, such a risk was definitely present; hence the central leaders insisted that the CCP in Manchuria follow the strategy of a united front from below. It is clear, however, that the cadres in the front line did not find this strategy appropriate. Dogmatic enforcement of such a strategy led them nowhere. More flexibility was clearly needed. Therefore, in spite of repeated admonitions from the central leaders, the Manchurian cadres followed a more flexible course.

From the Comintern's perspective, however, the risk of the Communist groups being smothered by other groups would have been worth taking. For the main concern in Moscow was the defense of the Soviet Union. While the Comintern would have preferred the Communists to assume leadership of the anti-Japanese movement in Manchuria, this would have been a matter of secondary importance to them. The Soviet leaders perceived Japan's presence in Manchuria and northern China as a real threat on the Far Eastern front. The anti-Japanese movement in Manchuria needed to be revived. When the CCP leadership demurred, however, the Comintern leaders were willing to settle for a compromise.

The central leaders in Kiangsi, on the other hand, may have feared that yielding to Ch'en's—and Comintern's—views would lead to the relinquishing of control over the party organization in Manchuria. As the appointment of Li Yao-k'uei in Moscow indicates, the CCP Central Committee had already given up some of its powers in Manchuria. Allowing the Manchurian Committee to follow the different strategy advocated by Ch'en would have been tantamount to yielding control to Moscow.

More importantly, perhaps, the call for a separate policy in Manchuria violated the sacred principle of a single, unified Chinese nation. For the Chinese Communists, who had come to communism not only because of their sense of justice but also because of their desire to modernize China and to restore the integrity and grandeur of the Middle Kingdom, the idea of devising different policies for different regions—thus in fact creating autonomous party branches—was repugnant. For the Chinese, who were just emerging from the warlord era, this would have been simply too much to bear. They would have been much more sensitive to this issue vis-à-vis Manchuria, not only because the three northeastern provinces were the last to be integrated into the Republic of China but also because China's hold on that region was very precarious in the early 1930s.

7 | Radicalism versus United Front among the Guerrillas

IF THERE WAS ONE THING THAT COMMUNIST LEADERS everywhere could agree upon with respect to the Communist movement in Manchuria in the early 1930s, it was that the party had theretofore been ineffective in building a viable foundation. Repeated attempts to build an organizational base among the proletariat had been squashed by the hostile police. The party had failed to establish a firm footing, even though the Central Committee had dispatched to Manchuria some of the more experienced cadres who had proven their ability in other parts of China. Building the party foundation was, therefore, the principal task facing the Chinese Communist Party (CCP).

Communist leaders would also have agreed that the party needed to play a more active and positive role in the anti-Japanese movement. The party's hope to assume leadership of the movement, of course, was still a distant dream.

While they could agree on these needs and weaknesses, the leaders were in disagreement regarding the means to improve the situation. The central leaders consistently blamed the local cadres for their failure to build the proletarian foundation, but the fact that even the experienced leaders were not able to make headway indicated that forces far greater than individual cadres were working against them. While the local cadres may have recognized the need to build a party based on the proletariat, they probably felt that the central leaders underestimated the harshness of the environment in Manchuria.

The difference of views on strategies toward the anti-Japanese movement, on the other hand, was much more visible. Ch'en Shao-yü in Moscow and the local cadres in Manchuria were of the opinion that anti-Japanese sentiment and the resolve to resist Japanese imperialism were much more widespread in Manchuria than the CCP's central leaders perceived them to be. Ch'en and the local leaders also favored a broad united front involving all anti-Japanese groups and individuals, while the central leaders insisted on the so-called "united front from below" strategy.

We have examined aspects of debates on these matters in the two preceding chapters. We shall now review the actual course of events in Manchuria, first examining the efforts of the Manchurian Provincial Committee to build a base among the urban workers to determine whether the committee indeed neglected its assigned task and failed to faithfully implement party instructions as the central leaders alleged, and then examining the successes and failures of the Communists in Manchuria in building a guerrilla force. The events of the period from 1932 to 1934 are particularly interesting and important in this regard because the Communist cadres in different regions pursued different policy lines. Since directives from Moscow and Shanghai ordered two different kinds of strategies, this was perhaps inevitable. Personalities and local conditions, therefore, played a much more important role in determining the strategies and tactics employed in different regions.

The General Condition of the CCP in 1933

We have noted earlier that the Communists in Manchuria suffered a major blow in October 1932, when many Communists were arrested in Mukden, Dairen, Harbin, and elsewhere. Lo Teng-hsien was recalled to Shanghai in December, and Li Yao-k'uei was dispatched from Moscow in May 1933 to direct the movement in Manchuria. What was the condition of the party when Li arrived on the scene?

No major party document of this period has yet come to light, but a resolution adopted by the Manchurian Provincial Committee of the Communist Youth Corps (CYC) on March 29, 1933, a month or so before Li's arrival, reveals the condition and aspirations of the party and the CYC. While the goals of the CYC were not identical with those of the party, particularly with regard to recruitment, the leadership of the two organizations frequently overlapped, and the information revealed in the CYC resolution may be used as an approximate guide to ascertain the general condition of the party as well.

The purpose of the March resolution was to turn the month of May 1933 into "the Month of Red Assault," when the "raging tide of national revolutionary war was to reach a new height,"[1] but most of it was devoted to a review of the situation in Manchuria. Evidently the purge of the Manchurian Committee, launched soon after the Northern Conference of June 1932, continued through early 1933, and it was conducted on a wide scale. Neither the provincial committee cadres nor the local cadres seem to have been spared. Indeed, the purge and rectification of the cadres and members was one of the major goals of the "winter assault season." The resolution said that, under the correct leadership of the Central Committee and the Comintern, "elementary results" had been attained in the struggle against the opportunist line of the provincial committee. The new provincial committee then established the "correct" leadership line; major CYC branches in Harbin, Mukden, Panshih, Chuho, Hailung, and Suining began to "shed opportunism and defeatism"; local corps in Panshih, Hailung, and Chuho also countered their earlier defeatism and escapism and overcame the weaknesses and decay in their organizations, becoming stronger and making progress in some sectors. In Panshih and Hailung, some progress was made in activities directed toward the guerrillas, and operations were also begun in Kirin and Changchun. The Chuho branch also produced great results in the area east of the Sungari River, particularly at Weishaho, where it led the revolt of 500 soldiers. In Harbin, the struggle against the counterrevolutionary faction and the Korean factional elements lodged in the provincial committee was launched, and "although it was still in the preliminary stage, the corps in Harbin was no longer in a state of grave crisis."[2] Inspection of the nine major districts under the provincial committee, including those at the Chinese Eastern Railway, Chuho, Panshih, the Kirin–Changchun Railway, and the Hulan–Hailun Railway showed that considerable results had been obtained.[3]

In the course of criticizing itself for past defects, the Manchurian Committee of the CYC revealed the state of affairs:

1. The struggle for the national revolutionary war continued to remain an empty slogan, and no visible result has been attained. Activities directed toward the Volunteer Army and the organization of the young

---

1. A Japanese translation of the resolution was sent from the consul general in Harbin (Morishima Morito) to the Japanese ambassador to Manchukuo on May 13, 1933. See AJMFA reel S382, file S9452-12, pp. 1218–1250.
2. Ibid., pp. 1223–26.
3. Ibid., p. 1226.

volunteer army and the young vanguards (*shao-nien hsien-feng-tui*) achieved no substantial results.
2. Activities in the factories have been abandoned, and the struggle of the young workers has not been given firm leadership. The union movement has been abandoned, and no result has been attained in the operations directed toward the unemployed youth.
3. There have been no accomplishments in the work regarding the protection of the Soviet Union, the Chinese soviet, and the Red Army.
4. There has been no result in the expansion and consolidation of the corps. The organizational foundation of the corps is very narrow, and the young workers occupy a very weak position within it. Nothing was accomplished through the "New Year's Struggle" or in the campaign for new members commemorating the anniversary of the Japanese invasion of Shanghai (January 28).
5. Because of the lack of resolve to select cadres and because of the absence of detailed educational activities, there is a shortage of cadres.
6. An extremely difficult situation emerged in the Harbin organization because of the bad influence of liberalism within the previous provincial committee. The committee suffered considerable loss, and the membership of the corps actually decreased. The district in the outskirts of Harbin has collapsed as a result of opportunistic leadership, and the central city district has only recently resumed its activities after a long period of stagnation.
7. There has been no progress in the corps branch in Mukden, and the corps membership there is very small.[4]

This was a very dismal picture indeed. Hence, the provincial committee of the CYC designated the month of May as a special "Month of Red Assault" to overcome the defects of the past. Since all the defects of the past were attributed to the wrong attitudes of the former leadership in Manchuria, and since a new leadership had been installed, it was logical to hope for the "raging tide" to reach a new height. The tasks of the corps members—and those of the CCP members—were clear-cut. The resolution stated:

4. Ibid., pp. 1227–28.

The CYC in Manchuria, under the leadership of the party, must rapidly lead and organize the young worker-farmer masses in Manchuria, join in the national revolutionary war and expand it, assume leadership of the national revolutionary war, establish soviet districts, organize red armies, elect governments of the masses, protect with arms the Soviet Union and the Chinese Soviet Red Army, and lead the young working masses and save them from starvation.[5]

Did the "Month of Red Assault" improve the situation for the party? Particularly, did the party and youth corps respond to the exhortations of the central and provincial leaders to arouse and organize the urban workers?

Evidence indicates that the cadres in Manchuria did indeed heed the criticisms of the central leaders and attempt to organize the urban workers as much as possible. But, as in the past, the Japanese and Japanese-directed Manchukuo police were much too efficient for the cadres to circumvent. Using the slightest of clues, the police tenaciously pursued the organizers, making it quite impossible for the party to plant roots among the workers. There were other factors, such as the nature of the appeals used by the CCP, but these were overshadowed by the problem of police suppression.

For example, T'ao Ho-hsiang and several others had been working among the miners in Fushun and had organized the Fushun Coal Mine Workers' Labor Union. They had advocated the improvement of the treatment of miners and had planned to organize a general strike on the anniversary of the May 30 Incident, but the Japanese military police discovered the secret network and rounded up five cadres of the CCP on April 11, 1933.[6]

The Manchurian Committee also dispatched three cadres to Penhsihu, another important mining center near Fushun, where efforts were made to recruit sympathizers, but the alert police destroyed the organization, not only in Penhsihu but also in Mukden, one of the most important centers of Communist activities in Manchuria. Since this incident reveals the thoroughness with

---

5. Ibid., p. 1224.
6. Okamoto Goichi, "The Chinese Communist Party and the Communist Bandits in Manchuria," in Shihō-shō, Keiji-kyoku (Bureau of Criminal Affairs, Ministry of Justice, Japan), *Shisō jōsei shisatsu hōkokushū, 4: Manshū ni okeru kyōsanshugi undō* [Reports of Inspection Tours of Ideological Conditions, 4: The Communist Movement in Manchuria] (Tokyo, 1938), pp. 8–9. This source does not say on what date the Fushun union was established.

which the Japanese pursued subversive elements, some details should be provided.

On May 1 and May 30, the anniversaries of May Day and the May 30 Incident, the Japanese authorities in Penhsihu discovered leaflets, posters, and magazines issued in the name of the Penhsihu Special Branch of the CCP and the CYC. Although we do not know the content of the leaflets and posters, copies of two issues of *Lien-ho-pao* [United News] issued in the name of the CYC Penhsihu branch indicate the general line of propaganda. Short articles in them emphasized the low pay and long hours of the workers and the heartlessness and brutality of the Japanese and Chinese foremen and supervisors. One out of the five articles in each of the issues also dealt with the anti-Japanese theme, recalling the Japanese "massacre" of the Chinese in Tsinan in 1929 (May 3) and the Twenty-One Demands pressed on the Chinese government by the Japanese in 1915 (May 7), the acceptance of which had virtually subordinated China to Japan's will. The need to organize an anti-Japanese army was strongly emphasized.[7] Needless to say, the police were alerted, and the search for the culprits began.

On June 18, a Japanese police officer arrested a suspicious Chinese at an athletic meet celebrating the second anniversary of the establishment of Manchukuo. Upon interrogation, he confessed that he had joined the Anti-Japanese National Salvation Society (Fan-Jih Chiu-kuo Hui) upon the recommendation of Yang Yü-tien, a clerk in the mining company. The arrested man, a young man of 21 years, had been attempting to enlist other mine workers in his group. During the interrogation, however, the man committed suicide. The police went to arrest Yang, but he had resigned his post in April and had already left for Mukden. The police, however, discovered that Yang's brother was working in another mine nearby, and arrested him on June 19. The police quickly learned that Yang Yü-tien was teaching at the First Normal School in Mukden and that while in Penhsihu he had communicated with a man named Wang Yü-nan. The First Normal School in Mukden obviously became an object for search.[8]

The police did not find Yang Yü-tien there, but they did locate Wang Yü-nan, who confessed that Yang had been his schoolmate,

---

7. The contents of two issues of *Lien-ho-pao* [United News] (No. 2, May 18, 1933, and No. 3, May 30, 1933), the organ of the Penhsihu Special Branch of the CYC, are preserved in Japanese translation in AJMFA reel S382, file 9451-12, pp. 1323–1341.

8. Okamoto Goichi, "Chinese Communist Party and Bandits," pp. 9–11.

and that it was upon his recommendation that Wang had joined the Anti-Japanese National Salvation Society in early May. The police also learned that Wang had been meeting Wang Shu-te, also a schoolmate and member of the society, twice a week at a botanical garden. Wang Yü-nan was taken to the garden at the regular rendezvous hour. When Wang Shu-te showed up, he was given an eye signal by his friend and began to move away, but the police arrested him. It was subsequently learned that Wang Shu-te was the head of the propaganda department of the Mukden Special Committee of the Communist Youth Corps, and that Wang Yü-tien, the man whom the police had sought in Penhsihu, was the head of the printing department of both the youth corps and the party. It was only a matter of time before other leading cadres of the special committee were rounded up. By June 28, the police had taken 38 cadres into custody, including the head of the party's special committee, Yang I-ch'en, and six members of the Penhsihu Special Branch.[9]

The Japanese found that the CCP's Mukden Special Committee had produced significant results since its destruction by the Japanese military police nine months before in September 1932. They learned, for example, that the special committee had established seven branches in various industrial enterprises and schools, including at least seven and perhaps more than a dozen secondary schools, the Mukden Arsenal (more than ten), the Mukden Textile Mill (approximately 30), the railroad stations (20), and the police (number unknown).[10] Aside from the party and the youth corps, a number of peripheral organizations had been established, such as the Mukden General Labor Union, the Anti-Japanese National Salvation Society, the Mutual Aid Society, and the Youth Vanguard Society. Activities directed toward nonparty organizations had just begun, however, and the memberships of these societies were still minute. For example, the union had only approximately 20 members, the anti-Japanese society (organized in May) only a handful, and so on. The Mutual Aid Society was

9. It appears, however, that the Japanese gendarmes and Manchukuo police had other leads. On June 18, for example, a Chinese policeman in the employ of the Manchukuo police in Mukden learned the general area frequented by Yang I-ch'en and narrowed the search. It was learned somehow that Yang was to meet the head of the engineering office of the Mukden–Shanhaikuan Railway at the Mukden railway station on June 21. A police sergeant was sent in disguise to meet Yang. At the rendezvous, Yang agreed to bring other party members on the following day. On June 22, Yang was arrested with thirteen kinds of documents in his possession. See "Detailed Report on the Arrest of the Chinese Communist Party [Members]," AJMFA reel S386, file 9452-15, p. 13.
10. Ibid., p. 7.

dissolved in April because its leader was arrested by the police on April 10.[11]

The activities of the Mukden Special Committee were not confined to the city of Mukden alone, however. It had branches in a number of cities and towns in the vicinity, such as Changwu, Peichen, Taian, Liaochung, Liaoyang, Antung, Penhsihu, and Fushun. The total membership is listed by Japanese interrogators as 1,600 to 1,700, but it is quite possible that the figures include those recruited into various peripheral organizations.[12]

In addition to recruiting activities, the party cadres had also frequently mimeographed and distributed propaganda leaflets and pamphlets. At least eighteen different kinds of leaflets bearing party declarations and slogans were distributed during the nine months, the number of copies distributed on each occasion being between 150 and 200. The special committee also issued a publication, first called *Workers' Life* (*Kung-jen sheng-huo*) (November 1932) and later changed to *Workers' Way* (*Kung-jen chih lu*) (No. 1, February; No. 6, May, 1933). Various cadres also traveled to such places as Penhsihu to confer with cadres there.[13] Considering the number of members recruited and the quantity of propaganda materials produced and distributed, much seems to have been accomplished in Mukden. The cadres had also taken considerable precautions against detection by not maintaining a roster of membership and keeping the names and addresses of the members secret, even among the members.[14] This prevented the Japanese police from rounding up all those connected with the party. The party members had also been forewarned not to divulge party secrets if arrested. Indeed, they had been told that they would be executed by the party after their release from jail if they confessed to the enemy.[15] But the Japanese interrogators were thoroughly familiar with human frailties. Be they Chinese, Japanese, or Korean, very few of those arrested by the Japanese police for subversive activities managed to outwit their interrogators.

Cadres in other cities were also being arrested. On May 13, the Japanese military police rounded up twenty-three youth corps members in Kirin. The Japanese and Manchukuo police had been on the alert since March, when subversive leaflets were discovered in various locations in the city. Most of those implicated

11. Okamoto Goichi, "Chinese Communist Party and Bandits," p. 16.
12. "Detailed Report," p. 16.
13. Okamoto Goichi, "Chinese Communist Party and Bandits," pp. 15–18.
14. "Detailed Report," p. 30.
15. Ibid., p. 32.

were students of secondary schools in which the organization of youth corps branches had been in progress since 1931.[16]

Thus, the situation in the cities was precarious for the CCP and CYC cadres, and the continuing arrests had a demoralizing effect on the surviving members. Indeed, one of the cadres in Mukden was so discouraged and demoralized that he surrendered to the Japanese police on October 8, 1933, causing the destruction of the party organization in Dairen. Yü Chi-hsien, 27 years old in 1933, had joined the party in 1931 at his home town in Shantung, where he served as a cadre in district and *hsien* party organizations and was later appointed a political commissar of the Lunan Red Guerrillas. When the unit was crushed by the local warlord, he fled to Shanghai, and after six months training there, he volunteered for activities in Dairen, arriving in April 1933. Many former comrades from Lunan were active in Dairen, and he found it easy to adapt to the situation there. But on September 28 he was transferred to Mukden by Chang Yu-ts'ai, the newly appointed secretary of the Mukden Special Committee. Yü was so discouraged by the situation in Mukden that only ten days later he surrendered himself to the Japanese.[17]

The Japanese police should have been elated. Using the leads provided by Yü, they arrested Chang Yu-ts'ai and two other CCP cadres in Mukden who had been attempting to reconstruct the party. Then, on October 19, the police took Yü to Dairen and, using him as a guide, arrested eight cadres in Shahokou, where the largest machine manufacturing and repair plant of the South Manchuria Railway Company was located. The police found that the Dairen City Committee of the CCP had organized at least six branches, with several members in each branch. Among the arrested was the secretary of the Dairen City Committee, Chang Lo-shu, a party veteran since 1927. Judging from Chang's previous experience, the Manchurian Committee must have attached considerable importance to activities in Dairen. Chang, who was from Shantung Province and was 28 years old in 1933, had joined the Kuomintang in 1924 at the age of 19, and he worked in the Tsinan City Committee of the KMT. In 1927 he joined the CCP, and by 1928 he was serving as the secretary of the Kao-mi *Hsien*

---

16. *Chūgai Shōgyō Shimbun*, October 11, 1933. An article from this newspaper is in AJMFA reel S386, file S9452-15, p. 2. An article from the *Ōsaka Asahi Shimbun*, October 14, 1933, concerning the same incident, is on p. 72.

17. "Arrest of the CCP Dairen City Committee Members," report of the Chief of the Police Bureau, Kwantung Leased Territory, to various agencies, November 1, 1933, AJMFA reel S386, file S9452-15, pp. 74–87.

Committee. He was selected to go to the Soviet Union for further training in 1929 but was forced to return from Chita by a heart ailment. He was sent to Mukden in 1931 and later to Harbin, where he served as the head of the organizational department of the city committee. He was also given the important assignment of inspector of the CCP organizations along the Chinese Eastern Railway. It was under his leadership that the Dairen Special Branch was made a city committee, indicating the expanded level of activities there.[18] But a demoralized cadre nullified the efforts of Chang and his colleagues.

Communist party members in Harbin itself were not immune from arrest. On October 28, 1933, the Japanese consular police arrested Ch'en Ping-chang, the head of the propaganda and education department of the Manchurian committee of the youth corps. Ch'en, 22, had been a member of left-wing organizations in Shanghai, such as the Shanghai Writers' Union, and had been to Harbin in July 1931. But he soon returned to Shanghai to serve as the secretary of the youth corps' Kiangsu Provincial Committee. In December 1931, after the Japanese takeover of Manchuria, he was assigned to the Manchurian Committee of the CCP in Mukden. When the Manchurian Committee moved to Harbin, he was transferred there.[19]

If Ch'en told the truth to his Japanese interrogators, the overall condition of the CCP and the youth corps in Manchuria was not auspicious. The corps was supposed to receive 400 silver dollars a month from the Central Committee, but these funds did not arrive regularly. Ch'en told his interrogators that "because of the KMT's attack against the Chinese soviets in the South, the Central Committee tended to slight the Manchurian Committee." Ch'en also said that while there were 700 youth corps members in Manchuria, "very few of them understood communism." His assessment of his colleagues in the CYC Manchurian Committee was also quite low: "Their educational level is low and they are not qualified to lead corps members." It was not the CYC alone that was having difficulties. Ch'en said that the CCP activities in Manchuria were even weaker than those of the CYC.[20] The continuing arrests were having an effect.

In spite of these weaknesses and the continuing arrests, the cadres continued their organizational efforts. As soon as some

18. Ibid., p. 82.
19. Report of the Consul-General in Harbin to Foreign Minister, November 15, 1933, in AJMFA reel S386, file S9452-15, pp. 89–97.
20. Ibid., pp. 93–95.

of the leading cadres were arrested, others took their place and strove to rebuild the organization. But the odds were clearly against them. It was almost impossible for any Communist organization to elude the Japanese for more than a few months.

The Japanese records reveal additional arrests of Communist cadres in northern and southern Manchuria in April 1934. The police had detected the existence of party branches in Harbin, Mukden, Changchun, and Shuangcheng and launched a massive campaign to arrest the leading cadres on April 8. Hu Pin, the head of the Organization Department of the Manchurian Provincial Committee of the Communist Youth Corps, was arrested on the same day. Yang An-jen, the head of the propaganda department of the same committee, was soon netted, and so was Chou Hsiang-nan, the head of the secretariat of the committee. The printing department of the CYC committee was raided and important documents were confiscated on April 9. In Shuangcheng, where the CCP had its *hsien* committee as well as the important Eastern Kirin Bureau, the police arrested two Koreans and 22 Chinese cadres, confiscating some important documents as well.[21] In May, taking a cue from propaganda materials found at the Mukden Wool Company, the police arrested four Korean and 48 Chinese cadres in Mukden and nearby cities who had been active in organizing branches at various factories. One of those arrested was Yang Ta-ts'ung, the head of the Mukden Special Committee, who had been operating in Mukden since October 1933.[22] The Mukden committee, which had been under the direct command of the CCP Central Committee since July 1933,[23] not only lost its chief but the heads of the organization, propaganda, and secretarial departments.[24] Thus, the carefully rebuilt organizations were again completely demolished, although some leading cadres, including a cadre named Ma, who had been the acting secretary of the Manchurian Committee since Li Yao-k'uei's arrest, were still at large.

21. Japanese Ambassador to Manchukuo in Changchun to Foreign Minister, in AJMFA reel S386, file S9452-15, pp. 114–127. See also East Asia Bureau, Ministry of Foreign Affairs, Japan, *Shina oyobi Manshū ni okeru saikin no kyōsan undō shiryō* [Materials on the Communist Movement in China and Manchuria in the Recent Period] (Tokyo, 1934), pp. 151–161.
22. Japanese Ambassador to Manchukuo in Changchun to Foreign Minister, May 13, 1934, AJMFA reel S386, file S9452-15, pp. 133–145.
23. Ibid., p. 195.
24. Ibid., p. 134. Also arrested in May was Mun Kap-song, the head of the Liao-T'ai (Liaochung and Taian) *hsien* committee in Liaochung. Mun, a veteran Korean Communist leader, had played a leading role in organizing the guerrillas in Panshih and the anti-Japanese riot in Chientao. Mun and his wife had operated in Liaochung and Taian for approximately two years, having disguised themselves as Chinese. Ibid., pp. 137–138.

What was more damaging to the Communist movement as a whole was that the youth corps leaders in Harbin, such as Hu Pin and Yang An-jen, decided to collaborate with the Japanese and Manchukuo police after their arrests. Hu Pin told the police that the CCP had agents in the Manchurian government; he identified Li Yao-k'uei, who had been arrested in October 1933 on suspicion of being a bandit, as the head of the CCP's Manchurian Committee. The police naturally conducted a frantic search and found Li in a jail in Pinchiang, where he was serving a sentence of 14 months at hard labor.[25] Li had been a member of the CCP since 1925 and attended Sun Yat-sen University in Moscow from 1926 until he graduated in 1929.[26] Leads provided by Hu Pin also netted Li's "beautiful wife," Sung Lan-yün, a graduate of the Vladivostok Normal School, who was regarded as an influential party member. She edited the organ of the Manchurian Committee, *Tung-pei Min-chung-pao* [Manchurian People's News], and served as a liaison cadre between the party and the youth corps.[27]

Li's wife and some of the others arrested resisted all attempts to squeeze information out of them, and it was necessary for the police to feed Mrs. Li intravenously when she went on a hunger strike;[28] but the police did obtain some useful information from Li Yao-k'uei himself. They learned, for example, that at the time of Li's arrest on October 30, 1933, there were approximately 1,800 party members and 700 youth corps members throughout Manchuria, membership in both organizations overlapping in some cases. The party had only about 70 "combat unit members." The Manchurian committees of the party and the youth corps received 1,000 silver dollars a month from the CCP headquarters, of which 500 to 600 dollars was spent to operate the provincial committee. The Manchurian Committee also maintained a military committee to direct military operations.

Li Yao-k'uei insisted that there was no connection between the Manchurian Committee and the Comintern or the USSR but admitted that the Harbin branch of the Profintern's Pacific Secretariat provided guidance for the workers' movement among the Chinese and that there were approximately 100 "worker-comrades" in Harbin, probably meaning that these workers supported the party.

In view of the party's continuing concern to win over the anti-Japanese fighters in Manchuria, it is significant that, according to Li Yao-k'uei, the major task of the Eastern Kirin Bureau was to

25. Ibid., p. 149.   26. Ibid., pp. 185–186.   27. Ibid., pp. 156, 187.
28. Ibid., p. 166.

win over these fighters in eastern Manchuria along the Manchurian-Soviet border. By the time Li was arrested, the bureau had won over considerable numbers of anti-Japanese fighters, as follows:[29]

Wang Te-lin Unit	700–800
Ch'en Tung-shan Unit	500–600
Chin Shan Unit	700
Wu I-ch'eng Unit	300
Liu K'uai-t'ui Unit	800
Ch'ing Shan Unit	300
Chung Hou Unit	200
Chi Hsing Unit	80
Sun Ch'ao-yang Unit	400
Ta-p'ai Unit	40
Shanlin Unit (bandits)	20

We have examined the fortunes of the Manchurian Committee in the cities in some detail, particularly because of the repeated denunciations by the CCP headquarters of the alleged shortcomings of the Manchurian Committee. The facts, however, were not as simple as the central leaders made them out to be. The truth is that subversive organizers cannot make much headway when the government in power is determined to eradicate its opponents and possesses an efficient security system, and when socio-economic conditions are not so desperate that a large number of the populace would readily accept the challenges—and risks—presented by the revolutionaries. The CCP leaders in Kiangsi and elsewhere must have known that such indeed was the case. It was the efficient police system in the Kuomintang-occupied areas that forced the CCP to abandon any serious attempt to organize the workers in the cities of central and southern China and finally compelled the central leaders to retreat to safety in the Kiangsi hinterland. Their ideological appeals for the cause of proletarian revolution were largely unanswered by the workers.

Guerrillas in Eastern Manchuria

The central leaders' policy of stressing land reform in the rural sector as well as the adoption of the "united front from below" strategy with regard to the anti-Japanese groups underwent a severe test in Chientao in eastern Manchuria along the Korean

29. All the information attributed to Li Yao-k'uei is from ibid., pp. 184–195. Report of Japanese Ambassador in Changchun to Foreign Minister, May 22, 1934.

border. As we have seen in chapter 4, Chientao was the scene of a series of Communist-directed riots and other acts of violence in 1930. A large majority of the population in that region was Korean, and over 50 percent of the Korean farmers were indigent tenant farmers. Their economic condition in the early 1930s was much worse than before, particularly because of the worldwide depression, which had caused a drastic decrease in the price of soybeans grown for export.[30] Capitalizing on this situation, the East Manchurian Special Committee had vigorously pushed land reform since late 1930, confiscating the land and property of the landlords in some villages and distributing them to the indigent.[31] The slogans circulated by the committee called for confiscation of land belonging to landlords, seizure of political power from the "local rascals and oppressive gentry," abolition of exploitive taxes and sundry imposts, elimination of usury, annulment of debts owed to the credit department of the Japanese-operated East Asia Colonization Company (Tōyō Takushoku), and destruction of the Japanese imperial agencies. With these slogans, the party incited raids on the homes of landlords, usurers, and rich farmers in which houses, grain, and credit documents were burned. The party executed some landlords, anti-Communists, and pro-Japanese Koreans as lackeys of Japanese imperialism.[32]

The Communists also made an effort to employ the "united front from below" strategy in dealing with anti-Japanese groups while utilizing the anti-Japanese atmosphere created by the latter to maximum advantage. After the Japanese invasion in September 1931, Chientao was the scene of numerous rebellions of Chinese troops against the Kirin government (now under Hsi Hsia, who collaborated with the Japanese), involving 236 men in 1931 and 2,240 in 1932. Under the leadership of Wang Te-lin, these troops enlisted local peasants and workers and swept the entire region, fanning the already heightened anti-Japanese sentiment in the area. In the region under the new warlord who had sided with the Japanese, the Chinese government collapsed, and the Japanese consular personnel in Chientao were forced to evacuate, thus

30. In Chientao Province, which included Yenchi, Holung, Wangching and Hunchun *hsien*, 31.6 percent of the total crop in 1929 was soybeans. Gunseibu, Komonbu (Advisors' Department, Ministry of Defense, Manchukuo), *Manshū kyōsanhi no kenkyū* [Study of Communist Bandits in Manchuria] (n.p., 1937), p. 564. For the price of soybeans, see table 5, above.
31. Police Department of the Chü-chih-chieh Branch, Consulate-General in Chientao, "The Condition of the Communist Movement in Yenchi and Holung Hsien and Translations of Secret Party Documents," May 1931, in AJMFA reel S373–374, pp. 183–187.
32. *Manshū kyōsanhi no kenkyū*, p. 78.

creating a political vacuum. Utilizing the opportunity, the East Manchurian Committee dispatched propaganda and fund-raising units to various localities to mobilize mass support for the CCP. Subsidiary party organizations such as the Anti-Imperial League, the farmers' associations, and the Mutual Aid Society were mobilized to organize anti-Japanese soldiers' leagues and the "Association to Support the National Salvation Army" and to proselytize and recruit for the CCP. Evidently attempts were also made to organize a "Red Militia Army." The impression was fostered by propaganda units that Japan, because of internal problems and external pressures, would not be able to send large numbers of troops to Manchuria; that the anti-Japanese and anti-Manchukuo movements could be sustained for a long time; and that the Communists would become a dominant force—particularly because major elements of the Soviet Army allegedly stationed along the Russo-Chinese border were supporting the Chinese and Korean Communists. The CCP branches and auxiliaries organized frequent demonstrations and rallies, mobilizing 200 to 1,000 persons on each occasion.[33] Guerrilla units organized by the party also joined in the violence and destruction perpetrated by the rebels.[34] In the meantime, attempts were made to foment rebellion within the rebel groups, but these attempts only antagonized the anti-Japanese fighters.

The radical actions of the East Manchurian Committee, very much reminiscent of the events of 1930, produced three very damaging effects. First, the Japanese dispatched an army regiment from Korea to Chientao in April 1932 and, in cooperation with the local Chinese troops and police, conducted a "mop-up" operation, killing 1,200 persons and arresting some 1,500 by the end of the year.[35] Second, as in 1930, the Communists' radical policies against the landlords alienated the Chinese populace in general, particularly because most of the Communists were Koreans, and encouraged anti-Communist and anti-Korean tendencies among the anti-Japanese troops. Since the rank and file as well as the leaders of these groups shared affinity with the elements most harshly treated by the Communists, the outcome should not have been surprising. As the Japanese stepped up their suppression of the anti-Japanese groups and many groups began to surrender, some of the surrendering leaders attempted to win reprieves from

33. Consul-general, Chientao, to the Japanese foreign minister, March 31, 1932, in AJMFA reel SP103, file SP205-5, pp. 7795–96.
34. *Manshū kyōsanhi no kenkyū*, p. 78.
35. Ibid.

Table 14 Soviets in East Manchuria, 1932–1933

Location	Date established	Number of soviets	Persons in soviets
Wangyükou (Yenchi Hsien)	November 2, 1932	2 area soviets 9 village soviets	1,300
"Little Wangching" (Wangching Hsien)	November 2, 1932	2 area soviets 2 village soviets	800
Shihjenkou (Yenchi Hsien)	February 10, 1933	1 area soviet 1 village soviet	300
Huangkou (Hunchun Hsien)	December 21, 1932	1 area soviet 1 village soviet	300
Yentunglatzu (Hunchun Hsien)	December 21, 1932	1 area soviet 5 village soviets	1,800
Total			4,500

Source: Gunseibu, Komonbu (Advisors' Department, Ministry of Defense, Manchukuo), *Manshū kyōsanhi no kenkyū* [Study of Communist Bandits in Manchuria] (n.p., 1937), p. 80.

the Japanese by attacking the Communists. The party therefore strove to win over the "progressive" elements among the rebels by organizing groups under such names as the "Sino-Korean Anti-Japanese Soldiers' Committee," the "Sino-Korean Guerrilla Unit," and the "Military-Civilian Revolutionary Committee," but few rallied to the Communist cause. The original plan for a large Red Army, of course, did not materialize.[36]

On November 11, the Manchurian Provincial Committee issued an order to the East Manchurian Special Committee severely criticizing the left-wing errors committed by the latter. The party also ordered the Red Militia and the guerrillas to congregate in the hinterland, reorganize the scattered mass organizations there, and revive party activities in the towns. The East Manchurian Special Committee was also instructed to go underground to strengthen organizational and propaganda activities.[37]

The committee, however, was not able to make any headway in organizing the masses in the towns. In order to evade the Japanese army and the police, it led the people under its influence to remote locations and established "Red Districts" and soviet governments. In areas where the Communists did not have firm control, they established revolutionary committees. The soviets established by the East Manchurian Special Committee are listed in table 14.

36. Ibid.
37. Ibid., p. 79.

The "General Principles for Constructing Soviets" adopted by the East Manchurian Special Committee in January 1933 tended to reflect the directives issued by the central leaders at the Northern Conference, but evidently the committee was not able to discard its earlier radicalism. The "General Principles," for example, stated that soviets should be established only when the anti-Japanese and land reform movements already had broad mass support, considerable military power had been built up, and the geography of the locality was suitable for defense.[38] Clearly, these conditions were not met when the soviets were established. Instead of becoming solid revolutionary bases from which the party could expand its power, the soviets in eastern Manchuria in fact became temporary retreats for the party and its followers. The soviets did not serve to expand the party's influence,[39] and there is no indication that they could have withstood any prolonged onslaught by Japanese forces.

The wide gap between theory and practice was also displayed in the committee's pursuit of the land reform program. The "General Principles" specified that only the property of landlords and lackeys should be confiscated, and that lands belonging to rich and middle farmers should not be touched.[40] In practice, all lands, including those belonging to poor farmers, were confiscated, at least in the Peikou soviet in Hunchun *Hsien*, arousing widespread discontent.[41] The radical tendencies of the East Manchurian Special Committee thus alienated the masses, and the party was again forced to stand in isolation before the concerted attack of the Japanese.

Evidently, it was only after the arrival of Li Yao-k'uei from Moscow in May 1933 that the East Manchurian Special Committee was instructed to abandon its radical policies. By then, the Manchurian Provincial Committee would have received the letter of Ch'en Shao-yü as well as the January letter of the central leaders. In June, an inspector from the Manchurian Provincial Committee arrived in East Manchuria to order certain policy

38. Ibid., p. 81.
39. Ibid., p. 86. The Communist guerrillas, however, conducted frequent forays from the soviets, much to the annoyance of the Japanese. There were 40 reported forays in July 1932 and 70 in July 1933, according to a Kwantung Army staff officer. *Ōsaka Mainichi shimbun*, September 7, 1933, as quoted in South Manchuria Railway Company, Keizai Chōsakai (Economic Research Association), *Manshū kyōsantō undō gaikan* [A Survey of the Manchurian Communist Party Movement] (Dairen, 1935), p. 41; data on other months not provided.
40. *Manshū kyōsanhi no kenkyū*, p. 82.
41. Ibid., p. 85.

changes, including the conversion of the soviets to people's revolutionary governments, the establishment of a people's revolutionary army based on the red militia and guerrilla units, and the absorption of various organizations into the farmers' committees and the anti-Japanese armed groups.[42] In July, as noted in chapter 5, another cadre from the provincial committee, a man named P'an, convened a meeting in Tahuangkou to communicate the new policy lines of the Comintern and the CCP headquarters.[43] The gist of the new directive was to establish a broad united front by bringing together all anti-Japanese elements, including landlords and capitalists, and to establish people's revolutionary governments, farmers' committees, and the People's Revolutionary Army. The "Draft Political Platform of the Provisional Northeastern People's Revolutionary Government," issued in the name of the Wangching *Hsien* Committee on June 10, 1934, reaffirmed these policies. Unlike the constitution of the Chinese Soviet Republic adopted in January 1934 in Kiangsi, which called for the confiscation of all lands belonging to the landlords,[44] the Wangching draft platform merely called for the reduction of tenant fees to 20 percent.[45]

In spite of these instructions, however, the East Manchurian Special Committee did not abandon its radicalism. According to information gathered by the Japanese consul-general in Chientao in January 1933, the leftist faction in the committee insisted on continuing to engage in extremist or radical activities and even went as far as assassinating cadres opposed to their policy.[46] A report filed by the same consulate in February 1934 describes severe factional strife between the "military faction" and the "political faction," the former insisting on meeting the Japanese oppression by military action and the latter advocating "political action" to revive party strength. The differences of these two factions were not easily reconciled; the military faction, accusing its opponents of being lackeys of Japan, resorted to assassination. Some fifty cadres and important party members in the Holung *Hsien* committee who advocated "political action" were murdered, and many others surrendered to the Japanese.[47] A letter from Ch'en Hung-chang, the cadre in charge of the committee, to the Comin-

42. Ibid., p. 86.
43. See chapter 5.
44. Wang Chien-min, *Chung-kuo Kung-ch'an-tang shih-kao* [Draft History of the Chinese Communist Party] (Taipei, 1965), vol. 2, p. 325.
45. *Manshū kyōsanhi no kenkyū*, p. 89.
46. Ibid., p. 112.
47. Ibid.

Table 15 Communist Strength in Chientao, 1933–1934

	Sept. 1933	April 1934	Dec. 1934
Party members	580	360	465
Communist Youth Corps members	830	418	731
Anti-Japanese Society members	11,800	2,960	912
Guerrillas and People's Revolutionary Army personnel	560*	920	1,096

*The "Army" was not in existence in September 1933; the figure indicates the number of guerrillas.
Source: Report from the Chientao consul-general, as quoted in Gunseibu, Komonbu (Advisors' Department, Ministry of Defense, Manchukuo), *Manshū kyōsanhi no kenkyū* [Study of Communist Bandits in Manchuria] (n.p., 1937), p. 96.

tern's "Chinese liaison officer," Yang Ch'un-shan, which was intercepted by the Japanese in November 1935, spoke of the secretary of the East Manchurian Special Committee as "a man of the Li Li-san line" who distrusted "the comrades from the Soviet Union."[48] The East Manchurian Special Committee was undergoing problems in steering a new course.

In the meantime, the oppression of the landlords and rich farmers continued. In part this was a necessity because the party needed funds to conduct its operations and to support the destitute masses herded into the "soviets," and only the rich possessed what the party needed. As a result, the party committee won few new supporters among the Chinese; and as the political climate in Chientao changed, the party began to lose the support of the Korean population as well.

As we have discussed in chapter 4, the Koreans in Manchuria had suffered considerably under the discriminatory policies of the Chang Tso-lin regime since the mid-1920s; thus, despite strong anti-Japanese sentiment among the Korean immigrants, the advent of Japan in Manchuria was not totally inimical to them. This situation provided the Japanese with a powerful propaganda advantage in battling the Communists, and they did not lose a moment in utilizing the opportunity. Japanese propaganda combined with other counterinsurgency measures proved to be effective. The decline of mass support, particularly in the membership of the Anti-Japanese Society, was noticeable between September 1933 and April 1934, as shown in table 15. The number of defectors from the soviet areas in Chientao also continued to mount: 1,728 surrendered between February and December 1933, 1,195

48. Ibid., pp. 111–112.

between January and October 1934, and 1,179 between January and July 1935, a total of 4,102 in two and a half years.[49]

The Second People's Revolutionary Army in Manchuria was a product of this environment. As we have seen in chapter 5, the Communists in eastern Manchuria had been instructed at the Tahuangkou meeting in July 1933 to build a people's revolutionary army. The First People's Revolutionary Army was established in Panshih in southern Manchuria in September, but it was only in March 1934 that the East Manchuria Special Committee was able to establish the second army. Those present at the inaugural meeting of the First Division of the Second Army were Wang Te-t'ai, the head of the military section, and Yi Sang-muk, the head of the organization section of the East Manchuria Special Committee, in addition to leaders of guerrilla units under the committee as well as a number of non-Communist guerrilla groups. Evidently the Koreans outnumbered the Chinese among the armed men. Chu Chin, a Korean who had headed the party's guerrilla unit, became the commander of the First Division, and two of the three regimental commands and two other key posts—chief of staff and quartermaster—were given to Koreans. Wang Te-t'ai became the division's political commissar.[50] In May, when the Second Division was organized, command went to an unidentified Chinese, as did the three regimental commands; Koreans, however, occupied all the political commissars' posts at the divisional and regimental levels.[51] The First Division was assigned to operate in Yenchi and Hunchun *hsien* and the Second Division in Wangching and Hunchun *hsien* in the east. As can be seen from table 15, the total strength of the guerrillas and people's revolutionary army personnel in 1934 was approximately 1,000 men. According to a Korean veteran of this era, all of the Communist-led guerrillas were Korean youths. Some of these guerrillas rose to high positions in the North Korean power structure after 1945, most notably, Kim Il-sŏng, the president of the Democratic People's Republic of Korea, Ch'oe Hyŏn, defense minister, and An Kil, the first chief of staff of the North Korean army.[52]

Despite their continuing efforts, the Communist guerrillas were not able to expand their forces beyond the level reached in early 1934. Massive desertion from the Anti-Japanese Society and large-scale military attacks and surrender-inducement operations by the Japanese confined the Communist guerrillas to small areas

49. Ibid., pp. 110–111.   50. Ibid., p. 166.   51. Ibid., pp. 167–168.
52. Yim Ch'un-ch'u, *Hang-Il mujang t'ujaeng sigi rŭl hoesang hayŏ* [Recalling the Period of the Anti-Japanese Armed Struggle] (Pyongyang, 1960), pp. 21–34.

of the hinterland, and their position became increasingly untenable. Continuously deteriorating conditions and the machinations of the Japanese authorities led the Chinese cadres to suspect collusion between their Korean comrades and the Japanese enemy, and a massive purge was on. Thus, between November 1933 and January 1934, some 200 potential deserters and suspect individuals were murdered. The East Manchuria Special Committee itself is reported to have lost sixteen cadres in a purge in January 1934.[53] No one was immune once the witch hunt began. Suspicion was cast upon such top leaders as Chu Chin, commander of the First Division of the Second Army, and Yi Sang-Muk, the head of the organization department of the East Manchuria Special Committee, both of whom, fearing murder by their comrades, fled the Communist base in 1935 and surrendered to the Japanese.[54] Even the witch hunters themselves were later condemned and executed.[55] Having thus suffered from internal convulsions and external pressures, the Second Army units left their original territory in late 1935 and moved westward, one detachment joining the First Army in the west and the other the Fifth Army in the north.

Guerrillas in Southern Manchuria

In contrast to the situation in eastern Manchuria, where the party began with a relatively large following but steadily suffered major losses, the situation in Panshih improved considerably after 1933, and Panshih became the stronghold of the Communist-led guerrilla movement after the Japanese invasion. Although in south central Manchuria, and not remotely situated, being only 100 air miles south-southeast of Kirin, the Panshih area is mountainous and therefore not easily accessible from the outside. Economic conditions there also favored the Communists. Panshih *Hsien* was officially opened for cultivation in 1882, seven years later than some other parts of Manchuria, but many farmers had moved into the area to cultivate the fertile soil even before that time, and as a result there soon was a surplus farming populace, many of whom were landless (74 percent of the total farming population, according to a study conducted in 1934).[56] Having to pay

53. *Manshū kyōsanhi no kenkyū*, p. 109.
54. Ibid., p. 114.
55. For details, see my "Witch Hunt Among the Guerrillas: The Minsheng-t'uan Incident," *China Quarterly*, April–June 1966, pp. 107–117.
56. *Manshū kyōsanhi no kenkyū*, pp. 344–358.

high rents to landlords, they were in financial distress when the worldwide depression after 1929 worsened their plight. Panshih's agricultural crops consisted of soybeans to an extraordinarily high degree, 46.5 percent of the total cultivated area.

Another factor favoring the Communists' progress was the presence of a sizeable number of Korean farmers, who had already been influenced by a strong current of both nationalist and Communist movements.[57] As early as August 1923, a socialist organization called the Korean Labor Party (Hanjok Nodong-dang) had been organized in Panshih, with a membership exceeding 1,500 by the mid-1920s. It was no coincidence that the Korean nationalist leaders in southern Manchuria held their representatives' conference in Panshih Hsien in August 1927, and that some of the left-oriented leaders among them organized a farmers' league (nongmin tongmaeng). The latter had considerable support from the farmers in Panshih, most of whom had immigrated from impoverished farms in southern Korea, where they had been under the influence of a group of Korean Communists known as the "M-L" (Marxist-Leninist) group. In May 1930, when the CCP established its Panshih Hsien committee, a farmers' association (nung-min hsieh-hui), and an anti-imperial league (fan-ti t'ung-meng), the Koreans in the area became key members of these new organizations.[58]

Frequent mutinies among the local Chinese troops against the puppet regime of Manchukuo also provided a fertile recruiting ground for the new CCP organizations. In April–June 1932, several companies of Chinese soldiers stationed in Panshih and nearby Itung left their barracks and joined the anti-Japanese forces.[59] Not all the rebellious troops were willing to listen to the Communists, but at least some of them were susceptible to Communist propaganda.

57. See Manchukuo, Minseibu, Sōmushi, Chōsaka (Research Section, General Affairs Division, Civil Government Department), *Zaiman Chōsenjin jijō* [Condition of the Koreans in Manchuria] (Changchun, 1933), p. 222.
58. *Manshū kyōsanhi no kenkyū*, pp. 336–338. The Manchurian General Bureau of the Korean Communist Party ("M-L group"), under the direction of Pak Yun-sŏ, had been located at Panshih since early 1928. Along with the party organization, the Koreans also had a branch of the Communist Youth Association there. This group of Korean Communists had advocated the need for military action to bring about an independent and communized Korea. In order to provide necessary military training, the bureau had established its own military department in 1929. See Kōtō Hōin, Kenjikyoku (High Court, Prosecutor's Bureau, Government-General of Korea), "The Preliminary Trial of the Chientao May 30 Incident Concluded," *Shisō geppō* [Thought Monthly], vol. 1, no. 4 (July 15, 1931), in AJMFA, reel S355, p. 179.
59. *Manshū kyōsanhi no kenkyū*, p. 340.

The mood in the Panshih area was evident in an incident that took place just outside the town of Panshih early in April. On April 2, the Japanese consular police in Panshih dispatched a few officers to nearby Panku to hunt for Korean Communists. While returning from a successful mission, the police were surrounded by some 300 Korean villagers, who forced them to release their captives. The Japanese police dispatched an additional 12 men, along with 20 mounted Chinese civil guards (pao-wei-t'uan) and a company of Chinese infantrymen serving the Manchukuo regime to protect the harassed policemen, but on the afternoon of April 4 the Chinese soldiers killed one of the Japanese policemen and a Korean "guide" at Santaokou, forcing the other Japanese to flee for their lives.[60] The Chinese soldiers had been under strong pressure from the villagers, who shouted anti-Japanese slogans and appealed to patriotism.[61]

The Japanese officials did not know at the time that the Korean villagers had been led by a Korean Communist, Yi Hong-gwang, characterized as a "simple and very brave Korean farmer" by his former comrade.[62] Early in 1932, Yi had organized a "dog-beating" unit (ta-kou tui) of seven men to serve as a guard unit for the hsien committee, "dog" in this case referring to the "running dogs" of the Japanese. In March, under instructions from the Manchurian Provincial Committee, the original group was renamed the Anti-Japanese Worker-Farmer Guerrilla Unit (Fan-Jih Kung-nung Yu-chi-tui), Yi again becoming its head and an agent from Harbin, Yang Tso-ch'ing, becoming its political commissar. The unit had raided landlords' houses for weapons, and by the time the Panku incident took place, it had some 30 armed men.[63]

The victory at Panku boosted the morale of the party leaders and affected the Chinese soldiers serving the puppet regime. The battalion commander of the unit that was involved in the Panku incident mutinied and fled to the hills with his men, perhaps fearing punishment from the Japanese. Other soldiers responded to anti-Japanese propaganda and joined the Communist guerrillas. By May 16, the guerrilla unit contained more than 100 men.[64] The former soldiers trained their new farmer comrades in combat

---

60. Report from Consul-General Ishii in Chientao to Japanese Foreign Minister Saito, June 1, 1932, in AJMFA, reel S386, file S9452-16, pp. 53–68.
61. Yang Tso-ch'ing, "Panshih Rising Like A Gust of Wind," Chung-kuo Jen-min Chieh-fang-chün Shan-shih-nien Cheng-wen Pien-chi Wei-yüan-hui (Editorial Committee of the Literature on the Thirty Years of the Chinese People's Liberation Army), Hsing-huo Liao-yüan [Sparks Blazing over the Prairie], vol. 4 (Peking, 1959), pp. 384–386.
62. Ibid., p. 380.   63. Ibid., pp. 380–382.   64. Ibid., p. 386.

skills by day; by night a small group of leaders studied Sun Tzu's ancient war manual, *The Art of War*, having located a copy of it at the home of an old teacher. The guerrilla techniques that they learned from Sun Tzu were effectively applied against the Japanese forces.[65] The ranks of the guerrillas grew steadily, and by June the group numbered 170 men. In that month, the guerrilla unit was renamed the Farmer-Workers' Volunteer Army of Manchuria (Tung-pei Nung-kung I-yung-chün).[66]

In the meantime, in the spring of 1932, the Panshih *Hsien* Committee was elevated to the status of a "central *hsien* committee," with jurisdiction over seven *hsien* in the vicinity, and was placed directly under the Manchurian Provincial Committee. This was because the arrests of the cadres of the South Manchurian Special Committee in Mukden had made it impossible for that committee to provide adequate guidance to the movement in the guerrilla zone.[67]

Unlike the East Manchurian Special Committee, which stressed highly ideological programs in this period, the Panshih committee placed strong emphasis on anti-Japanese themes; ideologically oriented programs, such as land reform, do not appear in the extant records. The Communists in Panshih did wage severe struggles, which included kidnapping and killing, against some of the landlords, but it appears that the targets of struggle were carefully selected. In any event, there is no sign that serious damage was inflicted upon landlords at random, as was done in the Chientao region.

A lecture delivered by one of the important cadres of the Panshih committee, Han Chin (a Korean and one of the former leaders of the "M-L group"), is a good example of this. On July 17, 1932, Han reportedly led about 30 guerrillas to a place called Latzukang, where he told some 40 Korean and Chinese farmers the following:

> The Japanese imperialists took over Korea and Taiwan and oppressed them severely. This was not enough for the covetous Japanese, who wish to make Manchuria and Mongolia a second Korea. The Japanese deceitfully established the so-called Manchukuo, which is the same thing that they did in taking over Korea. They wish to enslave the thirty million people of Manchuria.

65. Ibid., pp. 387–388.
66. *Manshū kyōsanhi no kenkyū*, p. 340.
67. Ibid., p. 338.

Our party, which is of the workers and farmers, opposes the covetous devils of the East. In order to bring about freedom and liberation, our party supports the political principles and directive of the Comintern. . . . Through general mobilization, we will fight against the Japanese and destroy them. The duties of party members are: (1) to protect the secrets of the party; (2) to eliminate all national discrimination between Chinese and Korean workers and farmers, and to unite them according to the instructions of the party; (3) to report immediately to the guerrillas any appearance of the Japanese army or its running dogs; and (4) to kill all members of the [Japanese-sponsored] Pao-min Hui [Civil Protection Society] and their running dogs and families.[68]

The Panshih committee took steps to form alliances with other anti-Japanese groups, but not in the manner prescribed by the central leaders. The CCP Central Committee had repeatedly stressed the need to infiltrate anti-Japanese groups in order to separate the lower-echelon troops from their leaders. The Panshih committee proceeded to establish alliances with the leaders of these groups for various operations. Instead of the united front from below, for which the central leaders had called, the Panshih committee pursued the proscribed united front from above.

The Panshih *Hsien* Committee was reported to have held a meeting on June 28, 1932, at Hamahotzu, where some 300 persons gathered and adopted the following resolution:[69]

1. To destroy the bourgeoisie and the lackeys of Japan and Manchukuo, regardless of whether they are Chinese or Korean, and to repel the infiltration of Japanese forces.
2. To establish close ties with members of the Big Sword Society and the National Salvation Army and to mobilize soldiers, and obtain military funds for the Farmer-Workers' Volunteer Army of Manchuria.
3. To obtain compulsory donations of weapons from the rich Chinese gentry (*fu-hao*); if they do not comply, destroy them as lackeys of Japan.

68. Director, Police Affairs Bureau, Kwantung Territorial Government, to various agencies, July 28, 1932, in AJMFA, reel S386, file S9452-16, pp. 97–99. This report is based on a report from the Manchukuo Government Police Department, Kirin Province.
69. *Manshū kyōsanhi no kenkyū*, p. 341.

4. To organize a plain-clothes unit (*pien-i tui*) to reconnoiter the Japanese agencies in Panshih and thus facilitate attacks against them.

Although there were some difficulties, the Communists managed to establish alliances with various anti-Japanese groups. Thus, when word of an imminent Japanese attack reached the Panshih committee in July, leaders of several groups reportedly held a meeting to discuss the situation. It was revealed at the meeting that an alliance had been forged with the National Salvation Army under Fu Tien-ch'en, a former bandit leader with 4,000 to 5,000 men under him.[70] (The Big Sword Society had refused to collaborate because it regarded all Koreans as lackeys of Japanese imperialism.) To resolve misunderstandings and explain the views of the party, the committee dispatched three delegates, including Han Chin, to the Big Swords.[71] Evidently negotiations were successful, since about this time the "Red guerrillas" were reported to have expanded their forces by collaborating with the Big Swords in nearby Chinchuan *Hsien* and with the National Salvation Army in Tunghua and Liuho *hsien*.[72]

Details of arrangements between the Communists and the Big Swords were noted by the Japanese in August. In late July an agent of the CCP reportedly approached Wang Feng-ko, the head of the Big Sword Society, who was now known as the head of the Self-Defense Army, and concluded the following agreement:

1. The CCP shall provide necessary rifles and ammunition to the Self-Defense Army.
2. The Self-Defense Army agrees to act as the executors of military actions planned by the CCP.
3. The CCP shall harass the enemy and carry out reconnaissance activities to assist the military actions of the Self-Defense Army.
4. Communist party agencies may be established within the Self-Defense Army.
5. The 3,000 *yüan* provided by the CCP shall be used for relief of the indigent in order to win the support of the people for the Self-Defense Army and the Communist party.[73]

70. Yang Tso-ch'ing, "Panshih Rising," p. 383.
71. *Manshū kyōsanhi no kenkyū*, p. 341.
72. Ibid., pp. 341–342.
73. Director, Police Affairs Bureau, Kwantung Territorial Government, to various agencies, August 30, 1932, in AJMFA, reel S386, file S9452-16, pp. 45–47.

The Japanese report added that 14 distribution points for relief rice were set up in Tunghua and Liuho to implement this part of the agreement, but no information on the implementation of the other points was given. About 1,200 members of the Self-Defense Army under Wang Feng-ko and 150 Chinese and Korean CCP members were operating in the region. Since Communist leaders from Chientao and Tungpientao were said to be congregating there, it was thought that the Self-Defense Army in the Tunghua region was likely to be influenced by the Communists in the future.[74] Unlike the distant central leaders of the CCP, the Japanese authorities were inclined to believe—as did the Communist cadres in Panshih—that alliances with anti-Japanese groups such as the Big Sword Society would eventually work for the benefit of the Communists.

These developments were reflected in the numerical growth of the Communist army. Anti-Japanese sentiment was very strong in the region, and the party's position evidently appealed to some of the aroused populace. Particularly in September, the rebellion of a Chinese battalion and its commander in the town of Panshih led to an assault upon and the occupation of that town by 4,600 men from a variety of groups, including the rebellious battalion that had departed from the town, Red Spear Society members, railway guards, and several bandit groups.[75] Some teachers and students of the Panshih Middle School and some railway workers also took part. In October, when a counterattack by Japanese and Manchukuo forces dispersed these anti-Japanese groups, the Panshih committee absorbed some of the teachers, students, soldiers, and workers, increasing its strength to 230 men, including 80 Koreans.[76] The Communist army was renamed the South Manchurian Guerrilla Unit of the 32nd Army of the Chinese Red Army (Chung-kuo Hung-chün Ti-san-shih-erh Chün Nan-Man Yu-chi-tui); this force, which had 300 rifles and pistols and a mortar, was commanded by Yi Hong-gwang. Yang Ching-yü, a veteran organizer of the Red Labor Union in Fushun in 1929 who had been active as a leader of the Anti-Japanese Society in Harbin, assumed the position of political commissar.[77]

The Panshih *Hsien* Committee was thus in the process of gradually expanding its guerrilla forces when the January 1933 letter of

74. Ibid.
75. *Manshū kyōsanhi no kenkyū*, pp. 340–341.
76. Ibid., p. 341.
77. Chang Lin, "The Story of General Yang Ching-yü," *Hung-ch'i P'iao-p'iao* [Red Flag Waves], no. 8 (July, 1958), p. 68.

the Central Committee and Ch'en Shao-yü's letter reached Manchuria, and the Manchurian Provincial Committee instructed that the existing guerrilla group in Panshih be expanded into a people's revolutionary army. The campaign to win over the anti-Japanese groups, local bandits, and other Chinese in the service of the puppet regime of Manchukuo, either as soldiers or policemen, was intensified, and by September 1933, the Communists commanded 720 men in sixteen units. They also had under their influence some 1,000 troops of allied forces.[78] According to a Japanese source, the First Division of the First Army was established on September 18, 1933, the second anniversary of the Manchurian Incident; but it is more likely that the First Army was established in early July.[79]

A declaration issued in the name of the First Army on July 10, 1933, is of some importance, particularly in view of the fact that it appealed to various anti-Japanese groups in the area for an "anti-Japanese operational alliance." After surveying the massive efforts of the Japanese to encircle and destroy all the anti-Japanese forces, and denouncing the Kuomintang for selling out the nation and assisting the Japanese by concluding a truce with the Japanese in northern China and continuing the extermination campaign against the Chinese soviet, it set forth three conditions for concluding an alliance:

1. Do not surrender and do not betray the nation. Fight to the end against the Japanese bandits and their lackey, Manchukuo.
2. Support all struggles and movements of the farmers and workers and all anti-Japanese masses, including their strikes, demonstrations, collection of funds for

78. *Manshū kyōsanhi no kenkyū*, p. 342.
79. *Tou-cheng* [Struggle] (Juichin edition), no. 26 (September 15, 1933), pp. 1–3, carries a declaration of the First Army of the Panshih People's Revolutionary Army of Manchuria, dated July 10. *Tou-cheng* (mimeographed Shanghai edition), no. 52 (August 20, 1933), p. 17, refers to the People's Army of Manchuria in Panshih, adding that this was the new name of the 32nd Army of the Worker-Farmer Red Army of Manchuria. Chi Yün-lung's "Brief Account of the Great National Hero Yang Ching-yü," *Chi-shih* [Knowledge], no. 4 (September 1946), p. 7, dates the founding of the People's Revolutionary Army as September 18, 1933, but the content of the article indicates that the author relied heavily on *Manshū kyōsanhi no kenkyū*, which gave the same date. While some authors have alleged that the People's Revolutionary Army was established in the spring of 1933, this is also erroneous. A news item on the "New Victory of the Red Guerrilla Unit in Southern Manchuria," dated June 15, 1933, reports that the 32nd Red Army Guerrilla Unit was in the process of expanding into the People's Revolutionary Army. *Tou-cheng* (Juichin edition), no. 26 (September 15, 1933), p. 18.

farmers, struggle against taxes and imposts, and struggle to obtain food. Confiscate all property of Japan and traitors. Confiscate Japanese goods and use them for relief of the calamity-stricken people and the unemployed. Use them also for the fight against Japan. Protect all anti-Japanese and anti-imperial organizations, labor unions, farmers associations, etc.

3. Permit and assist the people to arm themselves; assist their anti-Japanese operations.[80]

All the anti-Japanese groups were invited to reply to the appeal and to dispatch representatives immediately in order to establish an alliance.

Because of a massive extermination campaign launched by the Japanese forces in October, the First Army dispersed its forces, dispatching the second and third regiments westward to Tungpientao. Since other anti-Japanese groups were also under strong pressure from the Japanese, and since the benefits to be gained from coordinating their activities were obvious, the appeals of the Communist guerrillas seem to have been well received, and efforts to form alliances continued. According to a Japanese account, the Communists concluded an agreement in July 1933 with such bandit chieftains (now heads of anti-Japanese groups) as Fu Tien-ch'en and Mao Kuo on the territory of operation of respective groups and the ways in which joint operations were to be conducted.[81] The Japanese also reported the establishment of the "Staff Office of the Anti-Japanese Allied Army" (K'ang-Jih Lien-ho-chün Ts'an-mou-ch'u) on May 22, 1933, which was supposed to have been elevated to the level of General Command (Tsung Chih-hui-pu) of the Anti-Japanese Army in March 1934.[82] But as we have seen in chapter 6, the General Command became an object of the central leaders' criticism in their February 1934 letter, being regarded by them as an organization which had colluded with the chieftains rather than implementing the strategy of a "united front from below." The possibility is very strong, therefore, that many more groups responded to the First Army's appeal of July 1933 and that the General Command was established soon after the appeal was issued. By March 1934 the General Command had ceased to exist, probably because of repeated desertions

80. *Tou-cheng*, pp. 1–3.
81. *Manshū kyōsanhi no kenkyū*, p. 428.
82. Ibid., pp. 343, 430.

of non-Communist leaders and because of the CCP headquarters' criticism.

The arrival of Yang Ching-yü's forces in the mountainous and inaccessible region where "daylight cannot be seen all day because it is always covered by shadows [of giant trees]" and where "only gloom pervades"[83] gave a boost to Communist party activities. Party branches in Huinan, Chinchuan, Chingyüan, Liuho, Mengchiang, and Tunghua suddenly became active, and on November 5, 1934, representatives of these branches established the Southern Manchuria Provisional Special Committee as a step toward reviving the defunct Southern Manchuria Special Committee.[84] On December 11, the Tunghua *Hsien* Committee was elevated to the status of a central *hsien* committee, with authority over districts of Tunghua, Liuho and Hailung.[85] In spite of the criticism of the Central Committee, collusion with the leaders permitted the party to dispatch political agents to various guerrilla groups to conduct propaganda and organizational activities.[86]

The Communist guerrilla unit remaining in Panshih, the First Regiment of the First Army, also engaged in united front activities with considerable success. In May 1934, the General Command of the Anti-Japanese Allied Army North of the [Sungari] River (Chiang-pei K'ang-Jih Lien-ho-chün Tsung Chih-hui-pu) was established by consolidating various units. Approximately 1,000 guerrillas were placed under the command of Yüan Te-sheng, the head of the First Regiment. Yi Hong-gwang served as the chief of staff.[87] The forces were organized into eight guerrilla companies,[88] and a number of coordinated attacks were planned. This formula also permitted the Communists to dispatch their agents into various guerrilla units to conduct propaganda and organizational activities, and in some cases the Communists were able to win over substantial numbers of guerrilla troops. The First Regiment grew in numbers, and the Communist leaders decided to expand it into the Second Division of the First Army in November 1934.[89]

Thus the Panshih committee was much more successful in absorbing rebellious troops and bringing various anti-Japanese

83. Ishigaki Sadakazu, "Pacification Activities in the Communist Bandit Area: Personal Reflections," in Office of Information, Department of General Affairs, Council of State, Manchukuo, *Sembu geppō* [Pacification Monthly Report], vol. 4, no. 4 (April 1939), as translated in Chong-Sik Lee, *Counterinsurgency in Manchuria: The Japanese Experience, 1931–1940* (Santa Monica, 1967), p. 218.
84. *Manshū kyōsanhi no kenkyū*, p. 343.
85. Ibid., p. 343.   86. Ibid., p. 430.   87. Ibid., pp. 430–431.
88. Ibid., p. 431.   89. Ibid., p. 343.

groups under its wing. But these achievements were largely due to its emphasis of the anti-Japanese theme that had been stressed by Ch'en Shao-yü. It is probably no accident that the Manchurian Provincial Committee had better control over the Panshih committee than it had over the East Manchurian Special Committee. Both Yang Tso-ch'ing, the man who aided Yi Hong-gwang in the initial stage, and Yang Ching-yü, who later assumed the leadership role, were dispatched from Harbin by Lo Teng-hsien, who had followed the line established in Su Kuang's article in *Hung-ch'i Chou-pao* of November 1931,[90] which had concentrated on the anti-Japanese theme. Lo was replaced by Li Yao-k'uei, but he was a follower of the Ch'en Shao-yü line, as we have seen in the previous chapter. What the central leaders in southern China denounced as "collusionist" or "chieftain's line" served the local Communists well. Only when the united front had been established at the top level were the Communist cadres able to infiltrate these groups. When the local cadres overemphasized the "united front from below" strategy in response to the repeated exhortations of the Central Committee, strong hostility was generated among the other anti-Japanese groups, jeopardizing the entire united front effort. It deserves to be noted again that the Communists in Panshih downplayed Communist concepts and jargon.

The Panshih committee also strove to organize anti-Japanese societies to serve as a popular base for the guerrillas. This had been emphasized by the February 1934 letter of the Central Committee. Thus, on August 20, 1934, the South Manchuria Anti-Japanese General Society (Nan-Man Fan-Jih Tsung-hui) was established at a meeting of a dozen or so representatives of various anti-Japanese groups in Panshih *Hsien*.[91] In conjunction with the CCP and the People's Revolutionary Army, this society engaged in anti-Japanese and anti-Manchukuo propaganda, collected funds and foodstuffs for the People's Revolutionary Army, organized armed groups, recruited troops for the revolutionary army, and collected intelligence on the Japanese security forces. The value of this organization for the party cannot be exaggerated. According to a report of the Japanese Ministry of Foreign Affairs, there were 3,589 members of the Anti-Japanese Society under the Panshih Central *Hsien* Committee as of the end of October 1934.[92]

90. Su Kuang, "The Central Task of the Manchurian Party Headquarters in the Struggle against the Japanese Imperialist Occupation of Manchuria," *Hung-ch'i Chou-pao* [Red Flag Weekly], no. 23 (November 20, 1931), pp. 9–16.
91. For details, see *Manshū kyōsanhi no kenkyū*, pp. 366–368.
92. See table 16, below.

But the Panshih leaders evidently bowed to the central leaders' repeated exhortations to apply the "united front from below" strategy in 1934, and the carefully built alliances were rendered precarious. The strategy of the united front from below was inherently self-limiting. The Communist strategy would have become obvious to everyone sooner or later. The non-Communist leaders had adequate reason to shun the Communists as long as their aim was to subvert other groups. It is also very likely that the leaders of the non-Communist anti-Japanese groups in Manchuria were informed of the continuous struggle between the Kuomintang and the Communists in southern China and that they shared the Kuomintang's hostile attitude toward the CCP. As long as the Communists openly denounced the Kuomintang and Chang Hsüeh-liang's forces as traitors and advocated subversion of the military groups, the local Communist groups were obliged to fight both the Japanese and the local military groups.

Thus skirmishes between Communists and other forces continued. In some instances non-Communist groups surrounded and attacked Communist guerrillas, and Communist agents were captured by non-Communist opponents. The Communists, on their part, attacked some anti-Japanese groups with whom they had formed alliances. Wang Feng-ko, the influential leader in Tungpientao and head of the Big Sword Society, was hostile to the Communists, and his groups and Communist units often engaged in skirmishes.[93]

Guerrillas in Northern Manchuria

Meanwhile, Communist guerrilla units were springing up in other regions of Manchuria. In eastern Manchuria, the party established the Eastern Kirin Bureau in May 1933 for the purpose of directing the activities of the East Manchuria Special Committee, the Suining Central *Hsien* Committee, and *hsien*-level organizations in places such as Mishan, Hulin, and Jaoho, located near the Soviet border. It was also charged with facilitating communication between the Manchurian Provincial Committee and the Comintern agencies in Vladivostok. Another duty of the bureau, as Li Yao-k'uei had told his interrogators, was to win over the anti-Japanese groups and to organize the red guerrillas.[94] Chou Pao-chung, who later became a hero of the anti-Japanese move-

93. *Manshū kyōsanhi no kenkyū*, pp. 433–434.
94. Ibid., p. 156.

ment in Manchuria, reportedly served as the head of the military committee of the bureau.[95]

It was Chou who organized the red guerrillas in the Tungning-Ningan area in early 1933. This mountainous region, situated in the north of Chientao, had its share of Korean nationalists and Communists. The Red Spear Society also had influence there, and after 1931 thousands of former Kirin warlord troops under Li Tu, Wang Te-lin, and others operated in this area against the Japanese. Chou, a native of Yunnan, had been a soldier since 1918, and had considerable military experience, having risen to the rank of deputy division commander in the National Revolutionary Army before he was dismissed in 1928 for refusing to implement an order to suppress Communist-led peasant uprisings.[96] He joined the CCP in the same year, and after the Japanese launched the operation to conquer Manchuria in 1931, he went to Manchuria, joining the forces of Li Tu and Wang Te-lin in 1932. According to Chou's own account, anti-Japanese leaders were hostile to the Communists and held him in suspicion initially, but they valued his ability and made him chief of staff of the Joint Headquarters of the Self-Defense Army and the National Salvation Army, comprised of the forces of Li Tu, Wang Te-lin and others.[97] In early 1933, however, "more than one hundred thousand" troops of these two armies, disunited among themselves, were routed by the Japanese, and Li Tu and Wang Te-lin fled to Siberia with 20,000 men. Chou and some of his comrades who had been working among these units gathered some of those remaining and organized the Shan-lin Tui, or "Mountain-Forest" unit.[98] A contemporary Japanese source reported the establishment of a "Mountain-Forest Farmers-Workers' Volunteer Unit" (Shan-lin Nung-kung I-wu Tui) in January 1933, consisting of 200 anti-Japanese soldiers and professional bandits in addition to forty Korean Communists.[99] This group expanded during the summer months to a force of some 500 men, and later, in late 1933, or early 1934, changed its name to the Ning-an Anti-Japanese Guerrilla Unit (Ning-an Fan-

---

95. Ibid., p. 160.
96. For the background of Chou Pao-chung, see Howard Boorman et al., eds., *Biographical Dictionary of Republican China* (New York, 1967), pp. 43–44, and Donald W. Klein and Anne B. Clark, *Biographic Dictionary of Chinese Communism, 1921–1965* (Cambridge, Mass., 1971), vol. 1, pp. 225–228. For Chou's own account, see Chang Lin, "The Story of a General in the United Resistance Army," *Hung-ch'i P'iao-p'iao*, vol. 2 (July 15, 1967), pp. 188–195.
97. Ibid., p. 195.
98. Ibid.
99. *Manshū kyōsanhi no kenkyū*, pp. 158–159.

Jih Yu-chi-tui).[100] It is quite likely that the new united front strategy was abetting the cause of Chou Pao-chung. This unit was reorganized into the Fifth Anti-Japanese Allied Army in February 1935.

In December 1933, the Communists also set up a small guerrilla unit in the Mishan-Hulin area north of Ningan, across the Soviet border from Iman. This area had been a stronghold of Li Tu, who had some 80,000 men in the Mishan area alone. The CCP had had a *hsien* committee in Mishan since 1930, and in 1932 it organized the Mishan Anti-Japanese General Society. On these foundations, a red guerrilla unit was organized in December 1933, with forty members of the CCP and the Communist Youth Corps, of whom nearly thirty were Koreans.[101] In Jaoho, north of Mishan, the CCP had established a *hsien* committee in 1930, but it had not prospered. In July 1933, a red guerrilla unit of some eighty men was organized.[102] Evidently all the members were Koreans. It is of interest to note that the name of the company commander of this unit was given as Kim Sŏk-ch'ŏn in the Japanese record.[103] There is a strong likelihood that this was Ch'oe Sŏk-ch'ŏn (Ch'oe Yong-gŏn) who later became the number-two man in the North Korean regime.[104]

In any event, the guerrillas in Jaoho joined with the anti-Japanese forces under Li Yen-lu to establish the Fourth Allied Army of Manchuria in September 1934.[105] Li had been a company commander under Wang Te-lin, who had been a battalion commander in the Kirin Army until the Japanese took over Manchuria in 1931, when he led the anti-Japanese forces. Even though Wang Te-lin joined other commanders in 1933 to beat a retreat to Siberia, Li Yen-lu remained with a small group of men to revive the anti-Japanese movement.[106] Unlike other anti-Japanese leaders, Li Yen-lu had frequent contacts with various anti-Japanese groups in Shanghai and Peking.[107]

---

100. Ibid., p. 159.   101. Ibid., p. 721.   102. Ibid., pp. 718–719.
103. Ibid., p. 718.
104. The presence of Ch'oe Sŏk-ch'ŏn (Ch'oe Yong-gŏn) in the Jaoho region is established by his delivering an address, "To the Officers and Soldiers of the Seventh Army," in 1939; the text of this address is given in Han Sŏl-ya, ed., *Pan-Il t'usa yŏnsŏljip* [Speeches of Anti-Japanese Fighters] (Pyongyang, 1946), pp. 21–28.
105. Sun Chieh, *Tung-pei K'ang-Jih Lien-chün ti-ssu-chün* [The Fourth Allied Army of Manchuria] (Paris[?], 1936), p. 116.
106. Ibid. See also Lei Ting, *Tung-pei, I-yung-chün yün-tung shih-hua* [Story of the Manchurian Volunteer Army Movement] (Shanghai, 1932), p. 127. This book's date of publication is erroneous; the book covers events after 1932.
107. Sun Chieh, *Tung-pei K'ang-Jih Lien-chün ti-ssu-chün*, pp. 14, 118.

Another small group of Communist guerrillas was organized in the vicinity of Chuho (now Shangchih), located southeast of Harbin, by Chao Shang-chih, who had been dispatched from Harbin in 1933. This had been the territory of the anti-Japanese leader Sun Ch'ao-yang, who had organized several thousand fighters under him, but concerted attacks by the Japanese army virtually decimated Sun's unit, and Sun was killed in action in the autumn of 1933. Chao, who had been Sun's chief of staff, gathered seven men under him and established the Chuho Anti-Japanese Guerrilla Unit, which grew to a force of some 300 men by the end of 1933.[108] The party subsequently dispatched more cadres to expand the unit, and, according to at least one Japanese estimate, by the end of 1934, the Chuho Central *Hsien* Committee had some 600 men under its command.[109] This was the beginning of the Third People's Revolutionary Army of Manchuria, which came into being in January 1935.

Tangyuan, to the northeast of Harbin and immediately west of Chiamussu, was another center of guerrilla activity. As in other areas, anti-Japanese forces (approximately 10,000 to 20,000 in 1934) had been active in the vicinity of Tangyuan. The CCP's Tangyuan branch became active after the spring of 1933, and under the leadership of Feng Chung-yün, the Northeastern Anti-Japanese Unit, consisting of about eighty men, half of whom were Koreans, was established in the summer of 1933.[110] This unit merged with the People's Self-Defense Army of Manchuria (Tungpei Min-chung Tzu-wei-chün) under the command of Hsieh Wen-tung, a landlord who had masterminded an anti-Japanese revolt of farmers in Tulungshan, Tangyuan *Hsien*, in March 1934, and established the Sixth Allied Army in the summer of 1935.[111]

Why were these groups able to expand their forces in the very region where large units of anti-Japanese armies before them had failed to survive? Li Tu and Wang Te-lin, for example, were forced to retreat to Siberia with the 20,000 men remaining under them in 1932, but Chou Pao-chung, Chao Shang-chih, and others began their movement afresh and built up a substantial force. How was this possible? The answer must be sought in the different charac-

---

108. Feng Chung-yün, *Tung-pei K'ang-Jih Lien-chün shih-ssu-nien k'u-tou chien-shih* [Brief History of the Fourteen-Year Struggle of the Anti-Japanese Allied Army of Manchuria] (Harbin, 1946), pp. 22–23; see also *Manshū kyōsanhi no kenkyū*, p. 631.
109. See table 16, below.
110. *Manshū kyōsanhi no kenkyū*, p. 753.
111. Ibid., pp. 756–757.

ter of the leaders and men involved and their overall strategies. Such leaders as Li Tu and Wang Te-lin were commanders of the former warlord army and were accustomed to the frontal engagements of regular armies; as such, when they encountered a more numerous, better-equipped and better-trained enemy, they were easily defeated. Moreover, although some of their men had been stationed in the region and they were now fighting a popular cause, their ties with the local population would not have been amicable. Under these conditions, the enormous task of feeding tens of thousands of men would have been reason enough for them to seek safety elsewhere. But, as we have noted, the guerrilla units sprang up in different localities among the masses, and hence their ties with the masses would have been of different character. As table 16 (infra) shows, the 600 armed men under the Chuho Central *Hsien* Committee (Chao Shang-chih's men) were backed by 1,500 members of the farmers' union and 1,700 Anti-Japanese Society members. The problem of supplying a far smaller number of guerrillas would have been much easier.

Since the guerrilla leaders were starting from virtually nothing, it would have been necessary for them to motivate each new recruit. The bond between leaders and followers under such conditions must be strong; the guerrilla leaders must not only articulate the grievances of their followers but inspire respect and trust.

The guerrillas, of course, could not have survived long unless they had the support of the local population, and therefore, the role of such peripheral organizations as the farmers' union and the Anti-Japanese Society would have been crucial. It is true that the regions where the anti-Japanese guerrillas operated were the very areas where brigands had formerly thrived; the brigands had held sway because government authority did not extend to these regions and because there was considerable collusion between them and the government forces. But such conditions no longer prevailed after 1931, and the guerrillas could not build their power on terror alone. Only if the guerrillas were able to convince the population of their raison d'être could they win the support of the masses, and such a condition could be realized only if the leaders instilled in their followers firm belief in their lofty aims and in the need to win the support of the masses.

One of the former participants in the anti-Japanese guerrilla movement left a vivid account of how the "Revolutionary Army" operated and what kind of problems it faced in this period. T'ien Chün's classic novel *Village in August* [Pa-yüeh te Hsiang-ts'un], written in 1934, was set in the region where Chou Pao-chung and Chao Shang-chih operated.[112] We find simple farmers, shoemakers, former soldiers, and former bandits among the rank and file of T'ien Chün's revolutionary army. The "general" of the 200-man force was a former soldier; one of the captains had been a bandit. These men were fired by hatred of the Japanese aggressors and Chinese officials, who had served the warlords but were now serving new masters with equal ease. The guerrillas are constantly exhorted by their captains, the general, and his adjutant (a young Korean woman), who remind them of their mission and the vision of the new world. They ambush a Japanese supply train, killing the Manchukuo officers but sparing the soldiers. They raid the walled and heavily guarded compound of a big landlord, execute the landlord and his wife, who had sought Japanese protection, and indoctrinate the tenant farmers. The peasants of the older generation put family concerns ahead of all other issues and turn a deaf ear to such guerrilla slogans as "Save the nation," "Drive out the Japanese soldiers," and "Farmland to the farmers." They are willing to pay taxes to whomever is emperor, to pay rent to whomever owns the land, and they wish to remain law-abiding "common people" until they are brutally trampled by the Japanese. The young are more easily agitated. They join the guerrillas in songs and discussions and eventually volunteer to join their ranks. But their lives as guerrillas are grueling. They must retreat over the mountains when the enemy pursues them with superior forces; they lack food and supplies, and there is little medicine for the wounded. They fear that the wounded may be captured by the enemy and betray them. But the guerrillas are determined not to yield; they are supported by the peasants, who share their hatred of the Japanese and are impressed by the guerrillas' behavior, which clearly sets them apart from the bandits and soldiers.

Thus, according to T'ien Chün's account, the guerrillas were focusing on the anti-Japanese theme, bringing up the issue of land ownership gingerly and in relation with the landlords' collabora-

---

112. The original Chinese work was published in 1935; the English translation by an unidentified translator and with an introduction by Edgar Snow was published in New York in 1943, and a reprint of the English edition was issued in 1974. In his introduction, Snow compares the work with *Uncle Tom's Cabin, Les Misérables*, and says further that he was in Peking when the novel appeared, and "suddenly every student I knew was talking about it," and that the influence of the book was especially pronounced among the exiled Manchurians, including the soldiers of Chang Hsüeh-liang stationed in northwest China. Chang was later to stage the famous Sian incident.

tion with the enemy. The CCP in this period was intent on arousing the Chinese masses against Japanese aggression rather than advocating a class war. It is quite possible, however, that the CCP was able to recruit new members among the guerrillas. All those supporting the revolutionary army were potential CCP recruits.

Compared to the utter failure of the CCP in the urban areas, the CCP's strength in the hinterlands was considerable. Table 16 presents the overall strength of the CCP at the end of October 1934. The table, compiled by the Japanese Ministry of Foreign Affairs for internal use, was based on confiscated or intercepted Communist documents.

Conclusions

As table 16 shows, the results of Communist efforts were mixed. Efforts to build party organizations in the cities and industrial areas were largely futile, particularly because the nascent party organizations provided clues to the hostile forces by distributing propaganda materials. It also appears that the CCP's emphasis on mobilizing the proletariat based on the traditional or orthodox Marxist line of arguments prevented it from making more effective use of the strong anti-Japanese sentiment among the urban youth.

The situation among the anti-Japanese fighters in the hinterlands was more encouraging from the Communist point of view, but there were hurdles to overcome. The left-wing radicalism of the East Manchuria Special Committee, abetted by instructions from the central leaders, alienated the party from the masses and weakened the party's ability to withstand the onslaught of Japanese forces. Had the CCP pursued a different course in building ties with the anti-Japanese masses in Chientao between 1932 and 1933, the Japanese would have encountered much greater resistance to their "pacification" of the region.

Developments in Panshih and elsewhere sharply contrasted with the situation in Chientao. Perhaps it was a fortuitous combination of environment, personality of leaders, and organizational ties with the Manchurian Provincial Committee that led the Panshih committee to avoid the mistakes of the East Manchuria Special Committee and to follow the new course established by Ch'en Shao-yü. In the Kiangsi soviet in Southern China, Mao Tse-tung was emerging as the principal leader in this period, overshadowing the other nonmilitary cadres. In southern Man-

Table 16 Communist Strength in Manchuria as of October 1934

Committees	Party branches	Party members	Labor Union members	Farmers' Union members	Anti-Japanese Society members	Youth Corps members	Armed men
East Kirin Bureau							
Muling	22	160	370			88	
Ningan	12	75	25	450	570	70	70
Mishan	17	110	4	75		70	
Tungning	4	30		15	100		
Jaoho	8	50		150			
East Manchurian Special Committee					(1,000+)*		700
Yenchi	52	189	40			143	
Wangching	45	190	65	350		260	
Holung	21	80	110	500		70	
Hunchun	27	100	90	100		176	
Antu	4	25	12	100		22	
Panshih Central Hsien Committee	75	292	21	1,490	3,589	223	720
Chuho Central Hsien Committee	11	117	13	1,500	1,700	45	600
Tangyuan Central Hsien Committee	12	82	5	50	40	70	
Harbin City Committee	20	100	230		380	75	
Harbin Railroad Area	16	67	37		10	23	
Totals	346	1,667	1,022	4,780	6,389	1,335	2,090

*Estimated membership of the anti-Japanese societies in Chientao; not included in total.
Source: East Asian Bureau, Ministry of Foreign Affairs, Japan, *Shina oyobi Manshū ni okeru saikin no kyōsan undō shiryō* [Recent Materials on the Communist Movement in China and Manchuria] (Tokyo, December 1934), table following p. 137.

churia, it was Yi Hong-gwang, a simple Korean peasant who had studied Sun Tzu's war manual, and Yang Ching-yü, the veteran of the organization movement in the Fushun mines, who began to exert greater influence on events. The leaders of the Manchurian Provincial Committee in Harbin also supported the policies pursued in Panshih. But the cadres in Manchuria were soon enjoined from pursuing their successful strategy and ordered to pursue the "united front from below" strategy, which threatened to undo all their previous accomplishments. Details concerning events of this period in northern Manchuria are not available, but a similar situation doubtless prevailed. A basic revision in the party strategy was needed if the Communists hoped to expand their forces and to assume leadership of the guerrilla movement in Manchuria.

8 United Front and Guerrilla Communism

WHILE COMMUNIST CADRES IN MANCHURIA WERE desperately trying to expand their still miniscule forces in the cities and hinterlands, momentous events were happening in southern China that had direct impact upon their future. As is well known, Communist forces in Kiangsi and neighboring provinces had been building a formidable army and soviet regimes to withstand the relentless onslaught of the Kuomintang since 1931, but the situation in Kiangsi became totally untenable by mid-1934. By October, the Central Soviet was abandoned, and the main armies of the Chinese Communist Party (CCP) headed west and northwest, setting out on the treacherous Long March. The central leaders and the many troops and civilians under them were forced to traverse remote regions of China, incessantly fighting a tenacious enemy in hot pursuit.

The central leaders were also forced to abandon their liaison point in Shanghai. Chang Wen-t'ien left for Kiangsi in 1933 at the latest, and more than fifty important Communists were reportedly arrested in Shanghai in April or May 1934.[1] As we noted earlier, the Shanghai Bureau of the CCP Central Committee ceased to exist after the middle of 1934.[2] Obviously the central leaders were not in a position to communicate with the Manchurian Provincial Committee, let alone to direct the movement in Manchuria.

By default, therefore, the task of guiding the Communist move-

---

1. Yoshihiro Motohiko and Takahashi Toshio, "Saikin ni okeru Manshū kyōsan shugi undō no jōsei" [Recent Status of the Communist Movement in Manchuria] (September 29, 1937), in Shihō-shō, Keiji-kyoku (Bureau of Criminal Affairs, Ministry of Justice, Japan), *Shisō jōsei shisatsu hōkokushū, 4: Manshū ni okeru kyōsan undō* [Reports of Inspection Tours of Ideological Conditions, 4: The Communist Movement in Manchuria], *Shisō kenkyū shiryō, 41* [Ideological Study Materials, Special Series, No. 41] (Tokyo, 1938), p. 185.
2. See my discussion in chapter 6, footnote 32.

ment in Manchuria fell upon Chinese leaders in Moscow. Ch'en Shao-yü, as we have seen in chapter 6, had been involved in directing the movement in Manchuria, and the Comintern itself had been involved since 1932. Li Yao-k'uei, the head of the Manchurian Provincial Committee, had been dispatched from Moscow in 1933. It was, therefore, an easy matter for the CCP delegation in Moscow to assume leadership of party activities in Manchuria. In order to facilitate liaison, a branch office of the Chinese delegation was established in Vladivostok in early 1935, although it was not meant to be an exclusive channel of communication between Moscow and Manchuria. At any rate, the Communist movement in Manchuria entered a new phase in early 1935.

The first act of the Chinese delegation, consisting of Ch'en Shao-yü and Chao Yün (better known by his alias, K'ang Sheng), was to effect a drastic change in the united front policy. As we have noted in chapter 6, Ch'en had argued since January 1933 that, given the new environment in Manchuria (i.e., the Japanese conquest of that territory), the CCP's united front policy must encompass all anti-Japanese elements in Manchuria rather than setting the low-level soldiers against the officers or the proletariat against the capitalists. In advocating this change, Ch'en ran counter to the CCP leaders in southern China, who insisted that the "united front from below" strategy must be the foundation of the CCP's united front policy. Ch'en must have been exasperated by the line of argument contained in the CCP central headquarters' directives to Manchuria issued in January 1933 and February 1934 (which had obliquely criticized Ch'en). Subsequent events in Panshih (see chapter 7) showed that Ch'en's policies were much more fruitful than the line that was followed in Chientao, where a more leftist strategy was implemented. Now that Ch'en and K'ang Sheng were in direct command of party activities in Manchuria, they had no reason not to bring about an abrupt change in strategy.

The order of the Chinese Comintern delegation enunciating the new policy was issued on June 3, 1935, in the form of a "Confidential Letter to the Comrade in Charge of Eastern Kirin Province."[3] We have a report indicating that the Chinese delegation

3. The text is available in Japanese translation in Gunseibu, Komonbu (Advisors' Department, Ministry of Defense, Manchukuo), *Manshū kyōsanhi no kenkyū* [Study of Communist Bandits in Manchuria] (n.p., 1937), appendix, pp. 47–57, and Nihon Kokusai Mondai Kenkyūjo, Chūgoku-bu (Chinese Department, Japanese International Problems Research Center), *Chūgoku kyōsantō-shi shiryō-shū* [Compendium of Materials on the History of the Chinese Communist Party] (Tokyo, 1971), vol. 7, pp. 506–517. Hereafter cited as *Shiryō-shū*.

had instructed the Manchurian Provincial Committee in May or June 1935 to terminate its relations with the CCP headquarters and receive orders from it.[4] This means that the line of communication between Moscow and Harbin was still open. Why, then, did the leaders in Moscow choose to send an important message to a person in charge of a province rather than the regional headquarters? Did they send similar letters to comrades in other provinces as well? We have no clear answers to either of these questions. But it will be helpful if we survey the status of the Manchurian Provincial Committee at this time.

The Manchurian Provincial Committee

The Manchurian Provincial Committee at this time was in a shambles. In many ways, the massive arrests of April 1934, involving Hu Pin and others, and the subsequent defection of key leaders to the Japanese side were fatal to the committee. This does not mean that the Communist movement in Manchuria came to an end, but the Manchurian Provincial Committee's role as the regional headquarters for the Communist movement in Manchuria effectively ended with the April arrests.

For one thing, the continuing arrests bred suspicion and distrust among the cadres within Manchuria; for another, the central leaders in Shanghai and the Chinese delegation in Moscow also came to doubt the integrity of some of the agents whom they themselves had dispatched. Needless to say, this was hardly conducive to a vigorous movement. In some regions of Manchuria, therefore, the Communist movement fell into the doldrums between April 1934 and the middle of 1935, although we must quickly add that the movement in other regions, particularly in the southern hinterlands under Yang Ching-yü and the northern hinterlands under Chao Shang-chih and Chou Pao-chung, expanded during the same period, having been unaffected by developments elsewhere.

There is no doubt that the Manchurian Provincial Committee had been infiltrated by enemy agents on different occasions. As we noted in chapter 5, the Japanese were very well informed about party affairs in 1932, and this could not have been possible unless someone in the party were transmitting copies of party reports to the Japanese. The Japanese tabulation of CCP strength in Manchuria as of October 1934 (as shown in table 16) also suggests

4. Yoshihiro and Takahashi, "Recent Status of the Communist Movement," p. 186.

that there was a leak in the CCP hierarchy. But the central leaders' distrust of Manchurian leaders in 1934 was due to another incident.

Soon after the April arrests in Manchuria, the Shanghai headquarters reportedly dispatched three agents to Manchuria to revive the movement there. None of the extant Japanese records reveal the full names of these agents, and the identity of the three is therefore unknown. In any event, immediately after the three left Shanghai, more than fifty important party members were arrested in that city, casting suspicion upon the three. Therefore, the central leaders in Shanghai—that is, whoever remained there—and the Chinese delegation to the Comintern refrained from sending any major directives to Manchuria. Eventually, in the early part of 1935, these three were summoned to Moscow for investigation, and "Lo," the new provincial secretary of the Communist Youth Corps, took over as acting head of the local party organization.[5] Evidently the central leaders dispatched other cadres to Manchuria, but the situation did not change for the better. According to a Japanese account, a cadre named Chuang was sent to the provincial committee from the party headquarters in China in October 1934 to head the organization department.[6] Also in the same month, Liu Shao-ch'i is said to have been sent back to Manchuria to head the provincial committee, but in March 1935 he was allegedly transferred to Vladivostok, where a branch office of the Chinese delegation to the Comintern had just been established.[7] Hatano Kenichi, a noted Japanese historian of the CCP, reports that Pien Shih-ch'i was newly appointed to head the provincial committee in December 1934, but was arrested in Tientsin while en route to his post.[8] In any event, we do know that the acting head, "Lo," remained in that position until January 1936.[9] Upon assuming the post of acting secretary in May 1935, "Lo" sent his wife to Shanghai to request additional personnel and possibly other aid, but there was no one in Shanghai to help her.[10]

Thus, the Manchurian Provincial Committee was in an anemic condition, and it was soon to be abolished. Probably it was for this reason that the leaders in Moscow decided to bypass the act-

5. Ibid., pp. 150–151, 185.
6. *Manshū kyōsanhi no kenkyū*, p. 38.
7. Ibid.
8. Hatano Kenichi, ed., *Chūgoku kyōsantō-shi* [History of the Chinese Communist Party] (Tokyo, 1961), vol. 6, p. 365.
9. Yoshihiro and Takahashi, "Recent Status of the Communist Movement," pp. 183–184.
10. Ibid., p. 186.

ing secretary in Harbin and communicate directly with local leaders.

Another interesting aspect of the "Confidential Letter" is that the strategy espoused in it is identical with the theme of the Seventh World Congress of the Comintern, which convened several weeks later in Moscow, between July and August of the same year.[11] Obviously, preparations for that congress had been made by early June, and both Ch'en Shao-yü and K'ang Sheng were informed of the direction in which the Comintern would be headed. It should be noted, however, that the close parallel between the strategies advanced in the "Confidential Letter" and by the Seventh World Congress suggests that the new strategy was not an expression of the personal preference of either Ch'en or K'ang but a decision reached by the Comintern leadership. (Recall in this context that Pavel Mif had participated in the 1933 decision to broaden the base of the united front in Manchuria.)

In the "Confidential Letter," Ch'en Shao-yü and K'ang Sheng reiterated the theme that Ch'en had stressed in January 1933. They noted, among other things, that the party and the guerrilla forces under its control were weak, and that there was extreme difficulty in establishing a united front.[12] The two leaders also saw that the immediate situation in Manchuria and elsewhere called not for a final contest against the enemy but for military and political preparation. Since the enemy was powerful and the Red Army in China and the foreign (Soviet Russian?) revolutionary forces were unable to provide direct support for the anti-Japanese movement in Manchuria, the Communists there would have to concentrate on arousing and expanding the anti-Japanese forces in the area, bringing them under the direct leadership of the Communist party and arming them.

Toward accomplishing this task, the two leaders in Moscow directed the Communists in Manchuria to abandon the strategy of the "united front from below" and to utilize all available methods to expand the united or popular front and the mass movement. The Communists in Manchuria were also instructed to abandon the fourfold classification of the guerrillas in Manchuria, which had governed the united front tactics of the Communists since the CCP letter of January 1933 was issued. Although K'ang Sheng had forcefully defended the correctness of the previous party policy toward Manchuria at the Thirteenth Plenum of the Executive

11. See Charles B. McLane, *Soviet Policy and the Chinese Communists, 1931–1946* (New York, 1958), pp. 61–63.
12. *Shiryō-shū*, vol. 7, pp. 506–517.

Committee of the Comintern in December 1933,[13] he and Ch'en Shao-yü (Wang Ming) now argued that the previous policy was a "fundamental error." It is interesting that the two leaders specifically vindicated the actions of Yang Ching-yü in establishing the General Command of the Anti-Japanese Allied Army in 1933. In doing so, the leaders in Moscow were reversing the position taken by the CCP leaders, who had criticized Yang in their February 1934 letter. The leaders in Moscow said:

> It was correct to organize the General Headquarters of the Anti-Japanese Allied Army. *But it is a fundamental error to argue, as some have done, that the superstructure can be established only upon the solid foundation of the infrastructure.* [Emphasis added.] It is an even greater mistake to dissolve the Allied Army's headquarters. The united front at the upper level should not be contrasted with that at the lower level. The upper-level united front must be advantageously utilized to facilitate the smooth operation of the activities directed toward the lower-level masses. Indirect operations toward the masses may be carried out without utilizing the upper-level united front, but there would be various dangers in direct operations [if the upper-level united front were not utilized].[14]

Along with this drastic change in basic policy, the leaders in Moscow also instructed the Communists in Manchuria to broaden the platform or slogans of the united front. The three points included in the "general standards" for the united front were: "Never surrender to the enemy—fight to the death against Japanese imperialism and Manchukuo," "Protect the interest of the masses—grant democratic freedom to the masses," and "Foster the anti-Japanese struggles of the masses through unity." Instead of isolating the counterrevolutionary groups among the anti-Japanese forces, the Communists in Manchuria were now directed to join hands with each and every group that opposed the Japanese:

13. See Kang Sin (K'ang Sheng), "The Development of the Revolutionary Movement in Non-Soviet China and the Work of the Communist Party," in *Theses, Reports, Speeches of the Thirteenth Plenum of the Executive Committee of the Communist International* (New York, 1934). Speeches of Wang Ming and K'ang Sheng were issued in a pamphlet, "Revolutionary China Today," and bound in the plenum volume. K'ang's discussion of the situation in Manchuria and the endorsement of the Central Committee's policy regarding the united front from below is on pp. 80–82.

14. *Shiryō-shū*, vol. 7, p. 509.

Even if groups contain elements addicted to opium or those who would undermine the good will of the masses, they should not be antagonized. These defects should be regarded as obstacles in the course of forming a united front. The provisional operational agreement should be regarded not as something apart from the united front but merely as the beginning stage in the establishment of a united front. By maintaining close liaison in combat and gradually bringing the groups under the command of the Allied Army Headquarters, temporary liaison can lead to permanent solidarity. . . .

Confuse the minds of those who, after their defection from the revolutionary camp, have been sent to subjugate the guerrillas: send them the slogan "Chinese Should Not Attack Chinese." Encourage them to revolt, and when they have returned to the anti-Japanese camp, assign them a designation bearing the name of the locality. . . .

In order to avoid the attention of the Japanese imperialists and to appeal to the broad masses, such terms as "red" or "soviet" should be avoided. Instead, such designations as the Anti-Japanese Army of National Salvation or the People's Revolutionary Army should be used.[15]

Thus, the two Chinese leaders in Moscow demanded an about-face in the CCP policy in Manchuria. There is no doubt that those in Moscow were encouraged by the developments in Panshih and that they wanted Panshih's successful policy emulated throughout Manchuria. Perhaps this was only natural, as the cadres in Panshih were following the line of policy Ch'en Shao-yü had set forth in January 1933.

Although Ch'en and K'ang were hostile toward Chiang Kai-shek, the struggle against the Kuomintang and the counterrevolutionaries was not the central concern of the leaders in Moscow.[16] Even if a group were under the influence of the Kuomintang, the Communists in Manchuria must now accept it in forming a

---

15. Ibid., p. 570.
16. In their letter, the leaders in Moscow advised the Communists in Manchuria to establish anti-Japanese regimes wherever possible. The platform of these regimes was to include the slogan "Oppose Chiang Kai-shek and other traitorous governments and establish ties with the masses and armies who are resisting Japan and opposing Manchukuo." No specific mention was made of the Kuomintang. See *Shiryō-shū*, vol. 7, p. 514.

united front to expand the anti-Japanese front. Of course, the purpose of the united front was not to surrender the Communist strength to the other anti-Japanese groups. The Communists in Manchuria were instructed to concentrate special efforts on improving their units so that they would have "power suitable for the nucleus of the anti-Japanese armed forces."[17] To this end, the leaders in Moscow issued detailed instructions on the political education of the cadres.

The major points of the June 3 letter were reiterated in Ch'en Shao-yü's speech at the Seventh Congress of the Communist International, delivered on August 7.[18] In his speech, Ch'en emphasized that

> under the conditions of the growing national crisis, there is no other means of saving China except the general mobilization of the whole of our great people for a decisive and relentless struggle against imperialism. And at the same time, the Communist Party has no other means for the general mobilization of the entire Chinese people for a sacred national revolutionary struggle against imperialism than the tactics of the anti-imperialist united people's front.[19]

Ch'en wanted all revolutionary elements, including "various political and military forces who constitute temporary, unstable, and wavering allies," to join the struggle.

Ch'en's criticism of his comrades who had consistently detracted from his earlier "proposals" or "directives" was mild. Even though the chasm separating his and the Comintern's policy from that of the CCP leadership was obvious for all to see, Ch'en openly stated that the CCP "has applied and is now applying the tactics of the anti-imperialist united front." The only fault, according to Ch'en, had been that the CCP "has not as yet succeeded in carrying out these tactics in a truly consistent and faultless manner."[20] Sharper criticism against the CCP leaders was to be launched by an underling named Yang Sung, who used such words as "wiseacres" and "left sectarians" in characterizing those leaders who had denounced the more successful attempts at alliance with the non-Communist elements.[21]

17. Ibid., p. 508.
18. "The Revolutionary Movement in the Colonial and Semi-Colonial Countries and the Tactics of the Communist Parties," *Communist International*, vol. 21, no. 17–18 (September 20, 1935), pp. 1323–1333.
19. Ibid., p. 1325.
20. Ibid.
21. Yan[g] Sun[g], "The Anti-Imperialist United Front in Manchuria: The Oc-

Evidently those in the Eastern Kirin Provincial Committee responded very quickly to the call from Moscow. In a book written by a cadre of the Fourth Army and published in 1936, we find the text of the "Declaration of the Anti-Japanese Allied Army of Manchuria to Compatriots in Manchuria Concerning the North China Incident," dated June 20, 1935.[22] The heads of the first to sixth armies and the anti-Japanese guerrilla units in Tangyuan and Hailun denounced the Kuomintang government for acceding to various demands of Japan in North China and echoed the theme of the "Confidential Letter." The declaration advocated the convening of an Anti-Japanese National Salvation People's Representatives' Conference to establish an anti-Japanese Manchurian government and called on all armed groups to join the Allied Army. It called on the soldiers and officers under the Japanese to kill the Japanese officers and join the anti-Japanese forces. It called on the workers, farmers, merchants, students, and women either to join the anti-Japanese forces or to support the cause of fighting against Japan. The three slogans presented were: oppose Japan and protect the fatherland, confiscate the property of the Japanese and their lackeys, and unite the people to oppose Japan and to save China.

These events were followed by the famous August 1 declaration, "Appeal to the Whole People to Resist Japan and Save the Country," issued in the name of the Chinese Soviet Government and the Central Committee of the CCP.[23] Although the leaders in Moscow borrowed the name of these two organizations in China proper, it is clear that the central leaders under Mao Tse-tung, then resting from the Long March in remote western China, neither approved nor agreed with the content of the "Appeal."[24] The

---

cupation of Manchuria and the Anti-Japanese National Liberation Movement," *Communist International*, vol. 13, special number (February 1936), pp. 171–183. Yang Sung subsequently published a two-part article, "On the Experience and Lessons of the Seven Years of the Anti-Japanese Guerrilla Movement in Manchuria," in the Chinese-language publication *Chieh-fang* [Liberation], vol. 1, no. 34 (April 5, 1938), pp. 4–9, and vol. 1, no. 38 (May 15, 1938), pp. 15–22. Between 1935 and 1936, Yang was located in Vladivostok at the Eastern Kirin Provincial Committee headquarters. See Yoshihiro and Takahashi, "Recent Status of the Communist Movement," p. 154. Evidently Yang moved to Yenan via Moscow in late 1937 in the company of Ch'en Shao-yü and K'ang Sheng.

22. Sun Chieh, *Tung-pei K'ang-Jih Lien-chün Ti-ssu-chün* [The Fourth Anti-Japanese Allied Army in Manchuria] (Paris[?], 1936), pp. 86–91.

23. An English version of the "Appeal to the Whole People to Resist Japan and Save the Country" (August 1, 1935) is in *International Press Correspondence*, no. 70 (December 21, 1935), pp. 1728–1729; the Chinese text is available in Wang Chien-min, *Chung-kuo Kung-ch'an-tang shih-kao* [Draft History of the Chinese Communist Party] (Taipei, 1965), vol. 3, pp. 42–45.

24. Gregor Benton, "The Second Wang Ming Line," *China Quarterly*, no. 61 (March 1975), pp. 62–67.

CCP leaders at this time were pursuing another strategy vis-à-vis the Kuomintang, and they were not ready to appeal for the unity of all forces, including the Kuomintang, to engage in the "sacred task of resisting Japan and saving the nation." Mao Tse-tung also objected to the provision in the "Appeal" that the property and land of national traitors alone would be confiscated and that all others, including landlords, would be permitted to continue to own land. This, of course, would have meant the end of the program of land reform being implemented by the CCP, and the central leaders were not prepared to make such a drastic change in policy. The gap between Ch'en Shao-yü in Moscow and Mao Tse-tung was not bridged until July 1936.[25]

The leaders in Moscow must have known beforehand that the formula presented in the declaration would not be acceptable to the CCP leaders. The likelihood of the Kuomintang's accepting the "Appeal" was even more remote, because it had almost succeeded in squashing the CCP forces in Kiangsi and was still hoping to put an end to the Communist movement throughout China. Was the August 1 declaration, then, issued simply as a corollary to the Seventh Congress? Was the call for the cessation of civil war and the establishment of an "All-China Unified National Defense Government" and an "All-China Anti-Japanese Allied Army" simply a propaganda ploy intended to gain legitimacy and win moral support for the CCP?

Close examination of the text of the "Appeal" suggests another possibility. There is reason to believe that the leaders in Moscow were very conscious of the potential effects of the "Appeal" on the popular front movement in Manchuria. Indeed, one is tempted to say that the August 1 declaration was intended primarily for the Manchurian audience. Preponderant references to events and individuals in Manchuria and exaggeration of the importance of organizations there suggest this. One could argue, of course, that Manchuria deserved special attention at this time because it was the only region in which the Chinese were fighting the Japanese. Even so, however, we find some of the details unusual.

It was natural, perhaps, that such figures as Cheng Hsiao-hsü, Chang Ching-hui, and P'u I, who headed the puppet regime of Manchukuo as either premier or emperor, were singled out as national traitors; but the listing of the following as "national heroes" who were allegedly leading several hundred thousand armed anti-Japanese fighters in Manchuria is a little out of the ordinary: Yang Ching-yü, Chao Shang-chih, Wang Te-t'ai, Li Yen-lu, Chou Pao-

25. Ibid., pp. 66–69.

chung, Hsieh Wen-tung, Wu I-ch'eng, and Li Hua-t'ang. The first six were the commanders of the first to sixth people's revolutionary armies respectively; the last two were the heads of volunteer armies, that is to say, armies which had not established formal ties with the Communists. We wonder whether the leaders in Moscow had ulterior motives in thrusting these partisan fighters onto the national stage as national heroes and thereby inflating their egos. At least four of the eight (Li Yen-lu, Li Hua-t'ang, Hsieh, and Wu) were non-Communists.

These leaders in Manchuria must have been enormously flattered to see that the "Appeal" treated their forces in Manchuria on an equal footing with the Red Army in China proper. The Red Army, according to the "Appeal," was to establish the All-China Anti-Japanese Allied Army by joining with the people's revolutionary armies and various anti-Japanese volunteer armies of Manchuria. The All-China Unified National Defense Government was to be established by the Chinese Soviet government and the "anti-Japanese governments throughout Manchuria." It is to be noted that such "anti-Japanese governments" were not yet in existence in Manchuria.

Thus, while the August 1 declaration was incongruous in the context of the CCP-KMT struggle in China proper, its utility in Manchuria was enormous. The non-Communist leaders would have been hard put to refute the logic of the "Appeal" that had so inflated their egos. It would not have been necessary for the Communist cadres to argue long to persuade potential allies of the need for a popular front; all they would have needed to do was to read them the text of the August 1 declaration.

The objective environment in Manchuria also favored a broad popular front. The anti-Japanese forces had numbered more than 300,000 in 1932 but had steadily declined since then in the face of determined efforts by the Japanese Army. The Japanese estimated the total number of anti-Japanese forces in 1933 to be 52,000; in 1934, 40,000; and in 1935, 21,000.[26] Particularly after December 1934, the Japanese Kwantung Army began to implement special techniques for counterinsurgency operations, including the establishment of "collective hamlets" designed to isolate anti-Japanese armed groups from the general population,[27] and the guerrilla armies were finding it increasingly difficult to continue the uncoor-

26. Manshūkokushi Hensan Kankōkai (Editorial and Publication Committee of the History of Manchukuo), *Manshūkokushi* [History of Manchukuo] (Tokyo, 1971), vol. 1, pp. 302–303.
27. For details, see Chong-Sik Lee, *Counterinsurgency in Manchuria: The Japanese Experience, 1931–1940* (Santa Monica, 1967), pp. 25–36, 79–183.

dinated struggle. Those remaining in the anti-Japanese front were undoubtedly the more dedicated and weathered individuals, but if they were to have any impact at all against the Japanese and survive the Japanese onslaught, they needed to combine their strengths.

On October 5, 1935, leaders of 24 armed groups in the vicinity of Panshih responded to the call of the CCP's Panshih Central *Hsien* Committee and established the Anti-Japanese Allied Army General Command North of the [Sungari] River (K'ang-Jih Lien-ho-chün Chiang-pei Tsung Chih-hui-pu) and signed an agreement on joint operations. The principal points of the 13-article agreement were: (1) not to surrender or to betray the nation, and to firmly engage in the anti-Japanese national salvation struggle and recover lost territory; (2) to support the anti-Japanese government and join the people's government; (3) to confiscate all property of the Japanese bandits and their lackeys and utilize it for the anti-Japanese war; (4) to engage in the anti-Japanese national salvation struggle by uniting with all people and all anti-Japanese armed units; and (5) to protect the interest of the anti-Japanese masses (i.e., to solicit donations from the rich and utilize them in anti-Japanese work).[28] On October 10, leaders of nine non-Communist anti-Japanese groups in the "Southern Manchuria Guerrilla District" issued a "Statement of Opinion Concerning the Establishment of the Anti-Japanese Allied Army of Manchuria," in which they expressed their "utmost agreement" with the idea of establishing a "Southern Manchuria Anti-Japanese Allied Army." The brief statement added that "Commander Yang [Ching-yü], as is well known, is a person of strong determination with a glorious record of anti-Japanese struggle, and is the most appropriate person to become the commander of the Allied Army. Comrades! Speedily join the Allied Army for the nation and facilitate the strengthening of the anti-Japanese forces."[29] The Communists also succeeded in establishing a close alliance with Wang Feng-ko, the single most important non-Communist nationalist leader of the Tungpientao region, in the spring of 1936.[30]

Not only did the anti-Japanese groups in Manchuria swiftly respond to the call for unity. The leaders of the principal armed groups in Manchuria issued, on October 11, an appeal for a nationwide united front and the establishment of the National

28. *Manshū kyōsanhi no kenkyū*, pp. 435–437.
29. Ibid., p. 441.
30. Ibid., p. 418. The agreement may have been concluded in April; see ibid., p. 444.

United Front and Guerrilla Communism 241

Defense Government and the General Headquarters of the All-Nation Anti-Japanese Allied Army. The appeal, addressed to all heads of government and military leaders and the people of China,[31] was issued in the names of the commanders of the first to sixth armies of the Anti-Japanese Allied Army of Manchuria and in the names of Wu I-ch'eng and K'ung Hsien-jung, commander and deputy commander, respectively, of the Volunteer Army of Manchuria (Tung-pei Yi-yung-chün), a non-Communist group. Also listed in the appeal were the Tangyuan Anti-Japanese Guerrilla Unit, the Hailun Anti-Japanese Guerrilla Unit, and the Anti-Japanese National Salvation Committee of Manchuria (Tung-pei K'ang-Jih Chiu-kuo Wei-yüan-hui). We do not know the exact circumstances of the drafting and issuing of the appeal or who actually gave consent to the use of their names, but the message it contained was very potent. It reproachfully reminded the reader that not a soldier had been dispatched from China proper in the face of the Japanese takeover of Manchuria; it advocated that Chinese stop killing Chinese and requested that troops be dispatched to Manchuria to counter the Japanese. We do not know how widely the appeal was circulated in Manchuria, but judging from the fact that the Japanese authorities obtained a copy of it in Shanghai in January 1936, there is no doubt that the text was circulated in China proper.[32] It would not be surprising if the appeal played an important role in the large-scale anti-Japanese demonstrations of students in Peking, Tientsin, Shanghai, and other major cities. The student movement supporting the theme of the August 1 declaration erupted in Peking on December 9, 1935, and continued well into the spring of 1936.[33]

The united front movement in the region east of Harbin was spearheaded by Chao Shang-chih, the head of the Third Army. Ever since the founding of the Third Army of the People's Revolutionary Army of Manchuria in January 1935 under the direction

31. The Chinese text of the appeal is available in Sun Chieh, *Tung-pei K'ang-Jih Lien-chün*, pp. 91–95; for a Japanese version, see *Manshū kyōsanhi no kenkyū*, pp. 437–439. The Japanese text gives December 12 as the issuing date.
32. See *Manshū kyōsanhi no kenkyū*, p. 439.
33. For details of the December 9 movement, see Nihon Kokusai Seiji Gakkai (Japanese Association of International Politics), *Taiheiyō sensō e no michi* [The Road to the Pacific War] (Tokyo, 1963), vol. 3, pp. 298–303. The major impetus for the movement was the Japanese attempt to detach the five northern Chinese provinces of Hopei, Chahar, Suiyuan, Shantung, and Shansi from the jurisdiction of the Nanking government by setting up an "autonomous government." See B. Winston Kahn, "Doihara Kenji and the North China Autonomy Movement, 1935–1936," in Alvin D. Coox and Hilary Conroy, eds., *China and Japan: Search for Balance Since World War I* (Santa Barbara, 1978), pp. 177–207.

of the Chuho Central *Hsien* Committee, Chao had been active in the effort to elicit the support of the numerous non-Communist armed groups in the area and had, in April of the same year, established the Allied Anti-Japanese Army of Manchuria. The party's attempt to win over the troops under the "united front from below" strategy and the animosity of the past had hampered his efforts,[34] but a Japanese report of June 1935 stated that, as the professional bandits were persuaded by Chao Shang-chih to join his forces, "the Chuho region gives the sense of being a Communist kingdom, and the bandit groups in this area are not to be easily exterminated; on the contrary, small bandit groups in various places voluntarily join with the political and ideological bandits [i.e., the nationalist and Communist bandits], and the public security of the region is increasingly deteriorating."[35] It is no wonder that the People's Republic of China honored Chao by renaming Chuho after him as Shang-chih.

A massive attack by the Japanese in the fall of 1935, however, forced Chao's forces to retreat further northeast to the more remote Ilan-Tangyuan area near the Soviet border. Chao and six other military leaders, including the heads of the fourth and sixth armies, held a meeting in late January 1936 in Tangyuan to establish the People's Anti-Japanese Allied Army General Headquarters of Manchuria and the People's Anti-Japanese Allied Army Provisional Government of Manchuria. The purpose of the general headquarters was to coordinate and direct the anti-Japanese movement in Manchuria. Under the command of Chao Shang-chih, the entire movement was to be "organized, politicized, and systematized." It was to be coordinated through command posts (*chih-hui-pu*) in Southern Manchuria, Eastern Kirin, Eastern Harbin, Hulin, Jehol, and Ningan.[36] A proclamation issued on February 20 in the name of the heads of the six armies of the Allied Army and the Tangyuan and Hailun guerrilla units called for the systematization of all armed groups under the six armies and various guerrilla units and for struggle for national salvation by all armed groups, regardless of religious, political, or economic differences; it also beckoned all armed groups in Manchuria to join the allied armies.[37] As we noted above, although the establishment of the provisional government was mentioned, no information is

34. *Manshū kyōsanhi no kenkyū*, pp. 684–694.
35. Ibid., p. 696, quoting from *Hizoku geppō* [Bandit Monthly], August 1935 issue; no other details provided.
36. *Manshū kyōsanhi no kenkyū*, p. 775.
37. Ibid., pp. 775–777.

available concerning it. Instead, the February 20 proclamation indicated that the allied armies would be directed by the Anti-Japanese National Salvation General Association of Manchuria.

The campaign to establish and consolidate the united front was pushed through in eastern Kirin, where the Fifth Army and a part of the Second Army were operating,[38] and even in Chientao, where the East Manchuria Special Committee had pursued radical left-wing policies. The directive issued by the Manchurian Committee was unequivocal. The major duty of the CCP was to drive out Japanese imperialism: never mind that the past policies had concentrated on strengthening the proletariat while alienating the revolutionary bourgeoisie and intelligentsia or that the policies of the past had eliminated the spirit of "opposing Manchukuo and resisting Japan" and destroyed the chance for the formation of a united front; all anti-Japanese elements, including the revolutionary bourgeoisie, must be united.[39] Receiving these instructions, the heads of the first and second armies met with the leaders of other armed groups in the Chientao area in February 1936 and actively moved toward fulfillment of the new strategy.[40] By the spring of 1936, very few armed groups remained in Manchuria that did not subscribe to the principle enunciated in the August 1 declaration.

The successful implementation of the united front policy not only contributed to the consolidation of strength and streamlining of command structure among the armed groups, but it also contributed directly to the improvement of relations between the armed groups and the general population. If the major defect of the Communists had been their attempt to win over the troops of other armed groups by separating them from their chieftains, one of the principal shortcomings of the small bands of guerrillas had been their bandit-like behavior, which drove a deep wedge between the armed groups as a whole and the general population; the leaders of the allied armies therefore emphasized the correct behavior of the armed men toward the population. A statement issued in 1936 by Ch'i Chih-chung, the head of an "independent division of the allied army," as an appeal to the leaders and troops of the armed groups to join his forces, was primarily a criticism of the "evil deeds" of various small groups:

> But among the guerrilla revolutionary armies, some small units have plundered the people and otherwise in-

38. Ibid., pp. 277–282.   39. Ibid., pp. 243–244.
40. Ibid., pp. 244–251.

flicted damage upon the people. Remembering these actions, some of the people thought evil of the anti-Japanese armies; not only did they not establish good relationships with us, but on the contrary, they opposed us. This has produced immeasurable obstacles to the future of our anti-Japanese armies. The leaders and troops of anti-Japanese armies must understand this fact well. If the armies and the people unite and bring into being a [truly united] anti-Japanese army, and if the army loves and protects the people, the future progress of the anti-Japanese army can be great. But if not, political and military relationships among various anti-Japanese units [and between the army and the people] will fall into disorder and the support for the armed units will be gravely affected. Many weak units are absorbed with the problem of strengthening armaments in their sector and are inflicting damage on the people.[41]

The qualitative change brought about by the united front upon the anti-Japanese forces in Manchuria was immediately noticeable to the Japanese authorities. The Japanese officer in charge of compiling the massive work on the anti-Japanese movement in Manchuria, *Manshū kyōsanhi no kenkyū* [Study of the Communist Bandits in Manchuria], noted in February 1937 that

the number of bandits at present is said to be somewhere around 20,000, and compared to the period immediately after the [Manchurian] Incident [i.e., the takeover of Manchuria by Japan in 1931], when the number exceeded 300,000, it seems that we are living in a different world. Thus, the trend has shown a decline in number [of bandits]. But we notice the prominent phenomenon that the tempo of decline during the past two or three years has been relaxed.

This was not because the hand of subjugation has been relaxed. In spite of the fact that great sacrifice has been made in terms of persons and funds as before, the effects of the efforts at subjugation have not been as good as anticipated. While we can expect improvement in public security in certain regions at certain times, the fundamental strategy to realize perpetual [tranquility throughout our domain] has not been established.

41. Ibid., pp. 781–782.

Table 17 *Anti-Japanese Fighters in Sanchiang Province, January 1935 – June 1936*

Month	Number of anti-Japanese fighters				Number of reported appearances	Cumulative number of men in action
	Communist	Non-Communist Nationalist	Former bandits	Total		
January 1935	1,000	350	560	1,910	—	—
February	1,069	350	608	2,027	—	—
March	1,110	400	515	2,025	61	4,011
April	1,350	420	360	2,130	125	9,368
May	2,450	1,540	470	4,460	164	9,299
June	1,420	500	450	2,370	155	9,059
July	1,206	513	601	2,320	186	8,588
August	1,283	570	522	2,375	201	8,436
September	1,288	575	437	2,300	152	9,581
October	1,298	604	336	2,238	160	8,694
November	1,298	594	308	2,200	143	8,931
December	1,530	728	251	2,509	126	10,244
January 1936	1,140	728	251	2,119	143	9,240
February	1,449	700	251	2,400	192	11,686
March	1,649	700	251	2,600	269	19,660
April	1,650	600	250	2,500	270	25,690
May	1,850	600	250	2,700	239	23,768
June	1,800	600	300	2,700	265	21,048

Source: Gunseibu, Komonbu (Advisors' Department, Ministry of Defense, Manchukuo), *Manshū kyōsanhi no kenkyū* [Study of Communist Bandits in Manchuria] (n.p., 1937), pp. 826–827 and 832–833.

This is to say that the pattern of bandit subjugation operation or public security operation that has been employed in the past has now reached its limit.

What then, is the basic reason for this kind of stalemate in public security operations? It lies in the qualitative change among the bandit groups in Manchuria, that is to say, the communization of the bandit groups and the control of other bandit groups by the Communist bandits.[42]

Not only had the quality of the anti-Japanese forces improved, but their numbers and the frequency of their attacks had increased. We do not, unfortunately, have detailed data concerning all areas of anti-Japanese operations, but table 17, concerning Sanchiang Province, the operational area of Chao Shang-chih, is

---

42. Ibid., preface, pp. 3–4. The foreword by Major General Sasaki Tōichi, who was the supreme advisor to the Manchukuo Army, conveyed the same message.

suggestive. The numbers of both Communist and non-Communist nationalist fighters had increased in late 1935 and early 1936, and this was probably due to the retreat of Chao Shang-chih's forces from the southeast. But the number of operations undertaken by the anti-Japanese forces in the spring of 1936 and the number of fighters mobilized for these operations were more than double those of the same season in the previous year. The strategy of the united front was making an impact.

Relations with the Masses

The strength of Communist guerrillas, of course, was due not only to their ability to bring the scattered armed groups under the umbrella of a united front but also to their ability to win the support of the masses. Without such support, the Communist guerrillas could not have maintained themselves, let alone effectively operate against the more powerful Japanese forces. And without displaying their strength against the enemy, they could not play the leading role among the various groups.

We have already cited the remarks made by Ch'i Chih-chung in 1936, when he admonished "small units" of the guerrilla armies for plundering the people or otherwise inflicting damage upon them. He argued that the armies and the people must unite and establish an anti-Japanese army, and that the army must love and protect the people. From an account presented by Okamoto Goichi, a Japanese prosecutor who was dispatched in late 1937 to investigate the conditions among the guerrillas, we can see that the Communist guerrillas paid close attention to this problem in terms of both propaganda content and the day-to-day behavior of the guerrillas toward the masses. The information presented below is evidently drawn from the area of operation of the First Army under Yang Ching-yü near the Korean border, but there is every reason to believe that similar circumstances prevailed in other areas.

According to Prosecutor Okamoto, the Red Army's propaganda was directed toward the general masses, particularly young men and boys. In their propaganda, the agents stressed the recovery of lost territory (i.e., Manchuria), the saving of the nation, and the love of the people before propagandizing communism. They also asserted that the various security facilities in Manchukuo only enslaved the people and did not bring them happiness. After instilling anti-Manchukuo thoughts, the agents propagandized communism. They asserted that when the revolution was completed, land and property would be equally divided among the people and stability of livelihood would be guaranteed. The lower-class residents were told that the activities of the Japanese and Manchukuo units should be reported swiftly and that rich rewards would be given to those who led the Red Army into advantageous situations.

Prosecutor Okamoto provided some examples of propaganda as follows:

a. The poisoned fangs of the Japanese bandits have closed upon the three provinces in the northeast. For this reason, the masses in Manchuria have fallen into distress. The only way to escape from the oppression of the Japanese devils is for the people to unite with the Revolutionary Army of Manchuria to drive out the Japanese devils and establish a Manchurian government under freedom and equality.
b. Have you forgotten the fatherland? Why do you not resist the oppression of the Japanese government?
c. Why are you afraid of Japan? Wake up and fight for the fatherland and against Japan. We take up rifles to resist Japan.
d. You should organize anti-Japanese organizations as our supporters.
e. Our organization is spread throughout Manchuria. Our organization is truly devoted to the cause of opposing the Japanese and saving the nation, and we have great strength. Villagers, join hands with our revolutionary army and swear to be anti-Japanese fighters. Otherwise we will burn the whole village down.
f. Young men should voluntarily join our Red Army and the general masses should unite and help us because the Red Army intends to recover Manchuria, destroy Japanese imperialism, and liberate the masses of Manchuria.
g. The Japanese imperialist army has already enslaved the farmers to repair the roads, burned small villages, and made the people live in collective hamlets. They are preparing to drop bombs from airplanes [on the hamlets] and slaughter the masses.
h. Manchuria is a part of China. We, the Army of Na-

tional Salvation, are striving to destroy Manchukuo, which has been established by Japanese imperialism through a war of robbery, and to rescue the masses in Manchuria from distress and starvation. It is the duty of all Chinese, regardless of sex or age, to assist us.

i. The Japanese armies come to the countryside and harass the good people. They are the enemies of the people. The Communist party is a true friend.

j. The only interest of the general Japanese population is in making money; they take all the property of the masses to Japan.

k. We, the Communist party, are an army of resistance to the Japanese and Manchukuo armies; we intend to recover Manchuria and return it to the masses of Manchuria. You young men should rise and act.

l. When communism is realized, the property of the rich will be divided among the poor and the distinction between the rich and the poor will be eliminated. Only then, for the first time, will the people live in peace and be content with their professions. The Russians will come to Manchuria, and all of Manchuria will be communized. A peaceful Manchuria will be established through the power of Russia.[43]

These messages, according to Okamoto, were conveyed through lectures, plays enacted in the villages, and leaflets.

Communist guerrilla behavior toward the villagers was also exemplary, according to the prosecutor. They moved from one friendly village to another and paid a fixed sum of money for their food. They never engaged in pillage. When a pro-Japanese or pro-Manchukuo individual was discovered, however, he would be looted for that reason. To be prepared for staying in destitute villages, all troops carried a day's ration of rice, flour, or corn. When they were stationed in a village, an officer in charge of food would purchase grain and had civilians cook the meal. Sometimes, however, food was coercively requisitioned. No salaries were paid to the troops, and officers and men ate the same food. All captured goods were allocated for the unit's use or sold for military funds.

43. Okamoto Goichi, "The Chinese Communist Party and the Communist Bandits in Manchuria," in Shihō-shō, Keiji-kyoku, *Shisō jōsei shisatsu hōkokushū,* 4: *Manshū ni okeru kyōsanshugi undō,* pp. 63–65.

Acquired grain was sometimes entrusted to members of the farmers' self-defense unit or the Anti-Japanese Society for storage.[44]

The behavior of the guerrillas was reinforced by ten rules of troop conduct memorized by all recruits. These rules were evidently enforced strictly. They were as follows:

1. Those abusing the masses will be punished.
2. Those destroying weapons will be punished.
3. Those informing for the enemy will be executed.
4. Those raping women will be executed.
5. Those deserting from the war front will be executed.
6. Those deserting with rifles will be executed.
7. Those departing from the army and disobeying orders will be punished.
8. Those concealing ammunition will be executed.
9. Those plundering property without instructions will be punished.
10. Oppose Japanese and Manchukuo to the death.[45]

To insure the proper conduct of the guerrillas, guerrilla units conducted lecture and discussion sessions at every opportunity, according to the prosecutor. Officers were instructed to weed out undesirable elements from their units and to explain problems in current affairs to their subordinates. Representatives of the party and the youth corps assisted unit commanders' efforts. Officers closely watched the troops' conduct lest they beat or abuse the masses. The troops were provided with indoctrination to possess class consciousness as well as to persevere in hardship. They were taught revolutionary songs to heighten their enthusiasm for opposing Japan and resisting Manchukuo.[46]

The Japanese prosecutor concluded that the attitude of the masses toward the Red Army was highly favorable.

> The population in the base area tends to welcome the insurgents, either because they have accepted the propaganda or because they wish to avoid being harmed by them. Some young men are voluntarily joining the insurgent groups. On the whole, the people have favorable feelings toward the insurgents and have been helping them. The power of the Red Army has spread among the masses far beyond expectation. The anti-Japanese societies and the anti-Japanese farmers' self-

44. Ibid., pp. 71–72.   45. Ibid., pp. 52–53.   46. Ibid., p. 73.

defense units are satellite groups of the Red Army. There is a strong tendency for the masses to rely on the insurgent groups for the protection of their lives and property because the power of the [civil] authorities does not extend to their area. The relationship between the insurgents and the people is very intimate, and it is difficult to distinguish one from the other.[47]

Reorganization of the CCP in Manchuria

While the armed groups in Manchuria were thus reorganized and rejuvenated under the new united front strategy, the CCP organization also underwent substantial changes. As noted earlier, the Manchuria Provincial Committee suffered from frequent arrests and internal suspicions, and Acting Secretary "Lo" merely kept the name of the committee alive without serving any useful purpose for the party.

This situation caused the Chinese delegation in Moscow to dispatch Han Shou-k'uei and several others in December 1935. Han had been in Vladivostok since August 1933, after having assisted his elder brother in Aihun (to the north of Harbin) for two years in collecting information for the Soviet intelligence services. Han underwent training at the University of the Toilers of the East in Moscow throughout 1935, with the understanding that he would subsequently be dispatched to Manchuria for party work. Others dispatched with Han were similarly trained.[48] Han's mission was to implement the popular front strategy, to reorganize the party in Manchuria, and to abolish the Communist Youth Corps and mobilize the young people under the broad guidelines of the new strategy.

47. Ibid., p. 70.
48. Yoshihiro and Takahashi, "Recent Status of the Communist Movement," p. 177. The four others were Fu Yu, Chang Te, Wei Cheng-min, and Tu Wen-yüan. While the backgrounds of the others are unknown, Wei Cheng-min was a well-known figure in Eastern Manchuria, having served as the secretary of the Eastern Manchurian Special Committee and as political commissar of the Second Army of the People's Revolutionary Army. He had served as the chief of the propaganda department of the Manchurian Provincial committee in 1932 (see ibid., p. 181) and as the committee's inspector in Eastern Manchuria in October 1934 (see *Manshū kyōsanhi no kenkyū*, p. 97). Evidently Wei had been recalled to Moscow for further training in 1935. The account provided by Yoshihiro and Takahashi, the two Japanese prosecutors who toured Manchuria and filed a report dated September 29, 1937, was based on information gathered from Han Shou-k'uei and others who were arrested between April and June 1937 (Han was arrested on April 16, 1937). Unfortunately for the historian, the two prosecutors provided only the bare outline of Han's activities. I have not been able to locate the police records and investigatory reports which would have provided the details.

The party organization in Manchuria was to be reorganized as follows: the Manchurian Provincial Committee of the party was to be abolished, and the existing organizations were to be regrouped under the Harbin Special Committee, the Eastern Kirin Provincial Committee, the Eastern Manchurian Provincial Committee, the Southern Manchuria Provincial Committee, and the Eastern Harbin Provincial Committee. Each committee was to act independently under the direct command of the CCP delegation in Moscow. The city committees in Dairen and Mukden were to be reorganized into special committees in the future, but until conditions warranted such a change, they were to be placed under the new Harbin Special Committee.[49]

Han arrived in Harbin on January 1, 1936, met Acting Secretary "Lo" on January 7, and dissolved the Manchurian Committee on January 9. On the same day, he established the Harbin Special Committee and began to establish contacts with party members in such cities as Harbin, Dairen, and Mukden and in such localities near Harbin as Hailun, Hulan, Payen, and Pin *hsien*.[50] For the next fifteen months Han strove to revive and streamline communication networks and to expand the various groups under the party. A massive arrest of party supporters in June 1936 destroyed the Anti-Japanese General Society and the National Salvation Youth Association, but the effort to mobilize elements of society continued. The following list of organizations under the direction of the Harbin Special Committee suggests the party's targets of mobilization.[51]

> *Harbin City Committee*
> National Salvation Youth Corps
> Anti-Japanese Society
> Rickshaw Men's Society
> Shop Clerks' Society
> Sewing Machine Operators' Society
> Women Workers' Society
> Horse Carriage Drivers' Society
> *Hulan Special Branch*
> National Salvation Youth Corps
> Anti-Japanese Society
> *Dairen City Committee*
> National Salvation Youth Corps

49. Yoshihiro and Takahashi, "Recent Status of the Communist Movement," pp. 177–178.
50. Ibid., pp. 184–190.
51. Ibid., pp. 191–193.

Women's Society
Red Workers' Society
Anti-Japanese Society
Payen Special Branch
Anti-Japanese Society
Mukden City Committee
Women's Society
Anti-Japanese Society
Soldiers' Committee
Hailun Hsien Committee
Women's Society
Anti-Japanese Society
Farmers' Committee

Extant information does not reveal the number of individuals mobilized by these organizations, but the meager funds distributed by Han Shou-k'uei suggest that the operation was of very modest scale. Before leaving Moscow, Han had heard that the Manchurian Provincial Committee had been receiving 200 U.S. dollars per month from the Comintern, and that the Harbin Special Committee would be receiving the same amount. When converted to local currency, this amounted to 650–660 Manchukuo *yüan*. While the members of the party and the Anti-Japanese Society were required to pay 10–20 cents a month as membership fees, the party collected only one *yüan* a month from this source, and Han was thus obliged to depend solely upon the Moscow funds. Beginning in January 1937, as the U.S. dollar exchange rate went up, Han received 700 *yüan* a month, of which 45 *yüan* was allocated to his own maintenance and operational expenses. The remainder was distributed as follows:[52]

Harbin City Committee:	170–180 *yüan*
Dairen City Committee:	130–140 *yüan*
Mukden City Committee:	120–130 *yüan*
Hailun *Hsien* Committee:	90–100 *yüan*
Hulan Special Branch:	100 *yüan*
Pin *Hsien* Special Branch:	15 *yüan*
Harbin Special Committee, Traffic Bureau:	80–100 *yüan*

The funds were undoubtedly distributed according to need or intensity of activities in different places. If this assumption is correct, none of the urban centers was bustling with activity; one or

52. Ibid., p. 195.

two hundred *yüan* allocated to various committees could not have carried them very far. It is also noteworthy that the Comintern's allocation to the Harbin Special Committee does not appear to have increased after Han's arrival in Harbin or during his fifteen months of operation there. This in itself says something about the scale of the movement. Of course, an increase in membership does not necessarily require a proportional increase in expenses; but if the scale of activity had expanded significantly, the party would have found it necessary to provide for the subsistence of additional key personnel and other increased expenses. But the Comintern continued to send only $200 a month.

Mukden party members, however, seem to have had an independent source of income, at least between 1934 and 1936, and perhaps we should not draw too close a parallel between the funds distributed by Han Shou-k'uei and the magnitude of operations in different localities. According to the Japanese military police in Mukden, Liu Yao-fen (also cited elsewhere as Liu Yao-chieh) and the head of the South Manchurian Special Committee of the CCP, an employee of the Ch'i-tung Tobacco Company in Mukden, received 30,000 *yüan* from Soviet Consul General Khazhinov in March 1934. With this fund, Liu and others allegedly opened the Li-hsing Company (Li-hsing Yang-hang), a sales agency dealing in tobacco. The sales agency's profit was to be used to carry out propaganda and other party activities.[53] In October 1935, Liu caused the principals of privately operated middle schools to organize the Mukden Education Special Committee (Feng-tien Chiao-yü T'e-pieh Wei-yüan-hui), which brought a number of other educators into the fold. At least ten secondary schools in Mukden were involved with the committee, and the Japanese authorities decided that the primary purpose of the committee was to "communize" the school children.[54] According to the same source, the South Manchurian Special Committee established or directed branches (*chih-pu*) in Dairen, Antung, Yingkou, Shanchengchen, Kirin, Changchun, and Ssupingchieh, and cells (*hsiao chih-pu*) and *hsien* committees in Penhsihu, Fushun, Hsinmin, Liaochung, Liaoyang, and Anshan.[55]

It seems incredible that the Soviet consul general was in a position to provide such a large sum of money for the operation in Mukden. At that time, 30,000 *yüan* was worth approximately

---

53. Okamoto Goichi, "Chinese Communist Party and Communist Bandits," pp. 18, 26.
54. Ibid., pp. 18–26.
55. Ibid., p. 21.

U.S. $10,000. The Japanese sources also do not provide any details concerning Liu Yao-fen or the educators involved. But whatever operation Liu had directed in Mukden came to an end in April 1936, when the Japanese military police cast a dragnet over the alleged Communists.

Han Shou-k'uei's activities in Harbin came to an end in April 1937, when he was arrested by the Japanese and Manchukuo authorities. Two hundred and six others were also arrested between April and June. Of those arrested, 109 were from Harbin, including those in the Harbin City Committee, and 47 were from the eastern Harbin district. While we do not know how representative the arrested were in terms of occupation and age distribution, the data presented in tables 18 and 19 provide a clue to the kinds of individuals associated with the Communist-directed movement in the Harbin region.

The data presented in table 18 are limited, but we can safely conclude that the individuals mobilized by the Harbin Special Committee were of diverse backgrounds and not from any particular segment of the population. The intelligentsia, represented by the teachers, constituted only 15 percent of those arrested. The presence of soldiers and policemen among the arrested merits attention in view of the fact that they were presumably in the ser-

Table 18 *Occupation of Chinese Communist Party Members and Party Affiliates Arrested in June 1937*

Occupation	Number	Percent
Soldier	13	6.3
Policeman	10	4.8
Teacher	31	15.0
Student	13	6.3
Railroad Worker	11	5.3
Laborer	17	8.2
Merchant	20	9.7
Farmer	23	11.1
None	20	9.7
Others	49	23.7
Total	207	100.0

Source: Yoshihiro Motohiko and Takahashi Toshio, "Saikin ni okeru Manshū kyōsan shugi undō no jōsei" [Recent Status of the Communist Movement in Manchuria], September 29, 1937, in Shihō-shō Keiji-kyoku (Bureau of Criminal Affairs, Ministry of Justice), *Shisō jōsei shisatsu hōkokushū: 4: Manshū ni okeru kyōsan undō* [Reports of Inspection Tours of Ideological Conditions: 4: Communist Movement in Manchuria] (Tokyo, 1938), p. 200.

Table 19 Age of Chinese Communist Party Members and Party Affiliates Arrested in June 1937

Ages	Number	Percent
Below 20	14	6.8
21–25	60	29.0
26–30	61	29.5
31–35	42	20.3
36–40	10	4.8
41–45	9	4.3
46–50	3	1.4
Above 50	8	3.9
Total	207	100.0

Source: Yoshihiro Motohiko and Takahashi Toshio, "Saikin ni okeru Manshū kyōsan shugi undō no jōsei" [Recent Status of the Communist Movement in Manchuria], September 29, 1937, in Shihō-shō Keiji-kyoku (Bureau of Criminal Affairs, Ministry of Justice), *Shisō jōsei shisatsu hōkokushū: 4: Manshū ni okeru kyōsan undō* [Reports of Inspection Tours of Ideological Conditions: 4: Communist Movement in Manchuria] (Tokyo, 1938), p. 200.

vice of the Manchukuo regime. The fact that merchants constituted 9.7 percent of those arrested is also significant because their participation proves beyond doubt that the party had broken away from the narrow confines of the proletarian movement and had successfully appealed to the wider public.

The age distribution of the arrested presents few surprises. Those in their 20s were the most active, followed by those in their early 30s. Those under twenty were perhaps students. It is regrettable that other socio-economic data on the arrested are not available.

The Japanese imposed harsh punishment against their enemies. Forty-two of the 156 arrested in Harbin and vicinity (including the eastern Harbin district) were sentenced to death[56] for the simple act of conspiring against Japanese imperialism, rather than plotting or implementing armed revolts or other violent acts.

The Communist movement in the urban areas suffered another blow on June 2, when 113 party members and affiliates were arrested in Dairen and Port Arthur (Lushun). The Japanese authorities discovered that the city committee had infiltrated various major industrial and transportation facilities in the two cities and maintained organizational activities through such innocuous

56. Katō Narimasa, "Conspiracy and Intelligence Gathering of the Soviet Union and China in Korea, Manchuria, and Northern China" (December 1937) in Shihō-shō, Keiji-kyoku (Bureau of Criminal Affairs, Ministry of Justice, Japan), *Shisō jōsei shisatsu hōkokushū, 4: Manshū ni okeru kyōsan undō*, p. 297.

groups as associations of fellow provincials (t'ung-hsiang-hui) and charities (chi-shan-hui). In Dairen the Communists were found on the docks, in the railyards, in the power station and electric company, and in chemical, cement, and oil companies, among others.[57] With the leads provided by those arrested, the Japanese continued to probe into Communist activities, arresting four additional soldiers in Harbin between July and August.[58] Presumably, more were arrested as interrogations continued.

The Eastern Kirin Provincial Committee was based upon the old Eastern Kirin Bureau, described at the end of chapter 7. The bureau had been reorganized into the Eastern Kirin Special Committee in November 1935, and directed Communist movements in Jaoho, Mishan, Ningan, Tungning, Muleng, and Poli, towns on or near the Ussuri River which constituted the Sino-Soviet border.[59] The Japanese authorities surmised that the Eastern Kirin Provincial Committee was reorganized between December 1935 and April 1936, and located in Vladivostok under the direction of a Shih Ta-kan [Stakhan?] who was concurrently in charge of the Vladivostok branch of the Chinese section of the Comintern's Far East Bureau and the secretariat of the Pan-Pacific Labor Union.[60] The Eastern Kirin Provincial Committee continued to serve as a major channel of communication between Moscow and the Communists in Manchuria.

The South Manchurian Provincial Committee was established in July 1936, at the Second Representatives' Conference of the "South Manchurian Party" held in the hinterland of Chinchuan *Hsien.* As we have seen in previous chapters, the South Manchurian Special Committee had been located in Mukden, but after the mass arrests there in the spring of 1932, the committee became defunct, and the Panshih Central *Hsien* Committee had served as the party headquarters in the region. Later, in December 1934, another "central *hsien* committee" was created in Tunghua to supplement the Panshih committee.[61] Unlike the regular *hsien* committee, the central *hsien* committees were immediately subordinate to the Manchurian Provincial Committee and directed operations in a number of *hsien* in the vicinity. At the First Repre-

57. Ibid.
58. Ibid.
59. *Manshū kyōsanhi no kenkyū,* pp. 715–717.
60. Yoshihiro and Takahashi, "Recent Status of the Communist Movement," pp. 154–155. Although this source says Shih Ta-kan was a Chinese, he was probably a Russian, "Stakhan."
61. *Manshū kyōsanhi no kenkyū,* p. 338.

sentatives' Conference, held in October 1934 in Chinchuan (near the border of Kirin and Fengtien provinces), the Communist cadres had decided on the revival of the South Manchurian Special Committee, placing Yi Tong-il, a Korean, in charge of the organization.[62]

The conference of July 1936 introduced a major change not only in the party organization but in the allied army as well. And the conference not only dealt with the party and military affairs in southern Manchuria but those in eastern Manchuria also. In fact, the CCP cadres decided not to establish a separate provincial committee in eastern Manchuria, as had been planned, but to place the party and army organizations that remained in eastern Manchuria under the South Manchurian Provincial Committee. This decision was prompted by a sequence of events requiring a brief review.

East Manchuria had been the stronghold of the Korean Communists ever since the early 1920s, and, as we have mentioned in previous chapters, the Korean Communists had played important roles in the CCP's operation there since their incorporation into the CCP in 1930. But the East Manchurian Special Committee suffered massive losses between 1933 and 1935 from the concerted assault of the Japanese authorities and the witch hunt launched by the Chinese leaders (see chapter 7). Particularly because of its loss of mass support, evidenced by the drastic decline of the membership of the Anti-Japanese Society, the Second Army, which consisted of some one thousand men, was forced to abandon its sanctuary and split into two groups, one proceeding to the north to join the Fifth Army and the other, numbering some 350 men, joining the First Army in the west.[63] In February 1936, Li Tsung-hsüeh, the acting commander of the Second Army, had met with Yang Ching-yü, the commander of the First Army, and the leaders of other non-Communist groups at Santaokou in Fusung *Hsien* to confer on the unification of all of the anti-Japanese armed forces in the region.[64] When Wei Cheng-min returned to East Manchuria from Moscow together with Han Shou-k'uei, he found the situation in that region hopeless; at least the strength of the CCP there was not sufficient for him to reorganize the local party branch into a provincial committee as he had been directed.

Therefore, the July conference decided on establishing the

62. Yoshihiro and Takahashi, "Recent Status of the Communist Movement," p. 156.
63. *Manshū kyōsanhi no kenkyū*, p. 446.
64. Ibid., pp. 445–447.

South Manchurian Provincial Committee, placing the refurbished East Manchurian Special Committee under it. Wei Cheng-min was appointed secretary of the provincial committee, and Yi Tong-il, the former head of the South Manchurian Special Committee, was appointed head of the organization department. The new provincial committee, in any event, faced formidable tasks. The Liuho *Hsien* Committee had suffered from the arrest of 69 activists between October and December 1935,[65] and its secretary was arrested in February 1937.[66] In January 1937, the Panshih *Hsien* Committee also suffered a major blow as its secretary and some 70 members were arrested.[67] The Japanese military police and the Manchukuo police were becoming increasingly efficient, even in the hinterlands.

The July conference also implemented a major change in the military organization. The General Headquarters (*Tsung Ssu-ling-pu*) of the First Route Army was created, and the first and second armies were placed under it.[68] Yang Ching-yü was appointed commander of the First Route Army.

The party organization in the Chuho and Tangyuan region where Chao Shang-chih had been directing the military and united front movements was also reorganized. As noted before, the Japanese had launched a major assault on Communist and other groups in Chuho, and the anti-Japanese forces were forced to retreat down the Sungari River to the vicinity of Tangyuan. Evidently the Chuho Central *Hsien* Committee suffered from these events and was dormant. Han Shou-k'uei dispatched Fu Yu, a colleague from Moscow, and in the late summer of 1936 the committee was reorganized into the Eastern Harbin Special Committee.[69] The Tangyuan Central *Hsien* Committee, however, was in a robust condition with the support of the Third Army under Chao Shang-chih. In September 1936, leaders of party organizations in Chuho and Tangyuan and those of the third and sixth armies held a joint conference in a mountain hideout in Peishan, Tangyuan *Hsien*, and established the North Manchuria Provisional Provincial Committee.[70] Feng Ch'ün, who had served as head of the propaganda department of the Chuho committee[71] and head of the political department of the Third Army under Chao,[72] was

65. Ibid., p. 448.
66. Yoshihiro and Takahashi, "Recent Status of the Communist Movement," p. 157.
67. Ibid.   68. Ibid., pp. 156–157.   69. Ibid., pp. 158–159.
70. Ibid., pp. 157–158.
71. *Manshū kyōsanhi no kenkyū*, p. 613.
72. Ibid., p. 632.

elected secretary of the new provisional committee and Chao was elected head of the military department.[73]

Thus, the Communist party in Manchuria had been completely reorganized, and the united front strategy was very successfully implemented when the Japanese invasion of the mainland of China was launched in July 1937. Chang Hsüeh-liang, the Young Marshal from Manchuria, was then in Sian; he had been in touch with Chou En-lai of the CCP Politburo since the summer of 1936, hoping to bring about a cease-fire between the KMT and the CCP in order to mount a unified opposition to the Japanese aggressors. While the CCP was accommodating, Chiang Kai-shek was adamant in exterminating the CCP first. This led to the famous Sian Incident of December, when the Young Marshal arrested the generalissimo and kept him captive until he acceded to his demands.[74] While complicated negotiations between the KMT and the CCP ensued, the Japanese attack left little alternative for Chiang. The two parties again established a united front, and China was at war against Japan.[75]

These events exerted a great impact on the anti-Japanese front in Manchuria. Yang Sung, former Communist cadre and member of the Eastern Kirin Committee, writing in March 1938, succinctly summarized the ways in which these developments in China affected the anti-Japanese struggle in Manchuria. First, the war in China considerably lifted the Japanese pressure against the anti-Japanese forces in Manchuria because the Japanese were obliged to divert their resources to China. Second, political feelings in Manchuria were greatly aroused, and a great number of people voluntarily joined the anti-Japanese armies while others actively provided support to them; officers and men from the puppet Manchukuo army also deserted their units and joined the anti-Japanese forces. Third, these events provided opportunities for the guerrillas to establish anti-Japanese bases, although this was still a hope rather than reality.[76] Chou Pao-chung, the leader in northern Manchuria, told a reporter in 1946 that after the war

73. Yoshihiro and Takahashi, "Recent Status of the Communist Movement," p. 158.
74. Ōkubo Yasushi, Chūgoku kyōsantō-shi [History of the Chinese Communist Party] (Tokyo, 1971), vol. 1, pp. 501–508; James Pinckney Harrison, The Long March to Power: A History of the Chinese Communist Party, 1921–72 (New York, 1972), pp. 268–270.
75. For details of events leading to the second united front between the CCP and the KMT, see Lyman P. Van Slyke, Enemies and Friends: The United Front in Chinese Communist History (Stanford, 1967), pp. 75–121; and Ōkubo Yasushi, Chūgoku kyōsantō-shi, pp. 508–538.
76. Yang Sung, "Experience and Lessons," pp. 8–9.

erupted in China the allied armies in Manchuria became more active, and their central task was assisting the anti-Japanese war in China proper by assaulting the enemy from the rear. They attacked cities, took over fortresses, and destroyed the transportation facilities of the enemy. They also attacked key points along the railways. In a battle along the Shaho River, the allied armies destroyed more than 700 Japanese and Manchukuo soldiers; at Muleng Railroad Station they blew up an enemy train and killed 700 enemy troops. In various places, particularly in the lower reaches of the Sungari River, whole regiments of Manchukuo troops surrendered.[77]

A publication by Japanese former officers of the Manchukuo puppet army commented that the war in China "threw all of Manchuria into an uproar, recalling the adage that blood is thicker than water." Rumors ran rampant, and those with money and property engaged in speculative buying and selling.[78] The situation was so serious that the minister of public security of the Manchukuo regime issued a statement on July 31 warning the public not to be swayed by the intrigues of the Comintern or the Chinese Nationalist Party.[79] While details are not provided, the same publication also mentioned the frequent revolt of Manchukuo army and police units.[80]

We have quoted Chou Pao-chung's brief statement concerning some of his accomplishments after the outbreak of the war. Information about other areas of operation is equally scanty, and a more complete chronicle of the struggle of the anti-Japanese forces remains to be written. But the information at our disposal is sufficient to enable us to draw a general outline of events. A Japanese source reported the discovery of a number of leaflets issued by various armies throughout Manchuria. These leaflets exhorted the people to engage in the struggle against Japanese imperialism, urged Chinese soldiers, police, and other armed men under Japanese control to revolt, demanded funds and materials to be used in the anti-Japanese struggle, and urged the people to oppose the "collective hamlet" program being enforced by the Japanese.[81] The same source also reported the decision of the First

77. Feng Chung-yün, *Tung-pei K'ang-Jih Lien-chün Shih-ssu-nien K'u-tou chien-shih* [Brief History of the Fourteen-Year Struggle of the Anti-Japanese Allied Army of Manchuria] (Harbin, 1946), p. 62.
78. Ran Sei Kai (Orchid Star Society), *Manshūkokugun* [The Manchukuo Army] (Tokyo, 1970), p. 273.
79. Ibid.
80. Ibid., p. 381.
81. Katō Narimasa, "Conspiracy and Intelligence Gathering," pp. 291–292.

Army in southern Manchuria to concentrate on destroying railroads to hamper Japanese war efforts in north China. In order to accomplish this aim, the First Army reportedly dispatched the 120 men of its First Division, commanded by Ch'eng Pin, and the 150 men of its Third Division, under Wang Jen-ts'ai, to the north to cover the Chingyuan and Tiehling regions. Army Commander Yang Ching-yü reportedly moved with his 200 men northwest to Liaoyang *Hsien*, and the commander of the Second Army, Wang Te-t'ai, along with the commander of the Second Division, Ts'ao Kuo-an, moved eastward to Kirin Province.[82]

Another Japanese report mentioned the attempt of contingents of the Sixth Army to move westward to Jehol Province and eventually to join with Mao Tse-tung's forces.[83] According to the same source, Chou Pao-chung, Wei Cheng-min, Chao Shang-chih, and Li Yen-lu held a meeting deep in the forest of Ilan *Hsien* in San-chiang Province in August 1937.[84] At this meeting it was allegedly decided to cause disturbances in Manchuria, to establish a political-military training institute,[85] and to destroy the railroads.[86] Wei Cheng-min was sent to Vladivostok to obtain funds for these undertakings.[87] Among the revolts of Manchukuo army troops, the

---

82. Ibid., p. 292. The Japanese obtained this information from two anti-Japanese soldiers captured on July 17. Chi Yün-lung, a Chinese author, writing in 1946, confirmed some aspects of this report, although his account differs with regard to some of the details. According to Chi, Yang Ching-yü, the commander of the First Route Army, decided to move the entire force under his command westward to the vicinity of the Chinese border. He wished to establish a link with the anti-Japanese forces in Jehol Province so that the forces in Manchuria would no longer be isolated. For this purpose, the First Route Army was organized into three divisions, each of which was to push through the South Manchuria Railway line and the great plains along the Liao River. The First Division succeeded in breaking through the enemy lines to reach the area of Kangping and Faku near the Inner Mongolian border; the Second Division reached Kaiping (south of Yingkou) but was forced to return to Huanjen in August; Yang Ching-yü, leading the Third Division, was unable to cross the Liao River and was forced to return to the original area of operation. See Chi Yün-lung, "Brief Account of the Great National Hero Yang Ching-yü," *Chih-shih* [Knowledge], no. 4, September 1946, p. 8.

83. Gaimushō, Tō-a kyoku, Dai-ni-ka (Second Section, East Asia Bureau, Ministry of Foreign Affairs), *Shina oyobi manshū ni okeru kyōsan undō* [The Communist Movement in China and Manchuria] (Tokyo, June 1938), p. 106.

84. Ibid., p. 100.

85. Ibid. The Political and Military School of the Anti-Japanese Allied Army of Manchuria was established under Chao Shang-chih. See ibid., p. 104.

86. Ibid., p. 106.

87. Ibid., p. 100. Chou Pao-chung stated later that sometime after the Sino-Japanese war erupted, responsible comrades from the eastern Kirin, northern Manchurian, and southeastern Manchurian provincial committees held a meeting which established the policy of preserving their power, laid plans for new guerrilla activities, decided on streamlining all the forces under the three route armies into eleven detachments, and resolved to continue their fierce struggles. No other de-

most noteworthy was the rebellion of the 29th Infantry Regiment of the Manchukuo Army. In November 1937, when the Japanese Kwantung Army was preparing a massive extermination campaign in Sanchiang Province, the Japanese officers suspected the loyalty of the regiment and decided to disarm it, whereupon the regiment commander took the 600 men under him and fled to Laoyeshan where he joined the forces of the Eighth Army of the Anti-Japanese Allied Army.[88] According to the Japanese account, news of these events brought about the "great agitation" of all Manchukuo forces in the region.[89]

Some of the statistics compiled by the Japanese authorities clearly show the favorable effect of the war on the anti-Japanese movement in Manchuria. Table 20 shows that the total number of anti-Japanese guerrillas increased from 24,481 in June to 27,039 in July and to 31,269 in August, 1937, an increase of nearly 7,000 men during the two months between June and August, reversing the previous trend of continuous decline.[90] Table 21 shows a phenomenal rise in the cumulative number of insurgents reported to have appeared in 1937 in comparison with the previous years.[91]

---

tails are provided. Chou Pao-chung, "Recollecting the Anti-Japanese Guerrilla War in Manchuria," *Hsing-huo Liao-yüan* [Sparks Blazing Over the Prairies], vol. 4 (Peking, 1961), p. 375.

88. *Manshūkokugun*, pp. 383–384.

89. Ibid., p. 384. The regiment, however, was persuaded later to return to the fold. The regiment commander served the Manchukuo well after his return, and was promoted from colonel to major general.

90. We do not know what kind of reporting system the Manchukuo regime used in tabulating the number of guerrillas. The Japanese sources, including the volume that provided the data for table 20, reported widely divergent data for the same period. Thus, according to p. 271 of *Manshūkokugun*, the total number of anti-Japanese fighters was 9,600 as of September 9, 1937, and 12,275 as of November 1937; the number declined to 8,786 in September 1938. Evidently, these were the figures provided by the Japanese Kwantung Army. According to p. 354 of the same volume, the Kwantung Army announced on March 3, 1937, that the total number of "bandits" in Manchuria was 9,600. It should be noted that the Police Affairs Headquarters of Manchukuo, from whose monthly report the data for table 20 are derived, was directly responsible for counterinsurgency operations, and hence the data cited in the table are more likely to be correct. *Manshūkoku-shi*, vol. 2, p. 303, copied these data from p. 354 of *Manshūkokugun*.

91. Table 21 shows a sevenfold increase in the cumulative number of insurgents reported to have appeared in 1937 compared to 1936. But, curiously, the figures of other columns, such as the total number of appearances or the casualties suffered by the insurgents, actually show a slight decline. There is a strong possibility, therefore, that the "increase" was the result of a typographical error rather than an actual increase. The figure "10,355,577" for 1937 perhaps should read "1,355,577" instead. Unfortunately, the source of our table does not indicate the origin of its data, and we have no other materials of a similar nature to corroborate the information. Even if the total for 1937 is erroneous, however, the overall increase in the number of anti-Japanese fighters in 1937 cannot be disputed. Table 17

United Front and Guerrilla Communism 263

Table 20 *Numbers of Anti-Japanese Fighters in Manchuria by Province, June–October 1937*

Region and province	June	July	August	September	October
Northern Manchuria					
Sanchiang	12,208	12,054	12,607	12,200	14,069
Lungchiang	215	118	373	265	105
Eastern Kirin					
Chilin	621	426	771	669	829
Mutanchiang	—	2,501	1,574	1,153	1,085
Eastern Harbin					
Pinchiang	4,067	3,204	5,530	5,015	3,219
Southern Manchuria					
Fengtien	2,613	2,148	2,338	2,680	1,429
Antung	4,030	1,727	1,946	2,117	2,564
Chientao	520	217	258	—	—
Tunghua	—	4,136	4,058	3,614	3,529
Chinchou	207	658	1,814	3,258	2,282
Others (3 provinces)	—	120	—	311	261
Total	24,481	27,309	31,269	31,282	29,372

Source: Manshūkoku, Keimushi (Police Affairs Headquarters, Manchukuo), *Chian gaikyō geppō* [Monthly Report on Public Security], 1937; cited in Ran Sei Kai (Orchid Star Society), *Manshūkokugun* [The Manchukuo Army] (Tokyo, 1970), p. 352.

There is no doubt that the anti-Japanese forces in Manchuria were reinvigorated by the war in China. According to Chou Pao-chung, contact between the allied armies and patriotic organizations and personalities in such major cities as Peking, Tientsin, Shanghai, and Nanking became more frequent between 1936 and 1937 than ever before.[92] Undoubtedly, this contact yielded not only moral support for the anti-Japanese guerrillas in Manchuria but some financial support as well.

If the hopes of the anti-Japanese fighters and the patriotic Chinese in Manchuria were aroused by the outbreak of conflict in northern China, their disappointment with the subsequent developments there was greater. To all appearances, the Japanese victory in China was decisive. The Chinese army under Generalissimo Chiang Kai-shek had been humiliated. Tientsin fell to the Japanese before the month of July was over, and the Japanese army

---

shows the number of anti-Japanese fighters in Sanchiang Province in 1935 and 1936 to be approximately 2,000; table 20 shows that the number in the same province increased to between 12,000 and 14,000 in 1937.

92. Feng Chung-yün, *Tung-pei K'ang-Jih Lien-chün*, p. 61. Feng's volume reprinted the full text of an interview Chou gave to a Chinese newspaperman.

Table 21 *The Anti-Japanese Struggle in Manchuria and Losses Suffered by the Anti-Japanese Forces, 1932–1940*

Year	Number of appearances of insurgents	Cumulative number of insurgents reported	Killed	Wounded	Captured	Total losses	Rifles captured	Ammunition captured (rounds)	Horses captured
1932	3,816	3,774,184	7,591	5,160	831	13,582	3,642	8,238	1,558
1933	13,072	2,668,633	8,728	2,381	1,461	12,570	5,970	174,288	2,731
1934	13,395	900,204	8,909	4,264	1,435	14,608	3,153	36,107	2,889
1935	39,150	1,783,855	13,338	11,815	2,703	27,856	6,265	91,780	7,248
1936	36,517	1,555,558	10,713	7,988	1,783	20,484	5,300	72,736	4,251
1937	25,487	10,355,577 [sic]	7,663	5,242	1,298	14,203	2,871	69,081	3,465
1938	13,110	468,884	3,693	2,876	799	7,368	2,609	57,182	1,721
1939	6,547	186,071	3,168	1,753	496	5,417	2,870	51,158	1,287
1940	3,667	132,660	2,140	1,873	545	4,558	1,807	48,274	997
Total	154,761	21,825,626	65,943	43,352	11,351	120,646	34,487	608,844	26,127

Source: Manshūkoku-shi Hensan Kankōkai (Society to Compile and Publish the History of Manchukuo], *Manshūkoku-shi* [History of Manchukuo] (Tokyo, 1971), vol. 2, p. 312.

marched into Peking on August 8. Paoting fell in September, and in November the central government in Nanking was evacuated to Chungking. The Japanese marched into Nanking in early December, massacring thousands of Chinese soldiers and civilians alike and provoking an international outcry.[93] This was not the kind of news that would have uplifted the morale of the men who had been fighting the Japanese army against all odds in the mountains and forests of Manchuria.

The leaders of the anti-Japanese movement were dedicated men whose determination would not have been swayed by the rapid succession of calamitous news. But the effect of the news from China on the anti-Japanese movement in Manchuria would have been disastrous, undoubtedly dampening the enthusiasm of a large proportion of the masses whose support was critically needed by the guerrillas. The movement obviously could not depend solely upon the heroic elements in society whose dedication to patriotism or Communist ideology transcended death, suffering, and pain. In any society, only a small number of individuals possess such qualities; for others, the guerrillas would have had to show that the risk involved in supporting them—either by providing needed materiel or intelligence or by joining one of the subsidiary organizations, such as the Anti-Japanese Society—was compensated by what their support would bring for their nation or for themselves. As long as there was some prospect of success in the guerrillas' mission, many of the masses aggrieved by Japanese colonialism would have been swayed to their cause; but when the prospect of success in destroying Japanese imperialism was absent, most of the populace would have shunned the guerrillas.

As Ch'en Shao-yü and K'ang Sheng stated in their "Confidential Letter," the immediate situation in Manchuria and elsewhere called not for a final contest against the enemy but for military and political preparation. One could hope for another Russo-

---

93. Wholesale looting, terrorism, violation of women, and wanton killing of Chinese by the Japanese troops in Nanking caused international indignation at this time. It is of interest to the students of Manchurian affairs that one of the Japanese generals who spearheaded the attack of Nanking and served as commander of the Nanking garrison was Sasaki Tōichi, who had been the supreme advisor to the minister of defense of Manchukuo between December 1934 and August 1937 before his dispatch to China. In this latter capacity, Sasaki had overseen the establishment of the Manchukuo Army and counterinsurgency operations in Manchuria. For his autobiography, see *Aru gunjin no jiden* [Autobiography of a Certain Soldier], expanded edition (Tokyo, 1967). The "disposition" of several thousand captured soldiers in Nanking is curtly recorded on p. 335. According to Sasaki, the Chinese suffered some 70,000 casualties in their unsuccessful defense of Nanking.

Japanese war, which could provide an opportunity to liberate Manchuria. After all, the first Russo-Japanese war of 1904–1905 was fought over Manchuria and Korea. Many Chinese in Manchuria and China proper had also hoped for another Sino-Japanese war, which would bring about the same result. But the Soviet sale of the Chinese Eastern Railway to Manchukuo in March 1935 cast considerable doubt on Soviet intentions in the Far East.[94] By selling the railway to Manchukuo, the Soviet Union tacitly recognized the status quo; if the Soviet Union had been about to engage the Japanese in another war, it would not have sold the railway to the puppet regime created by Japan.[95] On the other hand, the Chinese government had finally decided to mount an armed resistance to the Japanese, but the vast armies of China proved to be too feeble to repel the aggressors. If thousands of regular troops in China could not deal with the aggressors, what could a few unarmed and impoverished people in the remote mountains of Manchuria be expected to do? Why should they jeopardize their lives and those of their families by listening to the guerrillas, whose future seemed dim? What were the guerrillas preparing for now? The pessimists—or in Mao Tse-tung's parlance, capitulationists—would have found ample reason not to involve themselves with the guerrillas. Yang Sung noted that the Japanese propaganda about the invincibility of the Imperial Army reaped considerable success.[96] Chou Pao-chung stated that the rapid defeat and retreat of the Chinese forces caused great disappointment among the people in Manchuria about the war of resistance.[97] According to Chou, the people in Manchuria regained their confidence in victory only because the Eighth Route Army under Mao Tse-tung firmly continued its anti-Japanese war and when Mao Tse-tung published his essay, "On Protracted War."[98]

94. On the sale of the Chinese Eastern Railway, see *Taiheiyō sensō e no michi*, vol. 4, pp. 259–272.
95. An editorial in *Izvestiya*, March 24, 1935, published on the occasion of the signing of the agreement on the sale of the railway, stressed the Soviet desire to avoid conflict in the Far East. See ibid., p. 272.
96. Yang Sung, "Experience and Lessons," p. 9.
97. Feng Chung-yün, *Tung-pei K'ang-Jih Lien-chün*, p. 62.
98. Ibid. Mao Tse-tung's essay, "On Protracted War," was delivered as a series of lectures in Yenan between May and June 1938. We do not know when or how the content of the essay reached the hills of Manchuria. The Eighth Route Army's victory and continued resistance in northern China was the only bright spot for the Chinese in the early years of the war. In September and October of 1937, Mao's forces under the command of Lin Piao and Nieh Jung-chen engaged the Japanese forces in northeastern Shansi Province and inflicted severe damage. These victories markedly heightened the morale of the Communist forces in China, according to a Japanese source. See Bō-ei-chō Bō-ei Kenshūjo, Senshi-shitsu (Office of

Conclusions

Thus there is no doubt that the new directive from Moscow regarding the united front strategy ushered in a new era in the anti-Japanese movement in Manchuria. The limited information at our disposal clearly indicates that leaders and groups of diverse ideological, political, social, and ethnic backgrounds were able to work together for the common goal of inflicting damage upon the Japanese aggressors. This was in part due to the desperate situation confronted by all armed groups in the face of incessant attacks by the Japanese forces, but it was also because the non-Communist groups perceived a clear change in the CCP policy. They no longer sensed in the CCP strategy the motive to undermine other leaders' power, and found merit in the CCP's pattern of relationship with the masses and its organizational and operational skills. The CCP's de-emphasis of its ideologically oriented programs, such as land reform, helped to convince the non-Communists and anti-Communists of the desirability of cooperating with the Communists. We must also recognize the contributions of some of the key individuals: Yang Ching-yü, Chou Pao-chung, and Chao Shang-chih, the men who were given the leadership of the guerrilla forces in 1936, appear to have been men of exceptional quality. Starting with barely a handful of men between 1933 and 1934, each was able to muster a force of several thousand within a year or two in spite of party directives that were often inimical to their success. While we know very little about their personalities, their accomplishments clearly indicate that other men found them to be trustworthy.

But as Yang Sung noted in his March 1938 article, the movement in Manchuria lacked unified military and political guidance; operations directed at the populace were feeble; anti-Japanese bases had not been established; operations among enemy troops were very weak; and activities in the cities had suffered from numerous arrests, from which they had not yet recovered.[99] In the wake of the war in China, the guerrillas in Manchuria and the CCP leaders who directed the entire movement had serious tasks ahead of them.

War History, Defense Institute, Defense Agency, Japan), *Hoku-shi no chi-an sen* [Public Security War in North China] (Tokyo, 1968), vol. 1, pp. 33–34. For Mao's account of these victories, see his "Interview with British Correspondent James Bertram" (October 25, 1937), *Selected Works of Mao Tse-tung* (London, 1954), vol. 2, p. 51.

99. Yang Sung, "Experience and Lessons," p. 9.

9 | The Final Confrontation

THE OUTBREAK OF THE SINO-JAPANESE WAR REVERSED the previous four-year decline in the number of anti-Japanese guerrillas, and the movement as a whole acquired considerable vitality. The Chinese Communist Party, which had but a small and insignificant guerrilla unit under its command in 1932, came to have a dominant influence on the anti-Japanese movement in Manchuria by 1935, and by the following year there were few armed men in Manchuria who were not under its influence. Whatever misgivings they may have had in the past, even the most renowned anti-Japanese leaders of non-Communist and anti-Communist background had by this time established effective alliances with the Communists. Wang Feng-ko, the former head of the Big Sword Society who had been known as the king of Tungpientao region, worked with the First Army. Li Yen-lu, a former Kirin Army officer and a colleague of Wang Te-lin, the foremost figure in the anti-Japanese movement in the Chientao region between 1931 and 1933, became an important link in the entire movement in 1934, having established and headed the Fourth Army that year.[1] Hsia Yün-chieh, a man of non-Communist background and a former officer in the Kirin Army, became the first commander of the Sixth Army, although he was to be killed in action in early 1936.[2] Hsieh Wen-tung, the landlord who had led a

---

1. For a brief biography of Li Yen-lu, see Sun Chieh, *Tung-pei K'ang-Jih Lien-chün Ti-ssu-chün* [The Fourth Anti-Japanese Allied Army of Manchuria] (Paris[?], 1936), pp. 113–119. About Wang Te-lin and Li Tu, with whom Li Yen-lu maintained close contacts, see Li Chih, ed., *Tung-pei K'ang-pao lieh-chüan* [Biographies of Resisters of Tyranny in Manchuria] (Taichung, Taiwan, 1966), pp. 17–19, 99–103.

2. Gunseibu, Komonbu (Advisors' Department, Ministry of Defense, Manchukuo), *Manshū kyōsanhi no kenkyū* [Study of Communist Bandits in Manchuria] (n.p., 1937), pp. 753–754.

farmers' revolt against the Japanese in Tangyuan *Hsien* in March 1934, was serving as the commander of the Eighth Allied Army.[3] Li Hua-t'ang, a former officer in the Kirin Army, was leading the Ninth Army. Wang Ya-ch'en, a former bandit chieftain, organized the Tenth Army, and Ch'i Ming-shan (who changed his name to Chih-chung, "devoted to China," after allying with the Communists) reorganized his bandit group into the Eleventh Allied Army.[4] These and many others, some of whom maintained active liaison with Chang Hsüeh-liang's supporters now exiled in northwestern China as late as 1934 or 1935,[5] collaborated closely with the CCP-led forces in every phase of their activities.

Anti-Japanese sentiment in the guerrillas' theaters of operation was also very strong. The residents of these remote regions of Manchuria had been subjected to a continuous barrage of anti-Japanese propaganda from a variety of anti-Japanese forces, both Communist and non-Communist, since 1931, and they had witnessed the struggles of thousands of fighters in battles that had ravaged the economy of most areas. The raising of cash crops, such as soybeans, became unprofitable as prices continued to tumble after 1929, as we have shown in chapter 1, and in the confusion of continuous warfare no other means of supplementing the meager farm income could be found. The effect of the crash of the soybean market was particularly severe in the Third Army's region of operations east of Harbin.[6] The Japanese attempt to immigrate a large number of Japanese to Manchuria also aroused strong resentment, as shown by the revolt spearheaded by Hsieh Wen-tung. The Japanese authorities took away the Chinese-owned farms, paying only nominal prices, and allocated them to the new Japanese immigrants, who were there ostensibly to cultivate the vast virgin lands of Manchuria. In spite of the resistance, however, the Japanese Kwantung Army pushed through the colonization program, and by 1942 the land coercively taken away

3. Ibid., p. 756.
4. Feng Chung-yün, *Tung-pei K'ang-Jih Lien-chün Shih-ssu-nien k'u-tou chien-shih* [Brief History of the Fourteen-Year Struggle of the Anti-Japanese Allied Army of Manchuria] (Harbin, 1946), pp. 32–33.
5. For Japanese reports on Li Yen-lu's contacts with exiled political figures in China and patriotic groups there, see *Manshū kyōsanhi no kenkyū*, pp. 723–724.
6. Manshūkoku Gunji Komonbu (Military Advisors' Department, Manchukuo), *Kokunai chian taisaku no kenkyū* [Study of Domestic Security Measures] (Changchun[?], 1937), pp. 19–20. This volume carries a subtitle in parenthesis, "Manshū kyōsanhi no kenkyū taisaku-hen" [Study of Communist Bandits in Manchuria, On Countermeasures], and was thus a supplement to *Manshū kyōsanhi no kenkyū*.

from the Chinese reached 20 million hectares, or approximately 50 million acres, of which 3,510,000 hectares, or approximately 8.67 million acres, was land already cultivated by the Chinese. An irony of this program was that the Japanese colonizers cultivated only 200,000 hectares, or 5.7 percent of the farmland taken away from the Chinese, and allowed the remainder to lie fallow.[7] In most cases, the Japanese colonizers became landlords, simply turning over their farms to Chinese tenants.[8]

Other agricultural programs instituted by the Japanese brought no relief to the farmers. In 1937, the Manchukuo regime had adopted a five-year agricultural development plan, which included the nationalization or confiscation of all forests, fields, and swamplands that remained uncultivated; other lands whose ownership was not known were to be confiscated. The lands needed for Japanese colonization were to be forcibly purchased, and the sale and inheritance of land were to be placed under regulation.[9] For this purpose, the Manchukuo regime began a land survey project in 1937, which did not augur well for the original owners.[10] While details concerning the land survey project in Manchuria are not known, the experience in Korea, which the Japanese had colonized since 1910, has shown that the survey instituted by the Japanese government resulted in the loss of lands by original owners or an increase in taxation.[11] In any event, the Chinese farmers could not have reacted favorably to the intrusion of the new government officials and would have been only suspicious of the intent of the government even in the pacified areas.

Beginning in 1938, the Japanese rulers also instituted a program of compulsory purchase of grain,[12] and the price paid by the government was naturally far below the market price.[13] Japan needed grain to supply its vast army operating in China, and the Japanese also needed to export more millet to Korea, as they were drawing more and more rice from the Korean farms for consumption in Japan and elsewhere.[14] All these new burdens imposed on

7. Man Shi Kai (Society for the History of Manchuria), *Manshū kaihatsu yonjūnen-shi* [Forty-Year History of Development in Manchuria] (Tokyo, 1964), vol. 1, p. 700.
8. Ibid., p. 701.
9. *Kokunai chian taisaku*, pp. 24–25.
10. *Manshū kaihatsu yonjūnen-shi*, vol. 1, p. 780.
11. See Kim Yong-sŏp, "Survey of Plunder: Land Survey," Shin-gu Munhwasa, ed., *Han-guk hyŏndae-sa* [History of Modern Korea] (Seoul, 1969), vol. 4, pp. 96–130.
12. *Manshū kaihatsu yonjūnen-shi*, vol. 1, p. 731.
13. Ibid., p. 783.
14. Ibid.

Chinese farmers could not have endeared the new rulers to the Chinese regardless of whether the area where they lived was pacified or not.

The most onerous, and indeed calamitous, burden imposed on the Chinese population living in the "bandit-infested areas," as the Japanese called them, was the pacification programs instituted by the Japanese. Among these, the most disastrous—both to the ordinary farmers and the guerrillas— was the "collective hamlet" program, instituted since 1934. The idea behind it was simply to isolate the guerrillas from the general population, thereby cutting off their source of food, clothing, other supplies, and intelligence information. In order to effect this goal, the Japanese and Manchukuo troops destroyed every farmhouse or village they could find in remote locations and ordered the farmers to relocate to designated locations where "collective hamlets" were being established. As a Japanese civilian serving as vice-governor of Huanjen Hsien related in 1939, the program was "forced through mercilessly, inhumanely, without emotion—as if driving a horse."[15] Families were ordered to move from their farms upon little or no notice, even if the collective hamlets were not ready. Some farmers were forced to move just before the sowing season, making it impossible for them to plant any seeds that year, while others were ordered to move just before harvest. The Japanese were intent on eliminating the anti-Japanese guerrillas as quickly as possible. The collective hamlet program was launched in 1934, and by the end of 1937, 10,629 hamlets had been constructed, or at least so designated, and 5.5 million people herded into them. An additional 2,550 hamlets were planned for 1938.[16] Many more were to follow.

Not only were the farmers deprived of their source of food and livelihood, but they were forced to provide labor not only for the construction of walled hamlets and their new living quarters but the construction and repair of the so-called "security highways" that linked these hamlets. The impact of these programs is graphically depicted by contemporary reports published for internal use by Manchukuo agencies. In view of the importance of the role played by the collective hamlet program in the future of the guer-

15. Ishigaki Sadakazu, "Pacification Activities in the Communist Bandit Area," in Office of Information, Department of General Affairs, Council of State, Manchukuo, Comp., Sembu geppō [Pacification Monthly], vol. 4, no. 4 (April 1939), p. 38.
16. Department of Security, Police Affairs Headquarters, Manchukuo, "Public Security, Police and Propaganda," Sembu geppō, vol. 3, no. 10 (October 1938), p. 21.

rilla movement, and particularly because these reports depict the condition of the people living in the guerrillas' theaters of operation, two long excerpts are presented below:

Tunghua Hsien:

Because the people have been taken to the construction of collective hamlets or repair of security highways during the harvest season, crops still lie unharvested under ice and snow.

Although the scattered residents of the mountains have been congregated in the collective hamlets, much of their crops lies unharvested in the fields. Although the people wish to harvest their crops, it is now the season of the mop-up operation, and without certificates of residence and entry permits to uninhabited areas they cannot harvest their crops.

There are about 12 hamlets in the recent operation area [of the Pacification and Supervisory Team], comprising some 3,000 families and 20,000 persons. Of these, 380 families with 2,200 persons are lacking in food at present. Others will manage until about May, but May and June are sowing season. They can somehow struggle through with tree bark, etc., but they cannot till and sow for the food of the following year.

There were 13,000 starved families at the end of 1936, and most of the residents in Tunghua *Hsien* are expected to be in the same situation by the spring sowing season. . . .

Many of the collective hamlets in Tunghua *Hsien* still have not completed their enclosing walls, and the construction of the houses is totally inadequate. The roofs are of tree bark or straw and the walls are full of holes; these cannot possibly keep out cold wind and snow. The residents do not have [adequate] clothing; [their only lifeline is] the smouldering fire built in their houses. It is a wonder that there is no sickness among them. . . .

Because the collective hamlet system was started late, there are no houses in Hoshantzukou, Tunghua *Hsien*. All the people are living in caves. In Hotzu village there are some moving into the village as late as December 15. Several families sharing a house belong to the more fortunate category. Many of them live in the defense fortifications of the hamlets. . . .

In Shihitaokou, the location of the collective hamlet has been changed several times. The loss suffered by the farmers from destruction and construction of houses is appalling. Also, because of these frequent changes, the houses have not been completed even today. One can clearly see the white clouds and blue sky through the roof [from inside the room]. In this severe cold, one can imagine the sufferings of these people.[17]

Chian Hsien:
The life of the residents has been worn to the limit. Except in the town of Chian, half the residents will be short of food by the Chinese New Year [around March]. Even now, half the residents are short of food and lack bedding. Because the collective hamlets were hurriedly built, epidemics are prevalent. The destitution in the river basin area is the result of inability to cultivate the hinterlands and the consumption of crops from small areas by a large number of people. Because of the law against transport of grain, grain cannot be brought from the hinterlands, and other goods cannot come from the Antung area in exchange. On top of this, the Manchukuo army has stationed troops in the area in great numbers and has purchased food, aggravating the problem of shortages.[18]

The sudden concentration of great numbers of people in incomplete and inadequate houses in the collective hamlets also caused the spread of epidemics. In 1936 there were more than 2,000 cases of typhoid in Tunghua *Hsien* and 1,200 in Liuho *Hsien*. There were many others in the neighboring area.[19]

To these reports we must add an observation by the vice-governor of Huanjen *Hsien* made in early 1939. He was referring to conditions in his jurisdiction as a whole:

The food shortage continued year after year. Only a month after the harvest, petitions for food are flooding in upon the government. Without exception, those in the mountain villages are living on the bark of elm

17. Excerpts from the report of the Second Pacification and Supervisory Team of the Security Operations Committee; quoted in *Kokunai chian taisaku*, pp. 286–290.
18. Excerpt from the report of the First Motion Picture Team; quoted in ibid., p. 287.
19. Ibid., pp. 407–408.

trees. The situation is the worst between March and May, when neither trees nor plants show their buds. It is truly sad to see the farmers gathered around elm trees on the mountainsides. It sounds only charitable to say that the people do not possess animated countenances. The word "animated" has no relationship whatsoever to these people. They are turning from the dark blue color of zinc to that of earth. Death is real.[20]

Although these may not be the most typical examples, the situation in the vast majority of the hamlets could not have been much better, for it was impossible for the residents in the hurriedly organized collective hamlets to have better living conditions than the general population, which was suffering severely from losses by war and starvation and the consequent reduction in crops.

Even the relatively well-planned hamlets showed the damaging effects of the collective hamlets upon the farmers' livelihood. Farmed areas were reduced, distance between places of residence and farms were extended, more lands were rented than owned, tenant fees increased, public imposts and compulsory labor increased, and the farmers' debts were enlarged to the proportion of a "hell of debts." According to Japanese officials who studied the problems of the collective hamlets in detail, "contradictions and the resulting pauperization of the farmers [were] universal in all the collective hamlets."[21]

It should be remembered that the purpose of the collective hamlets was to isolate the guerrillas from the general population. The available literature on the collective hamlet program leads one to conclude, however, that while the hamlets did physically separate the guerrillas from the masses, the hamlet program in fact drove the masses closer to the guerrillas morally and spiritually. Note, for example, the following statement in a report of the Chientao provincial government in 1939:

> Even among the residents of the collective hamlets there are those looking for the opportunity to escape. Some of them fully accept the Communist propaganda and plan to stay in the hamlet permanently only in the belief that their safety can be guaranteed by their providing food and other conveniences for the insurgents.

20. Ishigaki Sadakazu, "Pacification Activities," p. 37.
21. *Kokunai chian taisaku*, p. 89.

Considerable numbers of residents sympathize with communism and secretly plan to join the insurgents.

If the situation were left to its own course, not only would the counterinsurgency operations of the armies and police have become more difficult, but various areas of this province would have been dominated by insurgents just as in the period prior to the founding of Manchukuo.[22]

The farmers in the theaters of guerrilla operation thus had ample reason to oppose the Japanese. In this connection, Vice-Governor Ishigaki's statements are worth noting:

The farmers are ignorant, but they are not so ignorant as to be unaware of the destitute condition into which they have fallen. The Communists have been appealing to the masses by stressing this fact. The farmers will never follow [the Communists] blindly on the basis of emotional appeals that are detached from actual life; but when the appeals are focused on actual problems concerning their livelihood, unremitting collective revolt may occur. . . . *The construction of collective hamlets and security highways, the continued emergence of wastelands, starvation, and the sudden reduction of the population to half the former figure are unsurpassed subjects for Communist agitation among the farmers.* . . . We are not afraid of Communist propaganda, but we are worried because the material for propaganda can be found in the farmers' lives. We are not afraid of the ignition of fire; rather, we are afraid of the seeping oil.[23]

In the above paragraph, Ishigaki was referring to the fact that the population in the Huanjen *Hsien* had declined from 220,000 before September 1931, when the Japanese launched their assault on Manchuria, to 120,000 in 1939. Of the total decline of 100,000 during these years, 30,000 were due to death.[24]

The endless suffering of the Chinese masses, particularly those living in the remote regions, made them a strong potential source

---

22. Chientao Provincial Government, "Pacification Operations Accompanying the Autumn/Winter Mop-up Operation," *Sembu geppō*, vol. 4, no. 10 (November 1939), pp. 92–93.
23. Ishigaki Sadakazu, "Pacification Activities," p. 39 (emphasis added).
24. Ibid., p. 37.

of recruitment and support for the anti-Japanese allied armies, whose numbers, as we have related, were quite substantial. Of course, in comparison with earlier years, 31,000 men in 1937 may appear insignificant; but as we have noted, the quality of the anti-Japanese fighters had improved significantly. It should also be remembered that the Communist Party in China proper had in 1937 only about 40,000 organized members and an army of some 30,000.[25] But the CCP was able to grow into a formidable organization with 800,000 members and nearly 500,000 armed men by 1940, at which time it could boast a population of 100 million people in its base areas, including those paying taxes to both the CCP and the Japanese.[26] Why could not the allied armies in Manchuria, already under the strong influence of the CCP, bring about similar results?

It should be said at the outset that the allied armies in Manchuria failed to expand much beyond the level reached in August 1937; indeed, by early 1941, they were completely destroyed as an organized force. This was in strong contrast to the experience in North China. Why such a contrast, when the allied armies in Manchuria were fighting against the same enemy as those in North China?

The crucial difference was in the importance attached by Japan to the two theaters of Communist guerrillas. Northwestern China, where the CCP established its main base after the Long March between 1934 and 1935, was of no intrinsic value to either the Chinese or the Japanese. The initial aim of the Japanese in China was only to inflict blows against the Kuomintang forces occupying the major political and economic centers of China in order to force the Chinese to sue for peace. Therefore, until Canton and Hankow fell to their hands in late October 1938, the Japanese paid little attention to the anti-Japanese bases being established by the CCP in their rear. It was only on December 6, 1938, that the Ministry of the Army in Tokyo decided on the annihilation of the "remnant anti-Japanese forces" in the occupied areas.[27] By then, the Japanese army had reached its limit in penetrative power. All the major metropolitan centers of China were already under Japanese control, and further expansion of the war front

---

25. Mao Tse-tung, "Our Study and the Current Situation" (April 12, 1944), *Selected Works of Mao Tse-tung* (London, 1956), vol. 4, p. 162.
26. Ibid.
27. Bō-ei-chō Bō-ei Kenshūjo, Senshi-shitsu (Office of War History, Defense Institute, Self-Defense Agency, Japan), *Hoku-shi no chi-an sen* [Public Security War in North China] (Tokyo, 1968), vol. 1, pp. 101–102.

would have brought no benefit. Once the Japanese had decided on mopping up the "occupied territories," however, their strategies and tactics proved to be costly to the CCP. As Mao Tse-tung related in April 1944, the CCP was placed in an "extremely difficult situation" between 1941 and 1942. "During this phase," according to Mao, "our base areas shrank in size, the population was reduced to under 50 million [from the height of 100 million in 1940] and the Eighth Route Army to about 300,000 men [from nearly 500,000], and the casualties among cadres were very heavy and our finance and economy were in dire straits."[28]

The Japanese, on the other hand, attached great importance to the regions occupied by the anti-Japanese forces in Manchuria. The fact that most of the anti-Japanese guerrillas operated on or near the Soviet border did not help the situation. This was because the Japanese military leaders were increasingly concerned about the possibility of war against the Soviet Union, and as the Soviet Far Eastern Army increased its strength and as border incidents became more frequent, the Kwantung Army came to pay increasingly more attention to the Soviet border. The Soviet Far Eastern Army was estimated to possess eleven divisions with 230,000 men in 1934, but by 1937 there were twenty divisions with 370,000 men, and by 1939 it was estimated to possess thirty divisions with 570,000 men.[29] The Kwantung Army, on the other hand, possessed only three divisions in 1936 and nine divisions in 1939. The Soviet Union also dispatched a great number of aircraft to the Far East, and the Soviet Air Force would have dominated the air in the event of a war.[30] As to border incidents, there were only 152 minor incidents such as kidnapping of Chinese across the border or illegal border crossings of soldiers between 1932 and 1934, but the number increased to 136 in 1935 and to 203 in 1936.[31] Some of these incidents involved skirmishes between small detachments of Soviet and Japanese armies.[32] In the incident of June 19–29, 1937, the Japanese sunk a Soviet gunboat.[33] As Soviet-Japanese relations deteriorated, the Japanese had begun

28. Mao Tse-tung, "Our Study," p. 163.
29. Nihon Kokusai Seiji Gakkai (Japanese Association of International Politics), *Taiheiyō sensō e no michi* [The Road to the Pacific War] (Tokyo, 1963), vol. 4, p. 76.
30. Ibid.
31. Ibid., p. 77. These are Japanese figures. The Soviet side revealed at the Far Eastern War Criminals Tribunal after the war that the Japanese had violated Soviet territory 191 times between 1932 and 1934, but 192 times in 1935.
32. Ibid., pp. 78–79, 278, 285–288.
33. Ibid., p. 80.

in 1934 to build fortifications along the Soviet-Manchurian border in such places as Hulin, Suifenho, and Tungning (northwest of Khanka), where the anti-Japanese guerrillas had operated. Military highways and supply depots were also constructed.[34]

In 1938 and again in 1939 the Japanese and Soviet armies engaged in major battles in Manchuria, heightening the morale of the guerrillas and intensifying Japanese determination to "pacify the rear." These were the Changkufeng incident or Khanka Lake incident of July–August 1938 and the Nomonhan (Nomenkan) incident of May–September 1939. During the Changkufeng encounter at the convergence of the Soviet, Manchurian, and Korean borders, the Japanese suffered 1,440 casualties, including 526 deaths; in the Nomonhan incident at the Mongolian frontier, the Japanese suffered more than 17,000 casualties, including 8,440 killed.[35] The Japanese had also mobilized the Manchukuo troops in this incident, the latter suffering 2,895 casualties.[36] Both incidents had been triggered and expanded by adventuristic officers in the Kwantung Army, and the Soviet army retaliated with massive numbers of men and equipment, defeating the Japanese. While the Japanese Kwantung Army would have strictly censored the press, most of the Chinese in Manchuria who were sensitive to political news would have surmised the outcome.[37]

Another reason for the Japanese to pay particular concern to the guerrilla-occupied areas was the rich natural resources buried in the hinterlands. The Japanese anticipated a war with the Soviet Union, possibly in 1940 or 1941, and this required the rapid industrialization of Manchuria.[38] Tungpientao, the First Army's

34. Ibid., p. 277. Quoting from Minami Jirō Denki Kankōkai (Association to Publish the Biography of Minami Jirō), *Minami Jirō* (Tokyo, 1957), pp. 356–357.
35. *Taiheiyō sensō e no michi*, vol. 4, pp. 82–110. About the Changkufeng incident, see also Alvin D. Coox, *The Anatomy of a Small War: The Soviet-Japanese Struggle for Changkufeng/Khasan, 1938* (Westport, CT, 1977), passim.
36. Ran Sei Kai (Orchid Star Society), *Manshūkokugun* [The Manchukuo Army] (Tokyo, 1970), p. 576.
37. Since the Changkufeng incident took place at the point of convergence of the Soviet, Manchurian, and Korean borders, some Koreans suffered from the battles. The Japanese police authorities studied the impact of the incident upon public opinion in Korea and found that many people, both Japanese and Korean, expressed indignation at the failure of the Japanese to use aircraft during the incident to counter Soviet air attacks. At least one of the Japanese respondents feared that the Japanese propaganda about the invincibility of Japan would not thenceforth be believed by the Koreans and Chinese. See Chōsen Sōtokufu Keimu-kyoku (Police Affairs Department, Korean Government-General), *Saikin ni okeru Chōsen chian jōkyō* [Recent Status of Public Security in Korea] (Seoul, 1938), pp. 174–187.
38. Manshūkokushi Hensan Kankōkai (Editorial and Publication Committee of the History of Manchukuo), *Manshūkokushi* [History of Manchukuo] (Tokyo, 1971), vol. 1, pp. 528–532.

theater of operation, was rich in such natural resources as lumber, iron, and coal. Two coal mines were already in operation before the Japanese arrived in this area, but after 1938 the Japanese discovered several other coal deposits with a total estimated reserve of 590 million metric tons.[39] The Japanese also knew of iron mines operated by the Koreans in the region during the Ch'ing Dynasty, and by pursuing these leads they discovered numerous locations where iron ore could be profitably mined. Subsequently, in 1942, the Manchukuo regime announced the iron ore deposit in the Tungpientao region to be 440 million metric tons.[40] Similarly, in Mishan, near the Soviet border (northwest of Lake Khanka), the Japanese discovered rich deposits of coal, estimated at 1,389 million metric tons.[41] Exploitation of these resources required pacification of the territory, which, of course, meant the extermination of the anti-Japanese guerrillas.

The Japanese had a number of advantages in Manchuria which they did not have in North China in fighting against the guerrillas. As we have seen in chapter 1, the Japanese had been engaged in wars in Manchuria ever since 1894 and had actively pursued their colonization programs after defeating the Russians in 1905 and establishing the South Manchuria Railway Company (SMR) in 1906. Not only had the Japanese been long involved in Manchuria; largely because of the SMR's research department, the Japanese had acquired a thorough knowledge of almost every aspect of Manchuria. As some of the sources cited for the present study will show, the SMR's researches ranged over economics, sociology, ethnography, business, politics, geography, geology, agriculture, botany, meteorology, and many other fields considered useful in ruling and developing Manchuria.[42] Of course, the research activities of the SMR were not confined to Manchuria. China and Siberia were of important interest to Japan, and hence many studies, including those related to military strategy, were conducted by the researchers of the company, who at one time numbered some 300.[43] Until 1941, when the military police began to suppress the Japanese intellectuals gathered in the SMR's research department and various government and other agencies in

39. *Manshū kaihatsu yonjūnen-shi*, vol. 2, pp. 198–201.
40. Ibid., pp. 233–235.
41. Ibid., pp. 202–206.
42. See John Young, *The Research Activities of the South Manchurian Railway Company, 1907–1945: A History and Bibliography* (New York, 1966). Young's 678-page work lists 6,284 items published by the company and located by him in the 1950s and 1960s. Undoubtedly, there are many more items to be located.
43. Ibid., p. 1.

Manchuria on suspicion of engaging in a "Communist movement," they produced "one of the great stores of knowledge on twentieth-century Asia."[44]

This tradition of preparatory research, or action based on thorough knowledge, was applied to the suppression of anti-Japanese guerrillas in Manchuria. Various Japanese organizations, including the SMR's research department, had published reports on Communist organizations and activities in Manchuria, but beginning in 1935, the Military Advisors' Department of the Manchukuo Ministry of Defense, which was staffed by Japanese officers from the Kwantung Army, launched a massive research project, dispatching personnel to all the war zones for information. Two years of what must have been intensive work resulted in the two monumental volumes, *Manshū kyōsanhi no kenkyū* [Study of Communist Bandits in Manchuria] and *Kokunai chian taisaku no kenkyū* [Study of Domestic Security Measures], both of which have been quoted extensively in the present study. Printed strictly for internal use, the first volume covered such topics as the socio-economic and geographic conditions of the "guerrilla-infested areas," the history of the Communist movements, the CCP's strategies, the backgrounds and other details of the leaders, the internal conditions of various armed groups, and the relationship between the people and the guerrillas, and presented much other information pertinent to anti-guerrilla operations. The second volume presented thorough analyses of various pacification measures used by the Japanese in Manchuria, including the collective hamlet program and surrender-inducement operations. It is evident that many of those participating in the project had received Marxist-oriented social science training. Many pages of both volumes are devoted to socio-economic analysis of the hinterlands, attempting to gauge the effect of socio-economic changes upon the political attitude of the masses. It would not be surprising if some of the staff members of the SMR's research department had been utilized for these studies.

44. Ibid. The details of the arrest and investigation of the Japanese intellectuals are available in Kantō Kempeitai Shireibu (Kwantung Army Military Police Headquarters), *Zai-Man Nikkei kyōsanshugi undō* [The Communist Movement among the Japanese in Manchuria] (Dairen[?], 1934), passim. The Japanese intellectuals did not engage in any organized activities. They were charged with crimes and punished for taking Marxist viewpoints in analyzing the conditions of the Chinese workers and farmers in Manchuria. There was no relationship of any kind between these Japanese Marxists and the CCP in Manchuria. For a personal account of his experience in the research department of the railway company between 1920 and 1945, including his prison life for ten months, see Itō Takeo, *Mantetsu ni ikite* [Life in the South Manchuria Railway Company] (Tokyo, 1964).

Particularly noteworthy in the second volume is a long chapter on Chiang Kai-shek's Communist extermination campaign against the Kiangsi Soviet between 1930 and 1934. The Japanese paid particular attention to the causes of Chiang Kai-shek's success in the fourth and fifth encirclement campaigns, conducted between June 1932 and August 1934, and attributed Chiang's success to unified action on the military, political, and economic fronts. By using massive numbers of troops and enormous amounts of money, the Kuomintang (KMT) forces completely sealed off the Communist area, thereby cutting off sources of weapons and ammunition, food and other necessities, and information. In the "recovered areas," the KMT government provided economic and medical relief along with improvement in the government administration and the land tenure system. While the landlords' right of ownership was guaranteed, the tenants' right to till the land was protected. Tenant fees were also regulated to prevent unfair exploitation of the tenants by the landlords. While the Communists in the encircled area implemented equally progressive policies to consolidate their strength, the Kuomintang's superior military strength together with its socio-political and economic measures led to the latter's victory. The study concluded by noting that the pacification operation in Manchuria, being faced with "Communist and political bandits," must reinforce political and economic programs in contrast to the past policies of emphasizing military action alone. The authors of this study drew a close parallel between the Japanese action in Manchuria and Chiang Kai-shek's operation in south China.[45]

Thus, armed with firm determination to exterminate the guerrillas and with detailed knowledge about the strength and weakness of each unit of the anti-Japanese forces, the Japanese pushed through the pacification campaigns.

The lessons acquired from the massive study were first applied in the northern Tungpientao region, including Huinan, Chinchuan, Liuho, Tunghua, Mengchiang, Chian, Fusung, Linchiang, and Changpai *hsien*, the area in which the South Manchurian Provincial Committee and the First Route Army were operating. As one might expect, the Kwantung Army placed the entire "security operation," involving military, economic, and political actions, under the single command of Major General Sasaki Tōichi, the supreme advisor in the Manchukuo Ministry of Defense. The principal aims of the operation were to exterminate the guerrillas

---

45. *Kokunai chian taisaku*, pp. 439–521.

and to turn the "semi-farming and semi-bandit residents" around. In order to accomplish these aims, the Manchukuo regime allocated funds for the construction of more collective hamlets and telephone and telegraph facilities, for relief of the indigent, and for farming, food, and housing. Emphasis was also to be placed on economic development and propaganda.[46]

On the military side, the Japanese for the first time sought to rely on the Manchukuo army units alone without Japanese Kwantung Army troops taking part in the operation. This was considered a test of the reliability and effectiveness of the Manchukuo troops,[47] and for General Sasaki, who had overseen the building of the puppet army since its inception, it was a personal test as well. The total number of Manchukuo troops gathered for the campaign was 16,000; there was a total of 2,280 guerrillas, including 1,500 Communists.[48] The campaign was launched in October 1936 and ended in March 1937, but small-scale anti-guerrilla operations continued.

The results of this campaign were mixed. Between October 1936 and February 1937, the Manchukuo troops engaged in 528 battles against 17,463 guerrillas and killed or captured 2,030 guerrillas.[49] They were able to capture Wang Feng-ko, the Big Sword Society chieftain and the leader of the non-Communist nationalist groups in Tungpientao, on March 27, 1937.[50] Although the Japanese annihilated most of the non-Communist groups, they were not successful in "completely overturning the foundation of the Communist army."[51] Indeed, the Communist guerrillas continued to harass the Japanese, as we shall see. The Japanese, however, succeeded in killing Wang Te-t'ai, the commander of the Second Allied Army, on November 7, 1936, and Chou Shu-tung, who had succeeded Wang as acting commander, on April 24, 1937.[52] The Japanese capture of some of the leading Communist cadres, such as Feng Chien-ying (chairman of the CCP's Liuho *Hsien* Committee), and An Kwang-hun (chief of staff of the First Army), and Hu Kuo-ch'en (head of logistics of the First Army) in February 1938, and particularly that of Ch'eng Pin, the com-

---

46. A detailed report of this campaign is available in ibid., pp. 233–438.
47. Ibid., pp. 234, 247 (quoting from General Sasaki's speech of November 24, 1936).
48. Ibid., p. 236. In the Tungpientao region as a whole, there were 5,520 guerrillas, including 2,590 Communist guerrillas.
49. Ibid., pp. 284–285.
50. *Manshūkokugun*, p. 350. Wang was executed on the following day with his wife and his small child who had accompanied him.
51. Ibid., p. 351.
52. Ibid., p. 350.

mander of the first division of the First Army, in June 1938, proved to be very detrimental to the Communist guerrillas later because these individuals decided to collaborate with the Japanese after their capture. They, of course, knew all the secrets of the Allied Army, including their strategies and tactics, sources of weapons and supplies, and various hideouts. The fact that they were not killed outright after their capture—the result of a new Japanese policy (adopted only in late 1936 or early 1937, after the campaign in northern Tungpientao was launched) designed to induce the surrender of Communist guerrillas—would have affected the resolve of many guerrillas. Until then, the Japanese Kwantung Army had ordered its troops to kill every Communist "bandit" they captured. Those who surrendered were treated as harshly as those captured.[53]

The non-military aspects of the campaign differed little from those of previous campaigns. People, farm animals, and materials were as randomly conscripted for the military campaign as before; collective hamlets underwent the same kind of damage and suffering; epidemics spread widely; poverty and hunger continued to prevail; and many residents were tortured and killed on suspicion of serving the guerrillas.[54]

The Manchukuo Army evidently suffered considerable losses, particularly because of counterattacks by a few hundred men led by Kim Il-sŏng and Ch'oe Hyŏn.[55] The Manchukuo troops were not trained for the kind of warfare they were forced to wage. The guerrillas evidently used ambush in the darkness as a means of survival.

In the Sanchiang or Three-River (Amur, Ussuri, and Sungari) region, where most of the anti-Japanese forces were congregated, the Japanese launched another massive extermination campaign in November 1937, continuing it until March 1939.[56] For this campaign, the Japanese Kwantung Army dispatched a division of its own and mobilized 25,000 troops of the Manchukuo Army. Unfortunately, details of this campaign are not available, al-

53. Ibid., pp. 343, 355; *Manshūkoku-shi*, vol. 2, pp. 336–337.
54. *Manshūkokugun*, pp. 353–354; *Kokunai chian taisaku*, p. 260.
55. *Manshūkokugun*, pp. 350, 354–355, 361. On November 13, 1937, a company of the Manchukuo Army ambushed and killed a man identified as "Commander Kim." Believing the killed man to be Kim Il-sŏng, the commander of the Kwantung Army and the Manchukuo minister of public security awarded 10,000 yüan to the company. It was discovered later, however, that Kim Il-sŏng was still alive. See ibid., pp. 372–373. For a Korean account of this period, see Yim Ch'un-ch'u, *Hang-Il mujang t'ujaeng shigi rŭl hoesang hayŏ* [Recalling the Period of the Anti-Japanese Armed Struggle] (Pyongyang, 1960), pp. 64–173.
56. *Manshūkokugun*, pp. 382–399, and *Manshūkoku-shi*, vol. 2, pp. 320–321.

though the outline of the "pacification plan" adopted in July 1937 is identical to the one used in northern Tungpientao.⁵⁷ Chou Pao-chung, the commander of the Second Route Army, recollected later that

> Between the winter of 1938 and the entire year of 1939 [sic], the Anti-Japanese Allied Army suffered great losses under the assault of absolutely superior enemy forces. When the enemy encountered Chinese masses recognized to have had ties with the allied army, they uniformly applied the policy of terror, burning all and killing all. In Fuyuan *Hsien* there were 5,000 to 6,000 homes, but the enemy destroyed them all and turned the place into a no-man's land. In the puppet provinces of Sanchiang and Mutanchiang, more than 600,000 houses were burnt down, the total loss reaching several hundred million *yüan*.
> In addition, the Japanese robbers built the "collective hamlets," building high walls and digging deep ditches. They strengthened their special service police to cut off our army's ties with the masses. The war of resistance in Manchuria entered an extremely difficult period. Most of our army was forced to live in the remote mountains and deep forests in the icy air and on the snow-covered ground.⁵⁸

The Second Route Army came into being in December 1937, subsuming the Fourth Army (Li Yen-p'ing, commander), the Seventh Army (Ching Lo-t'ing, commander), the Eighth Army (Hsieh Wen-tung, commander), and the Tenth Army (Wang Ya-ch'en, commander), but it was now under a massive assault.⁵⁹

Obviously, the anti-Japanese forces suffered grave losses. Chao Shang-chih, the founder and commander of the Third Army, was killed in action. Li Yen-p'ing, the head of the Fourth Army, was killed in Shulan.⁶⁰ Ch'ai Shih-jung, who had assumed the post of

57. *Manshūkokugun*, pp. 395–396.
58. Feng Chung-yün, *Tung-pei K'ang-Jih Lien-chün*, p. 62.
59. Imoto Taikichi, "Recent Communist Movement in Manchukuo," dated October 1939, in Shihōshō, Keiji-kyoku [Bureau of Criminal Affairs, Ministry of Justice, Japan], *Shisō jōsei shisatsu hōkokushū, 8* [Reports of Inspection Tours of Ideological Conditions, 8] (Tokyo, 1940), pp. 33–36, 50–54. Based on the testimony of Sung I-fu, former political commissar of the Fifth Army and the commander of the Second Division of the same army who surrendered to the Harbin Police on August 25, 1938.
60. Li Yen-lu, the original head of the Fourth Army, was reportedly in China

commander of the Fifth Army after Chou Pao-chung was elevated to that of the Second Route Army,[61] was killed in Ilan.[62] Many other important leaders either surrendered or were captured. The most notable among these were: Hsieh Wen-tung, the hero of the Tulungshan revolt in Tangyuan *Hsien* and the commander of the Eighth Army, who was persuaded to surrender on March 20, 1939;[63] Li Hua-t'ang, the head of the Ninth Army; and Cheng Lu-yen, the commander of the Fourth Division of the Fourth Army. Many other division commanders also surrendered.[64] There is no doubt that the death, capture, and surrender of these leaders were preceded by grave losses among the rank and file. As we have noted in table 19, the guerrillas throughout Manchuria suffered 14,203 losses (of which 7,663 were killed) in 1937; 7,368 losses (of which 3,693 were killed) in 1938; and 5,417 losses (of which 3,168 were killed) in 1939. It is not possible to determine how many of these losses were from the Sanchiang region, but one can easily surmise from these statistics that fierce battles were fought in the Manchurian hinterlands.

The limited number of accounts presented in both Japanese and Chinese sources indicate that the remnants of the anti-Japanese forces abandoned their base areas in Sanchiang Province and moved into the Lesser Khingan Mountains in the northwest. A Japanese source indicates that the remnants of the Third Route Army established their base in Nanpeihoyuan, located directly east of Peian and north of Tiehli, and resumed their activities. The Third Route Army refers to the forces that were under Chao Shang-chih, commander of the People's Anti-Japanese Allied Army. They had been reorganized in August 1938.[65] The Japanese detachments established their headquarters in Peian and Hailun in 1940 and continued to pursue the guerrillas. Feng Chung-yün, former cadre in the Third Route Army, on the other hand, speaks of the Anti-Japanese National Salvation Societies in Noho, Tetu,

---

proper at this time; Li Yen-p'ing was his younger brother. See Feng Chung-yün, *Tung-pei K'ang-Jih Lien-chün*, pp. 26–27.

61. Ibid., p. 28.
62. *Manshūkokugun*, p. 385.
63. Ibid. The Japanese officer in the Manchukuo Army who undertook the risky task of singlehandedly going to Hsieh Wen-tung's hideout to persuade Hsieh was awarded 100 *yüan* by the minister of public security (p. 393). This was in sharp contrast to the award of 10,000 *yüan* to the company that killed "Commander Kim." The same officer had induced the surrender of some of the division commanders of the Eighth Army.
64. Ibid., p. 385; *Manshūkoku-shi*, vol. 2, p. 321.
65. Imoto Taikichi, "Recent Communist Movement in Manchukuo," pp. 18–19, 36–37, 54–56.

Peian, and Koshan being organized under the direction of the Third Route Army, and of that army's attacks on such towns as Noho, Koshan, and Peihsingchen.[66] These were towns located at the northwestern edge of Manchuria along the Inner Mongolian border, beyond which lie the inhospitable Greater Khingan Mountains. At least one small group of mounted guerrillas under Wang Ming-kuei moved in and out of Inner Mongolia between November 1939 and the spring of 1940, "moving around as supernatural beings," attacking police stations, raiding Japanese logging camps, and playing havoc with the pursuing Japanese. Wang's unit was reported in Putehachi, Ajungchi, Kannan, Koshan, etc.[67]

Other remnants of the Third Route Army also ventured into the plains just west of Harbin between 1940 and 1941 and caused the complacent Japanese much consternation. These incidents are collectively known as the "Three Chao" incidents because the attacks took place in Chaotung, Chaochou, and Chaoyuan *Hsien*. Although the last of these had been incorporated into Inner Mongolia and was known officially as Houkouerhlossu, the Chinese in the area continued to call it Chaoyuan. In any event, a small group of guerrillas, approximately 50 men, under Tai Hung-pin, the commander of the First Division of the Sixth Army, attacked Fenglochen, a small town in Chaochou *Hsien*, in August 1940. Another group of 100 men under Han Yü-shu ventured to Chaoyuan on October 11 and skirmished with a Manchukuo Army detachment. Then, on December 28, a group under Hsü Tse-min, known as the commander of the twelfth detachment of the Third Army, attacked the town of Chaoyuan, setting fire to the Mongolian banner government, massacring Japanese officials and their families, and taking away weapons, ammunition, clothing and grain.[68] On January 4 of the following year, some 100 airmen of the Manchukuo Air Force stationed at Wangkang on the southern outskirts of Harbin rebelled against the Japanese. They murdered Japanese officers and others and fled in three trucks to Szuchan in Chaoyuan *Hsien*, intending to join Hsü Tse-min's forces.[69] The

66. Feng Chung-yün, *Tung-pei K'ang-Jih Lien-chün*, pp. 38–39. A Japanese report of 1940 also says that the North Manchurian Provisional Provincial Committee established a large new guerrilla district in Lungchiang Province and a part of East Hsingan Province in the summer of 1939. See Gaimushō, Tō-a-kyoku (East Asia Bureau, Ministry of Foreign Affairs, Japan), *Shina oyobi Manshū ni okeru kyōsan undō gaisetsu* [Outline of the Communist Movement in China and Manchuria] (Tokyo, 1940), p. 75.
67. Ibid., p. 39; *Manshūkokugun*, pp. 393–394.
68. *Manshūkoku-shi*, vol. 2, p. 325.
69. *Manshūkokugun*, p. 419.

airmen were captured before they joined the guerrillas and were court-martialed.

These incidents, according to a Japanese account, aroused much sympathy among the Chinese. The Communist groups had been active in organizing the masses, and their operations among the Manchukuo troops had also been effective. They had distributed many leaflets bearing the slogan "Chinese don't kill Chinese," and "this slogan carried enormous potential for destruction."[70]

Japanese retaliation, of course, was very swift. Japanese and Manchukuo troops and police units were dispatched to destroy the guerrillas. The Japanese military police and the Manchukuo police searched for accomplices, arresting several hundred residents, and Hsü Tse-min was eventually apprehended in Chaochou.[71] According to Feng Chung-yün, the people in Chaoyuan, who had welcomed Hsü Tse-min's guerrillas and joined them in raiding the government granaries, suffered dire consequences. The Japanese dispatched Yeh Yung-nien, the chief detective of the Harbin Police Bureau, who sent nearly 1,000 people to the "ice caves" in the Sungari River.[72] We are not familiar with this form of punishment mentioned by Feng Chung-yün, but it is clear that a great number of people suffered gravely. A Japanese source also states that more than ten Communist agents apprehended in Chaochou were murdered on their way to Harbin.[73] Later, the Japanese brought in their experts on pacification from Tungpientao to "pacify" the region. These were the last of the "plains operations" of the Third Route Army.

Between October 1939 and March 1941, the Japanese conducted another massive extermination campaign throughout the southern rim of Manchuria, extending from Chientao in the east to the Tungpientao region in the west. The sources of Japanese concern and the targets of their campaign were obvious. The authorities put up monetary rewards ranging from 3,000 *yüan* to 10,000 *yüan*[74] for the principal military and political leaders of the region.

10,000 *yüan*:
- Yang Ching-yü: general commander of the First Route Army and commander of the First Army.

70. Ibid., p. 418.
71. Ibid., pp. 419–420; also see *Manshūkoku-shi*, vol. 2, p. 419.
72. Feng Chung-yün, *Tung-pei K'ang-Jih Lien-chün*, p. 39.
73. *Manshūkokugun*, p. 420.
74. Ibid., p. 402.

- Ts'ao Ya-fan: commander of the first front army of the route army; concurrently head of the Second Division of the First Army.
- Kim Il-sŏng: commander of the second front army of the route army.[75]
- Ch'en Han-chang: commander of the third front army.
- Ch'oe Hyŏn: regiment commander, Second Army.

5,000 *yüan*:
- Pak Tŭk-pŏm: regiment commander
- Fang Chen-sheng: chief of staff, First Route Army.

3,000 *yüan*:
- Wei Cheng-min: chairman, South Manchurian Provincial Committee, CCP.
- Chŏn Kwang: political commissar, Second Army.

The Tungpientao region, as discussed before, had undergone numerous extermination campaigns, including the one between 1936 and 1938, but approximately 3,000 guerrillas under the command of various Communist leaders not only survived the onslaught of the Japanese and Manchukuo forces but inflicted severe damage to them. It is also evident from the Japanese account of the campaign that the guerrillas returned to the Chientao region in the east.

Approximately 3,000 Communist troops and bandits under Yang Ching-yü (armed with mortars, heavy and light machine guns, and pistols) rampaged the [Chientao, Kirin and Tunghua] region, and as a result, government authority did not easily penetrate there and public security was in complete chaos. The activities of Kim Il-sŏng and Ch'oe Hyŏn were most outstanding.

We have learned that in 1939 the Anti-Japanese Al-

---

75. According to Yim Ch'un-ch'u, a North Korean veteran of the guerrilla wars, Kim Il-sŏng had been the commander and political commissar of the Sixth Division of the Second Army since March 1936. But after Wang Te-t'ai was killed (in November 1936, and presumably after Chou Shu-tung, known to the Japanese to have been the acting commander of the Second Army, was killed in April 1937), Kim Il-sŏng served as the acting commander of the Second Army. In November 1938, at the Nanpaitzu conference in Mengchiang Province, Kim was designated the commander of the Second Army. This conference also divided the First Route Army into three front armies (*fang-mien-chün*) and appointed Kim as the commander of the Second Front Army. Yim Ch'un-ch'u, *Hang-Il Mujangshigi*, p. 152.

lied Army held an officers' conference at a certain place and decided that the guerrillas should hinder military activities of the Japanese and Manchukuo armies by [concentrating on] the destruction of military facilities, transportation and communication facilities, and the enemy's blockade line, even if this required a certain degree of sacrifice in the activities directed toward the masses.[76]

The Kwantung Army evidently believed that much of the disturbance was caused by "picked troops" trained and dispatched by the Soviet Union after Soviet-Japanese tension mounted following the Changkufeng incident of the summer of 1938. The Japanese also inferred a close link between intensified guerrilla activities and the war in Nomonhan that raged between May and September 1939.[77] Although there is no indication in extant records that such ties existed, the guerrillas evidently learned of the Soviet-Japanese encounters from local newspapers[78] and redoubled their efforts against the Japanese. The official historians of Kim Il-sŏng's units refer to numerous attacks against superior enemies sent to destroy them. Yim Ch'un-ch'u even boasted that during 1939 the guerrillas killed, wounded, or captured more than 30,000 enemy personnel, including police and self-defense unit members.[79] Ch'oe Hyŏn's unit alone, according to Yim, captured more than 3,000 enemy rifles and machine guns after August 1937.[80] While the numbers cited appear to have been exaggerated, there is no question that the guerrillas were a source of great concern to the Japanese. Weakly defended collective hamlets, logging camps, and Manchukuo outposts appear to have been the favorite targets of the guerrillas. Yang Ching-yü's units also attacked coal mines, railroad construction sites, and other outposts. In 1938 alone, according to a Tunghua Provincial Government report, "Yang's group perpetrated 80 such attacks, and because of its fero-

---

76. *Manshūkokugun*, p. 400. The information provided here is based on materials provided by Kitabe Kunio, lieutenant colonel in the Kwantung Army, who served as the principal braintrust in the extermination campaigns of the Sanchiang region between 1937 and 1939 and in Kirin, Chientao, and Tunghua provinces between 1939 and 1941. In 1968 Kitabe wrote about the latter campaign: *Manshūkoku-shi*, vol. 2, p. 338, lists "Kichirin Kantō Tsūka Sanshō chian shuksei no gaikyō" [Pacification of the Three Provinces of Kirin, Chientao, and Tunghua], March 1968; but I have not been able to consult his manuscript.
77. *Manshūkokugun*, p. 400; *Manshūkoku-shi*, vol. 2, p. 321.
78. Yim Ch'un-ch'u, *Hang-Il mujang shigi*, p. 216.
79. Ibid., p. 224.
80. Ibid., p. 219.

city, a part of Chian *Hsien* along the Korean border had to be abandoned to it."[81] Evidently, his group's propaganda was effective: on June 15, 1938, when his group attacked a railroad construction project, more than 300 Chinese workers joined the guerrillas. His group was well armed; it had 90 light machine guns in 1938.[82]

The railroad construction projects would have been very vulnerable to the guerrillas. In order to exploit the natural resources of the Tungpientao region, the Japanese began a large-scale railroad construction project in 1937.[83] Although the construction and logging teams were protected by armed guards, the guerrillas would have had the advantage of selecting their targets and of surprise.

The North Korean source also sheds some light on the conference of Allied Army leaders mentioned in the above quotation. According to Yim Ch'un-ch'u, a conference of army and party leaders, including Yang Ching-yü, Wei Cheng-min, and Kim Il-sŏng, was held in November 1938 at Nanpaitzu, Mengchiang *Hsien*. The principal items on the agenda were military strategies to counter the enemy's large-scale assaults, and the organization of the army, party, and people in enemy-occupied territory. The conference decided to opt for large-scale attacks of several hundred men each in view of the strengthening of armaments in the collective hamlets; otherwise, the guerrillas could not obtain the food, clothing, and supplies they needed. The First Route Army was also divided into three front armies (*fang-mien-chün*). The party was to expand its political activity toward the masses.[84]

The Japanese master plan for the extermination campaign was carefully drawn. Lieutenant Colonel Kitabe Kunio, an experienced soldier who had fought against the anti-Japanese forces since 1932 and had directed the Sanchiang area campaign, served as the principal staff officer under Major General Nozoe Shōtoku. Kitabe demanded 30 million *yüan* for the campaign—in contrast

---

81. Tsūka Shōkōsho (Tunghua Provincial Government), "Report on the Result of the Reconstruction Operation in 1938," *Sembu geppō*, vol. 4, no. 4 (April 1936), p. 184. For an English translation of this report, see Chong-Sik Lee, *Counterinsurgency in Manchuria*, pp. 271–306. See also Chi Yün-lung, *Yang Ching-yü ho K'ang-lien Ti-i-chün* [Yang Ching-yü and the First Anti-Japanese Allied Army] (n.p., 1946), pp. 54–60.
82. Tsūka Shōkōsho (Tunghua Provincial Government), "Report on the Result of the Reconstruction Operation in 1938," p. 184.
83. *Manshū kaihatsu yonjūnen-shi*, vol. 1, pp. 246–247.
84. Yim Ch'un-ch'u, *Hang-Il mujang shigi*, pp. 222–227. The conference was held on or about January 12, 1939, near Shihpaitzu (Tunghua provincial government report, loc. cit., p. 185).

to the 3 million *yüan* proposed by the Kwantung Army headquarters—and drew up a thorough plan. It appears that approximately 6,000 to 7,000 Japanese troops, 15,000 to 20,000 Manchukuo troops, and 1,000 police combat units were mobilized.[85] In addition to the "security highways" built previously, Kitabe caused more highways to be built. Both sides of the highways and railways were cleared of trees and tall crops such as corn and sorghum for 200 to 500 meters, and telephone and telegraph facilities were reinforced. The Japanese invested 15 million *yüan*, or half of the budget for the campaign, in these preparations. The construction of the highways was to be completed by September 1940.[86] The Japanese and Manchukuo forces were divided into "guerrilla units" of battalion (for the Japanese) and regiment (Manchukuo forces) size, each of which was to identify a principal enemy target and pursue it to the end.[87] Sites for collective hamlets were more carefully selected in view of better living conditions for the farmers and to facilitate better defense. Large moats (4 to 5 meters deep and 4 to 5 meters wide) were dug around the hamlets, walls were made impregnable, and tall watchtowers were built at the four corners. Many rifles were distributed to the defense units. The collective hamlets were located within two hours' walking distance from each other so that police and self-defense units from one or more hamlets could provide reinforcements in case of a guerrilla attack.[88] The movement of people and goods was placed under more strict control to isolate the guerrillas. Two "special operations" units were organized under Japanese officers to induce guerrilla surrenders. One unit consisted exclusively of former guerrillas; the other consisted of police personnel. Captured or surrendered guerrillas were to be given very lenient treatment.[89] The plan also called for relief programs, farming capital, food grain, and propaganda programs that were designed to win the support of the masses.

It should be noted that all the major anti-guerrilla operations were launched late in the year, just before the onset of winter. The severe cold of Manchuria is well known; the guerrillas by necessity operated in the mountainous regions, which were even colder. Under such conditions, they needed warm clothing and substan-

---

85. The number of troops is my estimate based on information provided in *Manshūkokushi*, vol. 2, pp. 323–324. These figures may be low.
86. *Manshūkokugun*, pp. 403, 413; *Manshūkoku-shi*, vol. 2, p. 332.
87. *Manshūkokugun*, p. 402.
88. *Manshūkoku-shi*, vol. 2, pp. 333–334.
89. *Manshūkokugun*, pp. 404–405.

tial stores of food to pass the winter; but as the collective hamlet program became more and more effective, the guerrillas were placed in increasingly more difficult positions. The strategy of having a counterinsurgency unit to cling to and pursue the enemy to the end—named by the Japanese as the *da-ni* ("tick") strategy—proved more effective. The guerrillas were not allowed to launch attacks against the walled hamlets and other targets that had provided them with food and clothing. They were also given no respite. The improved highway and communication systems enabled the pursuers to field additional support units at will.

Yang Ching-yü and Kim Il-sŏng had been pursued by special units of the Tunghua provincial police before the major campaign began. A police unit consisting of 150 men that included Ch'eng Pin, the former commander of the first division under Yang, as well as some of his former subordinates, had doggedly tailed Yang for six months in 1938, moving from Chian *Hsien* to Tunghua, Linchiang, Chinchuan, Mengchiang, Fusung, and Huatien *hsien* and engaging Yang's forces in nine battles.[90] Another unit of fifty men, all surrendered guerrillas, had shadowed Kim Il-sŏng's 200 men, moving in and out of Fusung, Changpai, and Linchiang *hsien*.[91] But now every guerrilla group was subjected to the same strategy. Perhaps this strategy aided the pursuers to discover and destroy more shacks and huts built by the guerrillas as hideouts than otherwise. Between October 1, 1939, and March 19, 1941, anti-guerrilla forces destroyed 2,923 such hideouts. During the same period, 8,148 *koku* (or 40,430 bushels) of rice, and 3,123 *koku* (or 15,496 bushels) of other food grains, and 531,845 catties (265,922 kilograms or 586,253 pounds) of vegetables were confiscated.[92] If, for rough measure, we take a *koku* of food grain to be equal to 150 kilograms or 330 pounds, then 1,690 metric tons or 3,719,430 pounds of food grain were confiscated. This grain would have provided 2.4 pounds daily to each of the 3,000 guerrillas during the seventeen months. The guerrillas also would have had more than one-third pound of vegetables each day. Little wonder that the lore of the Manchurian guerrillas is filled with stories about food or the lack thereof. As enemy encirclement tightened,

90. Tunghua provincial government report, loc. cit., p. 186.
91. Ibid., p. 187.
92. Nozoe Tōbatsu Shireibu (Nozoe Subjugation Headquarters), "Kichirin, Kantō, Tsūka Sanshō tōbatsu shuyō senka ichiranhyō" [Table of Principal Results of Subjugation in Kirin, Chientao, and Tunghua Provinces (October 1, 1939–March 19, 1941)] (March, 1941); available at the Office of War History, Defense Institute, Japanese Defense Agency. Also see *Manshūkokugun*, p. 411.

it became impossible for the guerrillas to cook, even if they had had food in hand; rising smoke was a sure invitation to the enemy, as the Japanese forces were employing a small number of aircraft for detection of guerrilla locations. The guerrilla forces suffered heavy losses in manpower under these conditions. By the middle of October 1940, when the second stage of the mop-up operations started, only some 300 guerrillas remained in the region.[93] By March 19, 1941, the headquarters of the extermination campaign reported the following results:[94]

Abandoned guerrilla corpses	1,282
Surrendered	1,040
Captured prisoners	896
Total guerrilla losses	3,218

Among the dead, captured, and surrendered were some of the principal leaders. Yang Ching-yü, the general commander of the First Route Army who had led the Communist guerrilla movement from its inception in 1932, was killed on February 23, 1940, and was given a hero's burial by the Japanese.[95] Ts'ao Ya-fan, the commander of the First Front Army, was killed on April 4. Ch'en Han-chang, the commander of the Third Front Army, was killed

---

93. "Manshūkoku tōnan sanshō ni okeru Nozoe Tōbatsutai sakumei tsuzuri" [File of Operation Orders of the Nozoe Subjugation Unit in the Three Southeastern Provinces of Manchuria], September 1940–March 1941. No pagination. *Manshūkokugun*, p. 405, presents the same information.

94. *Manshūkokugun*, pp. 411–412.

95. Ibid., p. 407. For the last hours of Yang Ching-yü, see ibid., pp. 415–417, quoting from Morizaki Minoru, *Tō-hen-dō* [Tungpientao] (no other information given, but evidently published before 1945). Yang's death can be attributed to starvation and fatigue. After fleeing from continuous enemy pursuit for 90 days and finally separated from all of his subordinates except two bodyguards, Yang asked two woodcutters he encountered to sell him food and clothing. Yang had 6,660 yüan with him. The woodcutters were sent to fetch food and clothing, but they suspected Yang to be a major guerrilla leader (with rewards on his head) and reported him to the police. Yang was surrounded and was urged repeatedly to surrender, but he chose to fight to the end. Chi Yün-lung, *Yang Ching-yü*, pp. 90–101, and idem, "Brief Account of the Great National Hero Yang Ching-yü," *Chih-shih* [Knowledge], no. 4 (September 1946), p. 8, present an identical account, as Chi used the same work by Morizaki. Yü Lien-shui provides a similar account in "General Yang Ching-yü Fights from White Mountain to Black Waters," *Hung-ch'i P'iao-p'iao* [The Red Flag Waves], no. 5 (December 15, 1957), pp. 124–131, but with some differences in detail. For example, Yü claims that Yang shot himself to death and that his body was subjected to an autopsy in Mengchiang. Max Perleberg, ed., *Who's Who in Modern China* (Hong Kong, 1954), p. 243, also speaks of an autopsy that revealed grass in Yang's bowels. Yang's final encounter took place in Mengchiang *Hsien*, and hence Mengchiang was renamed Ching-yü. For Yang's earlier activities in the Fushun mines, when he used the name Chang Kuan-i, see chapter 4, p. 105, above.

on December 8. Fang Chen-sheng, the chief of staff of the First Route Army, and Pak Tŭk-pŏm, the regiment commander, were both captured. Wei Cheng-min, the chairman of the South Manchurian Provincial Committee and deputy commander of the route army, outlasted the others but was killed on March 8, 1941. Chŏn Kwang, the political commissar of the Second Army, surrendered on January 30, 1941.[96] Of the nine principal leaders for whom the Japanese had put up reward money, only Kim Il-sŏng and Ch'oe Hyŏn remained at large. The Japanese learned in February 1941 that Kim had fled to the Soviet Far East with six other men.[97] The Japanese were never able to discover the whereabouts of Ch'oe Hyŏn, who had run rampant through Manchuria and the border towns in Korea for a number of years. At any rate, organized Communist and nationalist guerrilla activity in southern Manchuria ended in 1941. According to North Korean sources, the former guerrillas were divided into small groups to engage in underground activities in the Manchurian hinterlands and in Korea.[98]

In the face of the overwhelming and brutal assault by Japanese military and political power, it is perhaps superfluous to discuss the reasons for the guerrillas' failure. Would the outcome have been very different, for instance, if the guerrillas had received more support from the local people? Would the local farmers have been able to sabotage Japanese operations and provide the guerrillas with food, clothing, and information?

The guerrilla leaders in southern Manchuria evidently felt in the spring of 1940 that they did indeed receive too little support from the people, and that this was due to an error committed by themselves. Wei Cheng-min, the chairman of the South Manchurian Provincial Committee, wrote the following on April 10, 1940:

> When the South Manchurian Provincial Committee held its spring meeting to discuss various problems of the army and the party, it was unanimously agreed that the cause of our failure lay in slighting ideological operations directed toward the local masses. It was thus decided that, in order to overcome the error and to revive or lay the groundwork for local operations, some

96. For a map showing where and when these leaders were killed or captured, see *Manshūkokugun*, p. 406.
97. *Manshūkokushi*, vol. 2, p. 325.
98. Yim Ch'un-ch'u, *Hang-Il mujang shigi*, pp. 287–303.

middle- and lower-level officers should be assigned to organize assault teams for engaging in local operations. They would completely sever relations with the army and engage exclusively in local operations. In the past, responsible comrades have reported orally or through personal letters that they were engaging in local operations, but they had, in fact, not carried out the activities; thus, no results have been achieved for several years. At present, many of the anti-Japanese masses have not joined the united front. Since our errors and weaknesses have caused this phenomenon, there is a need to provide the broad masses with leadership in the task of resisting Japan and saving the nation.[99]

Wei Cheng-min attributed the failure of activities among the masses to three causes. The first was that the guerrilla leaders were absorbed with the task of building up their military might and slighted the need for work among the masses. While the importance of indoctrinating and organizing the masses was repeatedly stressed in documents and resolutions issued by guerrilla leaders, evidently no serious attention was paid to these tasks. While small units of guerrillas were charged with the task of working among the masses, they in fact became agents responsible for collecting materials needed by the guerrillas, thus in effect "unconsciously destroying" the ties with the masses.

The second cause of failure was the lack of trained cadres. Attrition of trained personnel was obviously very serious. According to Wei Cheng-min, there were no cadres among the guerrillas who had any experience in "local [party] operations," and because of the residence-certificate system instituted by the Manchukuo regime, the guerrillas could not infiltrate the villages. Those with local ties were recruited to man the guerrilla units, leaving no one to engage in activities among the masses. All the residents in areas under the influence of the guerrillas were moved away into the collective hamlets established in "secure" areas, and hence they were no longer accessible to the guerrillas.

The third cause of failure was the brutal policy of the Japanese

99. "Report of Wei Cheng-min, secretary of the South Manchurian Provincial Committee of the CCP and deputy commander of the First Route Army of the People's Allied Army of Manchuria, to the Chinese representatives at the Comintern, April 10, 1940," in Kōtō Hōin, Kenji-kyoku (Prosecutor's Office, High Court, Government General of Korea), *Shisō ihō* [Ideological Report Series], no. 25 (December 1940), p. 72. The Japanese evidently intercepted this letter, probably by capturing the person dispatched by Wei to deliver it to the Soviet Union.

in ferreting out those with ties to the guerrillas. This was made considerably easier for the Japanese by deserters from the guerrilla ranks. When such individuals were discovered, according to Wei, the entire village was arrested and massacred. When the Japanese knew of the existence of a contact person but could not identify him, all of the villagers would be tortured or threatened until the individual was identified.[100]

Had the guerrilla leaders paid more attention to the need to mobilize and organize the masses, had they stressed the need of secrecy among the mobilized, the situation would have been substantially different; however, such underground organizations would have been able to survive only if they did not overtly come to the aid of the guerrillas. But by the time the South Manchurian Provincial Committee had decided on such a course of action, the trend was almost irreversible.

By the time Wei Cheng-min wrote these words, not only had the guerrillas' ties with the people been severed, but their determination had also weakened. In fact, the situation had begun to deteriorate ever since the Japanese began to use surrendered guerrillas to induce others to follow in their footsteps. According to Wei,

> The enemy has openly engaged in activities to destroy us by causing divisiveness among us, using Ch'eng Pin, who went over to the enemy in the summer of 1938, and bringing about considerable change in the troops' thinking. In the past, in spite of the bitterness of war and the difficulty of our living conditions, there was no discontentment, and good morale was maintained. Because of the notion that those who surrendered would be punished severely [by the enemy], there were no incidents of betrayal. Through the enemy's use of Ch'eng Pin, however, it came to be known among the troops that those who surrendered would not be severely punished. As a result, a considerable change has occurred in the troops' morale. That is to say, everyone knows that if he surrenders he will not be executed. Some of the troops think that if they were to become lackeys of the Japanese bandits, they would not be killed. It seems that some of the men think that by surrendering they would be able to keep alive and es-

100. Ibid., pp. 72–73.

cape from the difficult life they are leading. These are the ones without the spirit of sacrifice, who seek to save their own meager lives.[101]

Evidently, the guerrillas in northern Manchuria shared similar problems. In August 1938, Sung I-fu, the secretary of the Eastern Kirin Provincial Committee, surrendered, having become discouraged at the prospects of the anti-Japanese movement.[102] In January 1939, Chou Pao-chung executed Kuan Shu-fan, a member of the executive committee of the same committee and commander of the First Division of the Fifth Army, on suspicion of planning to surrender. Chou also placed Ch'ai Shih-jung, the commander of the Fifth Army, in confinement, allegedly for a similar reason.[103]

Wei Cheng-min's revelation concerning the lack of attention paid to ideological work among the masses brings us to the relationship between the guerrillas and the party. What had happened to the CCP in Manchuria after 1936?

Aside from the Harbin Special Committee, which had taken charge of organizational activities in the cities until Han Shou-k'uei was apprehended, all three provincial committees in northern and southern Manchuria and in eastern Kirin were effectively merged with the three route armies operating in these areas. As more party cadres operating independently of the guerrilla forces were apprehended, and as it became more difficult to survive enemy attacks, the party was gradually relegated to the background and, except in northern Manchuria, for all practical purposes lost its identity.

In his report of 1940, Wei Cheng-min of southern Manchuria

---

101. Ibid., pp. 66–67. The Japanese barred no means in their attempt to induce the surrender of the guerrillas. The following is a quotation from Wei Cheng-min's letter (p. 69): "By the use of material enticements and sex, they are inducing backsliding elements within our army to leave the revolutionary ranks. Focusing on the difficulty of life among the troops (lack of rice, flour, liquor, and fish) and the problem of sexual life, they are striving to buy off the comrades in small units assigned to various areas. Both by dispatching relatively pretty prostitutes (eighteen- or nineteen-year-olds) to solve the sexual problem directly and by distributing photographs of lewd acts in our area of operations, they are inducing the surrender of young troops in our army. Individual photographs of surrendered troops are distributed to induce others to surrender. Taking the opportunity offered by the fact that our lines of communication have been severed, they send out agents to spread the word that such and such units have surrendered, thus creating uneasy feelings among our men. It should be noted that the number of those who surrendered during the 1939–1941 campaign was very large."
102. Gaimushō, *Shina oyobi Manshū* (February 1940), pp. 74–75.
103. Ibid., pp. 75, 78.

stated that the Panshih Central *Hsien* Committee had been restored in 1936, and that organizational work in parts of Tunghua, Huanjen, Hsingching, Fusung, and Changpai *hsien* had been successful. But after 1937 these local organizations were destroyed one after another, "mainly owing to informing of the enemy by traitors and the arrest and murder of local agents by the enemy."[104] Local activities were then slighted and no agents were dispatched to revive these organizations. "Some local operations still exist[ed]," but there was "no model branch in the cities or villages under the South Manchurian Provincial Committee where [comrades could] freely meet and carry out activities. Although branches exist[ed], they [were] branches in name only and most of them have individual contacts only."[105] Thus, outside of the army, there were no party members, and even within the army, political training seems to have been slighted.

The situation in eastern Kirin was very similar. Sung I-fu, former secretary of the Eastern Kirin Provincial Committee, told the Japanese after his surrender in 1938 that his committee had been officially established in March 1937 and that it directed *hsien* committees in Ningan, Muleng, and Mishan, but that these had been virtually destroyed that spring. Although the provincial committee drew up plans to send out agents, the lack of personnel and police surveillance made it impossible to implement these plans.[106] A Japanese report of February 1940 states that the Jaoho Central *Hsien* Committee and the Hsiachiang Special Committee under the Eastern Kirin Provincial Committee do not appear to have been reconstructed after they were dissolved in the fall of 1938.[107]

The situation of the North Manchurian Provisional Provincial Committee appears to have been much better. After Chao Shang-chih was removed in February 1938 (an episode to be described presently), the committee is said to have striven to consolidate itself, having solidified the unity of the army (the Third Route Army) and the party. It established a new guerrilla district in Lungchiang Province and part of East Hsingan Province.[108] The standing committee of the provincial committee held frequent meetings to discuss means of strengthening the party and the army. The minutes of the January 1939 meeting, obtained by the

104. "Report of Wei Cheng-min," pp. 71–72.
105. Ibid., p. 72.
106. Gaimushō, *Shina oyobi Manshū* (December 1938), pp. 98–99.
107. Gaimushō, *Shina oyobi Manshū* (February 1940), pp. 74–75.
108. Ibid., p. 75.

Japanese, showed that the provincial committee took pride in being the "most powerful organization of the CCP" in Manchuria and expressed the hope that the Allied Army of Manchuria might be accepted officially as part of the National Revolutionary Army headed by Chiang Kai-shek. Unlike the other provincial committees, the North Manchurian committee evidently maintained contact with authorities in the Soviet Union. It is also reported to have dispatched a liaison person to the CCP headquarters, presumably meaning Yenan, although details are not recorded in the report.[109] The Japanese report of February 1940 noted that the North Manchurian committee had the best ideological leadership ability in Manchuria and hence special vigilance must be taken of its operations directed toward the masses.[110]

What did the party and the army advocate when they approached the masses? What was the party's program other than fighting against Japanese imperialism? Were the cadres in Manchuria aware of the intense struggle waged among the top leaders of the party in Yenan regarding the united front between 1937 and 1938? These are some of the important questions that cannot be answered adequately here simply because the extant record provides little information. It is of interest to note, however, that throughout his long report, Wei Cheng-min made no reference whatsoever to any of the socio-economic and political programs that the CCP leaders in Yenan debated.[111] Other than the confiscation of the property of the Japanese imperialists and their lackeys, none of the extant records, including reminiscences of veteran guerrillas, refers to land reform or rent reduction programs. "Destruction of landlords and capitalists in the future" was a theme used by the Communist guerrillas in 1937, but this was a theme confined to the Korean villages in the First Army's area of operation.[112] Evidently, only nationalistic themes were used by the guerrillas in their propaganda directed at the Chinese masses.[113] These leaders, who read the June 1935 letter from Ch'en Shao-yü

109. Ibid.
110. Ibid., p. 76.
111. For the debates in Yenan, see James Pinckney Harrison, *The Long March to Power: A History of the Chinese Communist Party, 1921–72* (New York, 1972), pp. 260–289.
112. Okamoto Goichi, "The Chinese Communist Party and the Communist Bandits in Manchuria," in Shihō-shō, Keiji-kyoku (Bureau of Criminal Affairs, Ministry of Justice, Japan), *Shisō jōsei shisatsu hōkokushū, 4: Manshū ni okeru kyōsanshugi undō* [Reports of Inspection Tours of Ideological Conditions, 4: The Communist Movement in Manchuria] (Tokyo, 1938), pp. 51–52.
113. Ibid., p. 51, and Ishigaki Sadakazu, "Pacification Activities," pp. 39, 44.

and K'ang Sheng, could have concluded that if all elements in the society, including the landlords and capitalists, were to be recruited into the united front, the party should not advocate any program that would be contrary to their interests.

The most prominent leader in Northern Manchuria, Chao Shang-chih, took exception to the new line of policy. His opposition was so strenuous that when a joint conference of the leaders of the North Manchurian and Eastern Kirin provincial committees met at Tangwangho in the summer of 1937, Chao ended up in a scuffle with Chou Pao-chung, who was concurrently head of the Fifth Army and the Eastern Kirin Provincial Committee.[114] The relationship between the two committees was so strained that they even engaged in military skirmishes against each other. Finally, Chao Shang-chih was summoned to the Soviet territory in January 1938; he was stripped of his military and party positions, being accused of engaging in left-wing sectarianism and opposing the Central Committee.[115] Having removed Chao, the Northern Manchurian Province Committee held a three-day meeting in May to criticize its past policies; the committee decided to reorganize the People's Anti-Japanese Allied Army General Headquarters into the Command Post (Chih-hui-pu) of the Third Route Army as of August 1, 1938.[116] Chang Shou-chien, who had been the political commissar of the Sixth Army, was appointed the commandant of the new route army.[117]

114. Gaimushō, *Shina oyobi Manshū* (December 1938), pp. 97, 102–103. According to this report, Feng Chih-kang was appointed acting commander of the Third Army. This was not the first time that Chao Shang-chih had opposed the new party line from Moscow. In January 1936, when Han Shou-k'uei arrived from Moscow and was implementing the reorganization plan, Chao accused Chang Te, the man from Moscow whom Han Shou-k'uei had dispatched from Harbin, as a spy and put him in confinement. Chao was opposed to the new reorganization plan, which abolished the Manchurian Provincial Committee, as well as the new line of policy. The organization of the North Manchurian Provincial Committee was therefore delayed for several months. See Shibata Kōzō, "General Status of Transportation Operations with the Soviet Union from Northern Manchuria," in Shihō-shō, Keiji-kyoku, *Shisō jōsei shisatsu hōkokushū, 4: Manshū ni okeru kyōsanshugi undō*, pp. 327–329.

115. Gaimushō, *Shina oyobi Manshū* (December 1938), pp. 97, 102–103; Imoto Taikichi, "Recent Communist Movement in Manchukuo," p. 37. Chao Shang-chih did return to Manchuria in the summer of 1939 with 320 subordinates, and used his former designation as the commander of the Third Army. He was killed in action soon afterward.

116. Imoto Taikichi, "Recent Communist Movement in Manchukuo," pp. 18–19.

117. Ibid., pp. 37, 54–56. According to Feng Chung-yün, former political commissar of the Third Route Army, the Third Route Army was established in early 1939. Feng Chung-yün, *Tung-pei K'ang-Jih Lien-chün*, p. 37. Feng provides a brief biography of Chang Shou-chien (alias Li Chao-lin) in ibid., pp. 68–76. Feng exalts

Thus it appears that the CCP and its guerrilla armies in Manchuria followed the line established by Ch'en Shao-yü even after 1938, even though Chou Pao-chung was in possession of some of the documents issued in Yenan in 1937.[118] But what kind of ideological programs, if any, did the party advocate toward its own members and new recruits? Unfortunately, not a single bit of information can be discovered on this question.

In the meantime, Ch'en Shao-yü and K'ang Sheng left Moscow, and this was to affect the CCP's policy toward Manchuria. Since Ch'en had assumed leadership of the party in Manchuria in 1935, we must now explicate the CCP's command structure in Manchuria.

As is well known, Ch'en Shao-yü and K'ang Sheng left Moscow for Yenan in late 1937 on a Soviet airplane, taking with them a number of other Chinese.[119] Now that all of China was at war against Japan, both Ch'en and the Soviet leaders probably felt that he should be at the scene of struggle rather than in Moscow. Ch'en reportedly carried instructions from Stalin and the Comintern.[120]

Once settled in Yenan, Ch'en might have resumed his previous role of leadership of the Communist movement in Manchuria, or he might have had the leaders in Yenan continue his policy; however, the situation in Yenan was too complicated for Ch'en to dictate party policy, and the leaders in Yenan had all the more reason now to integrate the struggle in Manchuria with that being waged throughout China. They also had different opinions regarding the interpretation and implementation of the united front with the Kuomintang. At least one Chinese author has asserted that Ch'en Shao-yü, Chou En-lai, and Chang Kuo-t'ao engaged in harsh argu-

---

Chao Shang-chih in connection with his early accomplishments in eastern Manchuria and with the Third Army; he also confirms Chao's death (p. 40). But neither *Hung-ch'i P'iao-p'iao* nor *Hsing-huo liao-yüan* [Sparks Blazing Over the Prairie], the two CCP publications devoted to the reminiscences of former revolutionaries, carried a single article devoted to Chao. As stated before, however, Chao was honored by the renaming of Chuho.

118. Gaimushō, *Shina oyobi Manshū* (February 1940), p. 74.

119. Some say that Ch'en Shao-yü's return was in October, and others say that it was in December. See James Pinckney Harrison, *Long March*, p. 284, and Nihon Kokusai Mondai Kenkyūjo, Chūgoku-bu (Chinese Department, Japanese International Problems Research Center), *Chūgoku kyōsantō-shi shiryō-shū* [Compendium of Materials on the History of the Chinese Communist Party] (Tokyo, 1971), vol. 9, p. 11. A Japanese source, written by an official in Peking in 1943, says October. See "Summary of the Chinese Communist Party's Activities toward Manchuria," Naimu-shō, Keiho-kyoku (Police and Security Bureau, Ministry of Home Affairs, Japan), *Gaiji keisatsu-hō* [External Police Report], no. 245 (June 1934), p. 25.

120. James Pinckney Harrison, *Long March*, p. 285.

ments with Mao Tse-tung and Chang Wen-t'ien at an activists' meeting on November 13, 1937.[121] In a speech at this meeting (published by the CCP in the 1950s), Mao issued a scathing attack against "class capitulationism" and "national capitulationism." Uncritical acceptance of the Kuomintang and the Chinese bourgeoisie were considered "class capitulationism" because of the KMT's attempt to place the CCP under its control and the bourgeoisie's propensity for compromise.[122]

Even if we disregard Mao's speech of November 13, the original text of which has not been discovered by scholars, we can find ample evidence that Mao's approach to the united front departed widely from that of Ch'en Shao-yü. For example, in his speech of September 29, 1937, entitled "Urgent Tasks after the Announcement of Kuomintang-Communist Cooperation," Mao criticized the KMT for carrying out the same policies toward the people that it had been pursuing for the last ten years and urged the KMT to implement speedily Sun Yat-sen's Three People's Principles, stating at the same time that "the agrarian revolution based on the principle of 'land to the tillers' is the policy proposed by Dr. Sun Yat-sen himself." He also urged the KMT to reform the government and the army, stressing the need to bring about "unity between officers and men, and unity between the army and the people."[123] Ch'en Shao-yü's writings before and after his return to China only stressed the positive aspects of the united front, urging the consolidation and expansion of the national united front.[124] All indications are that sharp differences of opinion existed among the CCP leaders on the united front, as they had since January 1933. It is therefore quite possible that Ch'en's previous directives on the united front in Manchuria and the reorga-

121. Kuo Hua-lun, *Chung-kung shih-lun* [History of the Chinese Communist Party] (Taipei, 1965), vol. 3, pp. 250–254.
122. "The Situation and Tasks in the Anti-Japanese War after the Fall of Shanghai and Taiyuan" (November 1937), *Selected Works of Mao Tse-tung* (London, 1958), vol. 2, pp. 65–71. Concerning problems in ascertaining Mao's attitude on the united front between 1937 and 1938, see James Pinckney Harrison, *Long March*, pp. 281–289.
123. *Selected Works of Mao Tse-tung*, vol. 2, pp. 33–44. The original text, "Urgent Tasks in Chinese Revolution After the Establishment of the United Front Between the Kuomintang and the Chinese Communist Party," was published in *Chieh-fang* [Liberation], vol. 1, no. 18 (October 2, 1937), pp. 5–8.
124. See "The Struggle of the Chinese People against the Japanese Aggressor, and the Great Socialist Revolution in the USSR," *Communist International*, vol. 14, no. 12 (December 1937), pp. 992–1001, and "Key to the Solution of the Situation," *Ch'ün-chung* [The Masses] (Hankow), vol. 1, no. 4 (April 1938), pp. 57–60. For a Japanese translation of the latter, see *Shiryō-shū*, vol. 9, pp. 31–40; see also our earlier discussions about Ch'en's policies.

nization of the party in 1936 came under sharp scrutiny and criticism. Whatever the outcome of the debate may have been, Ch'en took charge of the party's Yangtze Bureau, and went to Hankow to confer with the KMT government in his capacity as the head of the CCP's United Front Department and to serve as a member of the CCP delegation to the People's Political Council.[125] Ch'en was no longer in command of the Communists in Manchuria.

The task of directing affairs in Manchuria was assigned to the North China Bureau of the Central Committee, which was reestablished in Peking around the end of 1937.[126] According to a Japanese account, the bureau consisted of three provincial committees (Hopeh, Honan, Shansi) and two special district (*t'e-ch'ü*) committees (Manchuria and Inner Mongolia). The Manchurian Special Committee was further divided into the Liaoning District and the Jehol District.[127] The Politburo meeting of December 1937 reportedly decided to accelerate the work to expand party organization and guerrilla activity both behind Japanese lines and in the KMT territory,[128] but we do not know how this decision was translated into action. We know from Wei Cheng-min, in any event, that the central leaders in Yenan were not able to establish contact with the South Manchurian Provincial Committee before it was decimated. Wei's letter of April 1940 said the following:

> Since I received in the autumn of 1935 after the Seventh Congress [of the Comintern] a small booklet from Harbin, written by Comrade Wang Ming and entitled *Struggle of Free and Happy New China*, all relations with the central leaders and northern Manchuria have been severed. We have not been able to receive from the central leaders either detailed instructions or any document or communication. We have not seen even a trace of a book or newspaper addressed to the general masses. The sly and shrewd Japanese bandits have surrounded us on all sides and have been attacking us. All of our activities and struggles have been feeble. We are like a small boat on the ocean without a boatman. We are like small children who have lost their eyes [parents?] wan-

---

125. On Ch'en Shao-yü's career, see Donald W. Klein and Anne B. Clark, *Biographic Dictionary of Chinese Communism, 1921–1965* (Cambridge, Mass., 1971), vol. 1, pp. 127–134, particularly p. 133.
126. James Pinckney Harrison, *Long March*, p. 286.
127. "The Summary of the CCP's Activities Toward Manchuria," *Gaiji keisatsu-hō*, no. 245 (June 1943), p. 26.
128. James Pinckney Harrison, *Long March*, p. 286.

dering hither and thither, or it is as if we had been stuffed inside a sealed drum.[129]

As mentioned earlier, the North Manchurian Provincial Committee dispatched a man to the CCP headquarters in 1938, but we do not know whether he reached his destination. Chou Paochung's Eastern Kirin Committee, on the other hand, appears to have had a communication line open in 1937 because Chou had received party documents that year, but there is no indication that further contacts were made until 1940. Of course, Chou may have seen these documents in the Soviet territory while he was visiting there in 1938 to settle the Chao Shang-chih affair.

In January 1940, according to the Japanese, the CCP Central Committee decided to establish a special committee for Manchuria in order to push the cause there more vigorously. Li Te-fu, "former secretary of the Eastern Kirin Special Committee," was appointed the new committee's secretary, and Li Yen-lu, the former commander of the Fourth Army of the Allied Army, was placed in charge of propaganda and education.[130] This source also mentioned a "Party Affairs Committee of Manchuria" (Tung-pei Tang-wu Wei-yüan-hui) under the Politburo, but no other details were provided. The special committee was allegedly placed within the military unit under the command of General Lo Cheng-ts'ao, then operating in the central Hopeh region.[131]

Whichever organizational channel they used, the leaders in Yenan appear to have succeeded in establishing a link with the Eastern Kirin Provincial Committee in 1940, according to a Japanese report. In March of that year, the CCP Central Committee dispatched, "via the North China Bureau," Ni Yün-hai, former acting secretary of the Mishan *Hsien* Committee, who had been to Moscow for intensive training at the University of the Toilers of the East and who was one of the many who returned to Yenan with Ch'en Shao-yü. He was able to establish contact points or "traffic stations" in Harbin and Mutanchiang and to establish contact with the Eastern Kirin Provincial Committee. He is also said to have "confirmed" the existence of the Anti-Japanese Al-

---

129. "Report of Wei Cheng-min," *Shisō ihō*, no. 25, pp. 62–63. One of the reasons cited by Ch'eng Pin for surrendering in 1938 was the lack of instruction from the CCP headquarters during the previous six years. See Ishigaki Sadakazu, "Pacification Activities," p. 43.

130. "Summary of the CCP's Activities toward Manchuria," *Gaiji keisatsu-hō*, no. 245 (June 1943), p. 27.

131. Ibid. Lo Cheng-ts'ao was a former officer in Chang Hsüeh-liang's army but rose to prominence in the CCP.

lied Army, but we cannot determine what this "confirming" entailed. In any event, Ni Yün-hai returned to Yenan in the latter part of April and reported his findings.[132]

On July 30, Ni was sent back to Manchuria with instructions to strive to establish liaison with party branches in Manchuria and the Anti-Japanese Allied Army, to direct each party branch and the army to send a delegate each to the Seventh Plenum of the Central Committee to be convened in Yenan, and to redesignate the party branches in Manchuria and the allied armies there as "border region committees" (*pien-ch'ü wei-yüan-hui*) and border region armies and direct them to establish close ties with the party headquarters and the Eighth Route Army through the Kirin-Chahar-Jehol "Suicide Corps" operating in the Hopeh-Jehol region. Ni Yün-hai returned to Mutanchiang and then moved to Harbin, presumably attempting to broaden his contacts, but he was arrested in October.[133]

The leaders in Yenan, of course, had every reason to send more agents, and after Ni Yün-hai was sent on his second mission, five additional cadres, including two women, were dispatched.[134] We do not know the identity of these five, but in 1942 the Japanese military police in Tsitsihar, northwest of Harbin, arrested and tried 37 persons for "organizing" the North Manchurian Provincial Committee. They allegedly conducted propaganda activities directed at the employees of the railroad and collected information concerning the Japanese Army in the area for the "liaison headquarters" in Tientsin. The kingpin of this group was Wang Wen-hsüan, who had been dispatched from the CCP branch in Tientsin.[135] Wang and 44 others were arrested and tried three months later.[136] A group of 17, led by a "member of the CCP," Ts'ung Shih-ho, was arrested in either late 1942 or early 1943 for engaging in organization and propaganda in Tailai and the Chalainoerh Special Banner (*t'e-ch'i*) District on the border of Inner Mongolia,[137] but we do not know whether Ts'ung was one of those dispatched from North China.

It is highly likely that the CCP headquarters continued to send other agents. But they were on very precarious ground once they entered Manchuria. By 1940, the Japanese had streamlined the citizen registration and certification systems, the neighborhood

132. Ibid., p. 25.
133. Ibid. The Japanese authorities would have interrogated Ni and collected detailed information concerning every phase of his activities, but I have not been able to locate any relevant material.
134. Ibid. 135. *Manshūkokushi*, vol. 2, p. 420. 136. Ibid.
137. Ibid.

responsibility system (a modern version of the ancient Pao-chia system), military and labor conscription systems, and the food rationing system, all of which hindered the free movement of individuals. The control of civilian movements was tightened even more in eastern and northern Manchuria as the Japanese poured large numbers of troops into those regions in 1941 in preparation for the war against the Soviet Union that was anticipated to erupt momentarily. Surveillance of subversive elements would also have been intensified, and agents from North China would have found it extremely difficult to operate in such an environment.

Chou Pao-chung claimed later that he received a copy of *Hsin-Hua Yüeh-pao* [New China Monthly] published in Chungking and found articles on "Further Strengthening the Party Character" (Chia-ch'iang tang-hsing tuan-lien) and "On Rectification" (Cheng-tun san-feng) which provided great stimulus to the comrades. This would have been after 1942, since the rectification campaign was launched that year. He had not received any party publication for "many years" before this. Chou also revealed that, just before the end of the war, his group received a copy of Mao Tse-tung's April 1945 report "On Coalition Government."[138] But a Japanese report of 1942 located Chou in the Soviet territory, north of Khavarovsk, directing a training camp of Chinese and Korean guerrillas in exile.[139]

It is quite possible, in any event, that a number of Communist cadres were still operating in Manchuria, striving to organize and expand their followers, when the Japanese capitulated in August 1945. But all indications are that there were not many of them; whatever contact they had with the CCP headquarters in North China would have been very infrequent, and whatever directives were issued by the headquarters did not materially affect the course of events in Manchuria. Chou Pao-chung was undoubtedly right when he said that "embers of resistance against Japan were still burning on the soil of Manchuria"[140] when the Japanese capitulated, but the fire storm that had raged over the mountains and forests of Manchuria could not be revived before Japan was defeated by the Allies.

138. Chou Pao-chung, "Recollecting the Anti-Japanese Guerrilla War in Manchuria," *Hsing-huo Liao-yüan* [Sparks Blazing Over the Prairie], vol. 4, pp. 376–377.

139. "The Camp School in Khavarovsk," *Gaiji geppō* [External Affairs Monthly Report], November, 1942, pp. 85–86, as cited by Dae-Sook Suh, *The Korean Communist Movement* (Princeton, 1967), p. 291.

140. Chou Pao-chung, "Recollecting the Anti-Japanese Guerrilla War," p. 376.

10 | Summary and Conclusions

THE CHINESE COMMUNIST MOVEMENT IN MANCHUria went through many stages and pursued different aims and strategies. In the 1920s, the Chinese Communist Party (CCP) attempted to organize the urban proletariat, but to little avail. In 1930, under the slogan of protecting the Soviet Union, the party attempted to organize the peasants for armed revolt, but this strategy eventually created more problems for the party rather than advancing its cause. In the early 1930s, the party began to organize armed guerrillas in a more systematic manner, but when the CCP guerrillas were ordered to follow "the united front from below" strategy to wrest away anti-Japanese fighters in other groups from their leaders, they became isolated. Only the pursuit of the broadly based united front strategy against Japanese imperialism enabled the CCP to assume leadership of the entire anti-Japanese movement and rally a vast number of the rural masses under it. The concerted efforts of the Japanese military to eradicate the guerrillas in the late 1930s, however, finally decimated the guerrillas, and with them, the CCP organizations. We have discussed the merits and demerits of these strategies in the previous chapters; here, we shall recapitulate our previous discussion and attempt to answer other questions that did not receive adequate attention.

The CCP's attempt to mobilize the urban workers never got off the ground all through the period under study. The workers did not respond to the CCP's call to overthrow the capitalist system in the initial period, and few responded even when the party promoted the united front against Japan. Why was this so?

The economic condition of the working class was certainly miserable. The wages paid to Chinese workers by Japanese industries were never high, and rampant inflation rendered their livelihood precarious. This situation enabled the Communist cadres not only to attract hundreds of workers to the labor unions and party branches but to successfully change the mood of the laboring population. It is also reasonable to assume that the workers and others reached by the CCP's anti-Japanese messages in the later period were sympathetic to the causes advanced by the CCP. And yet, the CCP-directed movements in Manchuria among the workers simply did not expand beyond the conspiratorial stage. Manchuria did not witness massive and spontaneous workers' movements as did China proper.

A few explanations can be offered for this phenomenon. One factor to be considered is the subjective frame of reference of the Manchurian workers. While their wages were dismally low, and they could see the preferential treatment accorded to Japanese workers, most of the low wage earners were either transitory migrants or recent immigrants from North China. Even those who could be classified as natives by virtue of their longer residence in Manchuria could observe the continuous inflow of migrants from northern China and hear their sad tales of wretched conditions there. Therefore, most of the workers would have consoled themselves that they were better off than their compatriots elsewhere. In other words, many of the Manchurian workers would have compared their lot not with that of the Japanese or with some abstract and absolute standards but simply with conditions prevailing in northern China, and they would have considered themselves well off, as the continuous inflow of immigrants attested.

The detailed statistics compiled by Japanese corporations suggest that Japanese employers were sensitive to this issue. The South Manchuria Railway Company maintained a vast and highly sophisticated network of research organizations. As some of the reports cited in this study show, these researchers delved into virtually every aspect of the company's operations, including the workers' wages and living conditions. They also paid close attention to the wages paid by their rivals, such as the Chinese Eastern Railway, and were familiar with the conditions in northern China as well. It is only reasonable to assume that these statistics were effectively utilized to insure that the Chinese workers' discontent would not reach an explosive level. As we have seen, the SMR's managers also closely monitored the attitudes of the workers at every level and locality. This was a situation very difficult for the CCP to penetrate.

Not only did Japanese employers pay close attention to their workers, but the political structure behind them had the determination and means to suppress subversive elements. As we have noted, subversive movements cannot flourish under political regimes that have the determination and the means to suppress them; only if a political regime is sympathetic to a workers' movement or ineffectual in controlling it can the movement make headway. Even when they were suffering from dire conditions, the workers in Manchuria did not spontaneously rally behind a group that offered a cure. Only a small segment of the oppressed were willing to trade their present misery for a promised millennium. Unless the workers were assured of immediate gain through the CCP-led movements, they would not join them.

This brings us to a more fundamental question of the relationship between economic conditions and the "proletarian consciousness" or the propensity of the workers to engage in systematic revolutionary activities. In spite of their dismal conditions aggravated by rampant inflation, the workers in Manchuria did not move beyond "spontaneous" strikes demanding more wages and better livelihood. The Communist cadres had difficulty organizing even these strikes. Some of the workers did begin to be "awakened" by the notion of antagonism between the workers and employers, but they were far from becoming conscious of "irreconcilable antagonism of their interests to the whole of modern political and social systems," a condition defined by Lenin in his *What Is to Be Done?* as "social democratic consciousness." This "consciousness," according to Lenin, had to be brought "from without" by intellectuals, but the CCP cadres were shorthanded and gravely impaired by the security systems of their foes.

While the cadres in Manchuria were grimly aware of the security systems maintained by the Japanese and warlord regimes, the CCP cadres continued to provide clues of their presence to their enemies. We are referring to the pamphlets and leaflets distributed by the CCP organizations on numerous occasions which inevitably led to the arrest of Communist cadres. This distributing of printed matter was undoubtedly a legacy from the early stages of the Bolshevik revolution, but no other legacy was more damaging to the CCP in Manchuria than this one. The propaganda bearing revolutionary proclamations would have been useful, but only under certain circumstances. It could serve to inflame and direct the masses, but only if the masses were already inclined to follow the leadership of the revolutionaries. To anticipate that the masses in Manchuria would follow the CCP's leadership simply because of having read a leaflet was nothing more than illusory. In the Manchurian cities, the practice of distributing propaganda was simply suicidal, but the CCP cadres in Manchuria continued to engage in this practice.

The CCP cadres were directed to organize industrial workers, which meant that they had to operate in urban environments. But the urban areas, as it turned out, were the worst possible environment in which to organize subversive movements. Government mechanisms were most entrenched in urban areas, which were the centers of commerce, industry, and politics. Even though the cities provided temporary anonymity for the party agents, their position was precarious when the governments were determined to search out the subversives. As we have seen, the police of the Chang Tso-lin and Chang Hsüeh-liang regimes and those of the Japanese Army were too efficient for the CCP agents. Even though Manchuria was ruled by the warlords, the Japanese, and the Russians, the Communist cadres in Manchuria could not find sanctuary as did their counterparts in Shanghai, Canton, Hankow, and other major cities, where foreign concessions served as refuges for subversives.

The CCP's radical reform programs in the rural areas also proved to be damaging for the party. Even though many of the farmers in Manchuria were landless, they did not find the CCP's programs palatable. One of the reasons was that the Manchurian villages offered the new arrivals opportunities for upward mobility. A study by Ramon Myers has shown that in villages settled since 1909, one out of three families that moved into the villages as tenant farmers had already moved upward to landlord and owner-cultivator status by the early 1930s, and a third of the 82 families migrating to these villages had become tenant households.[1] The situation for the landless farmers, therefore, could not be said to be hopeless, even though much toil and suffering were necessary for upward mobility.

We must also take the traditional behavioral pattern of the Chinese farmers into account, that is, their habitual resignation to the status quo without resorting to revolutionary violence. Whether this was because of their primitive understanding of struggle, limited political horizons, spontaneous modes of protest, and tendency to strike out against personal abuses rather than the agrarian social system as a whole, as Marxists would argue, or because of the bonds of mutual obligations and responsibilities developed

---

1. Ramon H. Myers, "Socioeconomic Change in Villages of Manchuria During the Ch'ing and Republican Periods: Some Preliminary Findings," *Modern Asian Studies*, vol. 10, no. 4 (1976), p. 610.

between the landlords and the peasants[2] cannot be resolved here; but there is no denying that the Chinese peasants tended to be docile.

The CCP's call for land reform, of course, would have been tantalizing to many of the landless. But what the CCP offered was no more than an ideal that could be attained only by taking over government authority. Since the government could not be defied without overcoming the strength of the government army, the call for land reform was no different from a call to arms, which did not inspire the farmers. The CCP in Manchuria at this time, it must be added, was totally bereft of funds and weapons, and the party's proposals would therefore have sounded like pipedreams to most of the Chinese farmers—the alternative offered by the bandits was far more palatable. The essential prerequisite for land reform was an army that could protect the aroused masses from prolonged enemy assault; without such an army, the call for land reform was infantile.

Why, then, did the Korean peasants in eastern Manchuria respond to the Li Li-san line? Why were they unique among the peasants in Manchuria? The answer can be found in their special economic and political conditions. As we have seen earlier, economic destitution among the Korean peasants in Manchuria had been particularly severe. Unlike their Chinese counterparts, their chance of upward mobility was nil. They had also been subjected to abuse by the warlord government and the Chinese gentry, along with the Japanese Army and police and colonialists who followed them into Chientao. In addition, Chientao was a region in which the Korean nationalists had been very active even before Japan annexed Korea in 1910, and many of the local peasants had turned to communism in the hope of recovering Korean independence. Hence the peasants in this region had been inundated with nationalist and Communist propaganda.

Thus, many complicated factors were operating behind the revolt of the Korean Communists and Communist-led peasants in Chientao. It is possible to argue that the revolt was a case of the oppressed revolting against the oppressor, in pure Marxist class terms, but this would be glossing over the more complicated factors. The revolt was implicitly aimed against foreign oppressors, both Chinese and Japanese. The revolutionaries would not have displayed such ferocity had the nationalist factor not been pres-

2. Cf. Ralph Thaxton's review of Jean Chesneaux's *Peasant Revolts in China, 1840–1949*, trans. C. A. Curwen (London, 1973), in *Journal of Asian Studies*, vol. 33, no. 2 (February, 1974), pp. 279–288.

ent. The left-wing extremism of the Eastern Manchurian Committee must be seen in this context. As the CCP leaders were to criticize repeatedly later, the wanton and spontaneous revolt did not help the cause of the Communist Party. But the revolt of the Korean peasants did accentuate the potency of nationalism.

The strategy of the "united front from below," the practice of allying with the rank and file of armed groups and inciting them to overthrow their leadership, also proved to be a failure. This strategy was based on dubious assumptions about the leaders of various armed groups and their relationship with their followers. First, this strategy assumed that the leaders would be so inept that they would not know what was happening within their groups. This strategy could have succeeded only if the leaders were duped, but few leaders of armed groups were so culpable. The CCP's successes in one or two armed groups, in any event, would have warned the others what was happening. Second, this strategy also assumed that the leader-follower relationship in these groups was such that the followers could easily be persuaded by the CCP to betray their leaders. Undoubtedly, such a situation existed in some of the groups. By and large, however, armed groups, be they bandits, former warlord soldiers, or farmers, possessed closely knit ties of loyalty and friendship. The Communist cadres themselves must have understood the nature of human relationships among the Chinese: they themselves had been steeped in the deeply ingrained Confucian teachings about relationships between seniors and juniors and older friends and younger friends. More importantly, these men who had taken up arms for one purpose or another against the ruling authorities were dependent upon each other for their needs and self-protection. Each group undoubtedly had its share of slackers and malcontents, but the success of the "united front from below" strategy required much more. That strategy in the end built more roadblocks for the CCP in subsequent years than it served the cause of Communist revolution.

As we have seen in the first three chapters, the CCP cadres dispatched to Manchuria urged the party to focus its attention on the struggle against Japanese imperialism. They repeatedly sent their entreaties to the party headquarters advocating such a course. But, as we have seen, the party leadership held firmly to the notion that Japanese imperialism was not to be provoked and that even the warlord regime should not be directly confronted. The Soviet interest in protecting its Chinese Eastern Railway and its need to prevent a Japanese attack of the Soviet Far East dictated caution.

The rise of the CCP, obviously, was something that the Soviet and Comintern leaders considered important and desirable. But it is understandable that the national security of the Soviet Union took precedence. If the Chinese Communist movement jeopardized Soviet security in the Far East, the former must be sacrificed for the latter.

It is important, therefore, to consider the CCP movement in the context of East Asian international relations as a whole and, more specifically, in the context of Soviet relations with China and Japan. The most formidable enemy for the Soviet Union in East Asia between the October Revolution in 1917 and the Japanese capitulation in 1945 was Japan; the warlords in China and the Kuomintang paled in comparison. Until the Soviet Union was strong enough to resist Japanese aggression, Japan had to be placated at any cost. It would have been different had there not been a well-known tie between the Comintern and the CCP, but the CCP, along with all other Communist parties in what might be termed "developing countries" of that era, had been designated as a branch of the Comintern, and the relationship between the two was too well known. The Soviet Union had been criticized too often for actions taken by the CCP cadres in southern China against the "imperialist" nations of the West. In the case of Manchuria, in particular, any radical action taken by the CCP against Japan, including a surge of CCP strength there, would have provoked Japan against the Soviet Union.

The turning point came in 1933 because of developments in Japan, Manchuria, and the Soviet Union. By then, the Soviet Union had less reason to fear Japan, which was deeply mired in internal problems in the wake of worldwide depression while the Soviet Union had made phenomenal progress in its economy and defense. By 1931, Japan had become the object of international criticism while the Soviet Union was gaining in international prestige. United action by the Chinese against Japan would have also diverted Japanese attention and energy from the Soviet Union. It was, therefore, not only desirable but imperative to encourage the CCP to form a united front with any and all elements to struggle against Japanese imperialism. The Soviet Union had restored its diplomatic ties with the Kuomintang government in 1932 and instructed the CCP cadres in Manchuria to work toward a united front in 1933, but by this time the Comintern was not in a position to command the CCP, and the CCP leadership was not in a position to sue for peace with the KMT, which was determined to exterminate the Communists everywhere. Not until 1935, as we have seen, was the Comintern able to direct the CCP cadres in Manchuria to take the full step toward a united front policy. The CCP, as is well known, was mired in the Long March by this time.

As we have seen, the new strategy had a tonic effect on the Communist guerrillas in Manchuria. They were no longer hampered by the strategy to mobilize the proletariat, nor were they shackled by the strategy of a "united front from below" that had isolated the Communist groups. The Communist guerrilla armies in Manchuria did raise the "traditional" Communist theme of equal distribution of land and other wealth, but that slogan played an insignificant part in the guerrillas' appeal for mobilization. There is little doubt that patriotism was the foremost slogan of the anti-Japanese guerrillas; its success was phenomenal by any standard. The non-Communist armed groups flocked to the Communist-led guerrilla army, and the masses provided the support they needed. New recruits multiplied even in the face of relentless assault by the superior Japanese army.

Why do people participate in revolution? Our study of the Communist revolution clearly indicates that the people in Manchuria joined the revolutionary forces out of anger and the desire to repulse Japanese imperialism. Many of them undoubtedly joined the revolutionaries with the thought that the goals set by the anti-Japanese armies had a good chance of success; the guerrillas' propaganda certainly offered such a hope, even though it exaggerated their strength. The sudden increase of recruits after 1937 when China entered into a full-scale war against Japan also suggests this. Others were undoubtedly swayed by the exuberant atmosphere created by the guerrillas. There would have been others who joined the guerrillas for fear of reprisals, but they are likely to have known the high risks involved, particularly after the Japanese began to launch intensive mop-up campaigns. In spite of their high rate of attrition, however, the guerrilla armies kept attracting new recruits. These men joined the guerrillas not out of "rational choice" but because of their patriotism.

It is also possible that many young men joined the guerrillas simply because the Japanese actions left them no other choice. The scorched-earth tactics and collective hamlet program of the Japanese totally devastated the farmers' livelihood, and they had nowhere else to turn. The revolutionary armies offered them a cause as well as a means of survival, even if it was a highly risky one. By participating in the guerrillas' activities, they could find an outlet for their anger and frustration. In any event, it was the Japanese actions that led the masses to the guerrillas.

Why is it, then, that the non-Communist forces in Manchuria were not able to organize armies superior to the Communist-led ones, but were instead absorbed into the Communist-controlled forces? The answer lies in the Communist forces' superior organizational skill and their close ties with the masses. The caliber of leadership must also be taken into account. Let us recall some of the details.

The KMT-connected former warlord army troops in Manchuria had fought the Japanese a few years before the CCP began to organize their guerrilla forces, but by 1933 most of them had dissipated. Even the non-Communist guerrillas who had joined the Communist-led Allied Army dissolved more quickly than the Communist guerrillas in the face of enemy attack. In the latter case, the resolve, or lack of it, of the commanders probably played a significant role. But on the whole, the non-Communist forces paid less attention to the building of bonds with the masses. The former warlord armies had tried to operate in the same manner to which they had been accustomed before 1931. Large numbers of troops not only conducted military operations as before—in frontal engagements rather than hit-and-run guerrilla actions—but paid little attention to the building of ties with the local masses. There is no evidence that the armies under Ma Chan-shan and others tried to build a tight network of mass organizations at the grass roots level. It would have been difficult, in any event, to suddenly build a network that could supply tens of thousands of troops without the backing of a governmental system. The warlord armies, at any rate, were not accustomed to building mass organizations behind them.

The Communist guerrillas, on the other hand, emerged as armed units of local party organizations. Although the guerrillas in the end lost their ties with local party and people's organizations when they were preoccupied with the task of seeking food and supplies by attacking collective hamlets, the Communist guerrillas for a considerable period of time depended on the support of mass organizations. As we have seen, the Communist guerrillas paid meticulous care to indoctrinating the masses about their missions and goals. Anti-Japanese societies and farmers' self-defense associations were part and parcel of the guerrilla army; the guerrillas and the masses were often indistinguishable. In many ways, the guerrillas under the Big Sword chieftain Wang Feng-ko in Tungpientao possessed similar ties with the local masses. The Big Swords was an organization that sprang out of local needs. It is not surprising that the guerrillas under Wang's command offered the stiffest resistance against the Japanese.

The caliber of the leadership and the behavior of the rank and file are also factors not to be minimized. Yang Ching-yü, Chou Pao-chung, and Chao Shang-chih, the three top leaders of the Communist guerrilla forces in Manchuria, were veterans of organizational activities long before they became guerrilla leaders. These were not only dedicated revolutionaries of long standing but organizers and leaders of men under extremely adverse conditions. The very fact that they had been successful in gathering thousands of men around them bespeaks their caliber and character. No matter how persuasive an argument one may be able to advance, people normally do not rally around a risky cause when the advocate of the argument does not exude a sense of trustworthiness, unselfishness, acumen, and courage. This is particularly true before a revolutionary group has grown into a large organized movement and the weight of power possessed by the group has begun to command awe, respect, and fear, adding another dimension to the leader's relationship with potential recruits. At this stage, the leader's ability for organization and his ability to devise proper strategies and tactics for his group come to play a more important role. For most recruits and the masses, the top leader would become a remote figure with whom little direct contact would be maintained. Therefore, unless the top leader possessed all these qualities needed for leading small and large organizations, he would not have been able to start the organization and expand it into a large movement.

By the time the armed groups led by these men grew into large organizations, the relationship between the organization and the population around them would have been governed by what the men in the front line said and did before the masses. The messages and slogans advanced by the guerrillas, of course, would have been important. Without a persuasive argument, the people's emotions could not be aroused. But the behavior of the guerrillas would have played a crucial role. Just as the leaders could not attract the followers without exuding charismatic qualities, the guerrillas could not attract the masses without displaying exemplary behavior. The convincing arguments advanced by the guerrillas could have been negated by their own behavior. How could the masses have supported a guerrilla group ostensibly working for a patriotic cause if the very same men transgressed the interest of the masses? No wonder the guerrilla commanders paid close attention to the behavior of their men. A single infraction of the rules of conduct would have undone weeks if not months of propaganda. As far as can be determined, the Communist-led guerrillas behaved remarkably well. While Ch'i Chihchung's remarks of 1936, quoted in chapter 8, indicate that guerrillas did indeed loot and beat the people, we cannot determine whether these acts were committed by Communist guerrillas. Prosecutor Okamoto's 1937 report (see chapter 9) clearly shows that the Communist guerrillas' behavior was beyond reproach.

As is well known, such exemplary behavior by armed men contrasted sharply with the traditional behavior pattern of armed men in China, be they government troops or bandits. In fact, as we have seen in chapter 3, the masses feared government troops more than bandits. The bandits, at least, chose their targets for looting and kidnapping, and their atrocities were committed for the specific purpose of exacting more bounty. But the government troops—in the name of enforcing the laws—inflicted suffering on the people in a wanton and uncontrolled manner. Most of the indigent masses had not been the targets of the bandits, whereas government troops were not selective of their victims.

The harshness with which the Japanese troops treated the Chinese masses is widely known. We need not recount the atrocities committed by Japanese troops in China proper. Our study of the situation in Manchuria amply shows how grimly the Japanese troops treated the Chinese masses. Even if the Japanese troops had behaved in an exemplary way toward the masses, however, the very nature of their assigned missions would have precluded them from winning the support of the masses. How could a Chinese peasant remain unmoved when the Japanese and Manchukuo troops ordered him out of his home and set a torch to it? As we have seen, tens of thousands of Chinese peasants suffered this fate under the Japanese.

Seen in this context, Prosecutor Okamoto's report about the relationship between Communist guerrillas and the masses is entirely credible. The masses in the Manchurian hinterlands had witnessed the behavior of the bandits, the warlord troops, and the Japanese and Manchukuo troops. None of them offered the peasants anything but suffering and humiliation. But for the first time in their lives, they came into contact with groups of armed men who did not loot, burn, beat or rape them. These guerrillas also advocated a cause with which they could easily identify and were solicitous of their welfare. It would not have taken very much prodding or propaganda for the masses to come to the support of the guerrillas. The very fact that the guerrillas were on their side would have been sufficient. But the nationalist appeal of the guerrillas was potent. They could also easily agree that equal distribution of wealth would be a good thing indeed.

As the Japanese mercilessly enforced the collective hamlet program, however, the amicable relationship between the guerrillas and the masses deteriorated. As we have seen, the masses, herded into what actually amounted to concentration camps, held strong sympathy for the guerrillas, and most if not all of them would have welcomed a chance to depart from Japanese custody. But the guerrillas' raids on these hamlets would have aroused complex emotions. Initially, the purpose of guerrilla attacks against these hamlets was to hamper the overall pacification operations of the Japanese or to take the weapons stored in these installations. Later, as the Japanese implemented the scorched-earth tactic and pushed the collective hamlet program more vigorously, the guerrillas were forced to attack them simply for food. The only alternative for the guerrillas was to raid Japanese and Manchukuo supply convoys, which would have presented higher risks and fewer opportunities.

The guerrilla attacks for food presented the masses with an unenviable choice. If a hamlet were easily overrun, the Japanese and Manchukuo authorities would suspect complicity, thus inviting retributions; if resistance were stiff, it would have produced more casualties among the combatants and more damage would have been inflicted on the hamlet, which had to be repaired by the residents themselves. More importantly, for the non-combatant masses, food was scarce everywhere, and whatever food taken by the guerrillas would not have been replaceable.

From the guerrilla perspective, the taking of food and supplies was justifiable; after all, the collective hamlets were enemy installations, armed with Japanese supplies and weapons. But a sack of grain taken by the guerrillas would have meant a sack of grain lost to the residents. Food was strictly rationed, and in the face of severe shortages the Japanese would not have replaced food or supplies taken by the guerrillas. Thus, guerrilla attacks for food would have been adding salt to the wounds of the residents already suffering from starvation.

It is likely, therefore, that the peasants herded into the collective hamlets became weary of attacks by the guerrillas. Their very survival was at stake each time the guerrillas came for more food, and they were forced to make a choice not between the Japanese imperialists and the Chinese nation but between their own survival and that of the guerrillas. Moreover, as the Japanese relentlessly pursued the guerrillas and the prospect of their fulfilling their goals diminished, most of the masses would have stopped listening to anti-Japanese propaganda. And without the support of the masses, the guerrillas could not survive.

How do we then explain the contrast of fate between the Manchurian guerrillas on the one hand and the CCP army in northwest China on the other? This question received some attention in chapter 9. The most significant difference was the contrasting degree of importance attached by their enemies to the regions occupied by the two sets of anti-Japanese Communist armies. The Shensi-Kansu-Ninghsia region occupied by the Eighth Route Army (or the CCP Army of the Northwest) was one of the most desolate, impoverished, and sparsely populated in China; it lay far from the main route of the Japanese invasion of China and was of no interest whatsoever to the Japanese. On the other hand, the region occupied by the Manchurian guerrillas proved to be of utmost importance to the Japanese, both for security and economic reasons. Some of the guerrillas occupied areas adjacent to the Soviet border, where the Japanese began to fortify against the Soviet army; others occupied areas where the Japanese had discovered vital mineral resources. Furthermore, the Japanese were intent on ruling Manchuria as a Japanese colony, and the guerrillas presented security problems. The Japanese therefore expended massive human and material resources in exterminating the guerrillas in Manchuria. The Japanese did not find it necessary—or were not able—to expend so much resources against the Communist forces in northwestern China. The Japanese interest lay in the region east of the Shensi-Kansu-Ninghsia region. As in Manchuria, the Japanese had been intent on colonizing Shansi, Hopeh, and Shantung provinces.[3] When the forces under Mao Tse-tung ventured eastward in 1940, launching the Hundred Regiments campaign, the Japanese conducted the infamous "Three-All" campaign (kill all, burn all, and destroy all) between the spring of 1941 and the autumn of 1942, inflicting severe losses to the Communists.[4] Had the Japanese possessed more resources or time, the

---

3. Nihon Kokusai Seiji Gakkai (Japanese Association of International Politics), *Taiheiyō sensō e no michi* [The Road to the Pacific War] (Tokyo, 1963), vol. 4, pp. 154–157.

4. James Pinckney Harrison, *The Long March to Power: A History of the Chinese Communist Party, 1921–72* (New York, 1972), pp. 299–301.

Communist organizations remaining in that region would have been weakened even further.

The remoteness of their base area also served the CCP forces as a sanctuary from which they could conduct forays against the Japanese and KMT armies. The guerrillas in Manchuria, however, lacked such a sanctuary. No revolutionary base within Manchuria was beyond the Japanese reach. Until April 1941, when Japan signed a neutrality pact with the Soviet Union in preparation for the war against the United States, Japan had concentrated large forces in Manchuria which could search for and destroy all guerrilla bases. The Soviet-Manchurian border, of course, was tightly sealed by the Japanese. While the long border did permit some traffic of occasional emissaries, no large movement of personnel or supplies could go undetected. Even if the Soviet Union had been willing to support the Manchurian guerrillas, they could not have used the maritime provinces as a sanctuary. As we have mentioned, the Soviet Union was willing and able to engage Japanese forces in battle as they did in 1938 and 1939, but supporting the guerrillas by providing sanctuaries was another matter. This would have given the Japanese Army an excuse to provoke skirmishes with Soviet forces, which would have aggravated sensitive diplomatic relations. The Manchurian guerrillas' ability to damage Japan's overall military capacity was minimal, and the Soviet Union would not have found it advantageous to provide sanctuary to the guerrillas. In any event, the signing of the neutrality pact in 1941 and the German invasion of the Soviet Union in June of the same year made it impossible for the Soviet Union to pay any attention to the few Manchurian guerrillas then remaining. All that the Soviet Union could provide the last remnants of the guerrillas was an escape route.

Given the fact that the guerrillas in Manchuria were ultimately defeated by the Japanese, one might wonder whether the suffering and sacrifice of the guerrillas and the masses were in vain. Such a question, of course, belongs to the realm of philosophy rather than that of political analysis. It can be said, however, that contrary to the impression created by the inability of the central government in China under Chiang Kai-shek, Marshal Chang Hsüeh-liang's forces, and the CCP to mount a forceful resistance to the outside invaders in 1931, the people of Manchuria fought formidably in their own defense. The valor they displayed and the hardships they suffered in doing so can be compared favorably with any other historical situation. And, as we have shown, the Chinese Communists played an important part in this struggle, particularly after 1934, when conditions for the anti-Japanese guerrillas became more unfavorable; and the Communist guerrillas were the ones to continue the fighting to the bitter end.

The legacy of the Communist guerrillas in Manchuria played an important role in the subsequent history of China. As is well known, the Communist forces under Lin Piao regrouped and fortified themselves in the northern part of Manchuria between 1946 and 1947 before they launched the final assault against the KMT forces in December 1947. This was the region where the Manchurian guerrillas had been active. Their legacy is likely to have served the Communists well in their new recruitment program. General Lin Piao's Fourth Field Army crossed the Great Wall into North China in December 1948, and vanquished the last remnants of the KMT forces on the tropical island of Hainan in April 1950.

Glossary

Acheng	阿城
Aihun	愛琿
Ajungchi	阿榮旗
Amano Motonosuke	天野元之助
An Jo	安若
An Kil	安吉
Ankuang	安廣
An Kwang-hun	安光勳
Anhwei	安徽
An-kuo Chün	安國軍
Anshan	鞍山
Anta	安達
Antu	安圖
Antung	安東
Ch'ai Shih-jung	柴世榮
Chalainoerh	札賚諾爾
Chalantun	札蘭屯
Chang Chih	張知
Chang Ching-hui	張景惠
Changchun	長春
Chang Hsüeh-liang	張學良
Chang Jung	張榮
Chang Kuan-i	張貫一
Changkufeng	張鼓峯
Chang Kuo-t'ao	張國燾

Chang Lin 張麟
Chang Lo-shu 張洛書
Chang Meng-k'uan 張蒙寬
Changpai 長白
Changsha 長沙
Chang Shou-chien 張壽箋
Chang Te 張德
Chang Tso-lin 張作霖
Chang Wen-t'ien 張聞天
Changwu 彰武
Chang Yu-ts'ai 張有才
Chao Chih-ch'i 趙之啓
Chaochou 肇州
Chao Shang-chih 趙尚志
Chaotung 肇東
Chaoyang 朝陽
Chaoyuan 肇源
Chao Yün 趙雲
Chekiang 浙江
Chengchou 鄭州
Cheng-tun san-feng 整頓三風
Ch'en Han-chang 陳翰章
Ch'en Hung-chang 陳鴻章
Ch'en-kuang-pao 晨光報
Ch'en Kung-mu 陳公木
Ch'en Kung-po 陳公博
Ch'en Ping-chang 陳屏章
Ch'en Shao-yü 陳紹禹
Ch'en Tu-hsiu 陳獨秀
Ch'en Tung-shan 陳東山
Ch'en Tzu-chen 陳子眞
Ch'en Wei-jen 陳爲人
Chen Ying 震瀛
Cheng Hsiao-hsü 鄭孝胥
Cheng Lu-yen 鄭魯岩
Ch'eng Pin 程斌
Ch'i 旗

Chia-ch'iang tang-hsing tuan-lien	加強黨性鍛鍊
Chiamussu	佳木斯
Chian	輯安
Chiang-pei K'ang-Jih Lien-ho-chün Tsung Chih-hui-pu	江北抗日聯合軍總指揮部
Chiaoho	蛟河
Chi-Ch'a-Jeh Pien-ch'ü	冀察熱邊區
Ch'i Chih-chung	祁致中
Chienchang	建昌
Ch'ien Kung-lai	錢公來
Chienkuoerhlossu	前郭爾羅斯
Chientao	間島
Chi Hsing	吉興
Chihli	直隸
Chih-pu	支部
Ch'i Ming-shan	祁明山
Chin	斤
Chinchou	錦州
Chinchuan	金川
Ching Lo-t'ing	景樂亭
Ching-pei tui	警備隊
Chingcheng	慶城
Chingshan	青山
Chingyuan	清源
Chinhsien	錦縣
Chinhuangtao	秦皇島
Ch'in Pang-hsien	秦邦憲
Chin Shan	金山
Chi-shan-hui	積善會
Chi-ta te li-liang	極大的力量
Chi-tung-chü	吉東局
Ch'i-tung Tobacco Company	啓東煙草公司
Chiu-kuo Ch'ing-nien-hui	救國青年會
Chiu-kuo Chün	救國軍
Ch'iung-min-tang	窮民黨
Chi Yün-lung	紀云龍

Glossary

Ch'oe Hyŏn	崔賢
Ch'oe Sŏk-ch'ŏn	崔石泉
Ch'oe Yong-gŏn	崔鏞健
Chŏn Kwang	全光
Chou En-lai	周恩來
Chou Hsiang-nan	周向南
Chou Pao-chung	周保中
Chou Shu-tung	周樹東
Chuang	莊某
Ch'üan-sheng Ying-wu-ch'u Tsung-pan	全省營務處總辦
Chu Chi-ch'ing	朱霽青
Chu Chin	朱鎮
Ch'ü Ch'iu-pai	瞿秋白
Ch'u Chün	楚鈞
Ch'u Chün-feng	楚俊峯
Chuho	珠河
Chung Hou	忠厚
Chung-hsin ch'eng-tzu	中心城子
Chung-hsin hsien	中心縣
Chung-hua Ch'ing-nien-hui	中華青年會
Chung-hua Min-tsu Tzu-wei Wei-yüan-hui	中華民族自衛委員會
Chung-hua Yin-kung T'ung-chih-hui	中華印工同志會
Chung-Kung Yen-chiu Tsa-chih-she	中共研究雜誌社
Chung-kuo Ch'ing-nien	中國青年
Chung-kuo Hung-chün Ti-san-shih-erh Chün	中國紅軍第三十二軍
Chung-kuo T'ung-meng-hui	中國同盟會
Chungshan	中山
Chungyang	中央
Chu Teh	朱德
Chü-tzu-chieh	局子街
Ch'ü Wen-hsiu	曲文秀

Dairen	大連
Dairen Kikai Seisakusho	大連機械製作所
Deguchi Katsuji	出淵勝次
Faku	法庫
Fangcheng	方正
Fang Chen-sheng	方振聲
Fang-mien-chün	方面軍
Fan-Jih Chiu-kuo-hui	反日救國會
Fan-Jih-hui	反日會
Fan-Jih Kung-nung Yu-chi-tui	反日工農遊擊隊
Fan-Jih Tsung-hui	反日總會
Fan-Man k'ang-Jih	反滿抗日
Fengcheng	鳳城
Feng Chien-ying	馮劍英
Feng Chih-kang	馮治綱
Feng Ch'ün	馮羣
Feng Chung-yün	馮仲雲
Feng Lin-ko	馮麟閣
Fenglochen	豐樂鎮
Fengtien	奉天
Fengtien Chiang-chün	奉天將軍
Fengtien Chiao-yü T'e-pieh Wei-yüan-hui	奉天教育特別委員會
Feng Yü-hsiang	馮玉祥
Fu Ching-yang	傅景陽
Fuchou	復州
Fuhao	富豪
Fuhsien	復縣
Fujii Masuo	藤井滿洲男
Fukien	福建
Fukushima	福島
Fulaerhchi	富拉爾基
Fu Li-yü	傅立魚
Fushun Kung-hui	撫順工會
Fusung	撫松

328 *Glossary*

Fu Tien-ch'en	傅殿臣
Fu Yu	傅有
Fuyu	扶餘
Fuyüan	撫遠
Genrō	元老
Gotō Shimpei	後藤新平
Haicheng	海城
Haiching	海青
Hailar	海拉爾
Hailin	海林
Hailun	海倫
Hailung Hsien	海龍縣
Hamahotzu	蛤馬河子
Han Chin	韓震
Hanjok Nodong-dang	韓族勞動黨
Hankow	漢口
Han Pin	韓斌
Han Shou-k'uei	韓守魁
Han Sŏl-ya	韓雪野
Han Yü-shu	韓玉書
Harbin	哈爾濱
Hatano Kenichi	波多野乾一
Hayashi Masakazu	林正和
Heiho	黑河
Heilungkiang	黑龍江
Hengtaohotzu	橫道河子
Ho Ch'eng-hsiang	何成湘
Ho Hsiang-ning	何香凝
Hokang	何崗
Holung	和龍
Ho Meng-hsiung	何孟雄
Honan	河南
Hopei	河北
Hoshantzukou	何膳子溝
Ho Sheng	何生

Hosoya Chihiro	細谷千博
Ho Te	何德
Hotung	河東
Hotzu ts'un	河子村
Houkuoerhlossu	後郭爾羅斯
Ho Ying-ch'in	何應欽
Hsiachiang	下江
Hsiang	响
Hsiang Chung-fa	向忠發
Hsiang-tao Chou-pao	嚮導週報
Hsiao Chün	蕭軍
Hsiao kung-hui	小工會
Hsiao Tso-liang	蕭作亮
Hsia Yün-chieh	夏雲階
Hsieh Wen-tung	謝文東
Hsi Hsia	熙洽
Hsin-ch'ing-nien	新青年
Hsingan Hsi	興安西
Hsing-an-ling	興安嶺
Hsingan Nan	興安南
Hsingan Pei	興安北
Hsingan Tung	興安東
Hsingching	興京
Hsin-hua Yüeh-pao	新華月報
Hsinking	新京
Hsinmin	新民
Hsinpin	新賓
Hsiping	西平
Hsiuyen	岫巖
Hsüeh Wen	薛雯
Hsü Tse-min	徐澤民
Huang Fu	黃郛
Huangkou	荒溝
Huangkutun	皇姑屯
Huang Yün-t'eng	黃雲騰
Huanjen	桓仁
Huatien	樺甸

Hua Ying-shen	華應申
Hu-hai T'ieh-lu	呼海鐵路
Hu Han-min	胡漢民
Huinan	輝南
Hu Kuo-ch'en	胡國臣
Hulan	呼蘭
Hulin	虎林
Hunan	湖南
Hunchun	琿春
Hung-ch'iang-hui	紅槍會
Hung-ch'i Chou-pao	紅旗週報
Hung-ch'i Jih-pao	紅旗日報
Hung-ch'i Pao	紅旗報
Hung-ch'i P'iao-p'iao	紅旗飄飄
Hung hu-tzu	紅鬍子
Hung-se Chung-hua	紅色中華
Hu Pin	胡彬
Hwang Ch'ŏl-hwan	黃哲煥
Hyŏnjong	顯宗
Ilan	依蘭
Ikei Masaru	池井優
Imienpo	一面坡
Imoto Taikichi	井本臺吉
Ishigaki Sadakazu	石垣貞一
Ishii Kikujirō	石井菊次郎
Ishikawa Tadao	石川忠雄
Itō Takeo	伊藤武雄
Itung	伊通
Jaoho	饒河
Jehol	熱河
Jen-yin	壬寅
Juichin	瑞金
Kaifeng	開封
Kaiping	開平

Glossary 331

Kaishantun	開山屯
Kaitung	開通
Kaiyuan	開原
K'ang-Jih Lien-ho-chün Ts'an-mou-ch'u	抗日聯合軍參謀處
K'ang-Jih Lien-ho-chün Chiang-pei Tsung Chih-hui-pu	抗日聯合軍江北總指揮部
Kang P'ing	康平
K'ang Sheng	康生
Kannan	甘南
Kansu	甘肅
Kaoliang	高粱
Kaomi	高米
Katayama Sen	片山潛
Katō Narimasa	加藤成正
Khingan	興安
Kiangsi	江西
Kiangsu	江蘇
Kim Ch'ŏl	金哲
Kim Il-sŏng	金日成
Kim Kyu-hwan	金圭煥
Kim Sang-sŏn	金相善
Kim Sŏk-ch'ŏn	金石泉
Kim Yong-sŏp	金容燮
Kirin	吉林
Kitabe Kunio	北部邦雄
Kitakawa Shikazō	北川鹿藏
Kobayashi Hideo	小林英夫
Koku	石
Kokunai Chian Taisaku no kenkyū	國內治安對策の研究
Ko-ming-tang	革命黨
Kōmoto Taisaku	河本大作
Koryŏ	高麗
Koshan	克山
Kotung	克東
Kou-chieh	勾結

Ku Shun-chang	顧順章
Kuan Shu-fan	關書範
Kuan-chang lu-hsien	官長路線
Kuan-men chu-i	關門主義
Kuan-nien	觀念
Kuantien	寬甸
Kuantungchou	關東州
Kung Ch'u	龔楚
K'ung Hsien-jung	孔憲榮
Kung-ch'an-tang	共產黨
Kungchuling	公主嶺
Kung-jen chih lu	工人之路
Kung-jen sheng-huo	工人生活
Kuo Chen	國珍
Kuo Hua-lun	郭華倫
Kuomintang	國民黨
Kuo Sung-ling	郭松齡
Kurihara Ken	栗原健
Kwangju	光州
Kwangsi	廣西
Kwangtung	廣東
Kweichou	貴州
Lao-shih	老師
Laotoukou	老頭溝
Lao-tung-chieh	勞動界
Lao-tung Chou-kan	勞動週刊
Latzukang	拉子崗
Laoyeshan	老爺山
Lee Chŏng-Sik	李庭植
Lei Ting	雷丁
Li	里
Li Chao-lin	李兆麟
Li Chen-ying	李震瀛
Li Ch'eng-hsiang	李承相
Li Chien-nung	李劍農
Li Chih	栗直

Li Ch'un-shan	李春山
Li-hsing Yang-hang	利興洋行
Li Hua-t'ang	李華堂
Li Hung-kuang	李紅光
Li Li-san	李立三
Li Sung-lan	李頌蘭
Li Ta	李達
Li Ta-chao	李大釗
Li Te-fu	李德福
Li Tsung-hsüeh	李宗學
Li Tu	李杜
Li Wei-han	李維漢
Li Yao-k'uei	李耀奎
Li Yen-lu	李延祿
Li Yen-p'ing	李延平
Liaochung	遼中
Liao Chung-k'ai	廖仲凱
Liaohsi	遼西
Liaoning	遼寧
Liaotung	遼東
Liaoyang	遼陽
Linchiang	臨江
Lin Piao	林彪
Lishu	梨樹
Liu Ch'eng-hsiang	劉承相
Liu Chin-yüan	劉金元
Liu I-ch'eng	劉一成
Liu K'uai-t'ui	劉快腿
Liu Li-ming	劉立名
Liu Shao-ch'i	劉少奇
Liu Yao-fen (chieh)	劉耀芬（芥）
Liuho	柳河
Liutaokou	六道溝
Lo	羅某
Lo Chang-lung	羅章龍
Lo Cheng-ts'ao	羅正操
Lo Fu	洛甫

Lo I-nung	羅亦農
Lo Mai	羅邁
Lo Teng-hsien	羅登賢
Lunan	盧南
Lüshun	旅順
Lungchiang	龍江
Lungching	龍井
Ma Chan-shan	馬占山
Manchouli	滿洲里
Man-chou-sheng Lin-shih Wei-yüan-hui	滿州省臨時委員會
Man-chou-sheng Wei-yüan-hui	滿州省委員會
Man-chou Tang-pu	滿州黨部
Manchukuo	滿洲國
Man Shi Kai	滿史會
Manshū kyōsanhi no kenkyū	滿州共產匪の研究
Manshū Nippō	滿州日報
Mao Kuo	毛國
Mao Tse-tung	毛澤東
Maruta	丸田
Matsuoka Yōsuke	松岡洋右
Mengchiang	濛江
Meng Chien	孟堅
Meng Yung-ch'ien	孟用潛
Mishan	密山
Mitsuya Miyamatsu	三矢宮松
Morishima Morito	森島守人
Morizaki Minoru	森埼實
Mou	畝
Mulan	木蘭
Muleng	穆稜
Mutanchiang	牡丹江
Mun Kap-song	文甲松
Nancha	南岔
Nanchang	南昌

Glossary 335

Nanking	南京
Nan-Man Fan-Jih Tsung-hui	南滿反日總會
Nan-Man Yu-chi-tui	南滿遊擊隊
Nanpaitzu	南牌子
Nanpeihoyuan	南北河源
Nenchiang	嫩江
Nieh Jung-chen	聶榮臻
Ni Yün-hai	倪雲海
Ningan	寧安
Ningan Fan-Jih Yu-chi-tui	寧安反日遊擊隊
Ning Hai	寧海
Nishikawa Torajirō	西川虎次郎
Noho	訥河
Nomonhan (Nomenkan)	訥門汗
Nongmin Tongmaeng	農民同盟
Nozoe Shōtoku	野副昌德
Nungan	農安
Nungkiang	嫩江
Nung-min Hsieh-hui	農民協會
Ogiwara Kiwamu	荻原極
Okamoto Goichi	岡本吾市
Okubo Yasushi	大久保泰
Omu	額穆
Omuso	額穆索
Otsuka Reizō	大塚令三
Oyüwan Pien-ch'ü	鄂豫皖邊區
Pai Yün-t'i	白雲梯
P'an	潘某
Panku	盤谷
Panshih	盤石
Pak Tŭk-nam	朴得南
Pak Tŭk-pŏm	朴得範
Pak Yun-sŏ	朴允瑞
Pao-an tui	保安隊
Pao-chia	保甲

Paoching	寶清
Pao Kuei-ch'ing	鮑貴卿
Pao-min hui	保民會
Paoting	保定
Pao-wei-t'uan	保衞團
Payen	巴彥
Peian	北安
Peichen	北鎮
Peichiao	北郊
Pei-ching Ti-fang Wei-yüan-hui	北京地方委員會
Pei-fang Ko Sheng-wei Tai-piao Lien-hsi Hui-i	北方各省委代表聯席會議
Peihsingchen	北興鎮
Peikou	北溝
Peishan	北山
Peiyang	北洋
Peking	北京
P'eng Teh-hwai	彭德懷
Penhsihu	本溪湖
Pien-ch'ü Wei-yüan-hui	邊區委員會
Pien-i-tui	便衣隊
Pien Shih-ch'i	卞士琦
Pinchiang	賓江
Pingkang	平崗
P'ing-min Chou-pao	平民週報
Pingtan	平旦
Pokotu	博克圖
Po Ku	博古
Poli	勃利
P'u I	溥儀
P'u-pien chu-i	普遍主義
Putehachi	布特哈旗
Sanchiang	三江
Santaokou	三道溝
Sasaki Hideo	佐々木日出男

Sasaki Tōichi	佐々木到一
Seimu Sōkan	政務總監
Seki Hiroharu	關寬治
Shaho	沙河
Shahokou	沙河口
Shanchengchen	山城鎮
Shangchih	尚志
Shanghai	上海
Shanhaikuan	山海關
Shan-lin Nung-Kung I-wu-tui	山林農工義務隊
Shan-lin-tui	山林隊
Shansi	山西
Santaokang	三道崗
Shantung	山東
Shao Hsing	邵興
Shao-nien Hsien-feng-tui	少年先鋒隊
Sheng Chung-liang	盛仲亮
Sheng Yüeh	盛岳
Shensi	陝西
Shentao School	神道學校
Shenyang	瀋陽
Shen Yin	沈寅
Shibata Kōzō	柴田孔三
Shidehara Kijūrō	幣原喜重郎
Shihitaokou	十一道溝
Shihjenkou	石人溝
Shihpaitzu	十牌子
Shih Ta-kan	史大幹（石達干）
Shimada Toshihiko	島田俊彦
Shuangcheng	雙城
Shulan	舒蘭
Shunchih	順直
Shuntien	順天
Sian	西安
Ssuchan	四站
Ssuping	四平
Ssupingchieh	四平街

Suematsu Takayoshi	末松高義
Suifenho	綏芬河
Suihua	綏化
Suileng	綏稜
Suining	綏寧
Suitung	綏東
Su Kuang	蘇廣
Su Ping-wen	蘇炳文
Su Wen	蘇文
Sun Ch'ao-yang	孫朝陽
Sun Chieh	孫杰
Sung Chen-hua	宋振華
Sung Ch'ing-ling	宋慶齡
Sunghua	松花
Sung I-fu	宋一夫
Sung Lan-yün	宋蘭韻
Sungpuchen	松浦鎮
Sun Tzu	孫子
Sun Yat-sen	孫逸仙
Swatow	汕頭
Szechwan	四川
Tahuangkou	大荒溝
Taian	台安
Tai Hsüan-chih	戴玄之
Tai Hung-pin	戴鴻賓
T'ai I	太乙（太逸）
Tailai	泰來
T'ai-tung Jih-pao	泰東日報
Taiyuan	太原
Takahashi Toshio	高橋敏雄
Ta-kou-tui	打狗隊
Talatzu	大拉子
Ta-lien Chung-hua Kung-hsüeh-hui	大連中華工學會
Tanaka Giichi	田中義一
T'ang Hung-ching	唐宏景

Tangku	塘沽
Tangwangho	湯汪河
Tangyuan Fan-Jih Yu-chi-tui	湯原反日遊擊隊
T'ang Yü-shan	湯玉山
T'ao Ho-hsiang	陶何祥
Tao-li	道裡
T'ao Ming-hsüan	陶明宣
Taonan	洮南
Tao-wai	道外
Ta-p'ai-tui	大排隊
Tapanshang	大板上
ta-pen-ying	大本營
Ta P'ing	大平
Ta-tao-hui	大刀會
Ta-tung Jih-pao	大東日報
T'e-ch'i	特旗
Teng Ho-kao	鄧和高
T'e-pieh-ch'ü chih-hsing-pu	特別區執行部
Tetu	德都
T'e-wei	特委
T'e-wu	特務
Tiao	吊
Tiehli	鐵驪
Tiehling	鐵嶺
Tien Ch'en	殿臣
T'ien Chün	田軍
Tien-t'ieh Ch'ing-nien-hui	電鐵青年會
Tientsin	天津
Ting Chün-yang	丁君羊
Tō-a	東亞
Toutaokou	頭道溝
Tōyō Takushoku Kabushiki Kaisha	東洋拓殖株式會社
Ts'ao Kuo-an	曹國安
Ts'ao Ya-fan	曹亞範
Tseng-chih	增智
Tsinan	濟南

Tsingtao	青島
Tsitsihar	齊齊哈爾
Tsung Chih-hui-pu	總指揮部
Tsung-Chung-kuo Min-tsu Wu-chuang Tzu-wei Wei-yüan-hui	總中國民族武裝自衛委員會
Tsung Lao-shih	總老師
Ts'ung Shih-ho	叢世和
Tsung Ssu-ling-pu	總司令部
Tsurumi Yūsuke	鶴見祐輔
Tuan Ch'i-jui	段祺瑞
Tuan Chih-kuei	段芝貴
Tu Chi-ts'eng	杜繼曾
Tuerhpote	杜爾伯特
T'u-fei	土匪
Tu Lan-t'ing	杜蘭亭
Tulungshan	土龍山
Tumen	杜門
Tumuho	獨木河
Tu Wen-yüan	杜文遠
Tungan	東安
Tungchiang	同江
Tungho	通河
T'ung-hsiang-hui	同鄉會
Tunghua	通化
Tungliao	通遼
Tung-nan T'e-wei	東南特委
Tungning	東寧
Tung-pei Fan-Jih Chiu-kuo Tsung-hui	東北反日救國總會
Tung-pei I-yung-chün	東北義勇軍
Tung-pei Jen-min Koming-chün	東北人民革命軍
Tung-pei K'ang-Jih Chiu-kuo Wei-yüan-hui	東北抗日救國委員會
Tung-pei K'ang-Jih Lien-ho-chün	東北抗日聯合軍

Tung-pei Min-chung-pao	東北民眾報
Tung-pei Min-chung Tzu-wei-chün	東北民眾自衛軍
Tung-pei Nung-Kung I-yung-chün	東北農工義勇軍
Tung-pei Tang-wu Wei-yüan-hui	東北黨務委員會
Tung-pei Tsao-pao	東北早報
Tungpientao	東邊道
Tung-san-sheng	東三省
Tunhua	敦化
Tzu-wei-hui	自衛會
Ugaki Issei	宇垣一成
Wai-chiao Hsieh-hui	外交協會
Wakatsuki Reijirō	若槻礼次郎
Wang Chien-min	王健民
Wangching	汪清
Wang Ching-wei	汪精衛
Wang Feng-ko	王鳳閣
Wang Jen-ts'ai	王仁才
Wangkang	王崗
Wang Li-kung	王立功
Wang Ming	王明
Wang Ming-kuei	王明貴
Wang Shao-po	王少玻
Wang Sheng-i	王繩一
Wang Shu-te	王樹德
Wang Te-lin	王德林
Wang Te-t'ai	王德泰
Wang Wen-hsüan	王文宣
Wang Ya-ch'en	王亞臣
Wangyükou	王隅溝
Wang Yü-nan	王毓南
Wei Cheng-k'uei	韋正奎
Wei Cheng-min	魏拯民

Glossary 341

Weiho	葦河
Wei-jen	爲人
Weishaho	葦沙河
Wengshenglatzu	甕聲拉子
Wenmiao	文廟
Wu Chün-sheng	吳俊陞
Wuhan	武漢
Wu I-ch'eng	吳義成
Wu P'ei-fu	吳佩孚
Wuyun	烏雲
Yada Shichitarō	矢田七太郎
Yalu River	鴨綠江
Yanaihara Tadao	矢內原忠雄
Yang An-jen	楊安仁
Yang Chih-yün	楊志雲
Yang Ching-yü	楊靖宇
Yang Ch'un-shan	楊春山
Yang I-ch'en	楊翼辰
Yang Sung	楊菘
Yang Ta-ts'ung	楊大聰
Yang Tso-ch'ing	楊佐青
Yangtze River	楊子江
Yang Yü-tien	楊于典
Yang Yü-t'ing	楊宇霆
Yeh Yung-nien	葉永年
Yenchi	延吉
Yenpien	延邊
Yentunglatzu	煙筒拉子
Yen Ying	岩英
Yi Chin-a	李眞雅
Yi Ch'ŏl-ho	李哲澔
Yi Hong-gwang	李紅光
Yi Hun-gu	李勳求
Yi Pŏm-sŏk	李範奭
Yi Sang-muk	李相默
Yi Tong-il	李東日

Yi Yŏng-nan	李瑛蘭
Yim Ch'un-ch'u	林春秋
Yingkou	營口
Yoshihiro Motohiko	吉弘基彦
Yoshizawa Kenkichi	芳澤謙吉
Yüan	元
Yüan Shih-k'ai	袁世凱
Yüan Te-sheng	袁德勝
Yü Chi-hsien	于冀賢
Yu Chi-wŏn	柳志元
Yüeh Sheng	岳盛
Yü Lien-shui	于連水
Yunnan	雲南
Yushu	榆樹

Index

Acheng, 108, 108n
"adventurism" of Li Li-san, 120
Agricultural development plan of Manchukuo, 270
Agrarian revolution, 102, 116
Aihun, 250
Ajungchi, 286
All-China Congress of the Soviets, 125, 176
All-China Federation of Labor, 109
All-China General Union, 126
All-China People's Armed Self-Defense Committee, 179–180
All-China Unified National Defense Government, 239
All-East Manchuria Riot Committee, 115
All-Manchuria Anti-Japanese Society, 150
Amano Motonosuke, 22
Anhwei: CCP membership quota (1927), 59; mentioned, 8, 129
An Kil, 208
An Kwang-hun, captured, 282
Anshan: CCP activities in, 253; workers' strikes in, 29, 30; mentioned, 14, 72, 105
Anshan Iron Works, workers in, 15
Anti-Bolshevism, 149
Anti-guerrilla operations. See Pacification operations
Anti-Imperial League: in Chientao, 143, 203; in Mukden, 124; in Panshih, 210
Anti-Imperial League: in Chientao, 143, 203; in Mukden, 124; in Panshih, 210
Anti-Imperial Student Association, 123
Anti-Imperialism. See Imperialism

Anti-imperialist struggle: 39, 44, 53, 84, 98, 110, 137, 138, 149, 169, 177, 179
Anti-Japanese Allied Army General Command, 240
Anti-Japanese Farmers' Self-Defense Unit, 249–250
Anti-Japanese National Salvation Committee of Manchuria, 241
Anti-Japanese National Salvation General Association of Manchuria, 243
Anti-Japanese National Salvation People's Representatives' Conference, 237
Anti-Japanese National Salvation Society, 194, 195, 285
Anti-Japanese political alliance. See United front
Anti-Japanese resistants: losses suffered by, 130, 160, 264; numbers of, 129, 129n, 130, 160, 239, 244, 245, 262–263, 262n; quality of, 245
Anti-Japanese Society: in Chientao, 207; in Dairen, 252; direction from, 208; in eastern Manchuria, 257; in Hailun Hsien, 252; in Harbin, 151, 152, 153, 215, 251; in Mukden, 252; numbers of members, 227; in Panshih, 219; in Payen, 252; mentioned, 132, 175, 176, 178, 224, 249, 315
Anti-Japanese Soldiers' League, 203
Anti-Japanese struggle: advocated by Ch'en Wei-jen, 71; cautioned by the CCP central leaders, 72–73; impact on the Soviet Union, 86–94 passim; international repercussions of, 86; polemic over, 78–84 passim; mentioned, 175, 177, 213
Anti-Japanese united front: CCP cen-

345

tral leaders on, 165–166; Ch'en Shao-yu on, 165
Anti-Japanese Volunteer Army, 163
Anti-Japanese Worker-Farmer Guerrilla Unit, in Panshih, 211
Anti-Korean feeling, 203
Antu: CCP strength in, 227; mentioned, 122, 142
Antung: CCP branch in, 253; number of anti-Japanese fighters in, 263; soldiers' revolt in, 152; mentioned, 105, 124, 196, 273
Arrests of Communist Party members: in Changchun (1934), 199; in Chientao, (1932), 203; in Chinchou (1928), 68; in Dairen (1927), 50–51, 62; (1928), 67–68; (1931), 147; (1937), 255–256; in Fushun (1929), 105; (1930), 125, 125n; (1931), 147; (1933), 193; in Harbin (1932), 153; (1933), 198; (1934), 200, 231; (1937), 254–255, 256; impact of, 69; in Kirin (1933), 196; Korean Communists (1930), 115n; (1930–31), 120; in Liaochung, 199n; in Liuho, 258; Liu Shao-ch'i, 107–108; in Lungang village (1930), 123n; Meng Yung-ch'ien, 107–108; in Mukden, (1928), 68; (1929), 104–105; (1930), 123–124, 125; (1931), 141, 146, 147; (1932), 153; (1933), 193–195, 195n, 197; (1934), 199; (1936), 254; in northern Manchuria (1932), 148; in Panshih (1937), 258; in Penhsihu, (1933), 193–195; (1938), 194; in Port Arthur (1937), 255; in Shahokou (1933), 197; in Shanghai (1934), 229, 232; in Shuangcheng, 199; supporters of the party (1936), 251; in Tailai (1942), 305; in Tsitsihar (1942), 305; in Yen-Ho (1930), 122; (1931), 29–30; in Yingkou (1928), 68
Association to Support the National Salvation Army, 203
August 1 (1935) Declaration of the CCP, 237–239
Avarin, V., quoted, 89, 90

Banditry and Communist guerrillas, 121
Bandits: in the anti-Japanese struggle, 129, 175, 201, 215, 216, 221, 225, 242, 269; CCP policy on, 76, 117; Comintern strategy toward, 162; Li Chen-ying on, 38; Mao Tse-tung's relationship with, 76n; negotiations with, 77; numbers of, 24, 73; polemic over the use of, 77–83 passim; reasons for the growth of, 24–25; relationship with government of, 25–26; socio-economic composition of, 82; mentioned, 94, 138, 224, 312, 317
Benton, Gregor, 237n
Berlin, 160
Bertram, James, 267n
Bessedovskii, Acting Soviet Ambassador in Tokyo, 91, 92
Big Sword Society: CCP Central Committee's analysis of, 171; CCP's policy toward, 81–82, 136; CCP's ties with, in Panshih, 213, 214, 220, 268; character and origins of, 74–75; government suppression of, 75; negotiations with, 77; polemic over links with, 77–81; rituals of, 74; social composition of members, 75, 82; spread of, 75; ties with the masses, 316; in Tunghwa, 75; mentioned, 94, 282
Blagoveschensk, oppression of the Chinese in, 32
"Bloody Sunday," commemorated, 29
Bolsheviks: activities in Manchuria, 26–35 passim; propaganda of, 31, 32–33, 34
Boorman, Howard, 221n
Border incidents, Soviet-Manchukuo, 277–278, 277n
Bourgeoisie: alliances with, 164, 165; destruction of, 213; exclusion of, from revolutionary organizations, 133; isolation of, 178; rejection of, by Mao Tse-tung, 302; struggle against, 110, 135, 163, 166; in the united front, 206; mentioned, 131, 169
Boxers, 74
Brandt, Conrad, 103n
Brigands. See Bandits
Bukharin, Nikolai, 65, 83

Cadres, shortage of, 183
Canton: uprising in, 77, 173; workers' movement in, 41; mentioned, 55, 56, 84, 109, 114, 146, 164, 276, 310
Capitalists. See Bourgeoisie
Central cities, 149
Central General Action Committee, 119
Central hsien committees, 149
Central Manchuria, landholdings in, 19

Index   347

Chahar, 241n
Ch'ai Shih-jung, 284–285, 297
Chalainoerh: miners' strikes in, 30; mentioned, 305
Chang Chih, 68n
Chang Ching-hui, 238
Changchun: CCP organizations in, 48, 63, 64, 253; Japanese military police in, 57; Kuomintang in, 53; Li Chen-ying on, 38; workers' strikes in, 29; mentioned, 10, 11, 105, 149, 191
Changchun-Kirin Railway: wages at, 16; workers at, 15; workers organized at, 64; mentioned, 191
Chang Hsüeh-liang: ascends to power, 13; attempts to take over the Chinese Eastern Railway, 95; establishes ties with Kuomintang, 95; in Harbin, 125; liaison with anti-Japanese groups, 269; losses suffered from encounter against Soviet forces, 96; offers no resistance against Japan, 129; struggle against, 133; mentioned, 123, 124, 146, 149, 168, 187, 220, 258, 320
Chang Jung, 162, 163
Changkuang Glass Factory, 51
Chang Kuan-i, 105, 105n, 150, 293n. See also Yang Ching-yü
Changkufeng incident, 278, 289
Chang Kuo-t'ao: on anti-Japanese struggle, 85–86; movements of, 129; quoted, 36; in Tientsin, 140–141; mentioned, 146n, 301
Chang Lin, 105n, 177n, 221n
Chang Lo-shu, 197
Chang Meng-kuan: arrested, 146n, 147; mentioned, 142
Changpai Hsien: organizational activities in, 298; pacification operation in, 281; mentioned, 74, 122, 142, 292
Changpai Mountains, 74
Changsha: uprising in, 77; mentioned, 120
Chang Shou-chien, 300
Chang Te, 250n, 300n
Chang Tso-lin: agreement with Japan on the Koreans (1925), 112; agreement with L. Karakhan, 11; army of, directed by the Japanese, 70; attitude toward communism, 57, 58; background of, 7–8, 25; defeated in north China, 80; denounced in Harbin, 53; effects of involvement in north China politics, 71; financial conditions under, 9; involved in Chinese politics, 8–9; Koreans under, 112; landholdings of, 18; Li Chen-ying on, 38; military expenditures of, 17; the police under, 57–58; policies toward the Koreans, 207; relations with Japan, 9, 10–11; relations with the Soviet Union, 10–11, 34, 88–90; revenues of, 16–17; as warlord, 8; mentioned, 85
Chang Wen-t'ien: at the Northern Conference, 134, 134n; in Shanghai, 129, 129n; in Yenan, 302; mentioned, 229
Changwu, 196
Changwu-Tungliao Railroad, 12
Chang Yu-ts'ai, 197
Chaochou, 286
Chao Shang-chih: accused of left-wing sectarianism, 300, 300n; activities of, 241–243 passim; assessment of, 316; killed, 284; mentioned, 223, 224, 225, 231, 238, 245, 258, 259, 261, 261n, 267, 285, 298
Chaotung, 286
Chaoyuan, 286, 287
Chao Yün, 230
Chekiang Province: CCP membership quota for (1927), 59; mentioned, 9
Chengchow, 42
Cheng Hsiao-hsü, 238
Cheng Lu-yen, 285
Ch'eng Pin: captured, 282; pursues Yang Ching-yü, 292; mentioned, 261, 296, 304n
Ch'en Han-chang: killed, 293; monetary reward on, 288
Chen-hua, 124n
Ch'en Hung-chang, 206
Ch'en-kuang-Pao, 37
Ch'en Kung-mu, 123n
Ch'en Kung-po, 36n
Ch'en Ping-chang, 198
Ch'en Shao-yü: in charge of the Yangtze Bureau, 303; disagreement with Mao Tse-tung, 238, 302–303; instructions from, in 1935, 230–236 passim; leadership questioned, 141; leaves for Moscow, 129, 129n; moves to Yenan, 301; speech at the seventh congress of Comintern, 236; speech of 1934, 184–186; on broad united front, 163–173 passim, 184–186, 302–303; mentioned, 139, 146n, 161, 175, 180, 184, 189, 190, 205, 216, 219, 226,

233, 234n, 265, 299, 303, 304
Ch'en Tu-hsiu: criticism of the CCP, Central Committee, on Sino-Soviet conflict, 98; encounter with Chang Kuo-t'ao, 36; letter of 1926, 50n; purged, 69; mentioned, 37n, 58
Ch'en Tung-shan Unit, 201
Ch'en Tzu-chen, arrested in Mukden, 125
Ch'en Wei-jen: background of, 37; in Dairen, 41, 42; disappearance of, 100; dispatched to Manchuria in 1927, 63; links with the bandits and the Big Sword Society, 73; in Manchuria in 1923, 36–37; 1927 report of, 48n, 55, 63–66, passim, 63n; on peasant insurrection, 70; revolutionary strategy of, 79–80; in Shanghai, 38; at the Third CCP Congress, 36; mentioned, 54, 60, 68, 130, 161
Chesneaux, Jean, 47n, 75n, 126n, 311
Chian: effect of pacification operation in, 273; pacification operation in, 281; under Yang Ching-yü's control, 290; mentioned, 74, 75, 273, 292
Chiang Kai-shek: Communist extermination campaign of, 281; the Northern Expedition of, 10, 12, 91; priorities of, 186; mentioned, 55, 69, 80, 85, 86, 159, 235, 235n, 259, 263, 299, 320
Chiang-pei K'ang-Jih Lien-ho-chün Tsung chih-hui-pu, 218
Chiaomussu, 223
Chicherin, Georgi U.: issues an ultimatum against Chang Tso-lin, 89; on the Soviet-Japanese Treaty of 1925, 87; mentioned, 11
Ch'i Chih-chung, 243, 246, 269, 317
Chieftain line, 174, 219
Ch'ien Kung-lai, 54, 55
Chientao: CCP in, 142–143, 162; CCP strength in 1934, 227; guerrillas in, 201–209 passim, 243, 288; Japanese consulate branches in, 12; Korean Communists in, 122, 157; Koreans in, 24, 111–112, 311; leaflets in, 145; May 1930 riot in, 114–116 passim; numbers of anti-Japanese fighters in, in 1937, 263; pacification operation in, 287–294 passim; soviets in, 204; mentioned, 199n, 215, 221, 226, 230, 268
Chientao Treaty (1910), 111
Chih Hsing Unit, 201
Chihli (Hopeh), immigrants from, 21

Chihli group, 8
Chilin. See Kirin
Ch'i Ming-shan, 269
China: relations with the USSR, 11, 96
Chinchou Province: numbers of anti-Japanese fighters in (1937), 263; pacification operation in, 281; mentioned, 214, 218, 256, 257, 292
Chinese attitude toward the Koreans, 112
Chinese Communist Party:
—Central Committee: abandons Shanghai headquarters, 128; August 1 (1935) declaration of, 237–239; August 7 (1928) resolution of, 70; on bandits in Manchuria, 76, 81–83 passim; Border Region Committee, 305; dispute on the united front, 301–303; fifth congress (1927), 50, 58; fifth plenum (1934), 176–177, 183; first party congress (1921), 40; fourth plenum (1931), 128; funds from, 50; Honan Special Committee, 303; Hopeh Special Committee, 303; Inner Mongolia Special District, 303; internal struggles, 129; on Japanese invasion of North China, 184; on Korean Communists, 111; on Korean farmers, 116; Manchurian Special District, 303; membership quota of, in 1927, 50, 58–59; North China Bureau, 303; Northern Bureau, 60; Party Affairs Committee of Manchuria, 304; Peking Area Committee, 63; Politburo, 59, 303; relationship with Kuomintang, 314; relationship with the masses, 121; resolution on Japanese takeover of Manchuria, 131; "Resolution on the Plan of Activities in Manchuria," (1927), 72–73; on revolution in Manchuria, 76–83 passim; second party congress (1922), 40; second plenum, sixth Central Committee (1929), 97; seventh plenum (1940), 305; Shanghai Bureau, 176n; Shansi Special Committee, 303; on the Sino-Soviet conflict in 1929, 97–98; sixth party congress (1928), 102, 121, 137; on the tasks of the labor unions, 40; third party congress (1923), 36, 37, 41; ties with the Manchurian Province Committee severed, 231; United Front Department of, 303; mentioned, 213

—Central Committee, instructions for the Manchurian Province Committee: (February 1928) 77–78; (May 1928) 80–83; (December 1932) 154–157; (January 1933) 163–173 passim, 205, 215, 230; (February 1934) 176–183, 217, 219, 230
—in Manchuria (General): in Dairen (1927), 63, 64; education and training of members, 67; fears among members, 67, 154; financial source in Mukden, 253; funds from the Central Committee, 200; funds, lack of, 154; influence of, in Yen-Ho Hsien (1931), 123; in Kirin (1927), 63, 64; Korean members, (1930), 122; leading cadres, 54; members, age distribution of, 255; members in Chientao, 207; members, number of, 227, 280; members, number of in eastern Manchuria, 142, 143; members, occupation of, 254; members, quality of, 64, 65; members in Yen-Ho Hsien, 123; in Mukden (1927), 63, 64; (1930) 124; reorganization of, 250–259 passim; strength of (1927), 48. See also Arrests of Communist Party members; Manchurian Province Committee
—in Manchuria (Local Organizations): Chalainoerh Special Branch, 305; Chuho Central Hsien Committee, 223, 224, 227, 258; Dairen Area Committee, 48–50, 100; Dairen branch, 144, 145; Dairen City Committee, 197, 251, 252; Dairen Special Branch, 198; Eastern Harbin Special Committee, 258; Eastern Harbin Provincial Committee, 251; Eastern Kirin Bureau, 199, 220, 227, 256; Eastern Kirin Provincial Committee, 230, 237, 237n, 242, 251, 256, 298; Eastern Kirin Special Committee, 256, 304; Eastern Manchuria Provincial Committee, 251; Eastern Manchuria Special Committee, 108, 120, 120n, 122, 142–143, 147, 149, 151, 154, 162, 202, 203–208 passim, 219, 220, 226, 227, 250n, 257, 258, 312; Fengtien branch, 36; Fengtien Provincial Committee, 68n; Fengtien Special Committee, 149, 152, 153, 157; Fushun branch, 125; Hailung Hsien Committee, 144; Hailun Hsien Committee, 252; Harbin City Committee, 65, 150, 154, 227, 254; Harbin Special Committee, 251, 252, 253, 297; Hsiachiang Special Committee, 298; Hulan Special branch, 251, 252; Liuho Central Hsien Committee, 298; Kwantung Prefectural Committee (Dairen), 67–68; Liuho Hsien Committee, 282; Mishan Hsien Committee, 304; Mukden City Committee, 252; Mukden Commercial District Committee, 144; Mukden Special Committee, 195; Northern Manchuria Provincial Committee, 258, 286, 298–299, 300, 304, 305; North Manchurian Special Committee, 108, 143, 144, 147, 148, 152–153; Panshih Central Hsien Committee, 227, 240, 257; Panshih Hsien Committee, 210, 212, 215, 298; Payen Special Branch, 252; Penhsihu Special Branch, 194; Pin Hsien Special Branch, 252; Southeastern Manchurian Special Committee, 81; South Manchurian Provincial Committee, 251, 258, 281, 294, 296, 298, 303; South Manchurian Special Committee, 142, 147, 149, 212, 218, 253, 256, 257, 258; Tangyuan Central Hsien Committee, 227, 256, 258; Tunghua Hsien Committee, 219; Wangching Hsien Committee, 206; Yen-Ho Hsien Committee, 122, 143; Yenpien branch, 115, 119, 120, 122, 139
—Manchurian Province Committee: abolished, 232, 251; cadres, quality of, 156; cadres, shortage of, 66; and the Central Committee, 229; contact lost with the East Manchurian Committee, 154; criticism of, 137–139, 176, 182, 191, 192; criticizes the East Manchurian Special Committee, 204; destroyed in 1930, 124; directives of, on united front, 162; financial condition of, 66; funds from the Central Committee, 154; funds from Comintern, 252; infiltrated by Japanese agents, 231; instructions from the Central Committee (see Chinese Communist Party, Central Committee, instructions for the Manchurian Province Committee); liaison with the Central Committee, 153–154; liaison with Northern Bureau, 66; purge of, 191; relocated, 153; resolution adopted by, in September

1930, 128; separatist movement of, 154; mentioned, 60, 63, 119, 143–147 passim, 150, 157, 198, 216, 219, 220, 226, 231–233, 250n, 256. See also Arrests of Communist Party members
Chinese Eastern Railway: Bolshevik attempt to take over, 27; Bolsheviks renounce rights over, 11; ceding of, to China, 33; under Chang Tso-lin, 10–11; Chinese Communist Party along, 198; Chinese takeover of, 34; Communist activities on, 151, 191; constructed, 10; joint administration of, 11; managerial practice of, under the Soviet Union, 65; revolutionary activities of the Russians on, 26–35 passim; and Soviet-Japanese relations, 87, 88; Soviet Union decides to sell, 158, 159; wages at, 16; workers at, 15; workers' demonstrations against, 39; workers discharged by, 38, 38n; workers' movement on, 64, 105, 149; workers' strikes at, 27–35; mentioned, 61, 308
Chinese Labor Union: cadres from, 44; in Dairen, 50; in Fushun, 51
Chinese Printing Workers' Comrade Association, 43
Chinese Red Army, 215
Chinese Seamen's Union, 41
Chinese Soviet Republic, 206, 237
Chinese workers, attitudes of, 45–46
Chinese Youth Association in Dairen, 42, 49
Chingcheng, 153
Ch'ing dynasty: immigration policy of, 22, 25; sale of Manchurian acreage by, 18; mentioned, 279
Ching Lo-t'ing, 284
Ching-pei-tui, 150
Ch'ing Shan Unit, 201
Chingyuan, 218, 261
Ch'in Pang-hsien, 129, 129n
Chin Shan Unit, 201
Chita, 198
Chitung-chü. See Eastern Kirin Bureau, of CCP
Ch'i-tung Tobacco Company, 253
Chi Yün-lung, 216n, 261n, 290n, 293n
Ch'oe Hyŏn: damages inflicted on Manchukuo troops by, 283; guerrilla activities of, 289; monetary reward on, 288; mentioned, 208, 294
Ch'oe Sŏk-ch'ŏn, 222, 222n
Ch'oe Yong-gŏn, 222, 222n

Chŏn Kwang: monetary reward on, 288; surrendered, 294
Chou-En-lai: children in Manchuria, 59; moves to Juichin, 128; mentioned, 133, 259, 301
Cho Hsiang-nan, 199
Chou Pao-chung: assessment of, 316; career of, 220–221, 222; clashes against Chao Shang-chih, 300; liaison with central leaders, 304; quoted, 259–260, 263, 266, 284, 306; mentioned, 223, 225, 231, 238, 261, 261n, 262n, 267, 285, 297, 301, 306n
Chou Shu-tung, 282, 288n
Chow Tse-tsung, 148n
Christianity, 39
Chuang, 232
Chu Chi-ch'ing, 54, 55
Chu Chin, 208
Ch'ü Ch'iu-pai: on anti-Japanese struggle, 85; installed as CCP leader, 69; strategy of, 77; mentioned, 174
Ch'u Ch'ün-feng, 148
Chuho: CCP strength in 1934, 227; Communist Youth Corps in, 191; mentioned, 108, 108n, 149, 223, 242, 258
Chuho Anti-Japanese Guerrilla Unit, 223
Chung Hou Unit, 201
Chung-hsin ch'eng-tzu, 149
Chung-hua Ch'ing-nien-hui, 49
Chung-hua Yin-kung T'ung-chih-hui, 43
Chungking, 265, 306
Chung-kuo ch'ing-nien, 42
Chung-kuo Hung-chün, 215
Chung-kuo T'ung-meng-hui, 54
Chu Teh, 99, 122n, 128
Ch'ü Wen-hsiu, 68, 68n
Clark, Anne B., 37n
Clubb, O. Edmund, 11n
Coal mines, in Tungpientao, 279. See also Fushun; Penhsihu
Collective hamlets: described, 284, 291; effects of, 271–274 passim; 283, 284, 292, 295, 318–319; mentioned, 239, 260, 282, 289
Comintern: on Chinese communism, 313; directive of, 206; Eastern Conference (1932) of, 161; Far Eastern Bureau, 256; funds for the Manchurian Committee, 252; on Korean Communists, 111, 113; policy on rich peasants, 110n; representatives in China, 65; Seventh World

Congress (1935), 233; Sixth World Congress (1928), 77; strategy of, 61, 173; support of, 213; ties with the CCP, 313; on united front, 160–163; mentioned, 140, 148n, 200, 206–207, 220, 230, 260, 301, 303 —Executive Committee: letter of 1929, 99; ninth plenum of, 83; thirteenth plenum of, 184, 233–234
Commerce in Manchuria, under Japanese control, 13, 14
Communist International. See Comintern
Communist Party of the Soviet Union: fifth congress (1927), 77; lack of cooperation with the CCP, 64, 65, 66, 86; racial prejudice of, 65; strategy toward Manchuria, 61
Communist Youth Corps: abolition of, 250; cadres arrested (1932), 153; funds for the Manchurian Province Committee, 198; Kiangsu Provincial Committee, 198; in Manchuria, 232; in Mukden, 124; Mukden Special Committee, 195; numbers of members in Manchuria (1933), 198, 200; (1934), 227; numbers, in Chientao (1933–1934), 207; numbers, in Yen-Ho Hsien (1931), 123; resolution of the Manchurian Province Committee of, 190; mentioned, 64, 101, 102, 137, 143, 150, 152
Conroy, Hilary, 129n
Coox, Alvin D., 129n, 278n
Counterinsurgency. See Pacification operations
Counterrevolutionary groups, strategy against, 234
Currencies, 17, 38, 39, 70, 252

Dairen: Ch'en Wei-jen in, 37; Chinese Communist Party in, 48, 63, 64, 176, 253; effect of the May 30 incident in, 48; Li Chen-ying's observation of, 38; soldiers' revolt in, 152; mentioned, 10, 11, 13, 51, 105, 109, 124, 125, 144, 145, 147, 149, 190, 197, 251
Dairen Area Committee, of the Chinese Communist Party, 48–50, 100
Dairen Ceramic Company, 51
Dairen Chinese Labor Union, 50
Dairen Chinese Workers' Study Association, 41, 42, 49, 50, 100
Dairen Docks (1925): attitude of Chinese workers at, 46; wages at, 16, workers in, 15
Dairen Kikai Seisakusho, 16, 46
Dairen Machinery Manufacturing Company, 51
Dairen Machine Works, South Manchurian Railway Company, 16, 46
Dallin, David J., 96n
December 9 Movement, 241n
Degras, Jane, 88n
Deguchi Katsuji, 91
Demonstrations: in Kirin (1926), 53; in Mukden (1925), 47; in Tangyuan, 152
Depression, effect of, in Manchuria, 130
Deutscher, Isaac, 3
Dog-Beating Unit, 211
Doihara Kenji, 241

East Asia Colonial Company, 116, 202
East Asia Printing Company, 51
East Hsingan Province, guerrilla district in, 286, 298
Eastern Kirin Bureau, of CCP, 199, 200, 220, 227, 256
Eastern Kirin Provincial Committee, of CCP, 230, 237, 237n, 242, 251, 256, 298, 300
East Manchurian Special Committee, of the Chinese Communist Party: activities of, 203; contact with the Manchurian Province Committee, 154; criticized by the Manchurian Province Committee, 204; purges within, 208; radicalism of, 205, 206; secretary of, denounced, 207; mentioned, 108, 120, 120n, 122, 142–143, 147, 149, 151, 162, 202, 219, 220, 226, 227, 250n, 257, 258, 312
Economy in Manchuria, 71
Eighth Route Army, 266, 277, 319
Electric power generation in Manchuria, 14
Electric Railway Youth Corps, 43
Epidemics, 273
Eudin, Xenia Joukoff, 87n
Exchange rates, 17, 252
Exclusionism, 156, 175, 178

Factionalism, 136
Fairbank, John K., 103n
Faku, 261n
Fang Chen-shen, monetary reward on, 288
Fan-Jih Chiu-kuo Hui, 194, 195

352   Index

Fan-Jih Kun-nung Yu-chi-tui, 211
Far Eastern Republic, 33
Farmers: burdens imposed on, by the Japanese, 271; in the CCP, 254; effect of pacification operations on, 283; livelihood of, 20, 38, 39; plight of, under the Japanese, 272–274; in the resistance movement, 129, 171; socio-economic composition of, 18, 19
Farmers' associations: in Chientao, 143; in Panshih, 210; mentioned, 110, 122, 152, 163
Farmers' Committees, 163, 252
Farmers' League, 122, 123
Farmers' movements, directives on, 110, 116
Farmers' Movement Institute, 66
Farmers' Union, 227
Farmer-Workers' Volunteer Army of Manchuria, 212, 213
Farm Workers, 20, 71, 110, 136, 176
February 7 (1923) massacre, 36, 37, 38, 56
Feng Chien-ying, 282
Feng Chih-kang, 300
Feng Chün, 258
Feng Chung-yün, 133, 134, 134n, 146, 146n, 223, 223n, 260n, 285, 286
Feng Lin-ko, warlord, 18
Fenglochen, 286
Fengtien. See Mukden
Fengtien Chiang-chün, 122
Feng-tien Chiao-yü T'e-pieh Wei-yüan-hui, 253
Fengtien Province: land tenure in, 19; numbers of anti-Japanese fighters in 1937, 263; population in, 22
Fengtien Special Committee, of the Chinese Communist Party: branches of, 152; leaders arrested, 153; mentioned, 149, 152, 157
Feng Yü-hsiang, 9, 56, 80
Fifth encirclement campaign, 173
Floods, 21
Foreign concessions, 56, 85
France: investment in Manchuria, 15; support for Chang Tso-lin, 91; mentioned, 56
Fu Ching-yang, 42, 42n, 49
Fukien Province, CCP membership quota for (1927), 59
Fukushima Spinning Mill, workers' strike at (1925), 43, 49, 50
Fu Li-yü, 49n
Funds: from Comintern, 252; from Communist Youth Corps Central Committee to Manchuria, 198; sought in Vladivostok, 261
Fushun: CCP branch in, 124; Communist activities in, 125, 253; described, 103–104; miners' strikes in, 29; organization of workers at, 104; mentioned, 14, 51, 72, 101, 105, 109, 176, 196, 227
Fushun Coal Mine Workers' Labor Union, 193
Fushun Labor Union, 104
Fushun mines, 14–15
Fushun Mining Workers' Union, 125
Fushun Repair Shop, South Manchurian Railway Company, 16
Fusung: organizational activities in, 298; pacification operations in, 281; mentioned, 122, 142, 257, 292
Fu Tien-ch'en, 214, 217
Fu Yu, 250n, 258
Fuyüan Hsien, total destruction of homes in, 289

Gapon, Father, 29
General Command of Anti-Japanese Army, 217
General Command of the Anti-Japanese Allied Army, 234
General Command of the Anti-Japanese Allied Army North of the River, 218
Germany, 56
Gillin, Donald, 2
Gladeck, Frederick G., 27n
Gold mining, 25
Gondatti, 32
Gotō Shimpei, 14n
Grains: compulsory purchase of, 270; lack of, 318
Great Britain: feelings against, 47; investment in Manchuria of, 15; severs relations with the Soviet Union, 91; support of Chang Tso-lin, 91; mentioned, 56
Great Cultural Revolution, 108n
Greater Khingan Mountains, 286
Guerrilla districts: in Lungchiang Province, 298; mentioned, 182
Guerrillas: activities toward, 191; analyses of, 168–175; behavior of, 243–244, 246, 248–249, 316–317; CCP on operations of, 121–122; comparison with those in north China, 276–279 passim; deprived of food grains, 292; development of, 135; in East Manchuria, criticism against, 120; effects of deserters,

296; hideouts destroyed, 292; in Khavarovsk, 306; lack of cadres among, 295; losses suffered by, 282, 284–285, 293; in northern Manchuria, 220–226 passim; organization of, decided, 118; in Panshih, 152, 211–212; "Principles of Unit Operations," 120n; propaganda of, 225, 246–248; quality of, 276; reasons for the failure of, 294–297 passim; relationship with the masses, 121–122; 243–244, 246–250 passim, 271, 274–275, 280, 294–295, 296, 315–319 passim; rules of conduct, 249; in southern Manchuria, 209–220 passim; surrender of, 297n; surrender inducement of, 283; in Yenpien, 119; mentioned, 138, 143n, 151, 163, 177n, 203, 205n, 206
—numbers of: (1932–1933), 215, 216; (1934), 207, 227; (1937), 244, 262–263, 262n, 282, 282n; (1939), 288. See also Anti-Japanese resistants
Guerrilla war: instigation of, 136; intensification of, 132; preoccupation with, 176; mentioned, 152

Hailun: Communist activities in, 153, 251; guerrillas in, 237; pacification operation in, 285
Hailun Anti-Japanese Guerrilla Unit, 241
Hailung: Communist activities in, 152, 191; mentioned, 144, 218
Hailun Guerrilla Unit, 242
Hailun-Hulan Railway, 149, 191
Hailun-Kirin Railroad, 12
Hamahotzu, 213
Han Chin, 212, 214
Hanjok Nodong-dang, 210
Hankow, 102, 164, 276, 303, 310
Han Pin, 113
Han Shou-k'uei: activities of, 250–254 passim; mentioned, 257, 258, 297, 300n
Han Sŏl-ya, 222n
Han Yü-shu, 286
Harbin: Bolsheviks in, 27–28; Communists arrested in, 153, 190, 198, 200, 231, 254–255, 256; effects of the May 30 incident in, 47, 48; Kuomintang branch in, 53; leaflets issued in, 144; Li Chen-ying on, 38; Lo Teng-hsien in, 146; organization of workers in, 28, 44–45; plan for riot in, 125; Red Labor Union in, 137; Soviet-Chinese conflict in, 89; Soviet consulate in, 35, 96; suffering of the Chinese in, 32; workers' strikes in, 27, 28, 29, 30; mentioned, 108n, 133, 147, 211, 219, 223, 231, 233, 242, 286, 305
—Communist activities in: (1927), 48, 50, 63, 64, 65–66; (1929), 101–102, 105, 108; (1930), 113, 114, 124; (1932), 149, 151; (1933), 176, 191, 192, 198; (1934), 227; (1936), 251; (1940), 304
Harbin Anti-Japanese Society, 144, 150
Harbin Comrades of Kuomintang, 48
Harbin Guard Unit, 150, 151
Harbin Locomotive Yard, workers' strikes at, 28, 30, 31
Harbin Machine Plant, workers' strikes at, 29, 30
Harbin Medical College, 152
Harbin Police Bureau, 287
Harbin Telephone Company, 155
Harrison, James P., 2, 37n
Hatano Kenichi, 177n, 232
Hayashi Masaaki, 8n
Heilungkiang Province: currency of, 17; land tenure in, 19; number of anti-Japanese resistants in, 129; population in, 22; mentioned, 8, 13, 122
Hirai Tomoyoshi, 158n
Ho Ch'eng-hsiang, 105, 150, 150n
Ho Hsiang-ning, 179
Ho Kan-chih, 47n
Hokang, 152
Holung Hsien: Communist strength in, 227; internal struggle of CCP cadres in, 206–207; mentioned, 111, 122, 202n
Ho Meng-hsiung, 128
Honan Province: CCP membership quota for, 59; mentioned, 134, 136, 137, 149
Hong Kong: workers' movement in, 41; mentioned, 109
Hopeh Province, 60, 134, 149, 183, 184, 241n, 304, 305, 319. See also Chihli
Horse Carriage Drivers' Society, 251
Horvath, General Dimitri L.: denounced, 32, 33; ties with Japan alleged, 33; mentioned, 27, 30, 34
Ho Seng, 63
Hoshantzukou, 272
Hosoya Chihiro, 88n
Ho Te, 177n
Hotzu village, 272

354   Index

Hou Kuoerhlossu, 286
Howard, Harvey J., kidnapped by bandits, 83n
Ho Ying-ch'in, General, 184
Hsiang, measurement, 18n
Hsiang Chung-fa: executed, 128; mentioned, 83
Hsiang-tao Chou-pao, 37, 42
Hsiao Wang-ching Soviet, 204
Hsia Yün-chih, 268
Hsieh Wen-tung, 223, 239, 268, 285, 285n
Hsi Hsia, 202
Hsin Ch'ing-nien, 37
Hsingching, organizational activities in, 298
Hsinmin, CCP activities in, 253
Hsi P'ing, 102
Hsüeh Wen, 146, 146n
Hsü Kai-yu, 128n
Hsün-yüeh-shih, 8n
Hsü Tse-min, 286, 287
Huang Fu, General, 184
Huangkou, soviets in, 204
Huangkutun, 147
Huang Yün-t'eng, 147
Huanjen: Big Sword Society in, 74, 75; organizational activities in, 298; pacification operation in, 271, 273–274, 275; mentioned, 261n
Huatien, 122, 292
Hua Ying-shen, 146n
Hu Han-min, 179
Huinan; pacification operation in, 281; mentioned, 218
Hu Kuo-ch'en, 282
Hulan, 251
Hulan-Hailun Railway, 149, 191
Hulin: anti-Japanese activities in, 222, 242; Communist activities in, 220; Japanese fortifications in, 278; Northern Manchuria Speical Committee in, 147
Hunan Province, 129
Hunchun: Communist activities in, 122, 142, 143, 227; guerrillas in, 208; Soviets in, 204, 205; mentioned, 202n
Hundred Regiment Campaign, 319
Hung-ch'i, 109
Hung-ch'iang Hui, 74
Hung-ch'i Chou-pao, 219
Hung-ch'i Jih-pao, 116, 117
Hung-ch'i Pao, 133
Hung hu-tzu, 83, 83n
Hung-se Chung-hua, 179
Hunt, Michael H., 8n

Hupeh Province: CCP membership quota, 59; mentioned, 129
Hu Pin, 198, 200, 231

Ikei Masaru, 9n
Ilan: Chao Shang-chih's forces in, 242; guerrilla leaders' meeting in, 261; Koreans in, 122; mentioned, 285
Iman, 222
Immigration into Manchuria, 21–24 passim; Japanese, 23, 269; Korean, 23, 24, 74, 210; subsidies for, 23
Imoto Taikichi, 284n
Imperialism: direct conflict shunned, 84, 85; feeling against, 47; influence of, on northern party branches, 135; struggle against, 39, 44, 53, 84, 98, 110, 137, 138, 149, 169, 177, 179. See also Japanese imperialism, struggle against
Industry, under Japanese control, 13, 14, 70, 278–279
Inflation, 16–17, 43, 71, 307
Intellectuals, Lenin on, 40
Intelligentsia, 64, 166, 182. See also Teachers.
International repercussions, of Communist movement in Manchuria, 77, 79, 86–93 passim
Iriye, Akira, 8n, 13n, 91n
Iron mines, in Tungpientao, 279
Ishigaki Sadakazu, quoted, 271, 273–274, 275
Ishii Kikujirō, 12n
Ishikawa Tadao, 131n
Itung, soldiers' rebellion in, 210
Itō Takeo, 15n, 280n
Ivanov, A. N., General Manager of the Chinese Eastern Railway, 88, 89
Ivin, Alexander, 76n

James, Henry Evan M., 22, 74n
Jaoho: CCP activities in, 152, 227; CCP organizations in, 149, 220, 222, 256
Japan: acquired the Kwantung Leased Territory, 11; against the Kuo Sungling rebellion, 9, 11; and Chang Tso-lin, 9–10, 11–13, 91; Chinese feelings against, 12, 12n, 71, 269; invasion of China, 183, 259; investment in Manchuria, 15; in Siberia, 10, 86
—Army: operations against guerrillas, 203, 239, 242; security system of, 57
—and U.S.S.R.: contemplated military

action, 92; Japan prepares for war, 306; military conflicts, 278; neutrality pact signed, 319; mentioned, 86–87, 92, 96
Japanese control of Manchuria: extent of, 13–14; importance of, to Japan, 277; initial stage of, 9, 10, 11–13; noted by Ch'en Wei-jen, 70; noted by Li Chen-ying, 38
Japanese currency in Manchuria, 17, 38, 39, 252
Japanese immigrants in Manchuria, 23, 269
Japanese imperialism, struggle against: polemic over, 71, 72, 78–84 passim; mentioned, 115, 131, 133, 134, 135, 145, 151, 165, 234, 247–248, 260, 312–313
Jehol Province: number of anti-Japanese resistants in, 129n; mentioned, 142n, 160, 242, 261, 305
Johnson, Chalmers, 1–2
Jones, F. C., 13n
Juichin, 174, 186

Kahn, B. Winston, 241n
Kaifeng, cadres in, demoralized, 141
Kaiping, 261n
Kaishantun, CCP members in, 143, 143n
K'ang-Jih Lien-ho-chün Chiang-pei Chih-hui-pu, 240
K'ang-Jih Lien-ho-chün Ts'an-mou-ch'u, 217
Kangping, 261n
K'ang Sheng: instructions from, 230, 233, 265, 300; moves to Yenan, 301; speech of, 234n
Kannan, 286
Kansu Province: CCP membership quota for, 59; mentioned, 319
Kantō. See Kwantung
Kantōgun. See Kwantung Army
Kaoliang: export of, 17; price of, 43
Kaomi Hsien, 197
Karakhan, Leo M.: signed agreement with Chang Tso-lin, 11; on the Soviet-Japanese Treaty, 87
Katayama Sen, 45
Katō Narimasa, 255n
Khanka, Lake, 278, 279
Khasan incident, 278
Khavarovsk: guerrillas in, 306; oppression of the Chinese in, 32; peace protocol signed in, 96
Khazhinov, Soviet Consul General in Mukden, 253

Kiangsi soviet: abandoned, 160, 229; CCP headquarters in, 176, 187; campaign against, 281; on landlords, 163n, 206; mentioned, 94, 128, 154, 201, 226, 238
Kiangsu Province: CCP membership quota, 59; mentioned, 198
Kilchak, Admiral A., 33
Kim Ch'ŏl, 115
Kim Il-sŏng: guerrilla activities of, 289; inflicts losses on Manchukuo troops, 283, 283n; monetary reward on, 288; position among the guerrillas, 288n; pursued by enemy units, 292; retreats to the Soviet Far East, 294; mentioned, 208, 290
Kim Sang-sŏn, 123n
Kim Sŏk-ch'ŏn, 222
Kirin: CCP activities in, 48, 63, 64, 105, 191, 253; Communists arrested in, 196; currency of, 17; effects of the May 30 incident in, 47; guerrillas in, 288; Kuomintang branch in, 52–53; land tenure in, 19; leaflets issued in, 144, 145; Li Chen-ying on, 38; number of anti-Japanese resistants in, 129, 263; pacification operation in, 289n; population in, 22; workers' strikes in, 64; mentioned, 13, 209, 261
Kirin Army, 168, 170, 185
Kirin-Changchun Railway: wages at, 16; workers at, 15, 64; mentioned, 191
Kirin government, 202
Kirin-Hailun Railroad, 12
Kirin-Tunhua Railroad, 116, 142n
Kiselev, 31
Kitabe Kunio, Lieutenant Colonel, 289n, 290–291
Kitakawa Shikazō, 27n
Klein, Donald W., 37n
Kobayashi Hideo, 17n
Ko-ming-tang, 8
Kōmoto Taisaku, 13
Korea: dispatch of Japanese troops from, 203
Korean Communist Party, Manchurian General Bureau, 210n
Korean Communists: absorbed by the CCP, 111–113 passim; in Chientao, 114–123 passim; guerrillas in Panshih, 152; legacy of, 142; in northern Manchuria, 221; preponderance of, 155, 157; socioeconomic backgrounds of, 123
Korean factional elements, 191

Korean Farmers' League, 122, 123
Korean Labor Party, 210
Korean nationalists, 112, 142, 210, 311
Korean potters, 103
Koreans: call for the leadership of, 136; in Chientao, attitude of, 123, 207; CCP slogans toward, 299; demonstrations of, in Tangyuan, 152; immigration of, 23, 24, 74, 210; number of, 24; in Panshih, 210; relationship of, with the Chinese, 121; as a revolutionary force, 70, 72; socio-economic condition of, 202, 311; under the warlord regime, 112, 207; unity with, 133
Koryŏ dynasty, 103
Koshan, 286
Kuan-chang lu-hsien, 174
Kuan-men chu-i, 175
Kuan Shu-fan, executed by Chou Pao-chung, 297
Kuantien, 74
Kung-ch'an-tang, 38
Kung Ch'u, 128n
K'ung Hsien-jung, 241
Kung-jen chih lu, 196
Kung-jen Sheng-huo, 196
Kuo-chen, 101
Kuo Hua-lun, 174n, 302n
Kuomintang: Allied army leaders denounce, 237; campaign against the Kiangsi soviet, 281; Ch'en Shao-yü on, 235; Chinese Communist Party leaders, on the struggle against, 131, 135, 145, 166, 177, 178, 238; dispute on joining, 36; Dairen branch of, 49; fifth encirclement campaign of, 160; the First Army denounces, 216; in Harbin, 53; Harbin Comrades of, 48; influence of, in Manchuria, 138, 168, 181; in Kirin, 52–53, 68; left wing of, 91; in Liaosi, 152; in Manchuria, 52–55 *passim*; Manchurian Province Committee denounced, 173; members arrested in Changchun, 53; members arrested in Mukden, 53; in Mukden, 52, 54, 55; offers no resistance against Japan, 129; pressures against the CCP, 128; restores diplomatic ties with the U.S.S.R., 164, 313; suppression of anti-imperial movement by, 132; Tsinan City Committee of, 197; Tangku Truce agreement concluded by, 183–184; mentioned, 69, 85, 98, 127, 128, 139, 159, 187, 198, 201, 220, 238, 260, 276
Kuo Sung-ling, rebellion of, against Chang Tso-lin, 9–10, 54n
Ku Shun-chang, defects to the Kuomintang, 128
Kwangju incident, 114–115
Kwangsi Province, CCP membership quota, 59
Kwangtung Province: CCP membership quota, 59; purges in, 149
Kwantung Army: against the Kuo Sung-ling rebellion, 9; against the resistants, 160; and Chang Tso-lin, 12n, 13; clashes against the Soviet Army, 278; concerns about the U.S.S.R., 277; negotiations with the Kuomintang, 184; Soviet fear of, 158; suspicion of Soviet support for the guerrillas, 289; treatment of the guerrillas, 283; mentioned, 262, 269
Kwantung Leased Territory: CCP Special Committee in, 108; described, 13; economic conditions in, 52, 56, 67; obtained by Japan, 11; police in, 57
Kweichou Province, CCP membership quota for, 59

Lands, confiscation of: by the Chang Tso-lin government, 71; by the Japanese, 269–270
Landless farmers: 1934–1935, 18, 19; in Panshih, 209
Landlords: alliance with, 164; in anti-Japanese struggle, 223; CCP policy on, 163; confiscation of the lands of, 139; confiscation of property of, 162; exclusion of, from revolutionary organizations, 133; in Kiangsi, 281; Manchurian Province Committee on, 173; Mao Tse-tung on, 238; property of, destroyed, 119; struggle against, 110, 135, 177, 182, 202, 206, 207, 211, 212, 225; in the united front, 206; mentioned, 71, 121, 131, 169
Land reform: criticized by Li Wei-han, 175; difficulty of implementing, 311; in East Manchuria, 202, 205; emphasized by central leaders, 132, 166, 177, 178, 182, 201, 238; Manchurian Province Committee on, 173; promised, 247, 248; mentioned, 138, 212, 225

Land survey: by Manchukuo, 270; in Korea, 270
Land tenure in Manchuria, 18-20; observation of Ch'en Wei-jen, 71
Laborers. See Workers
Labor movement in Manchuria, 28-35
Labor strikes. See Workers' strikes
Labor unions: members recruited, 44-45; numbers of members in 1934, 227
Laotaokou, CCP members in, 143, 143n
Lao-tung-chieh, 37
Lao-tung Chou-k'an, 37
Laoyeshan, 262
Lasswell, Harold D., 59n
Latzukang, 212
Left-wing errors, 155, 157, 162, 175
Lei Ting, 222n
Lenin, V. I.: on bourgeois intellectuals, 40; on proletarian class consciousness, 40; on revolutionary situations, 5
Lensen, George Alexander, 86n, 89n
Lerner, Daniel, 59 n
Lesser Khingan Mountains, 285
Liaochung: CCP activities in, 253; mentioned, 109, 196, 199n
Liao Chung-k'ai, Madame, 179
Liaohsi: party branches in, 152; mentioned, 142n, 147, 152
Liaoning Province, number of anti-Japanese resistants in, 129
Liaoning Textile Mill, 144
Liao River, 261n
Liaoyang: CCP activities in, 109, 124, 196, 253; Yang Ching-yü in, 261
Liaoyang Repair Plant, South Manchurian Railway Company: report of, 41-42; wages at, 16
Lien-ho-pao, 194
Li Ch'eng-hsiang, 142
Li Chen-ying: background of, 37-38; in Dairen, 42; report on Manchuria of, 38-40, 60; revolutionary strategy of, 39, 61; mentioned, 22, 54, 59, 148n
Li Chien-nung, 9n
Li Chih, 54n
Li Ch'un-shan, 113
Li-hsing Company, 253
Li Hua-t'ang, 239, 269, 285
Li Li-san: on armed uprisings, 99-100; on protecting the Soviet Union, 99; repudiated, 128; mentioned, 83, 140, 141

Li Li-san Line, 113-123, 139, 149, 207
Li Li-san Line cadres, 154
Linchiang: the Big Sword Society in, 74, 75; numbers of anti-Japanese fighters in (1937), 263; pacification operations in, 281; Yang Ching-yü pursued in, 292
Lin Piao, General, 266n, 321
Li Ta, 179
Li Ta-chao, 54n
Li Te-fu, 304
Little Wangching soviets, 204
Li Tu, 160, 168, 179, 180, 183, 221, 222, 223, 224, 268n
Litvinov, Maksim, proposes non-aggression pact with Japan, 128
Liu Chih-yüan, 143n
Liuho: pacification operation in, 281; typhoid in, 273; mentioned, 214, 215, 218
Liu I-ch'eng, 142, 147
Liu K'uai-t'ui Unit, 201
Liu Li-ming, 67-68
Liu Shao-ch'i: departed for Shanghai, 123, 141; in Manchuria, 100-102 *passim*, 107-108, 108n, 109; in Moscow, 37; in Shanghai, 38; in Vladivostok, 232; mentioned, 124n, 232, 253
Liu Yao-chieh, 253
Liu Yao-fen, 253, 254
Li Wei-han: article on Manchuria of, 174-176 *passim*, mentioned, 186
Li Yao-k'uei: attended a Comintern meeting, 161, 161n; background of, 161, 161n, 200; on the Eastern Kirin Bureau, 220; replaces Lo Teng-hsien, 219; mentioned, 162n, 164, 173, 187, 190, 205, 230
Li Yen-lu: background of, 222, 268, 268n; in China, 284n; contacts with political groups in China, 269 n; in 1940, 304; mentioned, 238, 239, 261
Li Yen-p'ing: commander of the fourth allied army, 284; killed, 284
Lo, 232
Lo Chang-lung, 128
Lo Cheng-ts'ao, General, 304, 304n
Lo Fu. *See* Chang Wen-t'ien
Lo I-nung, 37, 38
Lo Mai. *See* Li Wei-han
Lominadze, Besso, 69
Long March, 229, 276
Lo Teng-hsien: background of, 145-146; head of the Manchurian Prov-

ince Committee, 147; recalled to Shanghai, 149, 190; receives an instruction from Chou En-lai, 133; mentioned, 219
Lumber industry, 25
Lunan Red Guerrillas, 197
Lungchiang Province, guerrilla district in, 286, 298
Lungchiang village: CCP members in, 143; mentioned, 115
Lushun. See Port Arthur

Ma, 199
Ma Chan-shan: background of, 25; comment on, by Ch'en Wei-jen, 168; emerged in Berlin, 160; Japanese forces against, 147; mentioned, 153, 315
Malozemoff, Andrew, 10n
Manchouli, 96
Manchou-sheng Wei-yüan-hui. See Chinese Communist Party, Manchurian Province Committee
Manchukuo, 154, 158, 160, 165, 177, 194, 212, 238, 280
Manchukuo Air Force, rebellion of troops of, 286
Manchukuo Army: desertions from, 259; losses suffered by, 283; at Nomonhan, 278; in pacification operation, 282; revolt of, 261–262; troops surrendered, 260; 29th Infantry Regiment of, 262
Manchuria, independence of: declared by Chang Tso-lin, 9; urged on Chang Tso-lin by Japan, 12n
Manchurian-British-American Tobacco Factory, strike at, 137
Manchurian Christian College, 54
Manchurian Daily News, 50
Manchurian Province Committee. See Chinese Communist Party, Manchurian Province Committee
Manchuria Woolen Manufacturing Company, 51
Manchu tribe, homeland of, 74
Manshū kyōsanhi no kenkyū, preparation of, 244
Mao Kuo, 217
Mao Tse-tung: on the anti-Japanese war, 277; on August 1 (1935) Appeal, 237–238; contributes articles to Hsiang-tao Chou-pao, 37n; criticism of guerrillas under, 122; leads the Hundred Regiments campaign, 319; at Nanchang, 120; relationship of, with bandits, 76n; on secret societies, 75; strategies of, 1; on

united front, 302; mentioned, 94, 99, 128, 177n, 226, 261, 266, 306
Marine workers, 136
Marxism, introduced to workers, 42
Masses: alienation of, by the CCP, 205; anti-Japanese movement among, 132; arming of, 132; relationship of the guerrillas with, 157, 162, 172, 175, 178–179, 182, 183, 224, 226, 316–319 passim
Matsuoka Yōsuke, 15n
May 30 (1930) riot in Chientao, 115–116, 120
May 30 (1925) incident, effect of: in Manchuria, 47–48, 52; in Shanghai, 46–47
McCormack, Gavan, 8n
McLane, Charles B., 233n
Meadown, Taylor, 22
Mengchiang: CCP activities in, 142; guerrilla leaders' conference in, 290; Kim Il-sŏng in, 288n; pacification activities in, 281; renamed Ching-yü, 293n; Yang Ching-yü's guerrillas in, 218, 292
Meng Chien. See Meng Yung-ch'ien
Meng Yung-ch'ien, 101, 102, 102n, 108n, 124n
Mensheviks, 27
Merchants: CCP on, 73; in the CCP, 254; damages inflicted on, by guerrillas, 121; mentioned, 179
Middle level farmers: as CCP's allies, 110, 177; damages inflicted on, by guerrillas, 121; in East Manchuria, 205
Mif, Pavel: head of Comintern's Chinese Section, 161; leaves for Moscow, 129; mentioned, 233
Migration, to and from Manchuria, of Chinese, 23
Military-Civilian Revolutionary Committee, 204
Millet, export of, 17
Minami Jirō, 278n
Miners: conditions of, 38; organizational attempts at Fushun, 103; revolts of, 71
Minorities in Manchuria, 23
Mishan: coal deposit in, 279; CCP strength in, 227; Communist activities in, 108, 108n, 220, 256, 298; guerrillas in, 222
Mishan Anti-Japanese General Society, 222
M-L Group, of the Korean Communist Party, 210
Mongolia, 12n, 33, 92, 127

Mongolians, 23, 70
Morizaki Minoru, on Yang Ching-yü, 293n
Morley, James W., 88n
Moscow, 102, 161, 173, 187, 190, 200, 205, 230, 231, 233, 237, 237n, 250, 301
Mukden: anti-Japanese demonstrations in, 12n; arrests of Communists in, 68, 104–105, 123–124, 125, 141, 146, 147, 153, 193–195, 195n, 197, 199, 254; Chang Tso-lin in, 12–13; Communist activities in, 51, 101–102, 104–105, 109, 125, 144, 196; Communist organizations in, 124, 149, 152, 195–196, 197; Communist party members in, 48, 50, 63, 64; Communist Youth Corps in, 191, 192; Kuomintang in, 52, 53, 55; Lo Teng-hsien in, 133; Manchurian Province Committee in, 142; possibility of CCP's takeover, 71; students in, 54; workers organized in, 44; mentioned, 143, 176, 190, 198, 212, 251, 254, 256
Mukden Anti-Japanese Society, 144
Mukden Arsenal, 195
Mukden General Labor Union, 195
Mukden Hemp Company, workers' strikes at, 43, 50, 51
Mukden Machine Plant, wages at, 16
Mukden-Peking Railway, 152
Mukden-Shanhaikuan Railway, 149
Mukden Shen-tao School, 54
Mukden Spinning Mill, 51
Mukden Textile Mill, 195
Mukden Tobacco Factory, strike at, 137
Mukden Weaving Works, 51
Mukden Wool Company, 199
Mukden Young Men's Christian Association School, 47
Mulan, 122
Muleng: Communist activities in, 298; mentioned, 256, 260
Muling, Communist strength in, 227
Mun Kap-song, 199n
Mutanchiang: Communist activities in, 108, 108n, 304; numbers of anti-Japanese fighters in, 263; pacification operation in, 284; mentioned, 305
Mutual Aid Society, 151, 195, 203
Myers, Ramon A., 22n, 67n, 310, 310n

Nakamura Foundry, 51
Nanchang, 77, 120
Nanking, 55, 102, 263
Nanking incident, 91, 265, 265n
Nan-man Fan-Jih-hui, 219
Nanpaitzu conference, 288n, 290
Nanpeihoyuan, 285
National Railway Workers' Association, 42
National Revolutionary Army, 221, 299
National Salvation Army, 213, 214, 221
National Salvation Youth Corps, 251
Neumann, Heinz, 69, 77
Nicholas II, 27
Nieh Jung-chen, 134, 134n, 266n
Ningan: CCP organizations in, 149, 152, 256, 298; CCP strength in, 227; guerrillas in, 221; mentioned, 222, 242
Ning-an-Fan-Jih Yu-chi-tui, 221-222
Ninghsia, 319
Nishikawa Printing Office, 51
Nishikawa Torajirō, 12n
Ni Yün-hai, 304–305
Noho, 285, 286
Nomonhan incident, 278, 289
Nongmin tongmaeng, 210
Northeastern Anti-Japanese Allied Army: declaration of, 237; establishment of, 240; liaison with organizations in China, 263. See also Anti-Japanese Allied Army General Command
—the First Army: establishment of, 208; movement of, 208, 216, 217, 246, 257, 261, 268, 278–279
—the Second Army: establishment of, 208; movement of, 209, 243, 250n, 257, 261
—the Third Army, 223, 241, 258, 269, 286
—the Fourth Army, 222, 237, 237n, 268, 284
—the Fifth Army, 209, 222, 243, 257
—the Sixth Army, 223, 261, 268, 286
—the Seventh Army, 284
—the Eighth Army, 262, 269, 284, 285
—the Ninth Army, 269, 285
—the Tenth Army, 269
—the Eleventh Army, 269
—the First Route Army: established, 258; mentioned, 281, 287, 293
—the Second Route Army: established, 284
—the Third Route Army, 285, 286, 287, 298, 300
Northeastern People's Revolutionary Army. See Northeastern Anti-Japanese Allied Army

360 Index

Northeastern People's Revolutionary Government, Provisional, 206
Northeastern Volunteer Army, 177n
Northern Bureau, CCP, 60, 66, 140–141
Northern Conference, of the CCP, 134–140 passim, 148, 154, 155, 156, 175, 205
Northern Manchuria: landholdings in, 19; mentioned, 133, 151
Northern Manchuria Prefectural Committee (Bolshevik), 34–35
Northern Manchuria Provincial Committee, CCP, 258, 286, 298–299, 300, 304, 305
North, Robert, 59n, 87n
North Manchuria Railway, 158
Nozoe, Shōtoku, Major General, 290
Nung-min Hsieh-hui, 110, 122

October Revolution, anniversary of, 64
Okamoto Goichi, Prosecutor, 193n; quoted, 246–250
Ōkubo Yasushi, 259n
Omu, 122, 142
Onoda Cement Factory, 51
Opium farming, 25
Otsuka Reizō, 118n
Oyüwan soviet, 129

Pacification operations: in Chientao and Tungpientao, 287–294 passim; in Sanchiang Province, 283–284; the use of prostitutes in, 297n
Pai Yün-t'i, 179
Pak Tŭk-pŏm: captured, 294; monetary reward on, 288
Pak Tu-nam, 163n
Pak Yun-sŏ, 115, 119, 120, 210n
P'an, 162, 163, 206
Panku incident, 211
Pan-Pacific Labor Union, 256
Panshih: allied army established in, 240; anti-Japanese movement in, 155; CCP organizations in, 212; CCP strength in, 227; Communist Youth Corps in, 191; guerrillas in, 151, 152, 209–220; People's Revolutionary Army in, 216, 219; soldiers' rebellion in, 215; united front in, 173, 218; mentioned, 139, 184, 199n, 226, 230, 235
Panshih Middle School, 215
Panshih People's Revolutionary Army, 216
Pao-chia, 306
Pao Kuei-ch'ing, landholding of, 18, 33

Pao-min Hui, 213
Paoting, Hopei Province, 48, 205
Payen: CCP activities in, 251, 252; guerrilla activities in, 174–175; volunteer armies in, 155, 251
Pa-yüeh te Hsiang-ts'un, 224–225
Peasant insurrections, call for, 70
Peasant mentality, 121
Peasant question, 110. See also Farm workers; Landless farmers; Landlords; Middle level farmers; Poor farmers
Peasantry. See Farmers
Peian, 285, 286
Peichen, 196
Pei-ching Ti-fang Wei-yüan-hui, 63
Pei-fang ko Sheng Wei tai-piao lien-hsi hui-i, 134, 140
Peihsingchen, 286
Peikou, soviet at, 205
Peishan, 258
Peiyang clique, 8
Peking: anti-Japanese demonstrations in, 241; CCP cadres demoralized in, 140–141; CCP cadres dispatched from, to Manchuria, 60; CCP North China Bureau in, 303; contact with Manchurian guerrillas, 263; mentioned, 8, 9, 13, 44, 55, 87, 173, 265
Peking Fine Arts College, 48
Peking-Hankow Railway General Union, 37, 38
Peking Higher Normal School, 68
Peking-Mukden Railway, 105, 152
P'eng Teh-huai, 120
Penhsihu: Communist activities in, 72, 105, 109, 193–196 passim, 253; miners' strikes in, 29
People's Revolutionary Army: Manchurian Province Committee on, 173; organization of, urged, 163, 181, 235; in Panshih, 216, 219
People's Revolutionary Government: organization of, urged, 163, 177; political platform of, 206
Perleberg, Max, on Yang Ching-yü, 293n
Petty bourgeoisie: alienation of, 121; CCP on, 166, 172, 179; mentioned, 171, 178
Pien Shih-ch'i, 232
Pinchiang: numbers of anti-Japanese fighters in, 263; mentioned, 200
Pingkang, CCP activities in, 143, 143n
P'ing-min Chou-pao, in Harbin, 54
P'ing-tan Middle School, 121n

Pin hsien, 251
Po Ku. *See* Ch'in Pang-hsien
Poli, 256
Policemen: in anti-Japanese struggle, 216; in the CCP, 195, 254
Politburo, 129, 140, 146
Political-Military Training Institute, 261
Poor farmers: Ch'en Wei-jen on, 71; CCP's alienation of, 121; CCP policy on, 110, 177; lands of, confiscated, 205
Poor People's Party, 71, 72
Popular front strategy: implementation of, 250; instructed by Ch'en Shao-yü, 230, 233; mentioned, 307
Population: Chinese in Chientao, 142n; Koreans in Chientao, 142n; in Manchuria, 21–24 *passim*
Port Arthur: effect of the May 30 incident in, 48; mentioned, 10, 13
Pratt, Sir John, on the Chinese Eastern Railway, 93
Press, the: against imperialism, 47–48; controlled by the Japanese, 70
Printers' strike, 155
Profintern, 45, 200
Provisional Central Political Bureau, in Shanghai, 129
Public security in Manchuria, 38, 260
P'u I, 238
Purges in the CCP, 148, 149, 154
Putehachi, 286
Putschism, 77, 120

Railroads, 10, 11, 12, 13, 14
Railroad workers, 15, 16, 27–35 *passim*, 38, 64, 105, 136, 149, 254
Railway Employees' Union (Russian), 89
Railway Workers' Union, 53
Rebellion of Chinese soldiers, 202, 215, 261–262, 286
Red Army: plan for, in Chientao, 204; mentioned, 120, 166, 175, 193
Red beards, 82, 83, 83n
Red districts, 204
Red guerrillas, 172, 175
Red labor unions, 136, 137, 166, 176, 215
Red militia: in Chientao, 143, 204; mentioned, 163, 203, 206
Red Spear Society, 74, 171, 215, 221
Red Workers' Society, 252
Returned students, 128, 148, 176
Revolutionary Army, 91
Revolutionary base, 182, 205

Revolution in Manchuria, the role of, in China's revolution, 79, 80
Rice, export of, 17
Rich peasants, 110, 110n, 121, 136, 138, 162, 163, 177, 205, 207
Rickshaw Men's Society, 251
Right-wing deviation, 117, 154, 155, 157, 174
Riot in Eastern Manchuria, 202
Romanov, B. A., 10n
Roy, M. N., 65
Rubles: certain notes cancelled, 32; decline in value of, 31
Russia, Tsarist, 10
Russian Army, defeat of, in 1905, 26
Russian Communist Party membership, 39
Russians in Manchuria: revolutionary activities among, 26–35; as a revolutionary force, 70; mentioned, 248
Russo-Japanese War, 1904–1905, 10, 266

Sanchiang Province: abandoned by the guerrillas, 285; numbers of anti-Japanese fighters in, 245, 263, 263n; pacification operation in, 283–284; mentioned, 261, 262, 289n, 290
Santaokou, 211, 257
Sasaki Hideo, 142n
Sasaki, Tōichi, Major General: commands pacification operation in Tungpientao, 281–282; in Nanking, 265n
Schram, Stuart, 47n
Schwartz, Benjamin, 103n
Security highways, 271, 291
Seki Hiroharu, 27n
Selden, Mark, 2
Self-Defense Army, 214, 215, 221
Self-Defense Society, 171
Semenov, Grigorii Mikhailovich, General, 33
Sewing Machine Operators' Society, 251
Sexual lures, the use of, in counterguerrilla operation, 297n
Shahokou: Communist cells in, 72
Shahokou Rolling Stock Plant: wages at, 16; workers organized at, 41, 49; workers' strikes at, 30, 44; mentioned, 42, 100
Shaho river, 260
Shanchengchen, CCP branch in, 253
Shangchih, 223, 242
Shanghai: anti-Japanese demonstra-

tions in, 241; CCP headquarters in, 128, 176, 229; May 30 incident in, 47; workers' movement in, 41, 44; mentioned, 44, 45, 55, 56, 97, 101, 109, 110, 116, 154, 173, 190, 192, 197, 232, 263, 310
Shanghai Foreign Language Institute, 38
Shanghai massacre, 69
Shanghai Writers' Union, 198
Shanhaikuan-Mukden Railway, 149
Shan-lin Tui, 201, 221
Shan-lin Nung-kung I-wu Tui, 221
Shansi Province: CCP membership quota, 59; mentioned, 60, 241n, 266n, 319
Shantaokou, CCP members in, 143
Shantung Province: CCP membership quota for, 59; immigration from, 21; mentioned, 101, 134, 197, 241n, 319
Shao-Hsing, 161
Shapiro, Leonard, 87n
Sheng Chung-liang. See Sheng Yüeh
Sheng Yüeh, 63n, 161n
Shensi Province: CCP membership quota for, 59; mentioned, 134, 136, 319
Shanyang. See Mukden
Shen Yin, report of, 42, 43, 57
Shibata Kōzō, 300n
Shidehara, Kijurō, 91
Shihitaokou, 273
Shihjenkou soviet, 204
Shihpaitzu, 290n
Shih Ta-kan, 256
Shimada Toshihiko, 9n
Shop Clerks' Society, 251
Sian incident, 259
Siberia: oppression of the Chinese in, 32; as staging area for Communist expansion, 92; mentioned, 160, 221, 222, 279
Sino-Japanese war: of 1894–1895, 10; (1937), effect on anti-Japanese movement in Manchuria, 259
Sino-Korean Anti-Japanese Soldiers' Committee, 204
Sino-Korean Guerrilla Unit, 204
Slawinski, Roman, 75n
Socialist Revolutionary Party, Harbin branch, 27
Socialist Youth League, 37
Sola Pool, de Ithiel, 59n
Soldiers, Chinese: in anti-Japanese struggle, 129, 168, 216, 225; behavior of, 38, 75, 317; in the CCP, 254; gaining support of, 136; motive of, 82; rebellion of, 132, 152, 191, 210, 215; mentioned, 70, 169, 175
Soldiers' Association, 152
Soldiers' Committee, 151, 252
Solomenik, V., 28, 28n, 31
Southern Manchuria, landholdings in, 19
South Manchuria Medical College, 47, 124
South Manchurian Anti-Japanese General Society, 219
South Manchurian Provincial Committee. See CCP, in Manchuria (Local Organizations)
South Manchurian Railway Company: established, 11, 14; wages in 1925, 16; workers, condition of, 38; workers, number of, 15; mentioned, 39, 105, 149, 279, 308
South Manchurian Railway zone, 13, 57, 146
South Manchurian Special Committee. See CCP, in Manchuria (Local Organizations)
Soviet districts, establishment of, 132, 135, 193; mentioned, 136, 166
Soviet regime: in Chientao, 204, 206, 207; principles for constructing, 205; mentioned, 116, 118, 132, 133, 138, 145, 178
Soviet republic, 162, 177n
Soviet revolution in Manchuria, 166
Soviets, establishment of, 175, 204, 207
Soviet Union. See Union of Soviet Socialist Republics
Soybeans: effect of depression on, 130; export of, 17, 21; fall in the prices of, 202, 202n, 269; in Panshih, 210; wholesale price of, 21
Ssupingchieh (Ssupingkai), CCP branch in, 253
Staff Office of the Anti-Japanese Allied Army, 217
Stakan, 256
Stalin, Josef: on Chang Tso-lin, 88; on Soviet-Japanese relations, 88; strategy of, 70; and Trotsky, 93; mentioned, 65, 69, 83, 301
Strikes. See Workers' strikes
Student Anti-Japanese Society, 152
Students: agitated, 47, 48; in anti-Japanese struggle, 215; arrested in Mukden, 124; call for the mobilization of, 132, 179, 180; CCP on, 73, 152, 166; in the CCP, 197, 254; in

Mukden, 54, 152; mentioned, 169, 175
Suematsu Takayoshi, 74n
Suicide Corps, 305
Suifenho: Japanese fortifications in, 278; workers' strikes in, 31; mentioned, 149
Suining: Communist activities in, 191, 220; mentioned, 149
Suiyuan, 241n
Su Kuang, 132–133, 140, 219
Suleski, Ronald, 14n, 18n
Sun Ch'ao-yang, 173, 201, 223
Sun Chieh, 222n, 268n
Sungari River, 89, 153, 258, 287
Sung Ch'ing-ling, 179
Sung I-fu, 284n, 297, 298
Sung Lang-yün, 200
Sungpuchen, 153
Sun, Kungtu C., 18n, 22
Sun Tzu, 212, 227
Sun Yat-sen: memorial service for, 45, 53; Three People's Principles of, 48, 50, 54; mentioned, 9
Sun Yat-sen, Madame, 179
Sun Yat-senism, opposed, 166
Sun Yat-sen University, 66, 161, 200
Su P'ing-wen, 160, 168
Su Wen, 113
Swatow, uprising in, 77
Szechwan, CCP membership quota for, 59
Szuchan, 286
Szuping-Tiaoan Railway: wages in 1925, 16; workers in 1925, 15

Tahuangkou, 162, 206, 208
Taian, 147, 196, 199n
Tai Hsüan-chih, 74n
Tai Hung-pin, 286
T'ai I, 148
T'ai-tung Daily News, 42
Taiwan, 14, 212
Taiyuan, cadres in, demoralized, 141
Takahashi Toshio, 229n
Ta-kou tui, 211
Talatzu: CCP members in, 143, 143n
Talien. See Dairen
Ta-lien Chung-hua Kung-hsüeh-hui. See Dairen Chinese Workers' Study Association
Tanaka Giichi, General: Manchurian policy of, 12, 12n; mentioned, 91
T'ang Hung-ching, 100, 101, 102, 149
Tangku Truce, 160, 184
T'ang, Peter S. H., 10
Tangwangho, 300

Tangyuan Anti-Japanese Guerrilla Unit, 241
Tangyuan Hsien: anti-Japanese guerrillas in, 237; CCP activities in, 152; CCP strength in, 227; Chao Shang-chih in, 242; Hsieh Wen-tung in, 269; the sixth Allied Army organized in, 223; the third and sixth allied armies in, 258; volunteer armies in, 155
T'ang Yü-shan, 148
T'ao Ho-hsiang, 193
Taomukou, 120
Ta-p'ai Unit, 201
Ta-tao Hui. See Big Sword Society
Ta-tung Jih-pao, 51
Taxes imposed, 71, 177
Teachers: in the anti-Japanese movement, 215; arrested, 124; in the Communist movement, 64, 115, 253, 254
Tenant farmers: Chinese, in Chientao, 111–112; in Kiangsi Province, 281; Korean, in Chientao, 111; Li Chen-ying on, 39; living conditions of, 20; T'ien Chün on, 225; upward mobility of, 310
Teng Ho-kao: organized the Dairen Area Committee, CCP, 48; mentioned, 50, 51, 54
Tetu, 285
Textile industry in Manchuria, 14
Thaxton, Ralph, 311n
Third International. See Comintern
Thirty-second Army, 215
Thornton, Richard C., 77n
Tiao-an-Szuping Railway: wages, 16; workers in, 15
Tiehli, 285
Tiehling: guerrillas in, 261; workers' strike in, 29
Tien Chen, 173
T'ien Chün, 224–225, 225n
Tienpaoshan-Tumen Railroad, 115
Tien-t'ieh Ch'ing-nien-hui, 43
Tientsin: anti-Japanese demonstrations in, 241; cadres demoralized in, 141; Li Chen-ying in, 38; Northern conference in, 134; mentioned, 45, 109, 232, 263, 305
Ting Chün-yang: background of, 102; executed, 124, 124n; mentioned, 101, 149
Tō-a Tobacco Company, workers' strike at, 43
Tokyo, 145, 158
Toutaokou, 115

Tōyō Takushoku, 202
Troops. *See* Soldiers, Chinese
Trotsky, Leon, and Stalin, 93
Ts'ao Kuo-an, 261
Ts'ao Ya-fan: filled, 293; monetary reward on, 288
Tsarist government, 32
Tseng-chih School, 42
Tsinan, 102, 124, 194, 197
Tsinan incident, 4, 85
Tsingtao: workers' strike in, 44; mentioned, 109
Tsitsihar: Communists arrested in, 305; workers' strike in, 31; mentioned, 96
Tsung-Chung-kuo Min-tzu Wu-chuang Tzu-wei Wei-yüan-hui, 179–180
Ts'ung Shih-ho, arrested, 305
Tsurumi Yūsuke, 14n
Tsushima Strait, 26
Tuan Chih-kuei, 12n
Tuan Ch'i-jui, 8, 9
Tu Chi-ts'eng, 68
Tu Lan-t'ing, 124
Tulungshan, 223
Tumen-Tienpaoshan Railroad, 115
Tumuho, 147
Tunghwa Hsien: effect of pacification operation in, 272–273; number of anti-Japanese fighters in, 263; organization activities in, 298; pacification operation in, 281; typhoid in, 273; mentioned, 74, 75, 214, 215, 218, 288, 289, 292
Tungliao-Changchun Railroad, 12
Tungning: Communist strength in, 227; Japanese fortifications in, 278; mentioned, 108, 108n, 221, 256
Tung-pei Chao-pao, 53
Tungpei College, 52, 124
Tung-pei Jen-min Ko-ming-chün. *See* Northeast People's Revolutionary Army
Tung-pei K'ang-Jih Chiu-kuo Wei-yüan-hui, 241
Tung-pei K'ang-Jih Lien-chün. *See* Northeast Anti-Japanese Allied Army
Tung-pei K'ang-Jih Lien-ho-chün Tsung Chih-hui-pu, 242
Tung-pei Min-chung-pao, 200
Tung-pei Min-chung Tzu-wei-chün, 223
Tung-pei Nung-kung I-yung-chün, 212
Tung-pei Yi-yung-chün, 241
Tungpientao: anti-Japanese groups in, 215, 217; Big Sword Society in, 74; Koreans in, 24; natural resources in, 278–279; pacification operation in, 281–283, 287–294 *passim*; railroad construction in, 290; Wang Feng-ko in, 268, 316
Tunhua: CCP in, 142; guerrillas in, 120; under the East Manchurian Special Committee, 122
Tunhua-Kirin Railroad, 116, 142n
Tu Wen-yüan, 250n
Twenty-one demands, 194
Typhoid, 273

Ugaki Issei, General, 92
Ulie, Thomas R., 67n
Union of Soviet Socialist Republics (U.S.S.R.): army of, 203, 277; bolsters its defense in the Far East, 127; call for the protection of, 98–99, 131, 135, 145, 166, 173, 175, 178, 192; consulate in Harbin raided, 96; contact with the North Manchurian Provincial Committee of the CCP, 299; defends its policy against Chang Hsüeh-liang, 97; dispatch of guerrillas alleged, 289; economic policies, 91; embassy in Peking raided, 90, 91; first five-year economic plan, 159; and Great Britain, 91; impact of the Communist movement in Manchuria on, 86–94 *passim*; intelligence services, 250; international relations, 91; investment in Manchuria, 15; motive of leaders, 313; policy on the Chinese Eastern Railway criticized, 96; priorities of, 187; protection of the Chinese Eastern Railway, 312–313; relations with Chang Tso-lin, 88, 89; sells the Chinese Eastern Railway, 266; smuggling of arms into Manchuria rumored, 119; mentioned, 58, 79, 130, 140, 158, 160, 198, 200. *See also* Communist Party of the Soviet Union
—and China: diplomatic relations established (1924), 11; restored, 159; ruptured (1929), 96; mentioned, 313
—and Japan: military engagements between, 278; neutrality pact signed, 320; non-aggression pact proposed, 128; Soviet fear of Japan, 86–93 *passim*, 158; mentioned, 86–87, 88, 91–92, 277–278, 313
United front: advocated by Li Chen-ying, 39–40; Ch'en Shao-yü on,

184–186 passim; CCP's strategy of, 165–166, 171; struggle within, 166, 181
United front from above: 169, 172, 174, 180, 206, 213. See also Popular front strategy
United front from below: to be abandoned, 233; effects of, 242, 307; mentioned, 82, 136, 161, 169, 172, 174, 177, 178–181, 190, 201, 202, 217, 219, 220, 228, 230, 312, 313, 314
United States of America: consulate in Dairen, report from (1927), 51–52; consulate in Harbin, reports on Bolsheviks, 32, 34, 34n; investment in Manchuria, 15; mentioned by Karakhan, 87; on the Nanking incident, 91; support of Chang Tso-lin alleged, 91; mentioned, 320
University of the Toilers of the East, 250, 304
Urlich, Richard, S., 108n
Ussuri River, 256

Van Slyke, Lyman P., 259n
Village in August, 224–225
Vladivostok: branch of the Chinese delegation to the Comintern, 230; Comintern agencies in, 220; Eastern Kirin Provincial Committee in, 237n, 256; eviction of Chinese from, 32; Han Shou-k'uei in, 250; Liu Shao-ch'i in, 232; Wei Chengmin dispatched to, 261; mentioned, 10, 45, 200
Voitinsky, Gregorii, 65
Volunteer armies, 138, 151, 152, 153, 173, 177, 179, 191, 241

Wages: in Dairen, 43–44; in Mukden, 43; in 1925, 16; mentioned, 66, 307, 308, 309
Wakatsuki, Reijirō, 91, 92
Wales, Nym, 129n
Wang Chien-min, 36n
Wangching: CCP strength in, 142, 143, 277; Koreans in, 111; Korean Communists in, 122; the Second People's Revolutionary Army in, 208; soviets in, 204; soybeans in, 202n
Wang Ching-wei, 85
Wang Feng-ko: captured and executed, 282, 282n; hostile to Communists, 220; joins the Communists in united front, 240; Self-Defense Army under, 215; ties with the masses, 316; mentioned, 268. See also Big Sword Society
Wang I-shou, 22n
Wang Jen-ts'ai, 261
Wangkang, 286
Wang Li-kung, 49, 100, 101
Wang Ming. See Ch'en Shao-yü
Wang Ming-kuei, 286
Wang Shao-po, 49
Wang Sheng-i, 108
Wang Shu-te, 195
Wang Te-lin: emerged in Berlin, 160; rebellion of, 202, 221, 222, 223, 224; strength of forces under, 201; mentioned, 170, 268, 268n
Wang Te-t'ai: killed, 282, 288n; in the second People's Revolutionary Army, 208; mentioned, 238, 261
Wang Wen-hsüan, 305
Wang Ya-ch'en, 269, 284
Wangyükou, soviet, 204
Wang Yü-nan, 194, 195
Warlords, struggle against, 110
Wei Cheng-k'uei, 50, 51
Wei Cheng-min: in eastern Manchuria, 257; killed, 294; monetary reward on, 288; report on the condition of guerrillas, 294–298 passim, 297n, 299, 303–304 passim; returns from Moscow, 250n; secretary of the South Manchurian Provincial Committee, 258; mentioned, 261, 290
Weiho, soldiers' rebellion in, 174
Weishaho, 191
Wenmiao, 151
Wenshenglatzu: CCP members in, 143; indiscriminate killing at, 121
Whampoa Military Academy, 66
Wharf Laborers Company, 51
Witch hunt among the guerrillas, 209
Women's Normal School, Mukden, 47
Women Workers' Society, 251, 252
Workers: attitudes of, 56, 308; in the CCP, 64, 65, 254; in Dairen, restrained from rioting, 71; Li Chen-ying on, 38; organized in Dairen, 42; wage differential with Japanese, 71. See also Wages
Workers' strikes: call for, by Li Li-san, 99–100; in Dairen, 43; frequency of, 45, 109, 137, 176; in Fushun, 125; in Hokang, 152; Japanese comment on, in 1925, 44; in Kirin, 64; leadership for, 136, 166; in Mukden, 43, 44, 49; at Mukden Tobacco Factory, 137; results of, 135,

136; of the Russians, 27; at Shahokou Plant, 44; in Yingkou, 43
Wo Chün-sheng: background of, 25; landholding of, 18
Wuhan, 55, 59n, 69, 91, 114
Wuhan Labor Union, 68
Wu I-ch'eng, 201, 239, 241
Wu P'ei-fu, 9, 37

Yada Shichitarō, 12n
Yanaihara Tadao, 9
Yang An-jen: arrested, 199; defects, 200
Yang Chih-yün, 49, 50, 51
Yang Ching-yü: assessment of, 316; commander of the First Route Army, 258; elected to the Central Executive Committee of the Chinese Soviet Republic, 177n; extolled, 240; guerrilla activities of, 288, 289–290; in Harbin, 150; killed, 293, 293n; monetary reward on, 287; movement of, 261; in Pan-shih, 215, 219; pursued by enemy units, 292; in Tungpientao, 218; mentioned, 105, 216n, 227, 231, 238, 246, 261n, 267. *See also* Chang Kuan-i
Yang Ch'un-shan, 207
Yang I-ch'en, 195
Yang Sung, 236, 236n, 259, 266, 267
Yang Ta-ts'ung, 199
Yang Tso-ch'ing, 211, 211n, 219
Yang Yü-tien, 194, 195
Yang Yü-t'ing, warlord, landholding of, 18
Yeh Yung-nien, 287
"Yellow unions," 136, 137, 166, 181
Yenan, 237n, 299, 301, 304, 305

Yenchi: Communist activities in, 109, 122; Communist strength in, 143, 227; guerrillas in, 208; Koreans in, 111; May 30 riot in, 115; soviets in, 204; soybeans in, 202n; Wang Te-lin's rebellion in, 170; mentioned, 147
Yen-Ho Hsien Committee, CCP: guerrilla activities in, 122, strength, 143
Yenpien branch, CCP: established, 115; guerrilla unit organized under, 119; Northern conference on, 139; reorganized into the East Manchurian Special Committee, 120n
Yentunglatzu, soviets in, 204
Yen Ying, 73n
Yi Hong-gwang, 211, 215, 218, 219, 227
Yi Hun-gu, 112n
Yim Ch'un-ch'u, 208n, 290
Yingkou: CCP branch in, 253; soldiers' revolt in, 152; wages in, 16; workers in, 15, 46; workers' strikes in, 29; mentioned, 51, 105, 109
Yi Sang-muk, 208, 209
Yi Tong-il, 257, 258
Young, C. Walter, 10n
Young, John, 279n
Younghusband, Francis E., 74n
Yoshihiro Motohiko, 229n
Yoshizawa Kenkichi, 128
Youth Vanguard Society, 195
Yüan Shih-kai, 8, 12n
Yüan Te-sheng, 218
Yü Chi-hsien, 197
Yu Chi-won, 143n
Yü Lien-shui, 293n
Yunnan, CCP membership quota (1927) for, 59

Designer: Randall Goodall
Compositor: G & S Typesetters, Inc.
Printer: Thomson-Shore
Binder: John H. Dekker & Sons
Text: 10/12 Trump
Display: Trump bold italic